OXFORD PAPERBACK REFERENCE

The A–Z of Card Games

David Parlett is a freelance games inventor, researcher, consultant, and author of international repute. His books include the *Oxford History of Card Games*, the *Oxford History of Board Games*, the *Penguin Encyclopedia of Card Games*, and many others. He is a consultant to the *Oxford English Dictionary* on the terminology of games and gaming and is regularly consulted on the staging of historical games for period films and TV productions. His classic board game *Hare & Tortoise* has been published in more than a dozen languages since it first appeared some 30 years ago and has never since been out of print. A former language teacher, Parlett describes himself as 'a Londoner by birth and inclination, and a patriotic European'. He is also a Quaker, and is married, with two adult children and a grandson (to whom this book is dedicated).

Oxford Paperback Reference

The most authoritative and up-to-date reference books for both students and the general reader.

forthcoming

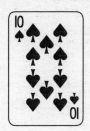

The A–Z of Card Games

  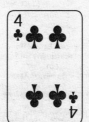 

DAVID PARLETT

OXFORD
UNIVERSITY PRESS

OXFORD

UNIVERSITY PRESS

Great Clarendon Street, Oxford OX2 6DP

Oxford University Press is a department of the University of Oxford.
It furthers the University's objective of excellence in research, scholarship,
and education by publishing worldwide in

Oxford New York

Auckland Cape Town Dar es Salaam Hong Kong Karachi Kuala Lumpur
Madrid Melbourne Mexico City Nairobi New Delhi Shanghai Taipei Toronto

With offices in

Argentina Austria Brazil Chile Czech Republic France Greece
Guatemala Hungary Italy Japan South Korea Poland Portugal
Singapore Switzerland Thailand Turkey Ukraine Vietnam

Published in the United States
by Oxford University Press Inc., New York

© David Parlett 1992, 2004

The moral rights of the author have been asserted
Database right Oxford University Press (maker)

First published 1992 as an Oxford University Press paperback entitled *A Dictionary of Card Games*
Reissued in new covers 1996
Second edition published 2004 as *The A–Z of Card Games*

British Library Cataloguing in Publication Data
Data available

Library of Congress Cataloging in Publication Data
Parlett, David Sidney.
    The A-Z of card games / David Parlett.–2nd ed.
        p. cm. – (Oxford paperback reference)
Rev. ed. of: A dictionary of card games. 1992.
ISBN 0-19-860870-5
    1. Card games. I. Parlett, David Sidney. Dictionary of card games. II. Title.
GV1243.P315 2004
795.4–dc22

                                            2004017034

ISBN 0-19-860870-5
2

Typeset in Minion and Meta by Kolam Information Services Pvt. Ltd, Pondicherry, India
Printed in Great Britain by Clays Ltd, St Ives plc.

Contents

KIRKLEES METROPOLITAN COUNCIL	
150117580	
Bertrams	11.12.05
795.403	£8.99
HU	CUL41024

For the eventual edification of Alexander Plunkett

I look upon cards in general as a rational amusement ... and while they amuse also supply matter for the exercise of genius.

Q. Quanti (1822)

Play smart, act dumb.

Anon.

Introduction

The aim of this book is simply to explain the basic rules of play for any card game you are likely to come across, or read, or hear about in the western world. It also covers several originating in the 'east'—ranging from Russia and Iraq to China—that have attracted enough of a following to show themselves worthy of wider popularity. Based on the *Oxford Dictionary of Card Games*, which was originally designed as a supplement to my *Oxford History of Card Games*, the book's change of title reflects a substantial change of approach and content. I have removed many defunct and complicated games that were only covered out of historical interest, and have rewritten almost every remaining entry to describe games more clearly, more economically, or more in accordance with the latest practices and up-to-date rules.

Despite omissions and reductions, the present collection is larger than before, with over 300 main entries, and as many cross-references and brief descriptions. It now includes 30 card solitaires in place of the previous single entry headed 'Patience', a greater number of children's games, a few more casino games, and several other games that have become prominent only in the past decade or so, such as Golf and Spades.

Being English, I naturally concentrate on games played throughout the English-speaking world. But that doesn't mean the content is restricted to British and American games. The British card-playing repertoire has always included many French games (as, of course, has that of Canada), and the American repertoire many of German and Italian origin, and all are well represented in this book. Many more have been drawn from other sources, and especially from other countries that have only recently been opening up communications with the wider world. With increased global travel, particularly by students in their gap year, and expanding international communications, especially via the Internet (where it is possible not just to read about exotic card games, but actually to play them live with people in other countries), the card-playing community is becoming increasingly internationalized. I therefore make no apology for including many exotic and off-beat games deserving of a wider audience.

To keep the contents down to a manageable size, I have included only games that either *are* normally played with the standard international 52-card pack (with suits of spades, clubs, hearts, diamonds, and face cards designated King, Queen, Jack), or else *can be* played with such cards even though they are normally played with a national or regional pack of some other design or constitution. The only exception I have made has been to include three tarot games: one played with French tarot cards, one with Austrian tarocks, and one with Italian tarocchi. These packs—not to be confused with fortune-telling cards—are now readily obtainable from specialist game shops, and the games played with them, albeit complicated at first sight, are too deep and rewarding to miss. (Tarot cards originated as trumps in trick-taking games and were only appropriated for arcane purposes several hundred years later.)

Researches made since the founding of the International Playing-Card Society in 1972 have revealed that every country, including Britain, harbours local communities, often quite small, who play games or variations unique to their region or locality, such as All Fours and Don in Britain. These are well described as folk games, not being recorded in books and subject to no universally accepted set of 'official rules'. Indeed, official rules only exist for games played in national or international tournaments, such as Bridge, Skat, and Poker, and even Poker has more folk variants than ever find their way into tournaments. Fortunately, they are now recorded and regularly updated by regular contributors throughout the world on John McLeod's award-winning 'Pagat' web site, where you will also find further information on most of the games described in this book, as well as many more that are not. Further information about historic card games can be found on my own web site (from which there is a link to my email address in case you spot any errors) and from the quarterly journal of the International Playing-Card Society.

I hope this book will enable you not only to rediscover the delights of some card games that you may have forgotten, but also to make the acquaintance of some brilliant and fascinating games that you may have heard of only in passing, or perhaps not even at all.

David Parlett   London, January 2004

Useful links:

http://www.pagat.com/
for rules of games and variants throughout the world

http://www.davidparlett.co.uk
for historic and original card games

http://i-p-c-s.org
for details of the International Playing-Card Society

http://www.playingcardsales.com
for national, regional, and other specialized playing cards

There are also links to specific game sites in the relevant entries.

Play your cards right …

The 'rules' of card games are not confined to explaining their mechanisms and objectives. They also include certain directions that are not specific to particular games but serve as a general code of good practice over the card-table. Their purpose is to keep things running smoothly and fairly, and to obviate disputes, so that nobody's enjoyment of the game is marred by embarrassment, ill behaviour, or time-wasting. The following points are worth taking into account.

Cards

Regular card-players prefer standard packs to fancy items with faces and garish advertisements. Always have fresh cards handy for replacement. A sloppy, old pack encourages sloppy, old habits, and cards should be abandoned when they get sticky or so marked with usage as to be identifiable from the back. It is good practice to alternate two packs of similar back design but contrasting colour, one of them being thoroughly shuffled for the next deal while the other is actually being dealt. It is a fact (not a superstition) that cards will sometimes run unfavourably to you for a long time. A traditional club rule is that anyone may call for new cards at any time in the session—but, also by tradition, at their own expense.

Cutting

Cards are cut to decide partners, choice of seats, first dealer, and so on. For these purposes you cut by lifting the top portion of the pack and turning it up to show its bottom card. Whoever cuts the highest card has first choice and deal. (A cut is also made before each deal—see below.)

Partners

In a fixed-partnership game, players may wish partners to be selected at random. This may be determined by cutting or drawing, the two highest ranks playing the two lowest, and having first choice of seats.

Seating

The order of seating around the table may be randomized by cutting, with highest cut conferring first choice of seat, and so on. This practice is rooted in superstition, the aim being to prevent players from fighting over 'lucky' seats or positions. There is, however, also a practical reason for it. Experienced players who know the company well can often adjust their play according to who is sitting on either side of them, and it is therefore only fair to randomize their relative positions.

Rotation

In some games, the turn to play passes to the left (clockwise), in others to the right. It makes no logical difference, but different countries have different traditions, so the rotation of a game often indicates its country of origin, and you might as well observe it. In this book rotation is to the left unless otherwise stated.

Dealer

Unless tradition or book-rules decree otherwise, the turn to deal passes from person to person in the same order as the turn to play. The first dealer may be selected by cutting or drawing the lowest (or highest) card. Normally, though not invariably, it is for the player next in rotation from the dealer—'eldest hand'—to play, bid, or bet first.

Shuffle and cut

Unless otherwise agreed, or specified by the rules, the cards should always be shuffled and cut between deals. Traditionally, anyone may shuffle, but the dealer has the right to shuffle last. If you cannot shuffle well, practise; and if this doesn't help, get someone else to do it. The important thing is the randomization, not the performance. Cutting is done as follows. Dealer places the pack face down on the table; the player at his right (in a clockwise game, otherwise vice versa) lifts the top portion and places it face down on the table; dealer then completes the cut by placing the previously lower half on top of it. The number of cards in the smaller half should be at least one tenth of the total number of cards in the pack.

Dealing

Unless otherwise agreed or specified, cards are dealt face down in rotation around the table, one at a time, starting with eldest and finishing with the dealer. In some games cards are dealt in batches of three or four at a time. This is not designed to produce 'more interesting hands' but rather to save time and effort. Custom should always be followed in this matter, as the dealer who fails to do so may be suspected of nefarious motives.

Play

It is bad manners to pick your cards up before the deal is complete. (It may put the dealer off his stroke, or cause a card to be faced, which is a waste of time and effort.) In play, restrict conversation to that which is necessary to the game—gossip can be left to between deals. Make bids clearly and audibly. Play cards smoothly rather than histrionically, decisively rather than hesitantly. If you have to stop and think, do so before touching a card in your hand, as the act of touching first one and then another may be construed as signalling to a partner, which is illegal. Do not criticize anyone for their play, especially a partner, or brag about or justify your own. If the rules of the game do not demand that players show the cards they have won, played, or discarded, do not insist on seeing them.

These procedures are open to relaxation in informal play, for example among close friends who are not playing seriously for money and know one another well enough to follow an intuitive code of behaviour. But it is as well to know and follow them, especially when a newcomer joins the group.

Go for your game

When choosing what to play, start by counting how many of you there are, as many games are designed for a specific number and may not work well for others. If the answer is four, decide whether to play a partnership game or everyone for themselves. Then decide whether or not you want to play a trick-taking game, as not everyone is partial to them. Finally, you might want to consider how easily or quickly a game can be learnt. For this, you need only look at the amount of space it takes to describe. Generally, a game with lots of rules is likely to be strategically deep and skill-rewarding, but it doesn't follow that one with few and simple rules is necessarily shallow, childish, or devoid of strategy.

Games for two
Trick games: Bezique, Bohemian Schneider, Bondtolva, Écarté, German Whist, Klaberjass, Marjolet, Penneech, Piquet, Put, Sedma, Sixty-Six, Tausendeins, Trappola, Truc, Tute.

Others: Basra, Canasta, Cassino, Challenge, Cribbage, Durak, Gin, Gops, Scopa, Spit, Spite and Malice.

Games for three
Trick games: Auction Pinochle, Bavarian Tarock, Belote, Bismarck, Black Maria, Booby, Bugami, Calabresella, Chinese Ten, Five Hundred, Jass, Knaves, Manni, Mittlere, Ninety-Nine, Reunion, Scarto, Sergeant Major, Six-Bid Solo, Skat, Skitgubbe, Spanish Solo, Tapp Tarock, Tarot (French), Terziglio, Tribello, Tysiacha, Zwikken.

Others: Cucumber, Gops, Oklahoma, Scopa, Tablanette, Zetema.

Games for four (solo)
Trick games: Barbu, Bassadewitz, Belgian Whist, Boston, Brandle, Bugami, Chinese Ten, Doppelkopf, Dutch Whist, German Solo, Hearts, Lórum, Nomination Whist, Oh Hell!, Pandur, Pinochle, Polignac, Slobberhannes, Solo Whist, Špády, Tarot (French), Tyotka.

Others: Dudak, Kaluki, Persian Rummy, President, Primiera, Svoyi Kozyri, Zetema, Zwicker.

Games for four (partnership)

Trick games: Alkort, All Fours, Aluette, Belote, Bid Whist, Bondtolva, Botifarra, Bridge, Calypso, Cinch, Coinche, Contract Whist, Don, Euchre, Five Hundred, Forty-One, Gaigel, Israeli Whist, Jass, Kaiser, Klaverjas, Madrasso, Manille, Minnesota Whist, Norwegian Whist, Phat, Pinochle, Quinto, Roque, Sedma, Spades, Sueca, Tressette, Truc, Two Hundred, Watten, Whist, Yukon.

Others: Basra, Canasta, Cribbage, Cirulla, Cuarenta, Persian Rummy, Pishti, Ristiklappi, Scopone, Tablanette.

Games for five

Bugami, Hearts, Nap, Oh Hell!, Pip-Pip, Slobberhannes, Poker, Twenty-Five, Yukon.

Games for six

Almonte (Euchre), Kemps (also for eight), Roque, Sixte, Sizette.

Games for 3–6 or more

Tricks: Best Boy, Briscola, Ciapanò, Coteccio, Femkort, Hearts, Hola, Julep, Knockout Whist, Loo, Manille, Nap, Oh Hell!, Phat, Pip-Pip, Polignac, Rams, Rolling Stone, Romanian Whist, Scotch Whist, Sift Smoke, Slobberhannes, Spoil Five, Toepen, Twenty-Five, Twenty-Nine, Yukon.

Others: Authors, Baccara, Brag, Caribbean Stud, Chase the Ace, Cícera, Commerce, Compartment Full, Contract Rummy, Crazy Eights, Cucumber, Delphi, Domino, Eleusis, Epsom, Farmer, Fifty-One, Go Boom, Go Fish, Golf, Hand and Foot, Hundred, Jubilee, Kemps, Kings and Queens, Let it Ride, Matrimony, Michigan, Muggins, Mustamaija, Newmarket, Ninety-Nine, Obstacle Race, Old Maid, Pai Gow, Paskahousu, Pink Nines, Play or Pay, Poch, Poker, Poker Patience, Pontoon, Pope Joan, President, Primiera, Progressive Rummy, Racing Demon, Red Dog, Ride the Bus, Rolling Stone, Rummy, Scotch Whist, Seven-and-a-Half, S**thead, Sift Smoke, Slapjack, Slippery Sam, Snap,

Speculation, Spinado, Stortok, Switch, Thirty-Five, Thirty-One, Tieng Len, Twenty-Five, Twenty-Nine, Two-Four-Jack, Vatican, Verish' ne Verish', Wan Maria, Whisky Poker, Yablon, Zetema.

See also ...
If you are looking for games of a particular type, other lists will be found in the entries for Children's Games, Gambling Games, Patience Games, and so on.

In this compiler's not very humble opinion, the well-educated card-player's repertoire should include at least half a dozen of the following games: **(for two)** Bezique, Cribbage, Gin Rummy, Klaberjass, Piquet, Scopa, Sixty-Six; **(for three)** Auction Pinochle, Ninety-Nine, Skat, Tysiacha, and some form of Tarot; **(for four)** Belote, Bridge, Canasta, Hearts, President, Scopone, Solo Whist, Spades, Whist; **(and, in general)** Contract Rummy, Eleusis (or Delphi), Oh Hell!, Pontoon (Blackjack), Poker, Vatican, Snap, and Old Maid.

Pick your pack

Most of the games in this book use the so-called international 52-card pack. These cards come in three sizes—'Patience' size (about 4.5 × 7 cm), 'Bridge' size (about 5.5 × 9 cm), for games where many cards make a hand, such as 13 at Bridge, and 'Poker' size (about 6.5 × 9 cm), for games where few cards are dealt, such as five at Poker, or six at Cribbage. It is worth getting the right cards for the game, and keeping on hand several different packs for different games—few things are more irritating than picking up your cards at Bridge and finding that the dealer last used them for playing Patience!

Many games use what appear to be stripped down packs. In fact, they mostly originate in countries with their own distinctive card-playing traditions manifesting themselves in different suit systems, different court or face cards, and a different range of numerals. In particular:

Games played with 40 cards are typically Italian and played with the Italian pack, with its suits of swords, batons, cups, and coins, court cards designated King, Knight, and Soldier, and numerals 7-6-5-4-3-2-1.

Spanish games use 48 or 40 cards, with suits of swords, clubs, cups, and coins, courts King, Knight, and Servant, and numerals (9-8-)7-6-5-4-3-2-1.

German games use 36, 32, or 24 cards, with suits of acorns, leaves, hearts, and bells, courts of King, Over-officer, Under-officer, numerals 10-9-(8-7-6), and another which is either an Ace or a Deuce.

In an ideal world you would use whatever pack is appropriate to the game you are playing. However, even if you are lucky enough to live near a specialist games shop, you may have difficulty in persuading everyone to learn to cope with an unfamiliar pack as well as an unusual game. In this collection, therefore, all such games have been 'translated' into the international pack for ease of comprehension.

The 'international' pack is in fact the Anglo-American version of what is basically and originally the French pack, with suits of spades, clubs, hearts, diamonds, and face-cards King, Queen, Jack. In France itself many native games are played with a standard 32-card pack, with an

Ace and numerals 10-9-8-7. The same pack is widely used throughout Europe, in either its 32- or 52-card form, or sometimes 36, especially in Russia.

If you are going to play any short-pack game regularly, it is advisable to keep separate packs of different lengths for specific games rather than to keep stripping a full pack—otherwise, when you restore (say) a 32-card pack to its original constitution, all the low cards will be identifiable by their relative cleanliness.

Key to headings

■●	one-player game (patience or card solitaire)		

● (two dots)	good for two players	○ (two circles)	playable by two but not ideal
▲ (triangle dots)	good for three players	△ (triangle circles)	playable by three but not ideal
●● ●●	good for four as individuals	○○ ○○	playable by four as individuals
❖ (four dots cross)	good for four as partners	(four circles)	playable by four as partners
(five dots)	good for five players	(five circles)	playable by five but not ideal
(six dots)	good for six players	(six circles)	playable by six but not ideal
(seven dots)	good for seven or more	(seven circles)	playable by seven or more

Type of game

Each game is identified as belonging to a family of similar or related games, so if you like one you will probably enjoy others of the same type. Each family name has its own entry, listing all games of the same type covered in this book. The family names are: Adding-up games, Banking games, Card-catch games, Climbing games, Collecting games, Gambling games, Going-out games, Patience games, Penalty-trick games, Plain-trick games, Point-trick games, Rummy games, Stops games, Vying games. There are also entries for Children's Games and Casino games, each with its own list of candidates.

Number of cards required

Card games are played with various numbers of cards to a pack according on their country of origin. The commonest are indicated as follows:

| 52 | = standard 'international' pack with A K Q J 10 9 8 7 6 5 4 3 2 in each suit. |

| 53 | = 52 plus one Joker, | 54 | plus two Jokers, etc. |

| 52 52 | | 54 54 | = two such packs shuffled together; | 52 52 52 52 | = four such packs, etc. |

| 40 | = K Q J 7 6 5 4 32 A in each suit, typical of Spanish and Italian games. May also indicate a standard pack shortened to A K Q J 10 9 8 7 6 5 in each suit. |

| 36 | = A K Q J 10 9 8 7 6, typically in games of Swiss, German or Russian origin. |

| 32 | = A K Q J 10 9 8 7, typical of French and many other continental games. |

| 32 32 | = two such packs shuffled together. |

| 24 | = A K Q J 10 9, mostly in games of German origin. |

| 24 24 | = two such packs shuffled together. |

Other numbers of cards are similarly indicated (such as | 65 | | 78 | etc). The exact constitution of each pack is always detailed in the text.

Accordion

Patience game

A simple and appropriately named solitaire, as you will see when it starts expanding and contracting.

Shuffle the pack and hold it face down. Turn cards one at a time from the top and deal them face up in a row from left to right. (Unless you're left-handed, in which case reverse all following left–right instructions.)

Whenever the card you play matches the suit or value of the card on its immediate left, put it on top of the matching card. Do the same if the card you play matches the suit of the card third along to the left—that is, not the one immediately to the left of the previous card, but the one to the left of that.

Treat a pile of two or more cards as if it consisted solely of its top card. Such a pile may never be split or separated.

When you play the last card from hand you will, if you are very lucky, be able to make matching moves to the left until all 52 cards finish up in a single pile. Count half a win for finishing up with just two piles.

Accordion. If the next card (dotted outline) is a club, a Five, a heart, or an Ace (but not a diamond or a Queen), it goes on whichever of the previous cards it matches.

Aces Up

Patience game

An entirely mechanical but maddeningly impulsive solitaire. Note that Aces are high, so the order of cards is 2-3-4-5-6-7-8-9-10-J-Q-K-A.

The aim is to finish with all four Aces in a row after eliminating the other 48 cards.

Deal four cards face up in a row. If two or more match suit, throw out all but the highest card of that suit.

Keep dealing rows of four cards at a time, each of them covering either the card beneath or an empty space. After each deal pause and see if any of the top cards are of the same suit. If so, eliminate all but the highest-ranking of them.

Keep doing this till all the top cards are of different suits, then deal four more, and so on.

Whenever you make a space by eliminating the bottom card of a pile you can fill it with the top card of any other pile. This is the only way of getting the Aces out to unblock the cards beneath them.

Acey-Deucey ▸▸ *Yablon*

Adding-up games

Games where each in turn plays a card to a common wastepile, announces the total face value of all cards so far played, and earns a score or penalty for hitting or overshooting certain totals. See individual entries for: Fifty-One, Hundred, Jubilee, Ninety-Nine, Obstacle Race, Twenty-Nine.

Agurk ▸▸ *Cucumber*

Alkort

Plain-trick game

This derivative of the ancient game of ▸ **Karnöffel** was Iceland's national card game until about a century ago, since when it has been swamped by Bridge.

Four players sitting crosswise in partnerships use a 44-card pack made by omitting Tens and Fives. All play goes to the left. Deal nine each in batches of three. The last eight go face down on the table and remain out of play. The aim is to win five of the nine tricks played, ideally the first five straight off.

Cards rank from high to low as follows:

1. Sevens always win the trick when led, but lose otherwise.
2. Six specific cards come next, namely (from high to low):

3. Aces, Jacks, Sixes, Eights (except ♠8) follow in that descending order, but regardless of suit.

The remaining cards (black Nines, three Fours, four Threes, three Twos, three Kings, four Queens) are all equal and have absolutely no trick-heading power, except that Twos beat Kings and Queens, and Threes beat Queens.

If you hold no card able to beat an Eight you may immediately declare yourself 'under-eight' (*friðufær*). This entitles you to discard eight cards from your hand and draw those undealt as replacements.

Before play, you all secretly show your partner your highest card. Eldest leads to the first trick and the winner of each trick leads to the next. Any card may be played; there is no need to follow suit. The trick is taken by the highest card played, or by the first played of cards equal in rank or equally worthless.

Play normally ends when one side has won its fifth trick, thereby scoring 1 point. However, if one side wins the first five straight off (a *múk*), play continues for as long as they continue to win tricks, after which they score from 5 to 9 points according to the number they won in unbroken succession. Six or more is called a 'stroke'.

All Fours

Point-trick game

52

All Fours first appeared as a tavern game of the Restoration, possibly of Dutch origin and brought over in the train of Charles II, and is of particular interest for attaching the name 'Jack' to what was previously only called 'knave'. In the eighteenth and nineteenth centuries it was regarded as a lower-class game and often castigated for its disreputability. Transported to America, it gave rise to extensions such as ▶ **Cinch**, and developed in other ways in the Caribbean islands. One form of it is now the national game of Trinidad. In Britain and Ireland it has produced other extensions in such games as ▶ **Don** and ▶ **Phat**, though it is still played in more or less its original form in Yorkshire and Lancashire. The following is described as for four, but if two play just ignore any reference to partners.

Four players sitting crosswise in partnerships play with a 52-card pack ranking A K Q J 10 9 8 7 6 5 4 3 2 in each suit. Cards are dealt round face up till someone gets a Jack. That player is the first 'pitcher' and the cards are dealt by his right-hand neighbour. The turn to deal and play rotates to the left thereafter.

The aim of the game is to peg most of the following four game points, namely one each for:

- **High:** the side dealt the highest trump in play;
- **Low:** the side dealt the lowest trump in play;
- **Jack:** the side that captures the trump Jack in a trick (if it is in play);
- **Game:** the side taking in tricks the highest total value of card-points, counting each Ace 4, King 3, Queen 2, Jack 1, Ten 10.

Deal six cards to each player in three rounds (2-2-2 or 4-1-1 or 3-2-1 in any order). The pitcher's partner may not look at their hand until the pitcher has 'pitched'—that is, led a card to the first trick. (There is a 4-point penalty for looking.) The suit pitched establishes trumps for that deal.

To the card led you may either follow suit or play a trump, as you prefer. Only if unable to do either may you discard. The trick is taken by the highest card of the suit led, or by the highest trump if any are played, and the winner of each trick leads to the next. The first trick goes face up in front of its winner, with a trump on top to serve as a reminder. Subsequent tricks are stored face down.

If you have no trumps left, no cards above Nine, and are not winning the current trick, you may indicate this to your partner by throwing all your remaining cards face up to the current trick, leaving your partner to play on alone.

At end of play points are scored as described above. There will normally be four, but one will be missing if the Jack is not in play, and the point for game is not scored in the (unusual) case of a tie for card-points.

The points are pegged on a special wooden peg board, and the first side to reach 11 points wins. In the event that both teams are close to winning, the points are always pegged in the order high, low, jack, game. So, for example, if the score is 10–10 the team holding the highest trump will win the match, even if the other team would have won the other three points.

Variant. Some play that the point for Low is awarded for capturing the lowest trump in a trick rather than for merely having held it.

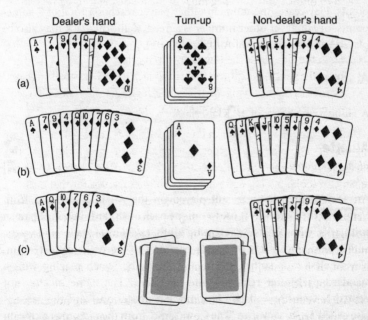

All Fours (two players). (a) Neither player accepts spades as trump. (b) Cards are run, and Dealer accepts the newly turned suit of diamonds. (c) The hands after discarding. Dealer scored for High, Low, and Game, but failed to win the Jack.

All Fives

is a two-player variant in which each player makes an additional score immediately upon capturing each of the following trumps: Ace 4, King 3, Queen 2, Jack 1, Ten 10, Five 5. Points for high, low, Jack, and game are scored as normal. Game is 61 up, scored on a crib board (*see* page 113).

California Jack (Shasta Sam)

is a trick-and-draw version for two. Deal six each in threes, turn the next for trumps, bury it in the pack, and stack the undealt cards in a squared-up pile either face up (California Jack) or face down (Shasta Sam). Non-dealer leads. Follow suit if possible, otherwise play any card; the privilege of trumping when able to follow does not here apply. The trick is taken by the higher card of the suit led, or by the higher trump if any are played. The winner of each trick draws the top card of stock, waits for his opponent to draw the next, then leads to the next trick. Score one point each for high, low, Jack, and game—'game' being 41 or more card-points. Play ceases the moment either player reaches a total of 7 game-points, or whatever other number is agreed. California Jack may also be played with the scoring of All Fives (above).

Alsós

A Hungarian variety of ▸▸ **Klaberjass**

Aluette

Plain-trick game

An ancient French game still played on the Atlantic seaboard from Vannes to the Garonne. It uses a unique pack of 48 cards bearing Spanish suitmarks, with courts representing kings, cavaliers (female) and valets, and depicting a variety of figures eccentric to the point of surrealism. Nevertheless it is sufficiently interesting to be worth playing with a standard pack after removing the four Tens. The name *aluette* (not related to *alouette* = 'lark') is somewhat mysterious, and the game is also called *Le Jeu de Vache*, 'The Cow Game', from the picture of a cow on the equivalent of the ♥2. The following description is based on several slightly divergent sources.

Four players sit crosswise in partnerships and play to the left. A game is five deals. The aim—an unusual one—is for both members of a partnership to play in such a way that one of them wins more tricks than any other single player.

Deal nine cards each in batches of three and stack the rest face down.

The eight highest cards are listed below from highest to lowest, together with their names, and the actions recognized as signalling their possession:

Aluette. Two of cups—the 'cow' card.

Luettes:	♦3	Monsieur	look up
	♥3	*Madame*	hand on heart
	♦2	*le borgne* (one-eyed man)	close one eye
	♥2	*la vache*	pout
Doubles:	♥9	*grand neuf*	raise a thumb
	♦9	*petit neuf*	raise little finger
	♣2	*deux de chêne* (two of oak)	raise index finger
	♠2	*deux d'écrit* (two of script)	mime writing

These are followed in order by Ace, King, Cavalier (Queen), Valet (Jack), 9-8-7-6-5-4-3 without distinction of suit. That is, all Aces are equal in value and beat Kings, which are equal in value and beat Cavaliers (Queens), and so on. Of these, the first four are called 'middlings' (*les moyennes*) and the rest 'inferiors' (*les inférieures*). Only two of the Nines and Threes are inferiors, the others being *luettes* or *doubles*.

Eldest hand leads first. Each in turn thereafter may play any card they please, without necessarily following suit. The trick is taken by the highest card, as explained above, and the winner of each trick leads to the next. If there is a tie for highest no one wins the trick: it is said to have 'gone off' (*être pourrie*) and is thrown away, the next lead being made by the same player who led to the tied trick. (But one account says by whoever played the first tied card.) A trick containing a *luette* or *double* cannot, of course, be tied.

You are allowed—indeed expected—to signal to your partner, preferably when the other side is not looking, your holding of any of the top eight cards. Only authorized signals are allowed, as listed above.

One game point goes to the side of the player who won most tricks individually, or, if tied, who took that number first. The turn to deal passes to the left, and the game is won by the side reaching 5 game points.

Mordienne (an exclamation equivalent to *gadzooks*!) is announced in the event that whoever won most tricks did so in unbroken succession up to the ninth and last—for example, by losing the first four but winning the last five. This scores 2 game points. (In one account, this only counts if it is bid in advance, and the opponents score 2 if the bidder fails.)

One account recognizes a feature called *le chant*, which may be played by agreement. After the deal and before the play, each in turn announces whether he is willing for the remaining cards to be dealt. If all agree, six each are dealt, in threes, to eldest and to dealer's partner. Each of them then examines his hand and makes six discards face down before eldest leads.

http://www.pagat.com/put/aluette.html
http://www.ouestnet.com/vendee/savoir/luette.cfm *(in French)*

A**ehole, A**hole ▸ *President*

As Nas

An old Iranian game wrongly considered ancestral to ▸ **Poker**. Four or five players receive five cards each from a pack of 20 or 25 and play as at Poker but without a draw. Only ranks count, there being four or five of each. The valid combinations are one pair, triplets, full house, fours, and five alike.

Auction *Auction Bridge* ▶▶ *Bridge*; *Auction Euchre* ▶▶ *Euchre*; etc

Authors
Collecting game

52

An old children's game—or, rather, an old game for children—related to ▶ **Donkey** and undoubtedly ancestral to Happy Families.

Shuffle and deal 52 cards one at a time as far as they will go. It doesn't matter if some players get more than others. The aim is to lose your cards by discarding them in 'books'. A book is four of a kind (Aces, Kings, etc). The first player starts by pointing to any other player and asking them for all the cards they have of a particular rank, which must be one of which the asker has at least one in his own hand. The player addressed must hand them all over if he has any. If so, the asker gets another turn and does the same thing, asking the same or another player for cards of any rank of which he holds at least one. This continues until the player addressed has none of the requested rank. He then replies 'None', and takes over the turn to ask somebody else. Whenever you get all four of a given rank you show them to the others and lay them down like a won trick. The winner is the first to run out of cards, whether by giving them away or discarding them in fours.

Baccara
Banking game

52 52 52

Spelt 'Baccarat' in Britain and Las Vegas, this is a more upmarket but less intelligent version of Twenty-One. It first appeared in nineteenth-century France and may be of oriental origin.

Casino play uses three or six 52-card packs shuffled together and dealt from a so-called 'shoe'. It consists essentially of a series of two-handed contests between a banker and a punter, though the punter may be any one of a table of players. Counting numerals at face value and courts 0, the punter's aim is to receive cards totalling closer to 9 than the banker's, for which purpose 10 or more counts only as its last digit.

The banker deals two cards to the punter and to himself. If either has a point of 8 or 9 he turns them face up. With under 5, the punter must call for a third card, dealt face up; with more than 5 he must stand; with exactly 5 he may do either. The banker must draw to a point under 3, stand with a point above 6, and may do either with a point of 3 to a punter's third-card 9, or 5 to a punter's third-card 4. Otherwise, he must draw or stand as dictated by the most favourable odds.

In basic Baccara, the house is the bank. In Chemin de Fer, or 'Chemmy', the bank passes from player to player. In Punto Banco, it appears to pass from player to player, but actually is held by the house.

Baker's Game (Patience) ▸▸ *Freecell*

Banking games

Gambling games typically played in casinos. They are essentially two-handers, in that one player, the banker, plays against one or more punters on an individual basis, there being no interaction between the punters themselves—in fact, they sometimes act as a single collective opponent of the banker. As the banker deals and usually has an inbuilt advantage, the bank is held in casinos exclusively by a house representative; otherwise, it passes from player to player by rote, by purchase, or by the occurrence of a winning hand. See individual entries for: Baccara, Caribbean Stud, Farmer, Faro, Lansquenet, Let it Ride, Monte Bank, Pai Gow, Pontoon, Quinze, Red Dog, Seven and a Half, Slippery Sam, Speculation, Trente et Quarante (Rouge et Noir), Pontoon (Blackjack, Twenty-One), Yablon.

Barbu
Penalty-trick game

52

Barbu is the most highly developed member of a series of compendium games based on ▸ **Hearts** which first appeared in the early twentieth century, apparently in Eastern Europe (*see also* ▸ **Lórum** and ▸ **Tyotka**), and was considerably expanded by French Bridge-players in the 1970s.

Le Barbu means 'the bearded one', and refers to the ♥K, which is the only heart with a beard. (Not the only King with a beard, as sometimes said. All French Kings have beards.)

Four players use a 52-card pack ranking A K Q J 10 9 8 7 6 5 4 3 2. A game is 28 deals. Scores are recorded on a specially ruled-up scoresheet (*see* below). Each in turn deals seven times in succession, dealing 13 cards to each player, one at a time starting at his left.

In each of his seven deals the dealer is automatically the declarer. He examines his cards and declares one of seven possible contracts, which must be one he has not already played. Of these, five yield negative scores to the value of −130 points in all, and two give positive scores to the value of +130 in all.

All the contracts listed below are trick-taking games except for the one called Domino, and the opening lead is made by the declarer (or, *variant*, by declarer's right-hand neighbour.) The five negative games are played at no trump. Players must follow suit if possible, otherwise may play any card. The trick is taken by the highest card of the suit led, and the winner of each trick leads to the next.

1. **No tricks**. Each trick taken scores −2 points.
2. **No hearts**. Each heart taken scores −2, the Ace of hearts −6. Hearts may not be led unless no other suit is held. Captured hearts are left face up so all can see which ones have gone.
3. **No Queens**. Each Queen taken scores −6. Captured Queens are left face up and play ends when all four are out.
4. **No King**. Taking ♥K (*le Barbu*) scores −20. Hearts may not be led unless no other suit is held. Play ends when the King is taken.
5. **No last**. Taking the last trick scores −20, the penultimate trick −10.
6. **Trump**. Each trick won scores +5 points. Declarer announces a trump suit and leads any card. If trumps are led, you must follow suit if possible and head the trick if possible. To a non-trump lead, you must follow suit if possible. If unable to follow, you must beat any trump that may have been played to the trick if you can, but, if none has been played, or you cannot beat it, you may play any card. The trick is taken by the highest card of the suit led, or by the highest trump if any are played, and the winner of each trick leads to the next.

7. **Domino**. Declarer announces 'Domino from …' and a rank, e.g. 'Domino from Eights', and plays a card of that rank to start the layout. He is allowed to call a rank he does not hold, in which case the layout is started by the next player to the left who has such a card. This forms the basis of a layout to which each player contributes in turn (if possible), and which will eventually consist of four 13-card suit sequences with one row per suit and one column per rank. The foundation card of each row must be put in place first, and each subsequent card placed to the right or left of the suit row to which it belongs. For example, if the first card played is ♥8, the next in turn must play either ♥7 or ♥9 to one side of it, or another Eight above or below it to start another row. You must play a card if you legally can, otherwise must pass. First out of cards scores +40, second +20, third +5.

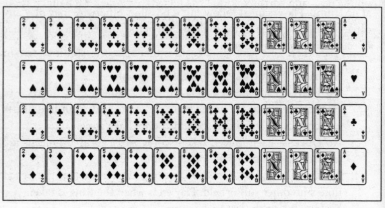

Barbu. The Domino layout. The suits may be arranged in any order.

Between the announcement of the contract and the play of the hand, each in turn has one opportunity to double one or more specific players, subject to the following rules:

- You must double the declarer at least twice in each seven-deal cycle.
- In a negative contract (but not in Trump or Domino) you may double any other player or players if you think you will achieve a better result than they will.

- You may redouble any player who doubles you. The announcement 'Maximum' means that you double everyone who doesn't double you, and redouble everyone who does.
- Declarer may not double independently, but may redouble an opponent's double.

A double amounts to a side-bet between two players as to which of them will do better than the other. A double must be noted on the scoresheet, and a double of the declarer is encircled to help ensure that everyone fulfils their quota of two such doubles per cycle of seven.

At the end of a hand everyone notes their score in the plus or the minus column as the case may be. The results of any doubling are then calculated for each of the six possible pairs of players. If only one member of a pair doubled the other, the difference between their two results for the deal is calculated, then added to the score of whichever of them did better in the deal, and correspondingly deducted from that of the other. If one doubled and the other redoubled, the same applies, except that the difference is doubled before being credited to one and debited from the other. This procedure ensures that all scores continue to sum to zero.

Example of scoring

	Annie			Benny			Connie			Denny				check	
Q	C -6 -6	-1		X 6 6 12	2		A -6 -6	-1		-1		-1	-2	2	2
			2			4			2	2			2	4	4	4
H	D 0 8	-4		-6 -2		16	-2 -1	-4		X -4 -8 2 16	-1		3	5
							0 6	8				8		0	4

In deal 1, declarer Annie declared No Queens (Q in the leftmost column). Benny, with a good hand for this bid, announced 'Maximum' to double everyone else. The 'X' for 'double all' is underlined to show that it includes the declarer. Connie doubled Annie (A), underlined to show that she has fulfilled one of her two requisite declarer doubles. Denny passed, having a hand too weak to risk redoubling Benny or doubling anyone else. Annie, finally, felt confident enough as declarer to redouble Connie (C), but not Benny, whose universal double implied unusual strength. This is indicated by 'C' in Annie's column.

In play, Denny took two Queens, for −12 points, and Annie and Connie one each, for −6 apiece. Now for the doubles. Annie was doubled by Benny, and did worse, causing her to score minus and him plus the difference between their two scores for Queens (6). Annie and Connie were mutually doubled and redoubled, but as they scored the same amount (−6) the difference was zero, so there is nothing to record. Benny doubled everyone, was not redoubled, and beat everyone, gaining 6 each from Annie and Connie, and 12 from Denny. As for the Connie–Denny pair, neither doubled the other. Each player's pluses and minuses are reckoned, and the total entered in their rightmost column.

In the first half of the check column is written the contract value of 24 (four Queens at 6 each). The second half is for the running total.

In deal 2, Annie chose No Hearts (H). Only Denny doubled ('Maximum'), but Annie then redoubled. Annie took no hearts, Benny took hearts worth −6, Connie −20, Denny −4, total −30, as entered in the check column. Denny did better than Benny and Connie, gaining a difference of 2 and 16 respectively. He did worse than Annie, however, who redoubled him, giving her twice the difference between their two totals ($2 \times 4 = 8$).

Variations.

Scoring. Different scoring schedules may be encountered, especially in the score for Domino. Whichever you follow or however you adapt, the important thing is to ensure that the five negative and two positive games retain a total yield of zero. This is useful for checking, and makes it easier to convert the result into hard score (cash).

Doubling. Some circles allow players to double only the declarer, not one another. Conversely, a declarer's redouble automatically applies to everyone who doubled, not just some of them.

Ravage city. An additional, negative contract played at no trump in the same way as the others. Whoever takes most cards in any one suit scores −36. In the event of a tie, with different players taking the same number of cards in (usually) different suits, it is divided evenly among them (−18, −12, −9). If Ravage City is admitted there will eight deals per player, making 32 in all, and the scoring schedule of other contracts will need adjusting to preserve the zero-sum feature.

http://www.pagat.com/reverse/barbu.html
http://www.barbu.co.uk

Basra

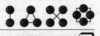

Fishing game

52

Iraqi version of a game widely played throughout the Middle East. The Lebanese version is called Ashush, which means Jack, but is also colloquial Arabic for imam. The Iranian equivalent is Passur.

From two to four may play, four usually in partnerships. The turn to deal and play passes to the right.

Deal four cards each, then four face up to the table (actually called the floor), not overlapping, and stack the rest face down. If the table cards include or ♦7 or any Jacks, put them at the bottom of the stock (they will eventually go to the dealer) and deal replacements. Whenever players run out of cards they are dealt four more so long as any remain.

At each turn you play one card to the table with the aim of capturing one or more table cards by pairing or summing.

Pairing means you play an Ace to capture one or more Aces, a King one or more Kings, and so on.

Summing means you capture two or more numeral cards that sum to the card you play. (For example, a Nine takes a Four and a Five.) Kings and Queens have no numerical value, and can only be taken by pairing.

You may make as many captures as you can with any one card. You must capture if the card you play is capable of doing so, but you aren't obliged to play a capturing card if you have one. If you play a non-capturing card, it merely becomes one of the table available for capture later.

Capturing all the cards from the table is a *basra*, and the capturing card is stored face up to mark it.

A Jack 'sweeps' all the cards from the table, but this does not count as a basra. So does ♦7, and this can count as a basra, but only if the table cards are all numerals with a total value not exceeding 10.

Any cards left on the table after the final capture are taken by the player who captured last, but this does not count as a basra.

Score 3 for cards, 1 per Jack, 1 per Ace, 2 for ♣2, 3 for ♦10, and 10 for each *basra*. Game is 101 points. A rubber is won by the first to win three games. If both players have won two, the fifth is usually played up to 150.

Bassadewitz

Penalty-trick game

32

(Or *Bassarovitz*): An old German game, still played domestically in parts of German-speaking Europe. Rules vary; these are typical.

Dealer puts up a pool of twelve chips and deals eight cards each from a 32-card pack ranking and counting as follows:

A	K	Q	J	10	9	8	7
11	4	3	2	10	0	0	0

Eldest hand leads to the first trick and the winner of each trick leads to the next. You must follow suit if you can, but may otherwise play any card. The trick is taken by the highest card of the suit led. There are no trumps.

Whoever takes fewest card-points wins 5 chips, second fewest 4, third fewest 3. Ties are settled in favour of the elder player, but a player taking no trick beats one who merely takes no card-points.

A player winning every trick is paid 4 each by the others; a player taking 100 or more card-points but failing to win every trick pays 4 each to the others. In these cases the pool remains intact and the same dealer deals again, as also if all four take the same number of card-points.

Variant. Ace counts 5 instead of 11, and each player adds 1 per trick to his total of card-points. (Probably the oldest form of the game.)

Basset

A notorious old Italian banking game once popular at the court of Charles II, but soon overtaken by its descendant ▸ **Faro**.

Bastard ▸ *Brag*

Battle

Card-catch game

52

An ancient game for children, like ▸ **Beggar my Neighbour** only simpler. Each player holds half the pack face down and at each turn plays the top card face up. Whoever plays the higher card, regardless of suit, wins and places both cards at the bottom of his pile. If both tie, they are laid aside and taken by the winner of the next untied pair.

Bauernschnapsen

A complicated partnership version of ▸ **Schnapsen**.

http://www.pagat.com/marriage/bauernschnapsen.html

Bavarian Tarock

Point-trick game

36

One of several German varieties of a game based on ▸ **Tarock** but played without the tarock cards. This version dates from the 1930s.

Players start by contributing 100 units each to a pot. A game ends when the pot is empty.

Deal 11 cards each in batches of 4 3 (3) 4, the bracketed 3 going face down to the table as a widow. Cards rank and count as follows:

A	10	K	Q	J	9	8	7	6
11	10	4	3	2	0	0	0	0

Each in turn, starting with Eldest, may pass or say 'Play'. 'Play' is an offer to take at least 61 of the 120 card-points in tricks after naming trumps and playing alone against the other two. If not overcalled, he declares whether he will play a 'pick-up' or 'hand' game. 'Pick-up' means he will take the widow and discard three unwanted cards before announcing trumps; 'hand' means he will play the hand as dealt. In either case, any card-points contained in the widow will count at end of play as if he had won them in tricks.

If he says 'Play', the next in turn (or, if he passes, the third player) may try to take the game off him by bidding 'hand'. The first bidder may then pass, or assert priority by bidding 'hand' himself. The latter may be contested by raising the amount bid in successive multiples of five ('And five', 'And ten', etc.; no jump-bidding permitted), until one of them passes. If the third player has yet to speak, he may bid the next higher multiple of five; and so on.

Eldest leads to the first trick. You must follow suit if you can and win the trick if you can, and if unable to follow must play a trump if you have any. A trick is taken by the highest card of the suit led or by the highest trump if any are played.

The soloist, if successful, wins a basic 5 units, plus 5 per whole or part of every 5 points he took in excess of his contract. If he loses, the minus value is 5 units per whole or part of every 5 card-points by which he fell short of it. (*Example*: In a basic contract, the value is 5 for taking 61–5, 10 for 66–70 etc, or minus 5 for 56–60, etc. In a 66-contract, it is 5 for taking 66–70, minus 5 for 61–5; and so on.)

For winning a pick-up, the soloist takes the appropriate amount from the pot; for winning a hand game, he receives the appropriate amount from each opponent, plus 10 units for each additional 5 points by which he raised his contract above 61.

For losing a pick-up, he pays out of pocket to one opponent, the other taking that amount from the pot; for losing a hand game, he pays it to each opponent instead.

The game ends when the pot is empty. If the last soloist wins, and the amount due from the pot is more than it contains, he can take only what is there. But if he loses, and the amount due from him is more than the pot contains, he need not pay one player more than the other can take from the pot.

Variant. If an opening bid is uncontested, and the bidder announces a hand game, he may raise the amount of his contract by any multiple of five.

Beggar my Neighbour

Card-catch game

52

Also called Beat your Neighbour out of Doors, or Strip Jack Naked. An extension of ▸ **Battle**. Each receives 26 cards and stacks them face down on the table. Each in turn plays the top card of his stack to a common pile. When one of them plays a Jack, Queen, King, or Ace, the other must play (respectively) one, two, three, or four cards immediately to the top of the pile. If they are all numerals, the pile is won by the other player and placed face down beneath his stack. If one of them is a pay card, however, the tables are turned, and the other must pay the appropriate number of cards. Whoever captures all 52 cards wins.

Bela ▸▸ *Clobiosh*

Belgian Whist

Plain-trick game

A popular continental game (*Wiezen, Kleurwiezen, Whist à la Couleur*) intermediate between ▸ **Solo Whist** and ▸ **Boston Whist**.

Four players use 52 cards ranking A K Q J 10 9 8 7 6 5 4 3 2 in each suit. Each player starts with the same number of chips or counters, and places an agreed small stake in the pool before each deal. The turn to deal, bid, and play passes to the left. Deal 13 cards each.

Each in turn may pass, make a proposal or a higher bid, or accept a proposal that has not been overcalled. Eldest hand has the additional privilege of checking ('*J'attends*'), in which case the opening bid passes to the left. A player who has passed may not bid again, apart from the first to speak (whether Eldest or the next player if he checked), who may accept a proposal if no one overcalled it.

The bids are listed below from lowest to highest. Certain bids may be overcalled by the same bid in a higher-ranking suit, for which purpose the suit order from low to high is ♠-♣-♦-♥.

1. **Proposal** in spades/clubs/diamonds/hearts. To win at least eight tricks with the aid of a partner, the caller to win at least five and partner at least three. Any subsequent player in turn to bid may offer support, provided that no intervening player has bid higher. A player may overcall a proposal, whether accepted or not, by proposing in a higher suit. A player whose proposal is followed by three passes may pass or raise the bid to a solo.

2. **Hole**. A proposal made by anyone holding three or four Aces. If three, whoever holds the fourth must reply 'Hole' and name a trump suit. If four, they announce this fact, then whoever holds ♥K must reply 'Hole', and the two play a Proposal in hearts. A player holding four Aces and ♥K may bid Hole, in which case whoever holds ♥Q becomes the partner in a heart contract. A bid of Hole may not be overcalled, and so becomes the contract.

3. **Solo** in spades/clubs/diamonds/hearts. To win at least six tricks, playing alone.
4. **Petite misère**. To lose all 12 tricks at no trump, after everyone has discarded one card before the first trick is played. Two players may bid this, but must then play cooperatively, as both lose equally if either takes a trick.
5. **Seven** in spades/clubs/diamonds/hearts. To win at least seven tricks, playing alone.
6. **Piccolissimo**. To win exactly two tricks, playing at no trump.
7. **Eight** in spades/clubs/diamonds/hearts. To win at least eight tricks, playing alone.
8. **Piccolo**. To win exactly one trick, playing at no trump. Two players may bid this, but must then play cooperatively, as both lose if one loses.
9. **Abundance**. To win at least nine tricks alone, playing at no trump, and leading to the first trick. It may be played open (the soloist playing with his hand exposed before the first trick) for a higher score.
10. **Grande misère**. To lose all 13 tricks, playing at no trump.
11. **Slam solo**. To win all 13 tricks alone, with a specified suit as trump, and leading to the first trick. It may be played open for a higher score.

If all pass, everyone stakes again to the pool and the same dealer deals again.

The opening lead is made by the soloist in an abundance or a slam, if any, otherwise by Eldest. You must follow suit if you can, but may otherwise play any card. The trick is taken by the highest card of the suit led, or by the highest trump if any are played, and the winner of each trick leads to the next.

If successful, the soloist wins the pool, plus an amount from each opponent that varies according to the contract and the result, as listed below. If partnered, both divide the pool equally and each receives the stated amount from one opponent. If unsuccessful, soloist doubles the pool and pays the appropriate amount to each opponent. If partnered, they double the pool between them—half each—and each pays the stated amount to one opponent. A typical schedule of pay-offs might be:

Proposal	4 + 1 per overtrick
Hole	4 + 1 per overtrick
Six solo	8 + 2 per overtrick
Petite misère	10
Seven solo	12 + 3 per overtrick
Piccolissimo	14
Eight solo	16 + 4 per overtrick
Piccolo	18
Abundance	22 or 44 if played open
Grande misère	28
Slam	100 or 200 if played open

Belle Lucie (Patience) ▸▸ *Fair Lucy*

Belote

Point-trick game

32

The French national card game, a variety of ▸ **Klaberjass**, first reached France in about 1914.

All forms of Belote are played with the 32-card French pack. The order of cards from highest to lowest, with their card-point value when captured in tricks, is as follows:

In trumps	J	9	A	10	K	Q	—	—	8	7
In plain suits	—	—	A	10	K	Q	J	9	8	7
Card-points	20	14	11	10	4	3	2	0	0	0

Card-points are also counted for holding certain melds (combinations) of cards in one hand, namely:

four Jacks	200	sequence of five +	100
four Nines	150	sequence of four	50
four Aces	100	sequence of three	20
four Tens	100		
four Kings	100	belote	20
four Queens	100		

A sequence is three or more cards of the same suit and in numerical order, for which purpose the order is always A K Q J 10 9 8 7 (regardless of the ranking power and point-value of the cards concerned).

Belote consists of the King and Queen of trumps in the same hand.

Belote for two

Whoever draws the lower-ranking card (A K Q J 10 9 8 7) deals first; thereafter, the winner of each hand deals to the next. Deal six cards each in threes and turn the next for trump. Whoever selects trumps becomes the declarer and aims to win more card-points in tricks than the other.

Elder (non-dealer) may either accept the turned suit as trump or invite Younger to do so. If both pass, Elder turns the odd card down and either proposes a different suit or allows Younger to do so. If both still pass, the hands are thrown in without play and the deal changes hands.

With trumps selected, Younger deals three more cards apiece and turns the bottom card of the stock face up (for information). If the original suit was accepted, either player holding the Seven may exchange it for the trump turn-up. This must be done before any melds are declared.

Upon leading to the first trick, Elder announces the highest he has of the melds listed above. If Younger cannot beat the declared meld, he says 'Good', whereupon Elder scores for it and any others he may have and is willing to show. If he can beat it, Younger in replying to the trick declares his best combination and scores for it, and any others he may have and is willing to show.

In deciding between melds a longer sequence beats a shorter; if equal, a higher beats a lower; if still equal, a trump sequence beats a plain; and if still equal, Elder's wins. When first announcing a sequence, Elder need only identify as much of it as is necessary to determine whose is better.

If either player holds K–Q of trumps, he scores 20 upon playing either of them to a trick and announcing *belote*. Later, upon playing the other, he must announce *rebelote*, otherwise the 20 is annulled.

The second to a trick must follow suit if possible, otherwise must trump if possible, and only otherwise may play any card. To a trump lead, the second must play higher if possible. The trick is taken by the higher card of the suit led or the higher trump if any are played. The winner of the last trick scores 10 for last (*dix de der*), or 100 for *capot* if he won all nine.

Both players then declare their respective totals for melds and card-points and count these towards game. However, if the declarer fails to take more than his opponent he counts nothing to game but adds whatever he did make to his opponent's total—unless they both took the same, in which case his score is held over and goes to the winner of the next deal.

Game is 1000 points.

Optional rules

1. A player dealt all four Sevens may annul the deal. His opponent then deals to the next.
2. If previously agreed, the game may cease in mid-play the moment either player claims to have reached the target score. The claimant must have won at least one trick before claiming. An incorrect claim loses the game.
3. Bids of *sans atout* and *tout atout* may be admitted, as in the partnership game (below).

Belote for three

As above, but the deal and the turn to play pass always to the right. If declarer leads a plain suit which neither opponent can follow, and the first of them plays a trump, then the other need not also trump but may renounce. If one player wins no trick, the others score 50 each for *capot*; if two take none, the third scores 100.

Partnership Belote

Four may play Belote independently, playing to the right and following the procedures described above, or in one of several partnership forms. In *Belote Coinchée* (or *Contrée*), bids are raised by stating the number of points one contracts to win with one's partner. *Belote Bridge* ranks the suits in Bridge order for bidding purposes, producing a hybrid concoction rightly eschewed by players of taste and refinement.

In basic Partnership Belote two new bids overcall a bid in the turned suit, as follows:

- In *sans atout*, or 'no trump', the cards of every suit rank A-11, 10-10, K-4, Q-3, J-2, 9 8 7 zero. A quartet of Aces counts 200, Tens 150, Kings, Queens, or Jacks 100 each. Nothing is counted for four Nines or a *belote*.

- In *tout atout*, or 'all trump', the cards of every suit rank Jack 20, Nine 14, A-11, 10-10, K-4, Q-3, others zero. All the usual melds are recognized, and there are four possible *belotes*, each consisting of the K-Q of the same suit. All trump is the highest possible bid.

The turn to deal, play, and bid passes always to the right. Deal five each (3 then 2) and turn the next for trump. There may be one or two rounds of bidding. Eldest starts. On the first round, each in turn may pass, name the turned suit as trump, bid no trump or all trump, double an opponent's bid, or redouble one's partner's bid if it has been doubled by an opponent.

If a bid is doubled and redoubled, the contract is established and the auction ends. If not, each in turn may bid again, provided that each bid, including the first, is higher than any which has gone before. In this case, however, a simple trump bid may no longer be made in the suit of the turn-up, but only in a suit of one's own choice. Bidding ends when a bid has been redoubled, or when three players successively pass. No player

Belote. West dealt, turning up ♦ 9 and accepting diamonds as trump on the strength of his two top trumps. Unfortunately, after three passes and the deal of three more cards each, North–South emerged with a majority of trumps as well as a heart tierce in South's hand (♥K-Q-J). The final score was North–South 107, plus 10 for last, plus 20 for the tierce, plus the paltry 45 made by East–West, giving them a grand total of 182.

may raise his own bid. If all four pass, the deal is annulled and the next in turn to deal does so.

The undealt cards are then dealt three to each player, the turn-up going to the player who named the contract. Eldest leads first. Each turn, on playing to the first trick, announces his highest meld (if any).

At the end of the trick, the player announcing the best meld shows and scores for it and any others he is willing to show; his partner also may show and score for any melds he has.

To a plain-suit lead players must either follow suit if possible or, if not, play a trump if possible. To a trump lead, players must follow suit and head the trick if possible, even if one's own partner is winning it. At no trump, all leads are plain. At all trump, logic demands that all leads count as if from trumps; but this rule is variable and should be settled beforehand.

The last trick counts 10 to the side taking it, or 100 in case of *capot*. If the contracting side scores more than the other, both score what they make; if equal or less, the other side scores both totals. This also applies in a redoubled contract, but not in a contract doubled once only. Equality here entitles the contracting side to score its points, as the double is construed as an undertaking by the other side to take a majority of points. Whatever the outcome, the score is doubled at no trump, or tripled at grand.

The game is won by the first side to reach 3000 points (or, since scores are usually recorded in tens, 300).

Besikovitch's Game ▸▸ *Challenge*

Best Boy
Plain tricks

An old but unusually interesting German game related to ▸ **Ecarté**.

Dealer puts five chips in the pot, deals five cards each in batches of three and two from a 32-card pack, and turns the next for trump. The highest trump is the Jack (called *Bester Bube*, meaning 'Top Jack', literally 'Best Boy'), followed by the other Jack of the same colour, followed by A K Q (J) 10 9 8 7.

Each in turn may make any number of discards and draw replacements from the stock (excluding the turn-up). Two rounds of discarding and drawing are permitted, so long as enough cards remain. Before play, dealer takes the turn-up in exchange for any discard.

Eldest must lead the Best Boy if held, otherwise any trump. Lacking trumps, he leads any card face down and announces 'Trumps'(!) Whoever holds the Best Boy must play it to the first trick—except for the dealer, who may retain it—and no one else need follow suit. The same rules apply at trick two, this time in respect of the second-best Boy. Thereafter any card may be led and played, still without obligation to follow suit.

Each player wins one chip per trick taken, but a player taking none pays into the pot the amount it contained at the start of the deal.

Bezique

Point-trick game

32 | 32

A nineteenth-century French game derived from ▶ **Mariage** and ▶ **Briscan** by the addition of a special and distinctive scoring feature—namely, the combination of a Queen and a Jack of different suits, which acts as a sort of illicit rival to a 'marriage', and goes under various names such as *besi, bésigue, binage, binocle*, etc., according to locality. The original game, also called Cinq Cents, was played with a single 32-card pack, but the most popular version is the classic Bezique played with two such packs shuffled together. In its heyday (early twentieth century) it gave rise to larger versions played with four packs (Rubicon or Japanese Bezique), six packs (Chinese Bezique), eight packs (no special name) and a significantly different two-pack variation called Polish Bezique, or Fildinski. The German form of the game reached America under the name *Binokel* and produced distinctive offspring now spelt ▶ **Pinochle**. For completeness, *see also* ▶ **Briscan** and ▶ **Marjolet**.

Two-pack Bezique

Two players each receive eight cards (dealt 3-2-3) from two 32-card packs shuffled together, ranking A 10 K Q J 9 8 7. The next card is turned for trumps and placed under the stock, face up and slightly projecting.

The winner is the first to reach 1000 points over as many deals as necessary, the players dealing alternately. Points are scored partly for capturing *brisques* (Aces and Tens) in tricks, but mainly for acquiring and declaring any of the following features:

Trump sequence (A-K-Q-J-10)	250
Marriages (K Q of same suit)	
Trump	40
Plain	20
Beziques (♠Q + ♦J)	
Single	40
Double	500
Quartets (four of a kind)	
Aces	100
Kings	80
Queens	60
Jacks	40
Dix (trump 7)	10

Non-dealer leads first. Second to a trick may play any card. A trick is taken by the higher card of the suit led, or the higher trump if any are played, or the first played of two identical cards.

Winning a trick entitles you to declare a scoring combination from the above list, if you have one, by laying the appropriate cards face up on the table before you, where they continue to remain part of your hand to be played from in subsequent tricks. In fact you can declare more than one than one combination upon winning a trick, but you may only score for one of them at a time: each of the others can only be scored upon winning another trick, and only so long as you have not played out any of its constituent cards to another trick.

The winner of each trick then draws the top card of stock, waits for the other to draw, and leads to the next trick.

Whoever wins the last trick before the stock is emptied may make one declaration before drawing the penultimate card. When both last cards have been drawn, no more declarations may be made, and each player takes all his cards back into hand.

In playing the last eight tricks the second must follow suit if possible, must win the trick if possible, and must trump (if possible) when unable to follow. Combinations are no longer declarable. The winner of the eighth trick scores '10 for last'.

Each player finally adds 10 for each Ace and Ten he has taken in tricks (*brisques*). If neither has yet reached 1000, the previous non-dealer deals to the next.

Special rules. Accounts differ. The following are typical:

Holding a Seven of trumps, you may, upon winning a trick, declare it for 10 points and exchange it for the turn-up (if different). This counts as a declaration (unless otherwise agreed—authorities are unclear about it).

Any card from a combination that you have declared and scored for may later be combined with one or more others from your hand or table to form a *different* type of combination, but you may not use it twice in the *same* type. For example, the Queen in a spade marriage may not be remarried to the other King, but may later be counted in a bezique or a quartet of Queens. Similarly, with 'eighty Kings' and 'sixty Queens' declared, each possible marriage may be scored on subsequent tricks so long as valid pairs remain intact. It is not (as sometimes claimed) illegal to make a meld entirely from cards already on the table, so long as it is different.

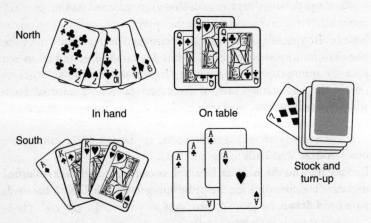

North

In hand   On table

South

Stock and turn-up

Bezique. A hand in progress. North has scored '60 Queens' and an earlier bezique, having since played the Jack; South has scored '100 Aces', plus 10 for exchanging the trump Seven, and has a marriage to score upon winning a trick.

If you score a trump sequence, you may not subsequently score the marriage it contains; but you may count the marriage first, and include it in a scoring sequence upon winning a subsequent trick.

You may declare double bezique by laying out all four cards at once, or by adding a second bezique to a single bezique already scored and still on the table; but if you score for two singles, you may not count the double as well.

Variations

1. Instead of turning a card, start at no trump and entrump the suit of the first marriage declared.
2. If spades or diamonds are trump, bezique may be redefined as ♣Q ♥J.

Fildinski (Polish Bezique)

Play as above, but with the following differences. You cannot meld the cards in your hand, but only those you capture in tricks. For this purpose you leave all the cards you win face up on the table in front of you. When you win a trick you may use either or both of its cards to create and score for a meld in conjunction with one or more cards already won. You may count two melds at a time, each using one card won in the trick, but you may not use the same card simultaneously in different melds.

Single Bezique (Cinq Cents, Binage)

The ancestor of two-pack Bezique, played with 32 cards and up to 500 points. Captured cards count Ace 11, Ten 10, King 4, Queen 3, Jack 2. Declarable combinations are: common marriage for 20, royal marriage 40, *binage* (♠ Q ♦J) 40, non-trump sequence 120, trump sequence 250. Quartets do not count.

Multi-pack variants

Bezique may be played with four, six, or eight 32-card packs shuffled together. The following general rules apply to all; see Table 1 for other scores and details.

Cards dealt. See following table. No card is turned for trump, and no score or significance attaches to the trump Seven.

Table 1 Table of scoring features for 4-, 6-, and 8-pack Bezique

	Four	Six	Eight
Deal to each	9	12	15
Carte blanche	50	250	–
Sequences			
Trump A K Q J 10	250	250	250
Non-trump	150	150	150
Royal marriage	40	40	40
Marriage	20	20	20
Quartets, quintets			
Any four Aces	100	100	100
Any four Kings	80	80	80
Any four Queens	60	60	60
Any four Jacks	40	40	40
Four trump Aces	–	1000	1000
Four trump Tens	–	900	900
Four trump Kings	–	800	800
Four trump Queens	–	600	600
Four trump Jacks	–	400	400
Five trump Aces	–	–	2000
Five trump Tens	–	–	1800
Five trump Kings	–	–	1600
Five trump Queens	–	–	1200
Five trump Jacks	–	–	800
Beziques			
Single	40	40	40
Double	500	500	500
Treble	1500	1500	1500
Quadruple	4500	4500	4500
Quintuple	–	–	9000
Winning last trick	50	250	250
Rubicon	1000	3000	5000
Add for game	500	1000	1000
Add for rubicon	500	Loser's total	Loser's total

Carte blanche. Except in eight-pack Bezique, a player dealt no court may show the hand and score for *carte blanche* (*see* Table 1). Thereafter, so long as the card he draws from stock after each trick fails to be a court, he may show the card and make the score again.

Trump suit. Play starts at no trump. The first marriage (or sequence) declared establishes a trump suit, which remains unchanged throughout.

Bezique no. If agreed, bezique may be redefined as the Queen of trumps and the appropriate Jack of opposite colour—spades with diamonds, clubs with hearts. In this case, the trump may be established as that of the Queen if a bezique is declared before a marriage. Also, the same suit may not be entrumped twice in successive deals. The score for a multiple bezique only obtains if all cards involved are on display at the same time.

Additional melds. Sequences may be declared in plain suits as well as trumps. In six-and eight-pack Bezique, trump quartets are declarable as shown in the table.

Re-forming melds. A meld that has been broken up by the play of one or more cards to a trick may be re-formed and scored again by the addition of matching replacements.

Brisques do not count in multi-pack variants, except to break ties in the four-pack game.

Game score. Final scores are rounded down to the nearest 100 and the winner scores the difference, plus a bonus if the loser fails to 'cross the rubicon'—that is, fails to reach the target score specified in the table for that purpose.

Bid Euchre ▸ *Five Hundred*

Bid Whist

An ancestor of ▸ **Bridge** (*see also* ▸ **Biritch**). Deal thirteen each from a 52-card pack. Each bids a number of odd tricks from one to seven, without mentioning trumps. Bidding continues until three pass in succession, when the last bidder announces trumps and his left opponent leads. A successful contract scores 1 point per odd trick taken, otherwise the opponents score 1 point per odd trick they took and the declarers deduct the amount of their bid.

Bid Whist

Plain-trick game

Modern Bid Whist is the national card game of Afro-Americans. Its popularity is phenomenal. Manuals (by Butch Thomas, R. Wesley Agee, and others) and websites confirm that it is now 'played by millions of people across the country at family or social gatherings. A number of big companies sponsor Bid Whist tournaments each year ... [It] has immense popularity on college campuses ... [and] is widely played by military service personnel and their families stationed around the world' (Agee). There is no universally accepted set of rules, but the following is typical.

Before play, it should be noted that the game has its own terminology for many otherwise standard features. In particular, a trick is a *book*, a non-trump suit is an *off-suit*, and *to cut* means to ruff (play a trump to the lead of an off-suit).

Four players sit crosswise in fixed partnerships and use a 54-card pack including two Jokers. The Jokers must be distinguishable from one another, one of them being called Big Joker and the other Little Joker.

Rank of cards

- In high bids ('uptown'), cards rank from high to low A K Q J 10 9 8 7 6 5 4 3 2.
- In low bids ('downtown'), cards rank from high to low A 2 3 4 5 6 7 8 9 10 J Q K.
- In trump bids, the top trumps are Big Joker, Little Joker, Ace, and so downwards to Two (uptown), or King (down-town).
- In no trump bids, Jokers are powerless and usually discarded before play begins.

Deal. 12 each in ones and six face down as a kitty.

Object. A contract is established by auction. If successful, the declarers score 1 per odd book, or 2 at no trump. Game is 5 or 7 points, as previously agreed.

Auction. Each in turn, starting at Dealer's left, may pass or bid once only. Each bid must be higher than the last. If the first three pass, Dealer must bid. The lowest bid is 'Three', i.e. to win nine books with a trump suit not yet specified. A bare number is understood to represent a 'high' or 'uptown' bid. This is beaten by 'Three low', which is the same but with reverse or 'downtown' ranking (Big Jo, Little Jo, Ace, Two, etc). This is beaten by 'Three no trump'—whether high or low not yet specified. Thus the bids from lowest to highest begin: Three high, Three low, Three no trump, Four high, Four low, and so on.

Taking the kitty. If playing in trumps, the highest bidder announces the trump suit, 'sports' the kitty by turning it face up for all to see, and adds it to his hand. If playing at no trump, he announces 'high' or 'low', and takes the kitty into hand without showing it. He then makes any six discards face down, and these count as the first of his side's won books. At no trump, anyone holding a Joker should then add it to the kitty and draw a replacement at random from it (face down, of course).

Play. Declarer leads to the first of 12 books. Players must follow suit if possible, otherwise may play any card. The book is taken by the highest card of the suit led, or by the highest trump if any are played, and the winner of each book leads to the next. (If anyone holds a Joker at no trump, it can never win a book, and may only be discarded when its holder cannot follow suit. If a Joker is led, the next card played establishes the suit to follow.)

Score. If successful, Declarer's side scores 1 point per book contracted. If not, they lose 1 point per book contracted; and if the opponents win seven or more, they score 1 point per book won above six. These scores are all doubled in the case of a no trump bid. The game ends when one side wins by reaching the target score, or loses by reaching minus the target score.

Winning all 13 books is a 'Boston', and scores quadruple.

Variants. With two Jokers, the lowest bid is sometimes 'Four'. Some play with only one Joker and a five-card kitty. Some play without Jokers and either a four-card kitty or none at all. In the latter case, 13 books are played and the lowest bid is 'One'.

Bierspiel

(Literally 'Beer Game') = any German ▸ **Drinking game**.

Big Ben (Patience) ▸ *Clock*

Big Two

A Chinese game (Choi Dai Di) similar to ▸ **President**, but extremely elaborate and with many variations.

http://www.pagat.com/climbing/bigtwo.html

Binage, Binocle, Binokel ▸ *Bezique*

Biritch

The earliest form of ▸ **Bridge**, first described by John Collinson in a four-page leaflet of 1886 spuriously entitled *Biritch, or Russian Whist*.

Bismarck ▸ *Dutch Whist*

Black Jack ▸ *Crazy Eights*

Blackjack ▸▸ *Pontoon* (the casino version of)

Black Maria (Finnish game) ▸▸ *Mustamaija*

Black Maria

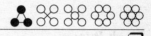

Penalty-trick game

52

A variety of ▸ **Hearts** devised by Hubert Phillips in the 1920s. Its popularity has waned in favour of Hearts, but you may find it preferable to Hearts when only three players are available.

Unless four play, start by stripping from the 52-card pack as many of the following cards as necessary to ensure that they will go round evenly: ♣2, ♦2, ♠2, ♣3.

The turn to deal and play passes to the left. Deal all the cards out one at a time. The aim is to avoid winning tricks containing hearts or any of the three highest spades—or, if the hand is strong enough, to win all 16 penalty cards.

Each player first passes three cards face down to his right-hand neighbour and receives the same number from his left. If more than four play, only two are passed.

Eldest leads first and the winner of each trick leads to the next. Suit must be followed if possible; if not, any unwanted or penalty card may be thrown without restriction. The trick is taken by the highest card of the suit led. There are no trumps.

At end of play each player scores penalty points for cards taken in tricks as follows:

each heart = 1   ♠ A = 7   ♠ K = 10   ♠ Q = 13

A player taking all 16 penalty cards deducts 43 points from his current penalty score.

The winner is the player with fewest points after an agreed number of deals, or when one player reaches an agreed limit, such as 100.

Black Peter ▸▸ *Old Maid*

Blackout ▸▸ *Oh Hell!*

Bleeding Hearts ▸▸ *Bugami*

Block Rummy

A variety of ▸ **Rummy** that ends when the stock runs out instead of allowing it to be reconstituted from the discard pile.

Bohemian Schneider

Plain-trick game

A Czech game said to be for children, but more interesting than it sounds.

Deal six cards each in threes from a 32-card pack ranking A K Q J 10 9 8 7 in each suit. The aim is to win a majority of 'honours', which are all the cards higher than Nine. Non-dealer leads. You don't have to follow suit; there are no trumps; and a trick can only be taken by the immediately next higher card of the suit led (♠7 by ♠8, ♦J by ♦Q, etc.). The trick-winner draws from stock, waits for the other to do so, and leads to the next trick. Taking eleven or more honours wins a single game, sixteen or more double, all twenty treble.

Variants

1. An Ace, normally uncapturable, may be taken by a Seven.
2. Cards count Ace 11, King 4, Queen 3, Jack 2, Ten 10, others zero. Play as above, but a trick is taken by any card exactly one rank higher than that led, regardless of suit. You win a single game or stake by taking 61 or more card-points, double for 91 plus, treble for all 120.

Bolivia ▸▸ *Canasta* (Bolivian)

Bondtolva

Point-tricks

24

Pronounced *boon-tolva*, and meaning 'farmer's dozen', Bondtolva is a Swedish game similar to ▸ **Sixty-Six**, but with a curious resonance of ▸ **All Fours**. The simplest version is for two:

Deal six each in threes from a 24-card pack ranking A 10 K Q J 9. Turn the rest face down as a stock. The winner is the first to reach 12 points over as many deals as necessary, each dealing in turn. Points are scored for declaring marriages, for winning the most 'matadors' (Aces and Tens), and for winning the last trick.

Elder leads to the first trick. Suit need not be followed. A trick is taken by the higher card of the suit led, or, when trumps have been made, by the higher trump. The trick-winner draws the top card of stock, waits for the other to draw, and leads to the next.

When leading to a trick (but not when following) you may declare a marriage by showing a King and Queen of the same suit and leading one of them. The first marriage, called 'trump', scores 2 points and establishes trumps for the rest of the deal. A subsequently declared marriage scores 1 point, but does not change the trump suit.

When the stock is empty no more marriages may be declared. Second to a trick must then follow suit if possible, head the trick if possible, and trump if unable to follow.

The winner of the last trick scores 1 point, as does the player who took a majority of Aces and Tens. If equal, that point goes to the player who took most card-points, reckoning each Ace 4, King 3, Queen 2, and Jack 1. If still equal, neither scores it.

Optional rule. You must make exactly 12 points to win. If the number you gain in a deal would take you over the 12, you deduct it from your current total instead of adding it.

Three or four players

The cards are all dealt out, and the rules of trick-play are those applying to the two-hander when the stock is empty, except that marriages are declarable throughout.

The four-hander is played in partnerships. Before trumps are established, the leader to a trick may do one of the following:

(a) If holding a marriage, show and lead from it. This scores 2 and fixes the trump suit.

(b) If not, ask if partner holds a marriage. If so, partner shows it for 2 and this establishes trumps. Any card may then be led.

(c) Holding one card of a marriage, ask if partner can pair it, by saying (for example) 'Hearts?'. If partner says 'Yes', the trump is established for 2 points and the qualifying King or Queen must be led. If 'No', any card may be led of that suit, but no other.

Note that only one marriage query may be made on the same turn. Given a negative to (b) or (c), the asker must win a trick and be on lead before asking again.

Subsequent marriages score only 1 each and do not change the trump. Upon leading, you may:

- declare a marriage yourself by showing and leading from it; or
- ask if your partner has one. If so, you must lead the stated suit in order to score the point; or
- lead a King or Queen and ask if your partner can wed it. If so, the marriage partner must be shown, but need only be played to the trick in order to comply with the rules of following—i.e. head the trick if possible, and trump if unable to follow suit.

☛ *Comment.* The first marriage is called a 'trump' for obvious reasons, and each subsequent marriage a 'score' (*tjog*). The latter reflects its original score of 20 points, as in Sixty-Six, Bezique, and others.

Booby

Plain-trick game

52

Hubert Phillips's adaptation of Contract ▶ **Bridge** for three players.

Deal 17 cards each and one face down to an eventual dummy. Each player examines his hand and makes four discards face down to the dummy, leaving all four hands with 13 cards each. Players bid to partner the dummy, following the usual procedure but with the addition of a nullo bid ranking between hearts and spades, and valued at 30 per trick. (One nullo is therefore a bid to win not more than six tricks at no trump, and seven nullos is a complete misère.) Whoever bids highest becomes the declarer, and, if necessary, changes seats with another player in order to play opposite the dummy and ensure that the defenders play alternately rather than consecutively. He then turns the dummy face up after his left-hand opponent has led.

Suggested variant. Try dealing 16 each and five face up to the dummy, to which each player then contributes three. Ignore nullos.

Boodle ▸ *Michigan*

Boonaken

A Dutch drinking-game variety of ▸ **Jass**.

> http://www.pagat.com/ jass/boonaken.html

Boston Whist
Plain-trick game

52

This great nineteenth-century card game was once played throughout the Western world apart from Britain—where, however, it later materialized in the descendant form of ▸ **Solo Whist**. Though appropriately named after a key location in the American War of Independence, it was probably devised in France in the 1770s by combining the 52-card pack and logical ranking system of partnership ▸ **Whist** with a range of solo and alliance bids borrowed from ▸ **Quadrille**. It produced many variants—Maryland, Boston de Nantes, Boston de Lorient, Russian Boston, etc.—and inventive bids with titles amounting to variations on a theme—*indépendance, souverain, concordia,* and suchlike. Described below is the highly developed version called Boston de Fontainebleau. As no two accounts are identical, the following rules can only be described as 'typical'. In particular, I have translated the hard-score into an equivalent soft-score system. As originally played, Boston required several thousand chips or counters, hundreds of which could be involved in complicated transactions between various players at the conclusion of every hand. Players nowadays are unlikely to have that many counters lying around, or tables big enough to accommodate them, or the patience to be forever fiddling about with bits of plastic.

Four players each receive 13 cards from a 52-card pack ranking A K Q J 10 9 8 7 6 5 4 3 2 in each suit. Eldest bids first and the highest bidder becomes the soloist, playing alone against the other three unless one of them bids to be an ally. Eldest leads first. Follow suit if possible, otherwise play any card. A trick is taken by the highest card of the suit led, or by the highest trump if any are played.

The contracts. Each in turn may bid or pass. A bid states the name of the proposed contract plus the suit of the proposed trump. Each bid must be higher than the preceding one in accordance with the schedule below, or equal in height but in a higher suit. For this purpose, suits ascend in the order spades, clubs, diamonds, hearts.

Although misère bids are actually played at no trump, a nominal suit must be stated for each one, as it can only overcall the positive bid ranking immediately below it if made in an equal or higher suit. For example, while 'six diamonds' may be overcalled by seven or more in any suit, a petite misère will only overcall it if said to be in diamonds or hearts. The nominal suit of a misère bid also governs the amount it wins or loses.

A player having once passed may not come in again, except to support a bid of from five to eight tricks, provided that it has not been overcalled. To support a bid means to ally oneself with the main bidder, thereby sharing in his win or loss.

The schedule of bids and values runs as follows:

1. *Five.* A bid to win at least five tricks with the named suit as trump. If supported, the ally must win at least three. Base value 4 (+1 per over/undertrick).

2. *Six.* To win at least six tricks with the named suit as trump. If supported, the ally must win at least four. Base value 6 (+2 per over/undertrick).

3. *Petite misère.* To lose every trick after making one discard face down and playing to twelve tricks at no trump. Base value 16.

4. *Seven.* To win at least seven tricks with the named suit as trump. If supported, the ally must win at least four. Base value 9 (+3 per over/undertrick).

5. *Piccolissimo.* To win exactly one trick at no trump. Base value 24.

6. *Eight.* To win at least eight tricks with the named suit as trump. If supported, the ally must win at least four. Base value 12 (+4 per over/undertrick).

7. *Grande misère.* To lose all thirteen tricks at no trump. Base value 32.

8. *Nine.* To win at least nine tricks with the named suit as trump. Base value 15 (+5 per over/undertrick).

9. *Four-ace misère.* Though holding four Aces, to lose all thirteen tricks at no trump, but with permission to revoke once in the first ten tricks. Base value 40.

10. *Ten.* To win at least ten tricks with the named suit as trump. Base value 18 (+6 per over/undertrick).

11. *Petite misère ouverte.* To lose every trick at no trump after making one discard face down, exposing one's hand on the table, and playing to twelve tricks. Base value 48.

12. *Eleven.* To win at least eleven tricks with the named suit as trump. Base value 21 (+7 per over/undertrick).

13. *Grande misère ouverte.* To lose all thirteen tricks at no trump, after laying one's hand face up on the table. Base value 56.

14. *Twelve.* To win at least twelve tricks with the named suit as trump. Base value 24 (+8 per over/undertrick).

15. *Boston.* To win all thirteen tricks with the named suit as trump. Base value 100.

16. *Boston ouvert.* The same, but with one's cards face up on the table. Base value 200.

Note. In any ouvert, the hand is exposed before the opening lead. In petite misère, only the bidder makes a discard, and only twelve tricks are played.

Scoring. In an unsupported contract, the amount won or lost by the soloist is found by taking the base value stated in the schedule above and increasing it as follows:

1. Except in misères and Bostons, add the stated 'overtrick' value for each trick taken in excess of the contract (or, if lost, for each trick short of the contract requirement).
2. Except in misères and Bostons, add the equivalent of two over-tricks if the bidder held three honours, or four overtricks if he held all four. The honours are Ace, King, Queen, Jack of trumps.
3. Multiply the result by two if the bid was made in clubs, three if diamonds, four if hearts.

In a supported contract:

- if both players either make or fail their individual contracts, each one's win or loss is calculated exactly as described above, but is then halved before being recorded. (For a supporter, an overtrick or undertrick is that in excess of, or short of, the three or four he personally contracted to win.)
- if only one succeeds, he scores zero. The other loses half the value of his lost contract plus half the value of his ally's won contract. (This correctly reproduces the equivalent payment in counters, but points up its unfairness. It would seem preferable for the successful ally to win half the value of his contract, leaving the other to lose half the value of his own.)

☞ *Comment.* French schedules include an apparent contract of *Boston à deux* ranking between bids of five and six tricks, but do not state how it arises. It is apparently not a bid but a premium score applied when, in a supported game, each makes his contract and both take all thirteen tricks between them. The base value is 50—i.e. half the value of a Boston contract played alone.

Botifarra

Point-trick game

48

A popular Catalan game named after a type of sausage.

The turn to deal and play passes always to the right. Four players sitting crosswise in partnerships are dealt 12 cards each in fours from a 48-card pack ranking 9 A K Q J 8 7 6 5 4 3 2 in each suit. (There are no Tens in the Catalan pack.) Each Nine, called *manilla*, counts 5 points, while A-K-Q-J count 4-3-2-1 respectively. An additional 1 point per trick makes 72 points in all, and the declaring side must take at least 37 to win.

The dealer may announce trumps, or declare *botifarra* (no trumps), or delegate this choice to his partner, who must then exercise it. Either opponent may double (*contrar*), either declarer or his partner may then redouble (*recontrar*), and either opponent may cap this with a double-redouble (announced as *St Vicens*). Doubling announcements must be made strictly in turn (to the right).

Eldest hand (dealer's right-hand neighbour) leads to the first trick and the winner of each trick leads to the next. The rules of trick-play are unusually strict, namely:

- You must not only follow suit if you can, but also, unless your partner is already winning the trick, try to win it yourself if you can (by playing a higher card of the suit led, or, if unable to follow, by trumping or overtrumping if possible).
- If unable to win the trick, or not obliged to because your partner is already winning it, your choice of play is still restricted by who is so far winning the trick, as follows:
  - If your partner is winning, you must play either a counter (9, A, K, Q, J), or the lowest card of whichever suit you play from.
  - If an opponent is winning, you must play the lowest card of whichever suit you play from—unless, however, you are playing second to the trick and cannot follow suit, when you are allowed to play a counter (hoping your partner will win the trick).

The winning side scores whatever it makes, doubled if played at no trump, and in any case doubled, quadrupled, or octupled to the extent that such doublings were made.

☞ *Note.* The unusual feature of the rules of play is not their actual content but the very fact that they are compulsory. What they require you to do is no more than what you would normally do as a matter of strategy. They merely prevent you from making an unorthodox play in order to bluff the opponents or encode information to your partner. In fact, the rules quoted are those of the eastern version of the game, which are stricter than those of the western.

Bouillotte

A game of the French Revolutionary period that achieved some popularity in nineteenth-century America before being ousted by Poker.

Bourré
Plain-trick game

A French-American relative of Nap, revived and promoted as the 'authentic Cajun game' by the National Cajun Bourré Association of Louisiana. (*Bourré* means 'stuffed'. It is sometimes spelt *Bouré*, which is meaningless, or *Booray*, which is illiterate.)

From three to seven players use a 52-card pack ranking A K Q J 10 9 8 7 6 5 4 3 2. Everyone contributes equally to a pool and receives five cards dealt one at a time. A trump suit is established by revealing the dealer's last card (or, in some circles, by exposing the next, undealt, card).

Everyone examines their hand and decides whether to pass or play. Anyone who decides to play must win at least one trick, otherwise they lose. In some circles, each player in turn announces which they will do. In others, everyone secretly put a chip in their fist if they want to stay in, or forms an empty fist if not, and when all are ready they open their fists simultaneously.

After this, each active player in turn may make any number of discards face down and receive replacements from the top of the stock.

The first active player to the dealer's left begins. Players must follow suit and head the trick if possible; must trump and overtrump if unable to follow; and may renounce only if unable to do either. The trick is taken by the highest card of the suit led, or by the highest trump if any are played, and the winner of each trick leads to the next. Anyone holding A, K, or Q of trumps must lead his highest trump as soon as possible.

A player who wins three or more tricks sweeps the pool. A player who wins none is '*bourréed*', and contributes to the next pool the same amount as the pool held when he lost. If two players win two each, it is a 'split pot' tie, and the pool is carried forward to the next deal.

Brag

Vying game

The British national representative of the ▶ **Vying** or 'bluffing' family of gambling games, and a major contributor to the development of ▶ **Poker**, Brag derives from the Elizabethan game of Primero and formed the subject of a treatise by Hoyle in 1751. Many different versions have been played throughout its long history. Their only common feature is the fact that they are based on three-card hands—as opposed to the four of Primero and five of Poker—and that the highest is three of a kind, though many also feature wild cards called 'braggers'.

Brag is played with a 52-card pack basically ranking A K Q J 10 9 8 7 6 5 4 3 2, and recognizes the following range of 'Brag hands', from low to high:

- **Pair.** Two cards of the same rank, the third unmatched.
- **Flush.** Three non-consecutive cards of the same suit.
- **Run.** Three consecutive cards, not flush. (As a deliberate oddity, 3 2 A beats A K Q, and the lowest is 4 3 2.)
- **Running flush.** Three consecutive cards of the same suit. (Again, 3 2 A is best.)
- **Prial** (= **pair royal**). Three of the same rank. (As a deliberate oddity, the highest is a prial of Threes, followed by Aces, Kings, etc.)

A higher combination beats a lower. If equal, that containing the highest top card wins, or second highest if equal. A hand containing one or more wild cards loses to a hand of the same type containing fewer wild cards, regardless of rank (e.g. 4 4 4 beats 5 5 W beats 6 W W). Nowadays Deuces may be wild, or the Joker added as a wild card. But they are often omitted altogether.

Several typical versions are described below, all individual rules being variable by agreement. Each can involve as many players as there are cards to go round. All are hard-score games, requiring coins or counters.

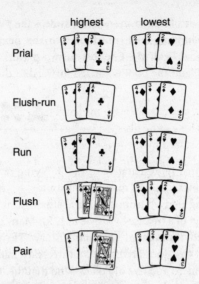

	highest	lowest
Prial		
Flush-run		
Run		
Flush		
Pair		

Brag. Brag hands from highest to lowest.

Basic Brag

The turn to deal passes to the left. A game ends at any time that everyone has made the same number of deals. Cards are shuffled before the first deal, but thereafter not between deals until a hand has been won with a prial. Before the deal, players may be required to ante one chip each (desirable if fewer than five play). It may be previously agreed to place a limit on the amount that may be bet at each turn. Deal three cards each, in ones, face down.

Each in turn, starting with Eldest, may drop out or make a bet by pushing one or more chips into the kitty. The number bet must be not less than that bet by the previous player, nor more than any limit that may have been previously agreed. (There is no need to equalize bets as in Poker, unless it has been agreed to follow Poker-style betting.)

Play continues until all but two have dropped out. The two remaining continue betting until either one drops out, whereupon the other wins the kitty without showing his hand, or one 'sees' the other by paying twice the amount legally required to stay in, whereupon both hands are revealed and the higher one wins.

The next dealer then gathers in all the hands, including those that have been dropped, and stacks them at the bottom of the pack without mixing them up. Only if the kitty was won on a prial does he shuffle them before dealing.

Betting blind. A player may leave his hand face down, untouched, and 'bet blind' for as long as he likes. So long as he does so, he need only add half the amount staked by the previous player, while any raise he makes must be doubled by those who follow. If *one* of the two final players is betting blind, the other may drop out but may not 'see' him until the blind bettor looks at his cards.

Covering. A player who runs out of chips but wishes to stay in the game may 'cover the kitty' by laying his hand face down on top of it. Subsequent players start a new kitty and continue playing for it. When one of them wins, his hand is compared with that of the covering player, and the better of them wins the original kitty.

Five-Card Brag
As above, but each receives five cards and discards two face down before play begins. A prial of Threes ranks between Deuces and Fours, but, by agreement, the top hand is a prial of Fives.

Seven-Card Brag
All contribute equally to a kitty and receive seven cards face down. If anyone is dealt four of a kind they win the kitty and there is a new deal. Otherwise, each discards one card face down and forms the other six into two Brag hands, laying the higher of them face down on his left and the lower face down on his right.

To play, Eldest turns up his left hand. Each in turn thereafter may pass, or turn his left hand face up if it beats the highest hand showing. Whoever is showing the best hand then turns up his right hand. Again, each in turn thereafter either passes or turns his hand up if it beats all other right hands.

The kitty goes to a player winning on both hands, or winning one and tying for best on the other. In the unlikely event of two players tying for best on left and right, it is divided between them. Otherwise, the kitty is not won but is carried forward to the next deal.

A prial of Threes counts between Deuces and Fours, the unbeatable top hand being a prial of Sevens.

Nine-Card Brag

As Seven-Card, except that each receives nine cards and arranges them into three Brag hands, which must be exposed in order from highest to lowest. All three must win (or at least tie for best) for a player to sweep the pool. The best hand is variously set at a prial of Threes or Nines.

Crash

Four players each receive 13 cards and arrange them into four Brag hands, ignoring the odd card. Each lays his hands out in a row face down before him. The hands are revealed strictly in order from left to right, the winner of each marking one point. The kitty is won by the first to reach seven over as many deals as necessary, but a player receiving four of a kind in one deal wins the game outright.

Bastard (Stop the Bus)

A cross between Brag and ▸ **Commerce** or ▸ **Whisky Poker**. Deal three cards each and a spare hand of three face up to the table. Each in turn must exchange one or more cards with the same number on the table. (In a particularly frustrating variant, a player may exchange one card or three, but never two.) Play continues until someone knocks, whereupon the others may—but need not—make one more exchange. Best hand wins the kitty, or worst hand pays a forfeit, or whatever.

Three-Stake Brag

Still recorded in books, but now defunct. Each player puts up three stakes and receives three cards, two face down, one face up. The first stake is won for the best up-card, or, if equal, by the elder of two tied players. The second goes to the winner of a round of bragging (betting, raising, etc.). All hands are then revealed, and the third goes to the player whose cards total closest to 31 without exceeding it. For this purpose Ace counts 1 and courts 10 each, and one or more additional cards may be drawn until a player is either bust or satisfied.

Classical Brag

An eighteenth-century version, though not according to Hoyle. Only prials and pairs are recognized. There are three wild cards or 'braggers': ♦A, ♣J, ♦9.

Brandle

Plain-trick game

28

Nap-players might like to try its German equivalent, actually called *brandeln*, meaning to smoulder. (I have Anglicized it.) Rules vary; the following are typical.

Deal seven cards each in batches of 2-3-2 from a 28-card pack ranking A K Q J 10 9 7 except in trumps, where the order is J 7 A K Q 10 9. (There are no Eights.)

The bids are:

Brandle (3 tricks)	1 point	Bettel (none)	5 points
Four	2 points	Mord (all seven)	6 points
Five	3 points	Herrenmord (7 NT)	7 points
Six	4 points		

Bettel and Herrenmord are no-trump games; in others, the bidder names trumps before leading.

Each in turn, starting with Eldest, may pass or bid. A player who has passed may not come in again. If all pass, there is no play and the deal moves round. Each bid must be higher than the previous one, but an earlier (elder) player may 'hold' the bid of a later one, thus forcing the latter to pass or go higher. The highest bid is *Mord* ('Death'): *Herrenmord* is not an overcall, merely a Mord played at no trump.

The soloist announces trumps (if any) and leads to the first trick. Follow suit if possible and head the trick if possible. If unable to follow, trump or renounce as preferred.

If successful, the soloist receives the value of his bid from each opponent, or scores the appropriate amount. There is no bonus for overtricks. If unsuccessful, he pays it to each opponent, or deducts it from his score.

Brazilian Canasta ▸▸ *Canasta*

Brelan

An old French vying game vaguely reminiscent of ▸ **Brag** and ancestral to ▸ **Bouillotte**.

Bridge
Plain-trick game

52

Contract Bridge (so called to distinguish it from Auction Bridge and earlier ancestors) is the international card game of the upper socio-economic classes, thus differing from nearly all other trick-taking games, which are national games played by all classes of society in their countries of origin.

Developed in the nineteenth century as one of several attempts to turn partnership Whist into a game with 'bidding' and 'suit hierarchy' like ▸ **Boston Whist**, Bridge enjoyed the advantage over comparable experiments (such as ▸ **Cayenne Whist** and ▸ **Vint**) of introducing the novel and enjoyable feature of the 'dummy'. This, once the bidding is over, in effect turns Bridge into a three -player game, with two playing as partners while the third, the declarer, plays an independent, prima donna role. Although tradition places the origins of Bridge in the Levant, the dummy feature should probably be credited to the French. Whether or not they invented it, it was certainly in the Parisian clubs that Dummy Whist enjoyed its greatest popularity.

Proto-Bridge was first described in English in 1885 under the spurious title *Biritch, or Russian Whist*. By 1900 it was called ▸ **Bridge-Whist** or simply Bridge, and had almost completely ousted ▸ **Whist** as the high-class club game of Europe and America. By 1905 it had been replaced by Auction Bridge, in which all four could bid instead of just the dealer's side. Contract Bridge, first developed in France (again) under the name Plafond during the First World War, came into its own in the early 1930s, following the application of technical improvements by millionaire

Harold S. Vanderbilt and a world-wide publicity campaign engineered by Ely Culbertson.

There being no shortage of books, clubs, classes, and web sites for those wishing to learn more than the basic essentials, only the basic essentials are given below. Contract is played in several different formats: 'rubber Bridge', the traditional domestic and informal game; 'Chicago', an American variation increasingly popular in Britain; and 'duplicate', the tournament game. (For adaptations for other numbers of players, *see* ▶ **Booby**, ▶ **Towie**, and ▶ **Honeymoon Bridge**.)

Rubber Bridge

Partners sit opposite each other. They are agreed in advance or decided by drawing cards, the two highest playing against the two lowest. The turn to deal, bid, and play passes always to the left.

The scoresheet is divided into two columns, one for each side, and into an upper and lower half by a horizontal line. Below the line are recorded scores made for tricks contracted and won; above it are recorded additional scores for extras, overtricks, and penalties, which do not count towards winning the game but may have some effect on the margin of victory.

A game is won by the first side to score 100 or more points 'below the line', over as many deals as it takes. When a game is won, another line is drawn beneath it across both columns, and the next game scored (from zero) below it.

A rubber is won by the first side to win two games. A side that has won one game is described as 'vulnerable', which makes it subject to higher scores for success and penalties for failure.

Deal 13 cards each, singly, from a 52-card pack ranking A K Q J 10 9 8 7 6 5 4 3 2 in each suit.

Play is preceded by an auction. Its main purpose is to decide what contract will be played and by whom, but it also enables partners to exchange information as to the lie of cards by means of conventions encoded in the bidding system being followed.

Each in turn, Dealer first, must either pass, or bid, or double an opponent's preceding bid, or redouble an opponent's preceding double. (In England a pass is normally announced as 'No bid', to avoid a possible mishearing of 'pass' as 'hearts'.) A pass does not prevent one from bidding next time round. If all pass immediately, the deal is annulled and a new one made by the next dealer.

A bid states the number of tricks above six which the bidder proposes to win from his partnership's two hands, and the suit he proposes as trump for the purpose. The lowest bid is 'one club'—an offer to win at least seven of the thirteen tricks played with clubs as trumps. Each bid must be higher than the last; that is, it must offer a greater number of tricks, or the same number but with a higher-ranking trump. For this purpose the ranking of trumps from low to high is ♣-♦-♥-♠ -NT (No Trump). 'One club' is therefore overcalled by 'one' anything else, but 'one no trump' only by 'two clubs' or higher. The highest possible bid is 'seven no trump'—to win a no-trump 'slam' of all thirteen tricks.

A player may 'double' the previous bid if it was made by an opponent and no other bid has intervened. A player may 'redouble' the previous double if it was made by an opponent and no other bid has intervened. These announcements respectively double and quadruple the eventual score if the proposed contract is actually played, but are automatically cancelled if followed by a higher bid.

The auction ends when a bid, double, or redouble has been followed by three consecutive passes. The last named bid is the 'contract'; whoever of the contracting side first named its suit is the 'declarer'; and the two opponents are the 'defenders'.

The opening lead is made by the player at Declarer's left, e.g. West if Declarer is South. As soon as West has led, North lays his hand of cards face up on the table as a 'dummy', with the four suits separate and each arranged from highest to lowest. North thereafter takes no active part, as South (the declarer) plays alternately from his own hand and from dummy.

Players must follow suit if possible, otherwise may play any card. A trick is taken by the highest card of the suit led or by the highest trump if any are played. When South wins a trick, he leads from whichever hand yielded the winning card.

Scoring details appear in Table 2. If the contract is made, the declaring side scores below the line for each trick bid and won, and above the line for overtricks and other bonuses. If not, the defenders score above the line for the number of tricks by which the declarer falls short of the contract.

Table 2. Contract Bridge: Table of scores

D = Doubled, R = Redoubled, V = Vulnerable, tv = trick value (20, 30, or 40)

IF CONTRACT MADE:

Declarers score below the line for each trick bid and won:

in a minor suit (♣ ♦)	20	40 D	80 R
in a major suit (♠ ♥)	30	60 D	120 R
at no trump, for the first trick	40	80 D	160 R
...for each subsequent trick	30	60 D	120 R

Declarers may also score above the line:

for each overtrick (if not vulnerable) *or*	tv	100 D	200 R
for each overtrick (if vulnerable), *plus*	tv	200 D	400 R
for making a doubled/redoubled contract	—	50 D	100 R
plus for making a small slam	500	750 V	
or for making a grand slam	1000	1500 V	

IF CONTRACT DEFEATED:

Defenders score above the line,

	if declarers not vulnerable:			if declarers vulnerable:		
undertricks	*und*	*dbld*	*rdbld*	*und*	*dbld*	*rdbld*
one	50	100	200	100	200	400
two	100	300	600	200	500	1000
three	150	500	1000	300	800	1600
four	200	800	1600	400	1100	2200
five	250	1100	2200	500	1400	2800
six	300	1400	2800	600	1700	3400
seven	350	1700	3400	700	2000	4000

HONOURS

Scored above the line by either side holding in one hand:

any four of A K Q J 10 of trumps	100
all five of A K Q J 10 of trumps	150
all four Aces at no trump	150

PREMIUM AT END OF PLAY

for winning the rubber, if opponents won no game	700
for winning the rubber, if opponents won one game	500
in an unfinished rubber, for winning the only game	300
...for the only part-score in an unfinished game	100

Independently of the contract, either side may score for holding (or, strictly, having held) 'honours' in one of their two hands before play began. Honours are, in a trump game, the five top trumps (Ace to Ten), and all four Aces in a no trump game.

Chicago or Four-Deal Bridge

This alternative structure is designed to speed the game up. A rubber is four contracts. (In effect, four deals; but if a deal is passed out, it does not count, and the same dealer deals again.) These are conducted on the following basis:

1. Neither side vulnerable.
2. Non-dealer's side vulnerable, dealer's not.
3. Non-dealer's side vulnerable, dealer's not.
4. Both sides vulnerable.

If and when either side wins a theoretical 'game' by making 100 points below the line, it adds an above-line bonus of 300, or 500 if vulnerable on the deal on which that total was reached. A new line is then drawn, and both sides start counting again (from zero) towards game.

If at the end of the fourth deal either side has a part-score (more than zero but less than 100 below the line), it adds a bonus of 100 above the line.

Various other scoring refinements may be applied.

Duplicate Bridge

A tournament system designed to increase the superiority of skill over chance in determining the overall outcome. Basically, four hands dealt randomly at one table are duplicated deliberately at another. If played on a team basis, two partnerships sitting at different tables but belonging to the same team receive not the same but the complementary hands of their fellow partnership.

Notes. Bridge is unique in that the auction is at least as weighty as the play—almost a game in itself. Bidding serves two purposes: to enable each side to work towards its highest and safest contract, and to exchange as much information as possible as to the lie of cards before play. For the second purpose, a strong hand will not necessarily be opened at a high level or in its best suit, as this would waste valuable 'bidding space' from which more detailed information could be gleaned about the complementary hand. The more progressively a contract has been worked towards, the higher and more accurate it is likely to be. The same purpose has also encouraged the growth of 'conventions', by which a particular bid may be made not as a serious suggestion for a contract, but as a device for requesting or conveying information. It is illegal in tournament play, and bad practice in home play, for partners to use

	WE	THEY	
g	50		
g	200		
f	500	150	c
e	100	60	c
a	30	100	b
a	60	100	c
f	120	80	d
g	80		
h	60		
h	500		
	1700	490	
	-490		
	1210		

Bridge. Example of scoring.

(a) We bid 2♠, made 3♠, scored 60 below for the bid of two and 30 for the overtrick.

(b) We bid 3♥, were doubled, and made only two. They scored 100 above for the doubled undertrick.

(c) They bid 3NT, made 5, scored below the line 40 for the first and 30 for each of the other two contracted tricks, plus two overtricks for 60 above. One of them held four Aces, scoring 150 for honours. They win the first game. Another line was drawn to mark the second.

(d) They bid and made 4♣ for 80 below.

(e) They bid 2♠ and made one, giving us 100 above for the undertrick (they being vulnerable).

(f) We bid and made a small slam of 6♦ for 120 below the line, giving us a game and making ourselves vulnerable. We also counted 500 above for the slam. Another line was drawn and a new game started.

(g) We bid 1NT, were doubled, and made three. This gave us 2×40 below the line, plus 200 above for the doubled overtrick (we being vulnerable), plus 50 'for the insult' (making any doubled game).

(h) We bid and made 2♥ for 60 below the line, giving us the second game and 500 for the rubber. Our margin of victory is 1210.

systems or conventions unknown to the other side, and each side must state at the outset what system it is using. The system most used by British players is 'Acol', named after the club in London where it was developed, while Standard American is based on a system developed originally by Charles Goren. The two are based on similar principles, and many players tend to use some sort of compromise between them. Further information must be sought from books devoted to Bridge, of which there are not a few. Helpful web sites include:

http://www.pagat.com/boston/bridge.html
A good summary of the essentials of all the major forms of Bridge and a jumping-off point for further exploration.

http://www.math.auc.dk/~nwp/bridge/laws/
National and international Laws of Bridge.

http://www.greatbridgelinks.com/
http://www.bridgetoday.com/
The Bridge Today University provides lessons by e-mail.

http://www.bridgeworld.com/
Home page of Bridge World magazine, which offers material suitable for beginners, as well as problems, a book list, etc.

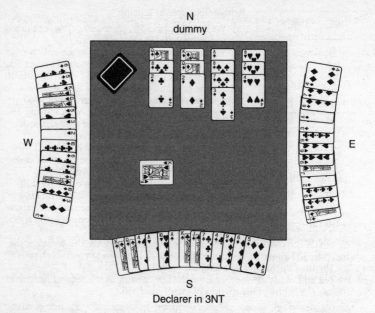

N
dummy

W

E

S
Declarer in 3NT

Bridge South opens 1♣, having 17 points and five of that suit. West intervenes with 2♥. North, after some thought, rejects no-trump and spade responses in favour of 3♣. East passes. South now counts at least 27 points between the two hands which is borderline for a game in clubs, but safer at no trump. This is duly bid; North passes, West attacks hearts by leading the King, dummy goes down, and this is the situation. It is usual for trumps to be set out to the left of dummy as seen by the Declarer, or clubs in a no-trump bid, as here. Declarer will probably make five clubs, one diamond, three spades and a heart, scoring 100 below the line and 30 above for the overtrick.

Bridge-Whist

The earliest form of Bridge, so called from about 1900. Virtually identical with ▸ **Biritch**.

Briscan

Point-trick game

32

Also called Brisque: a late eighteenth-century French relative of ▸ **Bezique**, with a vast range of scores and declarations.

Deal five cards each from a 32-card pack and play as at Bezique. Cards rank and count as follows: Ace 11, Ten 10, King 4, Queen 3, Jack 2, Nine 0, Eight 0, Seven 0.

Dealer scores 30 for turning an Ace as the trump card, 10 for turning any other card higher than a Nine.

Sequences of five, four, and three cards in the same suit score as follows, all doubled if made in trumps:

A K Q J 10	300	A K Q J	100	10 9 8 7	30	Q J 10	40
K Q J 10 9	150	K Q J 10	80			J 10 9	30
Q J 10 9 8	100	Q J 10 9	60	A K Q	60	10 9 8	20
J 10 9 8 7	50	J 10 9 8	40	K Q J	50	9 8 7	10

Note that for this purpose cards run in their natural order, not in their trick-taking order, and that a longer sequence is not scorable if any of its cards has already been scored in a shorter.

A quartet of Aces scores 150, Tens 100, Kings 80, Queens 60, Jacks 40.

A trump marriage scores 40, a common marriage 20. Either is also scorable for a *mariage de rencontre*, i.e. taking a Queen in a trick with the King of the same suit.

Score also 20 for a hand composed entirely of face cards (*carte rouge*), or 10 for one entirely devoid of face cards (*carte blanche*). You can keep scoring for *carte rouge* or *carte blanche* every time you draw another card of the same type.

The trump Seven may be exchanged for the turn-up at any time before the stock is exhausted, but attracts no score.

For taking the last card of stock, score 10.

For a hand consisting entirely of trumps when the last card has been taken, 30.

For winning the last five tricks, 30.

For winning nine or more in all, 10.

Winning all sixteen wins the game outright.

Finally, score for each Ace captured in tricks 11, each Ten 10, King 4, Queen 3, Jack 2.

Game is 600 points.

Briscola

Point-trick game

One of Italy's most popular games (with ▶ **Scopa** and ▶ **Tressette**), Briscola is a little-changed descendant of Brusquembille, the ancestor of ▶ **Briscan** and ▶ **Bezique**. It is known as Brisca in Spain.

All forms of the game are played with the Italian 40-card pack, with cards ranking and counting as follows:

Ace	11
Three	10
King (*Re*)	4
Queen (*Cavallo*)	3
Jack (*Fante*)	2
7 6 5 4 2	0 each

When three play, a Deuce is omitted from the pack. The following description is for two, three, and partnership four. Five should play Briscola Chiamata (see below).

The player cutting the lowest card deals first. The turn to deal and play passes to the right. Deal three cards each face down, turn the next card for trumps, and slide it face up and partly projecting from beneath the face-down stock. Eldest leads to the first trick. The winner of each trick draws the top card of the stock, and waits for the other(s) do to so in turn before leading to the next.

Suit need not be followed so long as any cards remain in the stock. A trick is taken by the highest card of the suit led or by the highest trump if any are played. Suit must be followed in the play of the last three tricks.

The game is won by the player or partnership taking most of the 120 card-points, the hands being played right through. A rubber is the best of five games (first to three). 60–60 or 40–40–40 is a stand-off. So, presumably, is a two-player tie when three play.

In the four-hander, partners may communicate certain trump holdings to each other by means of the following facial signals, preferably without being spotted by the opponents:

Ace	Go tight-lipped.
Three	Twist mouth sideways.
King	Raise eyes heavenwards.
Queen	Show tip of tongue.
Jack	Raise one shoulder.

They may also secretly show each other their final hand of three cards when the last card is taken from stock.

Briscola Chiamata

A modern alliance game for five (or, less happily, four). Deal eight cards each in fours, or 10 each (4-2-4) if four play. An auction follows to decide who will play against the others, either alone or with a secret partner. A bid is made by naming a card by rank only, the intention being that the holder of that card in trumps will become the bidder's partner when the trump suit is announced. Thus, a bid of 'Ace' means 'If I become the declarer I will name the trump suit, and the holder of the trump Ace will be my partner'. A bidder may name a card in his own hand if he thinks himself strong enough to play solo. Any bid can be overcalled by naming a lower-ranking card, Ace being followed by Trey, and so on down to Deuce. The player naming the lowest rank becomes the soloist and announces trumps. The holder of the called card may not reveal himself except through the play.

Eldest leads. Follow suit if possible, otherwise play any card. A trick is taken by the highest card of the suit led, or by the highest trump if any are played. The winner of each trick leads to the next.

If the declarer played alone and took 61 or more card-points, he scores 4 game points. If he and an ally took 61 or more between them, he scores 2 and his ally 1 point. Each opponent loses 1 point. These scores are doubled for winning every trick, and reversed if the declarer loses. The overall winner is the first to reach 11 game points.

Variant. A Deuce bid may be contested by raising the minimum number of card-points required to win, e.g. '66', '71'.

Briscolone

Two-hand Briscola with five cards each and no trumps. Theoretically, suit must be followed throughout; but, as the rule cannot be policed, players may agree to ignore it.

Brusquembille

Probable French ancestor of this family; played like Briscola but with a 32-card pack ranking A 10 K Q J 9 8 7.

Bristol ●

Patience game 52

One of several neat solitaires devised by Albert Morehead and Geoffrey Mott-Smith. It usually comes out, but you must be careful which move to make whenever you have a choice, as one false move can lead to disaster.

Deal eight fans of three cards each, all face up. The exposed card of each fan is always available for play, but the card immediately below it is not available until you have played off the card covering it. If any of the eight immediately available cards is a King, transfer it to the bottom of its fan. If this leaves another King exposed, do the same again.

If any available card is an Ace, take it out and set it up as the first card of a building pile. The aim of the game is to set up all the Aces as they become available, and to build each Ace up to a King in numerical order regardless of suit.

When you have played as far as you can from the opening position, hold the rest of the pack face down and deal the top three cards face up in a row, not overlapping one another. Regard each of these cards as the base of a wastepile.

The top card of each wastepile and the top card of each fan may be built on an Ace-pile whenever it correctly continues the sequence. Alternatively, you can build it on the top card of a fan if it is one rank lower. For example, if the top card of the fan is a Jack, you may build a Ten on it, then a Nine on that Ten, and so on. Note, however, the following things you may *not* do:

- You may not play a card to a wastepile from a fan or from another wastepile.
- You may not play more than one card at a time. (For example, if a fan is headed by a Three covering a Two, you may not play the Two-Three on top of an Ace.
- Having built a card on an Ace pile, you must leave it in place—you may not play it back into the game.
- When you take the last card of a fan, you may not start a new fan in its place. The number of fans can therefore only decrease.

When you can't play any further (or can but don't want to), deal three more cards across the tops of the wastepiles (or wastepile spaces, as the case may be), then pause and play again as far as you can and wish. Note that this is the only way in which cards may be played to wastepiles.

Brus

Plain-trick game

36

An eccentric game of ancient lineage (with resemblances to ▸ **Aluette** and ▸ **Karnöffel**) peculiar to the Swedish island of Gotland. Brus or Bräus underwent a brief revival in the 1980s for reasons possibly related to the touristic rediscovery of folklore and customs. This account is based on articles in various Swedish magazines, notably by Nils Lithberg and Göran Åkerman. Brus is also the name of a related Jutish game in Denmark.

Four players sit crosswise in partnerships, or six sit alternately in two partnerships of three. Four players receive nine each, or six players six each, dealt one at a time from a 36-card pack consisting of A K Q J 10 9 8 7 6 in each suit. Play to the left.

The ultimate aim is to win six game points, called 'strokes'. In each deal a stroke is scored by the side that wins six tricks, or five tricks if one of the partners holds ♣K. Winning six straight off is a lurch (*jan*) and earns two strokes. Ties are possible.

The pack consists of 'live' cards, which may be played to tricks, and 'duds', which may not (in Swedish respectively *spelbara* and *odugliga korte*). The top three live cards are called matadors (*makdorar*) and have individual names. Live cards rank from high to low as follows. Those equal in face value beat one another in the suit order shown (clubs highest):

♣	-	-	-	Jack	*Spit*
-	♠	-	-	Eight	*Dull*
-	-	♥	-	King	*Brus*
♣	♠	♥	♦	Nines	
♣	♠	♥	♦	Aces	
-	♠	♥	♦	Jacks	
♣	♠	♥	♦	Sixes	

The Sevens are winners, as explained below. All others—Tens, Queens, and unlisted Eights and Kings—are duds.

Eldest starts by laying face up on the table any Sevens he may hold. Each of these counts by itself as a won trick. He then leads a live card to the first trick. Each in turn thereafter must, if possible, play a higher live card than any so far played, otherwise pass. Whoever plays highest wins the trick, turns it face down, and leads to the next. Before leading, he may similarly lay out Sevens, counting each as a won trick. If a player on lead has no live card, the turn passes to the left until somebody has one and leads it.

Play ceases when one side has won six tricks, including any declared Sevens. That side scores 1 stroke, or 2 for the lurch. If neither has won six tricks when no live cards remain to be led, a side with five tricks scores 1 stroke if one of its members holds ♣K. Game is six strokes.

☛ *Comment.* The effect of dud cards is to distribute playing hands of unequal length, while camouflaging the number of live cards in each player's hand. Duds might as well be discarded before play begins, but this would spoil the fun. Certain cards other than matadors also have individual names, of varying degrees of formality and propriety. The ♣9 is commonly called *plågu*, literally 'torment', because it may force the play of a matador when its holder would have preferred to hold it back till later.

Brusquembille ▸▸ *Briscola*

Buck Euchre

(or Dirty Clubs): Non-partnership ▶ **Euchre** for various numbers of
players and with many variations.

Bugami
Penalty-trick game

52

Bugami, or Bleeding Hearts, is my more cut-throat version of ▶ **Hearts**,
in that you each declare which is your own penalty suit. It works best for
four, and is especially heart-rending in the 'shotgun wedding' variation,
which may force you into a partnership you do not really want.

Each player requires four bid-cards, one of each suit. Three players use
a 52-card pack from which the Tens, Nines, and Eights are removed for
use as bid-cards, leaving 40 in play. Four or more use a 52-card pack for
play, and an old or incomplete pack for bidding.

Deal all the cards out in ones until everyone has the same number.
Any surplus cards remain face down to one side. Cards rank
A K Q J 10 9 8 7 6 5 4 3 2.

The aim is to win as many tricks as possible that do not contain any
cards of what you have previously declared to be your 'bug' suit, while
trying to drop everyone else's bug cards on the tricks they win.

Everyone looks at their cards, decides on a bug suit, and selects a card
of that suit from their bid-cards. When ready, they turn their bid-cards
face up so everyone knows everyone else's bug suit. You can bid to take
no tricks at all (misère) by leaving all your bid-cards face down.

The player at dealer's left leads to the first trick. You must follow suit if
you can, but may otherwise play any card. A trick is taken by the highest
card of the suit led, and the winner of each trick leads to the next. There
is no trump suit. If any cards were left undealt, they are added to the last
trick, and go to the player who won it.

Score 10 per trick won, and divide this total by the number of bugs
taken, ignoring fractions. For example, four tricks containing one bug
scores 40, two bugs 20, three 13, and so on. If you win only clean tricks,
you don't divide by zero (which is mathematically meaningless) but by

one half, which is the same as doubling the value to 20 each. Winning four clean tricks, therefore, scores 80.

- Score 50 for winning no tricks, or 100 if you bid misère. But if you bid misère and win any trick, score zero.
- If you win every trick, and no one has bid misère, you score 100 and everyone else scores zero. But if someone did bid misère, you score zero for winning every trick.

Play up to any agreed target, such as 250 points.

One or more Jokers may be added to the pack, and these count as bugs when taken in tricks. Any cards left undealt are set face down and go to the winner of the last trick. You can only discard a Joker when unable to follow suit. If you lead one, it wins the trick, and opponents may discard as they please.

Shotgun Wedding

In this variation, two or more players who bid the same suit automatically become partners. Their tricks are kept together, and each member individually scores the score made by the whole partnership. This does not apply to misère bidders, who continue to score as individuals.

Bulka ▸▸ *Trappola*

Bullshit ▸▸ *Cheat*

Bum Game, the ▸▸ *President*

Bura

Point-trick game

36

A game played in Russian prisons, as discovered by Dr Alexey Lobashev. (Researcher, not inmate.)

Use a 36-card pack ranking and counting Ace 11, Ten 10, King 4, Queen 3, Jack 2, numerals Nine to Six 0.

When everyone has added an agreed stake to the pot, deal three cards each and stack the rest face down. Turn the next card for trump and half bury it under the stack.

The aim is to be the first to claim (correctly) to have captured cards totalling 31 or more.

Eldest hand leads first. The leader may play one, two, or all three cards, provided that they are all of the same suit. The followers must each play the same number of cards, but are not required to follow suit and may therefore play anything they like. A single trick is taken by the highest card of the suit led, or by the highest trump if any are played. If two or three cards were led, each one is played to as a separate trick. You can only win a multiple trick by winning both or all three tricks individually.

Example. Diamonds are trump. Alex leads ♠ K-J. Boris plays ♦9 ♣J, which beats one card (by trumping) but not the other. Grigori plays ♦A♠Q. This does beat Alex's play (♦A trumps ♠K, ♠Q beats ♠J), giving him a multiple trick worth 20.

Won tricks are stored face down and may not be referred to. After each trick, each in turn, starting with the trick-winner, draws cards from stock until all have three again. If not enough remain to go round, take as many as possible for all to have the same number and play the hand out without drawing any more.

Play ceases when someone claims to have made 31 or more, which must be done by memory and without checking. The claimant's cards are then examined. If the claim is successful, he wins the pot; if not, he doubles it. Each subsequent deal is made by the previous claimant, even if he claimed wrongly. If no one claims, the pot is added to and carried forward, and the same dealer deals again.

Certain hands entitle their holder to lead to the next round of tricks, even if they didn't win the previous trick. These are, from lowest to highest:

1. Three of a suit (*modolka*).
2. Three Aces.
3. Any three trumps (*bura*).

If you hold such a hand and wish to lead you must declare it before the previous trick-winner leads. If two or more players have the same special hand, priority goes to whichever of them would be playing earlier to the trick if it were led by the previous trick-winner.

Bust ▶ *Oh Hell!*

Butcher Boy ▶ *Poker*

Butifarra ▶ *Botifarra* (Spanish form of the Catalan name)

Butthead ▶ *President*

Calabresella ▶ *Tressette (Terziglio)*

Calculation

Patience game

This classic solitaire is quite maddening, as it requires intense concentration to get very far but may be blocked by an awkward distribution of cards, especially if the Kings come out too early.

Start by taking out any Ace, Two, Three, and Four and placing them face up as the bases of four building piles. Each of these cards is to be built up into a 13-card sequence, regardless of suit, headed by a King. The interval between each pair of cards built must be equivalent to that of its base card, namely one, two, three, four. The four sequences will therefore run as follows:

A-2-3-4-5-6-7-8-9-10-J-Q-K

2-4-6-8-10-Q-A-3-5-7-9-J-K

3-6-9-Q-2-5-8-J-A-4-7-10-K

4-8-Q-3-7-J-2-6-10-A-5-9-K

Turn cards from stock one by one and play them either to one of the building piles if it correctly continues the sequence, or to any one of four wastepiles. You can play the top card of any wastepile to a building pile when it fits, but may never shift it to the top of another wastepile.

California Jack ▸▸ *All Fours*

Calliente

Australian name for ▸▸ **Three in One**

Calypso
Plain-trick game

A cross between ▸ **Whist** and ▸ **Rummy** invented by R. W. Willis of Trinidad, perfected by Kenneth Konstam, and promoted by British playing-card companies in the 1950s as an additional attraction for Bridge and Canasta enthusiasts—without success, unfortunately, as it is a very good game. It still, however, has a following in Trinidad.

Use four 52-card packs of the same size, weight, and finish, and preferably of identical back design and colour. Shuffle them together very thoroughly before play. Cards rank A K Q J 10 9 8 7 6 5 4 3 2.

The players cutting the two highest cards are partners against the two lowest, and sit opposite each other. Whoever cut highest deals first and has the choice of seats, thereby determining his own and everyone else's personal trumps (see diagram).

Deal 13 cards each face down in ones, and stack the remainder face down to one side. These will gradually be used up in subsequent deals. A game consists of four deals, one by each player, the turn to deal passing to the left.

A calypso is a complete run of 13 cards of the same suit from Ace down to Two. Your aims are:

- to build calypsos in your personal trump suit,
- to help your partner build calypsos in his or her own suit, and
- to hinder your opponents from building calypsos in theirs.

The cards they are built from come only from cards won in tricks, not directly from the hand. The catch is that calypsos must be completed one at a time. That is, you may not start a second calypso until you have completed your first. If you win any cards in a trick that duplicate those already in the calypso you are currently constructing, you cannot (with one slight exception) hold them back for future calypsos. It is therefore practically impossible for anyone to complete all four possible calypsos, and even three will be something of a feat.

Eldest leads to the first trick, and the winner of each trick leads to the next. You must follow suit if you can, but may otherwise play any card. The rules of trick-taking are:

- If you lead a card of your personal trump suit, and everyone follows suit, you win the trick regardless of rank. However, if one or more players cannot follow suit and instead play a card of their own personal trump, then the trick is taken by the highest-ranking personal trump played.
- If you lead from any other suit, then the trick is taken by the highest card of the suit led, or by the highest personal trump if any are played.
- If the trick is being taken by two identical cards, or by personal trumps of different suits but equal rank, then the first such card wins.

☛ *Note*. If somebody else leads your personal trump suit, you cannot 'trump' it. You can only follow suit, and hope to win by playing the highest card.

When you win a trick, you extract from it any cards you need towards building your current calypso, and pass to your partner any cards needed for his. You then stack any unused cards face down on a pile of won cards belonging to your partnership, only one such pile being needed for each side. Unused cards will be those of your opponents' suits, and those of your side's suits that duplicate cards already contained in the calypso under construction.

When you complete a calypso you bunch all its cards together and stack them face up on the table in front of you like a won trick. You may then start building a new one, and for this purpose are allowed to use any valid cards in the trick you just won.

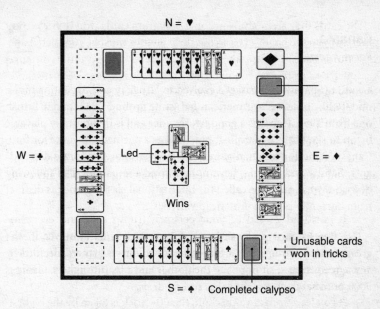

N = ♥

W = ♠

Led

Wins

E = ♦

Unusable cards
won in tricks

S = ♠ Completed calypso

Calypso. West leads the Eight of his personal trump, hoping to get the King he needs to complete a calypso. His partner obliges; but South, void in clubs, wins by playing a higher personal trump (♠9) than the only one so far played (♣8), thus completing his own calypso.

When thirteen tricks have been played, the next in turn to deal does so, and this continues until four deals have been played. Each side then scores as follows:

For each partner's first calypso	500
… second calypso	750
… each subsequent calypso	1000
For each card in an unfinished calypso	20
For each card in the winnings pile	10

☛ *Warning.* Avoid leading personal trumps at every opportunity for the novelty of winning easy tricks. Your opponents can easily thwart this approach by playing out cards that duplicate those in your current calypso, which will therefore be lost for ever.

Canasta

Rummy game

54 54

Canasta (Spanish for 'basket') evolved in Uruguay and Argentina in the mid-1940s, became an American fad game around 1948, and a British one from 1950. It makes a good two-hander and is theoretically playable by up to six, but is by far most practised as a partnership game for four. Canasta is no longer a fad game, and its even more elaborate descendants, Samba and Bolivia, have not survived the parent. The following describes what might be called the international classic game (as distinct from currently popular American varieties).

Use two 52-card packs and four Jokers, 108 cards in all. It doesn't greatly matter if the backs are of different colours. Partners, decided by any agreed means, sit opposite each other and play alternately. Game is 5000 points, which usually takes several deals.

Deal. After thorough shuffling, deal 11 cards each in ones and stack the rest face down. Turn the top card of stock and lay it beside stock to form the first card of the wastepile. This pile is known as 'the pack', and its top card as 'the upcard'. If the turned card is a Joker, a Two, or a red Three, cover it with the next card turned from stock. Keep doing so, if necessary, until it is some other card. Anyone dealt one or more red Threes must, on his first turn to play, lay them face up before him and draw replacements from stock.

Object. Each partnership's aim is to make melds and build them up into canastas. A meld is three or more cards of the same rank (other than Jokers, Twos, and Threes). A canasta is a meld of at least seven such cards. Melds and canastas made by a single partnership belong equally to either partner. When a partnership has made at least one canasta it may end the game by 'melding out'.

Card values and uses. Individual cards score as follows:

Each red 3	100
Each Joker	50

Ace, Deuce	20
K Q J 10 9 8	10
7 6 5 4 black 3	5

Threes have special uses, and are not normally melded together. All Jokers and Twos are wild, counting as any desired rank except Threes. A meld must always contain at least two natural (non-wild) cards and may never contain more than three wild ones. A canasta must contain at least four natural cards but may contain any number of wild ones.

The player at Dealer's left goes first and the turn to play passes to the left. On your turn to play, you:

1. must draw,
2. may meld, and
3. must then discard,

in accordance with the following rules.

Drawing. You may always draw the top card of stock. Alternatively, you may take the pack, in which case you must take the whole of it, and must use the upcard immediately. Furthermore:

If the pack is frozen, you may only use the upcard to start a new meld with at least two natural cards from your own hand. The pack is frozen to your own partnership until either of you has made an opening meld, and to both partnerships whenever it contains a wild card or red Three.

If the pack is unfrozen, you must still use the upcard, but may merely lay it off to an existing meld. This still prevents you from taking the pack if the upcard is a black Three, as they cannot be melded.

☛ *Note.* Red Threes are simple bonus cards. If you draw one from stock, lay it face up next to your melds and draw the next card as a replacement. If you are the first player to take the pack, and it includes a red Three, lay it out. Subsequent packs will not include red Threes, as they may not be discarded.

Melding. You can initiate a meld by laying face up on the table three or more cards of the same rank. It must contain at least two natural cards and not more than three wild. The first meld made by you or your partner must consist of cards totalling a required minimum of points. This minimum value depends on your partnership's current cumulative score, as follows:

Current score	Minimum value
Less than 0	no minimum
Less than 1500	50
1500 or more	90
3000 or more	120

At start of play, therefore, the minimum requirement is 50.

Once your side has made a meld, you and your partner may, on each of your turns to play, extend it by laying off to it one or more cards of the same rank, or one or more wild cards. When a meld contains seven or more cards, it becomes a canasta, and is squared up into a pile with a red card on top if it consists entirely of natural cards, otherwise a black one. (If you subsequently lay a wild card off to a 'red' canasta, it becomes a 'black' canasta, and its top card must be changed accordingly.)

You may make as many melds and lay-offs as you can and wish. In doing so, however, you may not reduce your hand to fewer than two cards unless you are legally entitled to meld out. You may not transfer a wild card from one meld to another, and you may never lay off to a meld belonging to the other side.

Discarding. You end your turn by making one discard face up to the top of the pack. If you discard a black Three, it prevents the next in turn from taking the pack. If you throw a wild card, you should place it sideways across the pack so as to project from it when subsequent discards are made. This shows that the pack is frozen.

Melding out. You go out, when ready, by playing the last card from your hand, whether as lay-off or discard. All play then ceases immediately. In order to meld out, however:

1. Your partnership must have made at least one canasta, and
2. You must have asked, and received, your partner's permission to go out. You may seek permission either before or after the draw.

You cannot go out if you hold two black Threes and nothing else. With just one, you can go out by discarding it; with three or four, you can go out by melding them. You can't use a wild card as a black Three.

If you have just one card left in hand, you may not go out by taking the pack if the pack also contains only one card (unless the stock is empty: *see* below.)

There is a bonus for going out 'concealed'—that is, by melding all eleven cards (or ten and a discard) without having previously made any melds or lay-offs. The hand must include a canasta, and no layoff may be made to any meld made by the partner.

End of stock. The stock very occasionally empties before anyone has gone out. If the last card drawn is a red Three it automatically ends the game, except that the player drawing it may first make as many melds and lay-offs as possible. (He may not discard.) If it is not a red Three, play continues without a stock. Each in turn must then take the upcard if he can meld or lay it off, and end his turn by discarding or melding out. This continues until someone either goes out or cannot use the previous player's discard. All play then ceases.

Score. Each side scores the total value of all cards it has melded, plus any of the following bonuses that may apply:

For each natural canasta made	500
For each mixed canasta	300
For going out	100 (200 if concealed)
For each red Three declared	100 (doubled if all four held)

Subtract from this the total value of cards left in both partners' hands. If the partnership has failed to make any meld, subtract also 100 per red Three possessed (or 800 for all four). Carry the score forward, and cease play if either side has reached or exceeded 5000. The winning margin is the difference between the two sides' final scores.

Penalties. The commonest penalties are the loss of 500 for holding an undeclared red Three, 100 for trying to go out without permission, 100 for being unable to go out after receiving permission to do so, 50 for taking the upcard when unable to use it legally.

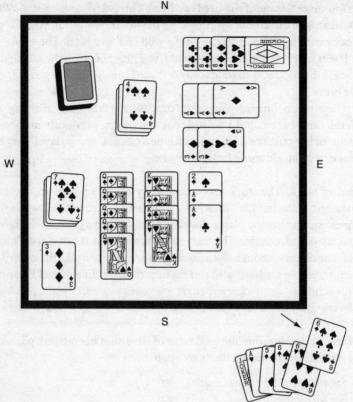

Canasta. South has just drawn ♠6 from stock and will, if his partner agrees, go out by melding three Sixes, laying off the Ace and Joker to the meld of Aces, and discarding ♠5. N–S will score 300 for the mixed canasta (Sevens), 50 for Queens, 40 for Kings, 130 for the Ace meld, 15 for the Sixes, 100 for the red Three, and 100 for going out, total 735 less whatever remains in North's hand. W–E have 90 for the Eight meld, 60 for the Aces, and 200 for the red Threes, total 350 less whatever remains in both hands.

Canasta for three
Deal 13 cards each and play as above, but without partnerships.

Canasta for two
Deal 15 cards each and play as above.

Variants. (1) You must have two canastas to go out. (2) You draw two cards from stock instead of one. (Recommended for players with large hands.)

Samba

The earliest of several variations in which you can meld suit-sequences, called sambas. Use three packs and six Jokers; deal 15 cards each; at each turn draw two from stock and discard one. The pack, whether frozen or unfrozen, may not be taken to start a sequence meld. A sequence meld is three or more natural cards in suit and sequence (Ace high, Four low). More may be added until it contains seven, whereupon it becomes a samba. No meld may contain more than two wild cards; sambas and sequence melds may not contain any. Two canastas are required to go out, for which purpose a samba counts as a canasta.

Game is 10,000. At 7000 the minimum opening meld requirement is 150. There is a bonus of 200 for going out (open or concealed), and of 1500 for each samba made. Red Threes count 100 each, or all six 1000.

Bolivia

As Samba, but with additional scores melds consisting solely of wild cards, minimum three. A *bolivia* is a meld of seven wild cards; it is stacked with a Joker on top and may not then be extended. A seven-card suit-sequence is called an *escalera* ('ladder'). Black Threes left unmelded in hand count −100 each.

Canfield ▸ *Demon*

Card-catch games

Games where the object is to capture cards by various methods, other than specifically trick-taking or fishing games. Most of them are ancient gambling games that have been cleaned up for children, notably: Battle, Beggar My Neighbour, Slapjack, Snap. A notable exception is the simple but highly skilled game of ▸ **Gops**.

Caribbean Stud

Banking game

So-called Caribbean Stud Poker is a casino banking game involving ▶ **Poker** hands. It is not a true Poker game, as it involves no vying or bluffing—nor, for that matter, the slightest degree of intelligence.

Everyone places a first stake (ante) of any amount and receives five cards face down. The banker/dealer receives four down and one face up. The players then look at their hands and either play or fold. Those who fold forfeit their stakes. Those who play must put out a second stake which is twice the amount of their first.

The dealer's cards are then faced and:

- If his hand does not contain a pair or better, or at least an Ace and a King, he pays each player the amount of that player's first stake and returns the second stake to him without matching it.
- If the dealer's hand beats a player's, the player loses both his stakes.
- If the player's hand beats the dealer's then both his stakes are paid off at evens (1/1), unless his hand is two pair or better, in which case the second stake is paid off at the following odds: Two pair 2/1, three of a kind 3/1, straight 4/1, flush 5/1, full house 7/1, four of a kind 20/1, straight flush 50/1, royal flush 100/1.

Tied hands are decided in the usual way (*see* ▶ **Poker**), but in case of absolute equality it is a stand-off and the player retrieves his stakes unmatched.

Casino games

The principal gambling card games in British and American casinos are banking games (Blackjack or Twenty-One, Baccara in the form of Chemin de Fer or Punto Banco), various forms of Poker (Five-card Draw, Five-card Stud, Seven-card Stud, Hold' em, Omaha), and hybrids of the two (Caribbean Stud Poker, Pai Gow Poker). Trente et Quarante, or Rouge et Noir (R&N), may still be encountered in some French casinos but is virtually extinct. *See also* ▶ **Gambling games**.

Cassino

Fishing game

(Also spelt Casino, which may be correct but is confusing.) This Italian game of the ▶ **Scopa** family is the only one to have penetrated the English-speaking world, via Italian immigrants to America. First recorded just before 1800, it seems to have been heavily elaborated in nineteenth-century American practice. It is mostly played by two, but works well for three. Four play in partnerships.

From a 52-card pack, deal, two at a time, four cards face down to each player and four face up to the table. When everyone has played their four cards the same dealer deals four more each, but none to the table. Similar deals ensue, the game ending when no cards remain in stock or in anybody's hand.

The aim is to capture table cards with cards played from the hand. The eventual scores will be:

For taking most cards	3 points
For Big Cassino (♦10)	2
For Little Cassino (♠2)	1
For taking most spades	1
For each Ace captured	1
For each sweep made	1

('Most cards' is 27 or more when two individuals or partnerships play, or more than either opponent when three play.)

Each in turn plays a card to the table, thereby either capturing one or more table cards, or building a combination with one or more table cards for capture on a subsequent turn. Captured cards, together with the card they were taken with, are stored face down in front of the player taking them.

A 'sweep' is the capture of all the table cards in one turn. As this is a scoring feature, you indicate it by storing one of the cards face up instead of down.

If you can neither capture nor build, you can only 'trail'—that is, add another card to the table cards so that it becomes available for being captured itself. Whenever you make a sweep, the next in turn to play can only trail.

On your turn to play, take a card from your hand and (unless forced to trail) do one of the following with it:

1. Capture one or more cards of the same rank as itself. Example:

You can take ♦3 with your ♠3 or ♣Q with your ♠Q.

2. If you have a pair, you can 'build' one of them on a table card of the same rank with a view to capturing both on your next turn. You must announce 'Building Aces' (or 'Twos', 'Kings', etc., whatever the rank may be). Example:

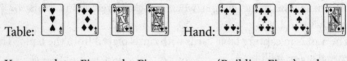

You can play a Five to the Five, announce 'Building Fives', and capture both on your next turn.

Cassino. With this hand you can sweep the board with a Seven. Better still, you can play a Seven to the Seven, announce 'Building Sevens', and sweep the board on your next turn—provided your opponent doesn't also hold a Seven with which to sweep it first. Note that you cannot increase the 2–5 or 4–3, as they form a multiple build.

3. Capture two or more numerals that sum to the value of the played card. The latter may simultaneously capture any number of single or combined cards equal in face value to itself. Example:

Table:  Hand:

By playing your ♠7, you can capture ♥A ♦2 ♣4 by combining and ♣7 by pairing, thus also making a sweep. Face cards cannot capture by summing, as they have no numerical value.

4. Build it on one or more table numerals to produce a total which you can capture with a single card that you already hold. Example:

Table:  Hand:

Put ♥2 and ♦3 together, add your ♠4, announce 'Building nine', and capture all three cards with ♦9 on your next turn.

5. Increase a build with it, provided that you already hold the capturing card. Example:

Table:  Hand:

You can play your Ace to the (2-3-4), announce 'Building ten', and capture them with ♦10 on your next turn. A build may not total more than 10, as no numeral card can capture it. You may not capture any single card forming part of a build, as the build itself counts as a single card.

Multiple builds—that is, more than one totalling the same amount—may not be increased individually: they can only be captured with a card of the same value. Example:

Table:  Hand:

You can't play ♠2 to capture ♥2, as the latter forms part of a build. Nor can you play it to build nines on one of the seven-builds, as each is part of a multiple build. But you can use one of your Sevens to capture the two builds and the Seven, thereby making a sweep. Better still, you can play one Seven, announce 'Building sevens', and sweep the lot on your next turn.

A build may be captured by another player, whether an opponent or a partner. In the partnership game, you may increase builds made by your partner without yourself holding a capturing card, provided that it is evident from his announcement that he can capture on the next turn. (*Example*: He plays a Four to a Three and announces 'Building seven'. You may play a Seven and announce 'Building sevens', even if you do not hold another Seven yourself.)

If you make or increase a build on one turn, you must either capture or increase it on your next. You may not trail, unless the build you were making has meanwhile been captured by somebody else.

When the last deal is played, whoever made the last capture adds to his won cards all the untaken table cards, but this does not count as a sweep unless it is one by definition.

Players then sort through their won cards and score as shown above. The game ends at the end of the deal on which a player or side reaches a previously agreed target score, typically 11 or 21.

Variants.

1. When two play, sweeps are sometimes ignored.
2. Some players allow a face card to capture only one card by pairing, or one card, or three, but not two. This is because, if two are captured, the fourth will be impossible to capture when it becomes a table card, thus preventing sweeps from being made. (If sweeps are not counted, there is no point in restricting court captures.)
3. It may be agreed that play ends the moment someone makes a capture that brings his score to the target.

Catch the Ten ⏵ *Scotch Whist*

Cayenne Whist

An ancestor of ▶ **Bridge** named after the capital of French Guyana.

Challenge

Going-out game

24 → 52

An unusual game in that both players start with equally balanced hands and perfect information as to what the other holds. So named and first described in print by Hubert Phillips, it was originally introduced into the card-playing circles of Cambridge University in the 1930s by Professor Besikovitch. Although Challenge is obviously a two-player relative of the Russian game ▸ **Svoyi Kozyri** ('Your own trump'), its unusual feature of perfect information, and the fact that no such game is known in Russia, point to Besikovitch himself as the inventor of this particular variation.

Use any number of cards which is a multiple of four, ranking A K Q J 10 9 8 7…etc, as far as they go. Phillips regarded 32 as standard (Seven low), and this is assumed below.

Object. To be the first to run out of cards, leaving them all in the other player's hand.

Trumps and deal. To start, each player chooses two suits and nominates one of them as his personal trump. Dealer then deals out half the pack (16 cards) face up in a row, extracts from them those of his own suits, and discards the rest. This gives him approximately half his playing hand. He then distributes to Elder, as the first half of his hand, all the cards of Elder's two suits which are exactly equivalent to those of his own two.

Example. Suppose Dealer chooses black suits and entrumps spades, leaving Elder with red suits of which he entrumps hearts. Then the cards might come out:

Dealer:

Elder:

To complete both hands, each player takes all the remaining cards of his opponent's two suits. Each player's hand is therefore a mirror image of the other's, and neither has a strategic advantage other than that of the lead—if such it be. Each hand should include at least two cards in every suit. If not, deal again.

Play. At each turn, one player leads a card of his choice. Elder leads first. The other must then either play a better card, in which case he leads next, or else take up all the cards so far played and add them to his hand, in which case his opponent leads next. A 'better' card is a higher card of the suit led, or any card of one's own personal trump (if different from the

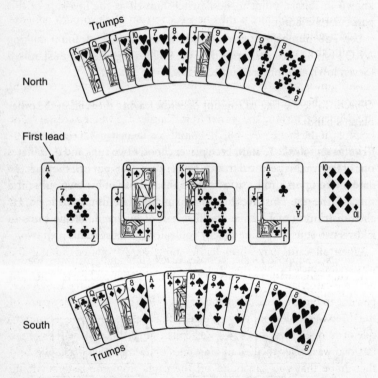

Challenge. North, with hearts as personal trump, leads ♦10 to the fifth 'trick'. South, though able to play ♦Q or a personal trump (clubs), prefers to take all the cards so far played and lead next. This results in a larger but more powerful hand, and it remains to be seen whether it will pay off.

suit led). Note that any card may be led at each turn; it need not relate in any way to the previous card played.

Winning. The first to play his last card wins. As this can take hours, it may be agreed that a player who falls asleep during play loses by default, unless the other is also asleep, in which case it is a draw.

Chaos

Patience game

This infuriating solitaire is the one-pack version of a two-pack patience called Higgledy-Piggledy.

Shuffle the cards and scatter them face down all over the table. Pick out any card at random and set it up as a base.

Your aim is to set up the other three cards of the same rank as and when they become available, and to build each one up into a 13-card suit-sequence, turning the corner from King to Ace where necessary. For example, if the first base is ♦8, the completed sequence will run ♦8-9-10-J-Q-K-A-2-3-4-5-6-7, and likewise in each other suit.

Turn up cards from the table one by one and play them either to the building piles if they fit, or face up to any of four wastepiles which you create as you go along. You may at any time build the top (uncovered) card of any wastepile whenever possible, thus freeing the one it covers.

When all cards have been either built or distributed among the wastepiles, pick up any one of the wastepiles and, holding it face up, deal the cards face up one by one to any of the other three wastepiles, pausing to build any cards whenever possible. That done, pick up any of the three wastepiles and play its cards off as before, either to a building pile or to one of the other two wastepiles. Finally, play off either of the last two wastepiles to the building piles or to the other wastepile, and then hope that you can build off the cards from the last remaining wastepile.

This rarely happens.

Chase the Ace

Gambling game

52

A primitive gambling or children's game, called Cuckoo in most European countries, though recorded in Cornwall as Ranter-go-Round. Much played in Scandinavia with specially designed cards (Gnav, Killekort, etc.).

Players deal in turn. Deal one card each face down from a 52-card pack ranking (low-high) A 2 3 4 5 6 7 8 9 10 J Q K. The aim is to avoid holding the lowest card at end of play. Suits are irrelevant; Ace is always low.

Each plays in turn, starting with the player at dealer's left. On your turn you may either keep your card (and must turn it face up if it is a King), or demand to exchange it with that of your left-hand neighbour. The latter may only refuse if he holds a King, in which case he shows it and says 'Cuckoo!'.

When it comes round to the dealer, he may either keep his card or cut a replacement from the pack. The cards are then revealed, and whoever has the lowest loses a life. Players tying for lowest all lose one.

Variants. If Dealer rejects his card, and then cuts a King, it counts lowest of all, and only he loses a life. Some do not cut, but take the top card of the pack. Some have a rule that a player passing an Ace, Two, or Three to his right-hand neighbour must announce that fact.

Cheat

Going-out game

Also called 'I Doubt It', Cheat is a good game for children if you want to teach them dishonesty. A more elaborate equivalent is the Russian game of ▶ **Verish' ne Verish'**.

Deal all the cards out. It doesn't matter if some have more than others. The aim is to be the first to run out of cards.

The first player takes one, two, three, or four cards from hand and lays them face down on the table, saying 'Aces'. The second does likewise, saying 'Twos'; and so on up to 'Kings'. If not challenged, the cards so played are left in a pile on the table.

Anyone may challenge an announcement by saying 'Cheat!', or 'I doubt it'. The cards just played are then turned up. If they are not all Aces (or whatever they were said to be), then whoever played them must take all the cards in the pile and add them to his hand; otherwise, they must be taken by the challenger. Play does not then continue from the left, but is resumed by whoever won the challenge.

One-Card Cheat
Similar, but more long-winded. Each in turn lays only one card face down on the table. The first may state any rank, for example 'Ten', the second to play must then say 'Jack', the third 'Queen', and so on. Anyone may challenge by saying 'Cheat!', whereupon the last card is turned up, and the loser of the challenge takes all the cards in the played-out pile. The winner of a challenge plays next, and may call it whatever rank he likes, which then starts a new sequence to be followed by the others.

Three-card Cheat
Distribute the cards equally as far as they will go and stack any remainder face down. The first player lays three cards face down on the table and declares them to be of any rank, for example 'Three Jacks'. The second would then do likewise and announce 'Three Queens', the next Kings, then Aces, and so on. Challenges are made and resolved in the same way as described above. When you have only two or three cards left, you make up three by drawing from the undealt cards.

Chemin de Fer (Chemmy) ▸▸ Baccara

Chicago ▸▸ Bridge (four-deal variant)

Children's games

This is not a technical classification, as so much depends on the child. Games suitable for children are (*a*) any with easily grasped rules and (*b*) any of insufficient depth to interest adults. Many are ancient gambling games that have been cleaned up for children. See, in particular: Authors, Battle, Beggar my Neighbour, Commerce, Donkey, Fifty-One, Go Fish, Golf (memory game), Gops, Hundred, Jubilee, Kemps, My Ship Sails, Ninety-Nine (adding-up game), Obstacle Race, Pelmanism, Slapjack, Snap, Thirty-One. Also suitable for children are many games of the Rummy, Stops, and Going-out families.

Chinese Poker

Gambling game

An apparent derivative of ▶ **Pai Gow Poker**, this is neither Poker nor a banking game—nor, for that matter, Chinese.

Deal thirteen cards each. Everyone arranges their cards in three tiers, a top row of three and two rows of five beneath. The lowest row must be the highest Poker hand of the three, and the top row the lowest. (For Poker hands, *see* ▶ **Poker**.) Each row is then revealed in turn, and each player wins or loses with each other according to their relative ranking. Anyone who fails to arrange their hands in the correct order loses. There is no strategy, no vying, and no sense in it at all.

Chinese Ten

Fishing game

An unusual member of the fishing fraternity.

From a 52-card pack deal 12 to each of two players, or eight to each of three, or six to each of four. Deal the next four cards face up to the table and stack the rest face down. It is usual, but not essential, to arrange the four table cards in a square with sufficient space between them to stack the rest of the pack in the middle, in the overall form of a quincunx (the pattern of five spots on a die).

Your aim is to capture cards from the layout, especially red cards and (if three or four play) ♠A, and (if four play) ♣A.

At each turn you play one card from your hand and either capture a table card with it, or leave it face up as another table card. You capture a numeral card by playing another numeral that makes up 10 with it. For example, an Ace captures a Nine, or vice versa, a Six captures a Four, or vice versa, and so on. You can only capture a Ten or a face card by playing another card of exactly the same rank: a Ten captures a Ten, a Queen a Queen, and so on.

When you capture, you place both cards face down in front of you. Note that you can only play one card from your hand at each turn.

Whether you capture or not, you end your turn by flipping the top card of the central pack face up. If it captures a card from the layout you take both cards; if not, you leave it in the layout. Either way, this ends your turn regardless of whether or not you made any captures.

If you played properly, the last card from the pack will always capture the last card from the layout and all 52 cards will end up distributed among the players' winning piles.

Finally, you score for the cards you won as follows:

low red numerals	face value (2–8)
red 9, 10, J, Q, K	10 each
red Aces	20 each
♠A	30 (only if three or four play)
♣A	40 (only if four play)

The amount you win or lose by is the difference between the score as determined above and the so-called 'tie' score, which is 105 if two play, 80 if three, or 70 if four.

Chinese Whist

Plain-trick game

52

Nineteenth-century Whist-players became fascinated with exposed hands, or 'dummies', which increased skill and calculation at the expense of chance and estimation and eventually gave rise to ▸ **Bridge**. This more lightweight relative recalls a period when anything unusual or eccentric was described as 'Chinese' (cf. Chinese finesse, Chinese snooker, etc). The partnership version is described first.

Players sitting opposite each other are partners. Each receives six cards, and, without examining them, lays them face down in a non-overlapping row. Six more are then dealt face up across the same row, so that each of the six pairs consists of a down-card partly covered by an upcard. The four remaining cards are dealt one to each hand.

The dealer, after examining his hand-card and upcards, announces a trump suit (without consulting his partner.)

Eldest hand leads to the first trick, and the winner of each trick leads to the next. Each may play his hand-card or any upcard at any time, but must follow suit to the led card if possible. The trick is taken by the highest card of the suit led or by the highest trump if any are played. At the end of each trick, any down-card uncovered by the play of an upcard is itself turned up.

Each side scores 1 point per trick taken above six. Play up to any agreed target.

Three players

Remove one of the Twos and deal each player eight cards face down, eight face up, and one in hand. Or (my suggestion): use a full pack and turn the last for trump, without dealing it to anyone. Score for each trick taken above five.

Two players

Each player receives 12 face down, 12 face up, and two in hand. Score for each trick taken above thirteen.

Ciapanò

Penalty-trick game

40

A Milanese game played with either French-or Italian-suited cards, Ciapanò (also called Rovescino, Traversone, Tressette a non Prendere, Perdivinci or Vinciperdi) is the trick-avoidance equivalent of ▶ **Tressette**. Following Italian practice, play rotates to the right. Eldest hand is therefore the dealer's right-hand neighbour.

Ciapanò is played with a 40-card pack ranking and counting as follows:

3	2	A	K	Q	J	7	6	5	4
$\frac{1}{3}$	$\frac{1}{3}$	1	$\frac{1}{3}$	$\frac{1}{3}$	$\frac{1}{3}$	0	0	0	0

Deal eight cards each if five play, ten each if four play, or 13 if three play. With three, the extra card goes to the dealer, who after examining his 14 cards makes one discard face down. This will be added to the last trick.

Eldest hand leads to the first trick. You must follow suit if you can, but may otherwise play any card. The trick is taken by the highest card of the suit led and the winner of each trick leads to the next. There are no trumps.

At end of play everyone except the winner of the last trick counts the value of all the counting cards he has taken in tricks and records this as his penalty score. Fractions are ignored, so a total of 3 or $3\frac{1}{3}$ or $3\frac{2}{3}$ counts always 3 penalty points, and so on. A total of less than 1 counts zero.

The winner of the last trick scores the difference between 11 and the total of the amounts scored by the other players. (This is because the total value of all counting-cards is $10\frac{2}{3}$, which is rounded up to 11.)

A player who wins all the points (not necessarily all the tricks), scores zero for *cappotto* and the others all score 11 penalty points each.

When after several deals you reach a cumulative score of 31 or more you drop out of play. The last players left in—whether one, two, or three, as agreed in advance—are the winners.

Variants. The target score may be set at 21 or 41. Some play that the winner is the player with the lowest score when one player reaches the target.

Cìcera

Fishing game

A decorative member of the ▶ **Fishing** family played in the province of Brescia with Italian-suited cards.

Play to the right. Deal 12 cards each and four to the table. Each in turn plays a card to the table and either makes a capture or leaves it to trail. Captures are made by:

- **pairing**—that is, a Two captures a Two, a Jack a Jack, and so on, or
- **summing**—that is, capturing two or more cards summing to the value of the capturing card, for which purpose each Jack counts 8, Queen 9, King 10.

Given a choice of captures, you may make any one of them (but not more). You are allowed to trail a card even if it could capture.

Points are scored during play for any of the following feats. These are indicated by leaving the capturing card face up in the partnership's pile of winnings.

Scùa = capturing all the table cards in one turn.

Picada = pairing the card just trailed by your left-hand opponent.

Simili = capturing one or more cards of the same suit as the capturing card.

Quadriglia = capturing three or more cards from the table.

More than one of these points can be scored with a single play. For example, if ♥9 captures ♥2-3-4 it scores 1 for *simili* and 1 for *quadriglia*, and, if no cards remain on the table, another 1 for *scùa*. It is obviously necessary to leave some of the captured cards face up to mark these points.

The last player to make a capture also wins any remaining table cards. At end of play, either side scores as follows:

2 for most cards (neither scores if split 26-26)
2 for most spades
3 for *napula*, which is the sequence ♠A-2-3 if the Four is not held.

If it is, *napula* scores the value of the highest card in unbroken suit-sequence from the ♠3 upwards.

1 for *mata* (♠2)
1 for ♦10
1 for ♥J
Play up to 51 points.

Cinch

Point-trick game

52

A descendant of ▸ **All Fours** and ▸ **Pitch**, Cinch originated in Denver, Colorado, around 1885 and was a popular club game until the advent of Auction ▸ **Bridge**.

Cards basically rank A K Q J 10 9 8 7 6 5 4 3 2, except that the Five of the same colour as trumps ('Left Pedro') ranks immediately below the trump Five ('Right Pedro'), thereby extending trumps to fourteen cards and reducing one plain suit to twelve.

Deal nine cards each in threes. Starting with Eldest, each in turn may pass or make a higher bid than any so far made. The possible bids range from one to fourteen, representing the number of points the bidder offers to win, with his partner, in return for choosing trumps. The 14 points accrue for winning certain trumps in tricks, namely:

Ace	1	Right Pedro	5
Jack	1	Left Pedro	5
Ten	1	Two	1

If all pass, dealer declares trumps, but this does not constitute a bid and hence there are no penalties for failure.

Declarer having named trumps, each in turn, starting with Eldest, discards from his hand all cards which are not trumps and is promptly dealt as many more as necessary to restore his hand to six. (Anyone dealt seven or more trumps must reduce his hand to six, discarded trumps being shown for information.) When the first three have been dealt with, dealer then 'robs the pack' by (in effect) adding the undealt cards to his hand and discarding down to six. The net result is that all fourteen trumps will be in play, and only ten plain cards.

Declarer leads first. Players may follow suit or trump, as preferred, but may only renounce if unable to follow suit. The trick is taken by the highest card of the suit led or by the highest trump if any are played.

Game is 51 up, or 61 if a Cribbage board is used. Scoring methods vary. For instance:

1. If the bidding side fulfils its contract, each side scores what it took in tricks. If not, the bidding side deducts from its score 14 plus the number of points it did take. If both sides reach the target on the same deal, the bidding side wins. Or:
2. If the bidding side fulfils its contract, it scores the difference between the number of points taken by each side. If not, the other side scores what it made plus the amount of the bid. This makes the game longer and prevents both from reaching the target simultaneously.

☛ *Note.* To 'cinch' a trick is to play in such a way as to prevent an opponent winning it with a Pedro—a key feature of the game, and hence the origin of its title.

Cinq Cents

1. A one-pack form of ▶ **Bezique**, played with 32 cards.
2. Swiss variety of ▶ **Klaberjass**.

Cirulla

Fishing game

An Italian relative of ▶ **Cassino** and ▶ **Scopa**, played around Genoa and Liguria, usually in partnerships and invariably with Italian-suited cards (swords, batons, cups, coins, equivalent respectively to ♠♣♥♦).

Deal three cards each and four to the table, and stack the rest face down. If the table cards include more than one Ace, bury them and deal again.

To trail is to play a card to the table without capturing anything. A sweep (*scopa*) means capturing all the table cards in one turn. This is indicated by leaving the capturing card face up in one's pile of winnings.

If all four table cards initially dealt total 15 exactly, the dealer takes them immediately, scores for a sweep, and leaves the next player to trail. If they total exactly 30, he does likewise and scores 2 sweeps. The ♥7, if among them, is wild, and represents any valid count the dealer wishes.

So long as cards remain in stock, deal three more each when all are out of cards. If, after any such deal or redeal, a player's three cards total less than 10, he may 'knock' by revealing them all. This counts as three sweeps, indicated by turning three captured cards face up. A player dealt three of a kind at any time may also knock for 10 points. In either case, the ♥7 may be used as a wild card for the purpose of knocking for a low total or three of a kind. It must be designated as a particular rank, and then played as such. For example, if it is called an Ace, it can be used to sweep the table.

Each in turn plays a card to the table and either captures with it or leaves it to trail. Captures are made by:

- **pairing**—that is, a Two takes a Two, a Jack a Jack, etc, or
- **summing**—that is, capturing two or more cards summing to the value of the capturing card, for which purpose each Jack counts 8, Queen 9, King 10, or
- **fifteening**—that is, capturing with a card that makes up 15 with the cards captured. For example, a Seven takes an Eight, or vice versa; a King takes a Two and a Three $(10 + 2 + 3 = 15)$; etc.

Given a choice of captures, you may make any one (but not more in the same turn). You are allowed to trail a card even if it could capture.

An Ace captures all the table cards, but only if there is not another Ace among them.

At end of play points are scored for the cards you or your partnership won as follows:

1 for each sweep
1 for most cards (unless tied)
1 for most diamonds (unless tied)
1 for *sette bello* (♦7)
1 for *primiera* (*see* below)
5 for *scala grande* (♦J-Q-K)
3 for *scala piccola* (♦A-2-3 if the ♦4 is not held. If it is, you score the value of the highest diamond held in unbroken sequence from the ♦3 up.)

Capturing all the diamonds wins the game outright. Otherwise, play up to 26, 51, or 101, as agreed.

For primiera, each side extracts from its won cards the highest-valued card it has taken in each suit, and totals their face values according to the following schedule: Seven 21, Six 18, Ace 16, Five 15, Four 14, Three 13, Two 12, face cards 10 each.

Whoever took the highest-valued card in each of the four suits scores 1 for primiera. A player who has only taken cards in three or fewer suits cannot compete for this point. (You rarely need to count these exactly, as it's usually obvious who has the best primiera by just looking at the Sevens and Sixes.)

Climbing games

Games where players try to run out of cards by playing them out singly or in combinations matching those of previous players. They are widespread in China and South-East Asia. *See* ▸ **Tieng Len**, ▸ **Viet Cong** (in the Tieng Len entry), and ▸ **President** (*aka* A**hole), the American version of Zheng Shàngyóu.

http://www. pagat.com/climbing/

Clobiosh

Or Clob, or Bella: Anglo-Jewish variety of ▸ **Klaberjass**.

Clock

Patience game

Several different solitaires are called Clock, as it is such an obvious theme. This one is also known as Big Ben.

Arrange the following twelve cards in a circle starting at the one o'clock position and going clockwise: ♠6 ♥7 ♣8 ♦9 ♠10 ♥J ♣Q ♦K ♠2 ♥3 ♣4 ♦5.

Deal the next 36 cards face up in twelve columns of three overlapping cards each, in such a way that each column radiates away from one of the first twelve cards without touching it. These columns form the layout, and the original twelve cards are bases.

Your aim is to build each base card up in suit and sequence, turning the corner from King to Ace where necessary, until the top card of the pile exhibits the number corresponding to its position on a clock face. For this purpose eleven and twelve are represented by Queen and King respectively.

In the layout columns, pack cards in suit and descending sequence, turning the corner from Ace to King where necessary but always moving only one card at a time (the card at the outer end of a column).

Turn cards from stock one by one and either play them if possible or else discard them face up to a single wastepile. Special rules govern the replenishment of columns when they become short or entirely consumed. A column containing fewer than three cards must he refilled up to three again using only cards taken from stock, not from the wastepile or from elsewhere in the layout. When you decide to make the refill, you must refill all the deficient columns at once, starting at the one o'clock position, proceeding in a clockwise direction, and restoring a column to three cards before dealing with the next.

There is no redeal.

Coinche

Point-trick game

32

France's national card game is an advanced form of ▶ **Belote** (also called *Belote Coinché*), a member of the ▶ **Jass** family with features borrowed from ▶ **Bridge**. Coinche means 'fist', and it is so called because if you make a bid, and an opponent doubles it—traditionally by banging a fist on the table—the auction ends, and you're stuck with it.

Four play in fixed partnerships, and, traditionally, to the right, but many now play to the left. Game is 3000 points, or 300 if counted in tens.

Cards and deal. Cards number, rank and count as at basic Belote.

trumps or 'all trump'	J	9	A	10	K	Q	—	—	8	7
plain suits or 'no trump'	—	—	A	10	K	Q	J	9	8	7
card-points	20	14	11	10	4	3	2	0	0	0

Shuffle before the first deal, but do no more than cut before each successive deal. Deal eight cards each in batches of 3-2-3. Do not turn a card for trump.

Contracts. Coinche allows contracts to be played with a suit as trump, or at no trump (*sans atout*), or at all trump (*tout atout*).

- In a suit contract, the total of trick-points is 62 in trumps, plus 90 in plain suits, plus 10 for last, total 162.

- At no trump, all Jacks and Nines rank in their plain-suit position, Jacks counting 2 each and Nines zero. The total of trick-points is therefore 120 for cards, plus 10 for last, total 130. There being no trump suit, there can be no belote.
- At all trump, all Jacks and Nines rank in their trump-suit position—that is, above Aces and Tens—and count respectively 20 and 14 each. The total of trick-points is therefore 248 for cards, plus 10 for last, total 258. Since every suit is a quasi-trump, the King and Queen of every suit counts as a belote.

Melds. Card-points are also counted for holding certain melds (combinations) of cards in one hand as shown below. The left column applies to the trump suit only, or to every suit at 'all trump'; the right column applies to plain suits only, or to every suit at 'no trump'.

four Jacks	200	– (*see below*)
four Nines	150	– (*not applicable*)
four Aces	100	200
four Tens	100	150
four Kings	100	100
four Queens	100	100
four Jacks (NT)	–	100 (*see above*)
sequence of five+	100	100
sequence of four	50	50
sequence of three	20	20

A sequence is three or more cards of the same suit and in numerical order, for which purpose the order is always A K Q J 10 9 8 7 (regardless of the ranking power and point-value of the cards concerned).

Finally, *belote* itself denotes the King and Queen of trumps in the same hand and scores 20 card-points.

Bidding. A bid is an offer to win both (*a*) more than half the trick-points available and (*b*) more points than the opposing side in tricks and melds. It consists of a number and a contract, e.g. '80 hearts', '90 all trump' etc.

☞ *Note*. A nominal bid of 80 is actually a bid of at least 82, as 80 is less than half of the 162 available. In some circles, the principle is extended, so that 90 requires at least 92, and so on. The number quoted is that of the actual score made after rounding the minimum requisite number of points down to the nearest ten.

Eldest speaks first, and each in turn may pass, bid, double, or redouble. Bidding may start at any level, but the lowest is 80, and each subsequent bid must quote a higher multiple of ten. Jump-bidding is allowed, and a player who has passed is still allowed to bid again later. A contract is established when a bid is followed by three passes, or by an opponent's 'Double', which may then be redoubled by the bidder or his partner.

If all pass on the first round, the deal is annulled and passes to the next in turn.

Announcing melds. Each in turn, upon playing to the first trick, announces his highest meld, provided that it is not lower than any already announced. If equal, he asks 'How high?', and the previous announcer details the rank of a foursome or the top card of a sequence, as the case may be. Whichever player has the highest meld notes the total value of all melds declared by himself and his partner. A meld declared at the first trick must be shown (on demand) at the second.

Play. Eldest leads first. Rules of trick-play vary, the laxest being those of eastern France.

- To a trump lead you must follow suit if possible and head the trick if possible. (*Variant*: If your partner is winning, you need not overtrump.)
- To a plain-suit lead you must follow suit if possible, but need not head the trick.
- If you can't follow suit, and an opponent is currently winning the trick with a trump, you must trump and overtrump if possible. (*Variant*: If you cannot overtrump, you need not undertrump but may discard at will.)

- If you can't follow suit, and your partner is currently winning the trick, you may play anything. (*Variant*: But may not undertrump if able to overtrump.)

The trick is taken by the highest card of the suit led, or by the highest trump if any are played, and the winner of each trick leads to the next.

Announcing belote. If you hold the King and Queen of trumps, and announce '*belote*' upon playing one of them and '*rebelote*' upon playing the other, your side scores 20 points. Belote is declarable in any suit in an all trump contract, but not at all in no trumps.

Score. At end of play each side calculates its total for trick-points (including 10 for last) and melds. To win, the declaring side must have scored more than their opponents and at least as many as they bid. If successful, both sides score (rounded to the nearest 10) the amount they took for tricks and melds, and the declarers add the value of the contract. If not, the declarers score nothing, and the opponents score 160 for trick-points, plus the value of their melds, plus the value of the lost contract. These scores are all affected by any doubling that may have taken place.

☛ *Note.* Belote players have been quick to exploit the possibilities of the bidding system for conveying information about their hands, using conventions along the same lines as those for Bidding at Bridge.

Collecting games

Games where you strive to collect cards that match one another in some obvious way, other than those better classified as ▶ **Going-out games** or ▶ **Rummy** games. Most are old and simple gambling games that have been cleaned up for children, notably Authors, Commerce, Donkey, Go Fish, and My Ship Sails. Others include Bastard (a form of Brag), Thirty-One, and the unusual partnership game of Kemps.

Comet

Stops game

52

An ancestor of the ▶ **Newmarket** family named after the 1682 appearance of Halley's Comet—possibly from the fancied resemblance of its layout to a comet's tail. The following, one of several different versions, greatly resembles the modern game of ▶ **Pink Nines**.

Remove ♦8 from a 52-card pack. Two players are dealt 20 cards each, three 14, four 11, or five 9, the rest being left out of play. The aim is to run out of cards before anyone else, thus winning the pool.

Eldest starts by playing any card face up to the table and adding to it as many cards as he can in ascending numerical sequence, regardless of suit. If he reaches a King he continues Ace, Two, etc. When he gets stuck, the next in turn continues the sequence from the next higher rank, and so on.

The ♦9, or 'Comet', is wild, being playable at any time. It is followed by the next above the rank it represents, or by a Ten, but a Ten ends one's turn. When no one can continue, the current player starts a new sequence.

If previously agreed, anyone holding the Comet when someone else goes out pays a fixed sum to the winner, and anyone going out by playing the Comet receives a bonus from everyone else.

Commerce

Gambling games

52

Several similar games are called Commerce. The earliest is a nineteenth-century French game, akin to ▶ **Thirty-One** and perhaps ancestral to ▶ **Whisky Poker** and ▶ **Bastard Brag**. Trade and Barter, sometimes also called Commerce, has the same combinations but a different way of acquiring them, and (to my knowledge) appears only in English books. Trentuno applies basically the same method of play to slightly different combinations.

Commerce

Use a 52-card pack ranking A K Q J 10 9 8 7 6 5 4 3 2. Players contribute equally to a pool. The aim is to finish with the best three-card combination. Traditionally, the turn to play passes to the right.

Deal three cards each and a three-card widow face up to the table. Before play, the dealer may exchange his hand for the widow. Thereafter, each in turn, starting with eldest, exchanges a hand card for a card in the widow. A player who is satisfied with his hand knocks on the table instead of playing, and play ceases as soon as two have knocked. The best hands are, from high to low:

Tricon. Three of a kind. Aces best, and so on down.
Sequence. Three cards in suit and sequence. Best is A K Q, lowest 3 2 A.
Point. The greatest value of cards in any one suit, counting Ace 11, courts 10 each, numerals at face value. If equal, a three-card beats a two-card flush. If still equal, the winning equal hand is that of the dealer if he is involved, otherwise that of the first in order of play after the dealer.

Trentuno (Thirty-One)

Use a 40-card pack lacking Eights, Nines, and Tens, and play (to the right) as above. The best hand when someone knocks is that containing cards of the same suit totalling 31 or the nearest below it. Three of a kind is a special hand ranking between 30 and 31.

Trade and Barter

From a 52-card pack deal three each (to the right) but no widow. The aim is to have the best Commerce hand (tricon, sequence, point) at a showdown. Each in turn, starting with Eldest, must exchange one card by announcing 'trade' or 'barter'. If he says 'trade', he passes a card face down to the dealer and receives the next one from the stock, paying the dealer one chip for this privilege. If he says 'barter', he exchanges one card with his right-hand neighbour, sight unseen, and without payment. Play continues until someone knocks.

Commit ▸ *Comet*

Compartment Full ✖️⭕◆❀

Rummy game

52 52

An unusual variety of ▸ **Rummy**, probably invented by B. C. Westall, who first published a description of it in about 1930.

Deal 10 cards each and stack the rest face down without an upcard. The aim is to convert one's hand into one or more melds and go down with all ten cards at once. A meld is three or more cards of the same rank, or three or more numerals in suit and sequence. Sequences run Ace low, Ten high. They may not include face cards.

The first player draws one cards from stock and makes one discard face up. Each in turn thereafter may draw from stock or take any one of the faced discards, which are not piled up but kept separate so all remain visible. If you take a faced card you may not discard it in the same turn. If the stock runs out it is not replaced, and play continues with just the discards. Play ceases when one player declares 'Compartment full' by laying down ten cards arranged into one or more valid melds and making one discard. That player scores 50 for going out plus scores for melds as follows:

eight Aces	50	eight K, Q, or J	25	sequence of ten	50
seven …	40	seven …	20	sequence of nine	25
six …	30	six …	15	sequence of eight	20
five …	20	five …	10	sequence of seven	15
four …	10	four …	5	sequence of six	10
				sequence of five	5

Sets of cards lower than Ten are not allowed. Sequences of three and four are, but score nothing. Everyone else also scores for their melds, and there is no penalty for deadwood.

Note that, although eight of a kind is worth having, it does not enable you to go out. Having got it, therefore, you should so play as to assist another player to go out before everyone gets a high score.

Compendium games

Games consisting of two or more independent games played in a fixed sequence. ▸ **Cribbage**, for example, consists of a partitioning phase (splitting the hand into two) followed by a phase of playing up to 31. Many traditional gambling games consist of three distinct phases, notably ▸ **Poch** and three-stake ▸ **Brag**.

Conquiàn

Rummy game

The earliest true ▸ **Rummy**, first recorded in Mexico and the south-western states from the mid-nineteenth century, was first described as 'Coon Can' in 1887 and as 'Conquiàn' in 1897.

Two players each receive 10 cards dealt singly from a 40-card pack ranking A 2 3 4 5 6 7 J Q K, the rest being stacked face down. The aim is to be the first to go out by melding *eleven* cards, including the last one drawn. Melding means laying them down in sets of three or more matched cards, each consisting of three or four cards of the same rank, or from three to eight cards in suit and sequence.

It is impossible to meld eleven in sequence, as there are only ten per suit. The longest possible is therefore eight, the other three forming a separate meld. Because Ace is low, and Seven and Jack consecutive, both A 2 3 and 6 7 J are valid, but Q K A is not.

Non-dealer starts by facing the top card of stock. He may not take it into hand, but must either meld it immediately (with at least two hand-cards) or pass. If he melds, he must balance his hand by making a discard face up. If he passes, Dealer must either meld it himself, leaving a discard face up in its place, or else also pass by turning it face down. In the latter event it becomes his turn to draw from stock.

Play continues in the same way. Whoever turns from stock has first choice of the card turned, and must either meld it, extend one of his existing melds with it, or pass. If both pass, the second turns it down and draws next.

In melding, you may 'borrow' cards from your existing melds to help create new ones, provided that those thereby depleted are not reduced to less than valid three-card melds. After melding, your discard becomes available to the opponent, who may either meld it himself or turn it down and make the next draw.

The game ends when one player melds both the faced card and all cards remaining in his hand, whether by adding to existing melds, making new ones, or both.

If you decline a faced card which can legally be added to one of your existing melds, you must meld it if your opponent so demands. In this way, it is sometimes possible to force a player into a situation from which he can never go out—a point of much interest to the strategy of play.

If neither is out when the last available card has been declined, the game is drawn and the stake carried forward.

Continental Rummy ▸▸ *Contract Rummy*

Contract Bridge ▸▸ *Bridge*

Contract Rummy

Rummy game

52 52

This is the most convenient heading for a group of closely related ▸ **Rummy** games with a variety of names (Combination R., Hollywood R., Joker R., King R., Liverpool R., Progressive R., Shanghai R., Zion-check, etc.), dating from the Contract ▸ **Bridge** boom of the 1930s. They were later swept aside by ▸ **Canasta**. Typically, a game is several deals, in each of which the first meld anyone can make—the initial meld or 'contract'—gets progressively larger. The following rules assume a knowledge of basic Rummy. Many variations will be found.

Three or four players use 105 cards (2×52 + Joker), five or more use 158 (3×52 + Jokers). Cards rank 2 3 4 5 6 7 8 9 10 J Q K A. The aim is to be the first to go out by melding all one's cards. Other players are penalized for cards remaining unmelded in hand, counting numerals at face value, courts 10 each, Aces and Jokers (or other agreed wild cards) 15 each.

The turn to deal and play passes to the left. A game is seven deals, the first four of 10 cards each, thereafter 12, dealt face down and 1 at a time after very thorough shuffling. Deal the next card face up to start the wastepile, and lay the rest face down as a stock beside it.

Each deal imposes the following requirement as to what every player must meld first before making any other play:

> 1st = 2 sets
> 2nd = 1 set + 1 sequence
> 3rd = 2 sequences
> 4th = 3 sets
> 5th = 2 sets, 1 sequence
> 6th = 1 set, 2 sequences
> 7th = 3 sequences using all cards held

A set is three or more cards of the same rank, regardless of suit. A sequence is three or more cards in suit and sequence. Ace normally counts high in sequences. If it is agreed to count it low as well, it is permissible to make a fourteen-card sequence using it in both capacities. Jokers are wild, and so are Deuces if agreed. Where two or more sequences are required, none may be consecutive and in the same suit. Thus ♣2-3-4, 6-7-8 is valid, but ♣2-3-4-5-6-7 counts as one sequence, not two.

Eldest plays first. Each in turn draws the top card of the stock or wastepile, may meld or lay off as the rules direct, and ends with a face-up discard to the wastepile.

If on your turn to play you do not want the upcard, the right to take it immediately passes to each other player in turn from your left until somebody exercises it. If anyone does take it, they must also draw the top card of stock, without discarding. You must then draw the top card of the stock, having already declined the upcard.

The first meld you make must comply with the schedule above. In later turns you may then lay off one or more matching cards to any meld or melds on the table, whether your own or someone else's, but may not start a new one.

Wild cards represent any desired card in a set or sequence, but only in sequences may they be replaced by the natural cards they represent. If you hold such a card you may substitute it for the Joker, and then either take the Joker into hand or shift it to one end of the sequence. In the latter case, it must stand for a real card with which it can be replaced to produce a valid meld. You may substitute a natural for a wild card at any time you can (not necessarily in turn), provided that you have made your requisite initial meld(s). If two players have the appropriate natural card, priority goes to whichever is next in turn to play. It may be agreed to limit the maximum legal size of sets to eight if two packs are used, twelve if three, whether or not including wild cards.

Play ceases as soon as any player goes out by laying off or discarding his last card. In the seventh and last deal you can only go out by melding your whole hand (with or without one discard) in one go, and making at least three sequences. The others are penalized by the value of cards remaining in hand, and the overall winner is the player with the lowest score at the end of the last deal.

Continental Rummy

A relative of Contract Rummy played by three or four with two 53-card packs, by five or more with three, by eight or more with four. Ace high, Jokers wild (sometimes also Deuces). Deal 15 each. Play as basic Rummy—but collecting only suit-sequences, not sets—until someone ends the game by melding all 15 cards in any of these sequence patterns:

$$(a)\ 3\ 3\ 3\ 3 \qquad (b)\ 4\ 4\ 4\ 3 \qquad (c)\ 5\ 4\ 3\ 3$$

No cards may be laid off or naturals exchanged for wild cards. The winner receives from (or scores off) each opponent 1 for going out, 2 per Joker melded, 1 per Deuce melded if Deuces wild. Other possible bonuses include 10 for going out without having drawn a card, 7 for having drawn only one, 10 for having melded only natural cards, 10 for melding 15 cards of one suit.

Contract Whist

Plain-trick game

52

A deliberate cross between traditional partnership ▶ **Whist** and Contract ▶ **Bridge** devised by Hubert Phillips around 1932. By eliminating the dummy and simplifying the scoring schedule he rid Bridge of many elaborate complications without reducing the skill factor. It will appeal to players whose tastes favour the elegant and classical over the romantic and dramatic.

Four players sit crosswise in partnerships. Deal 13 cards each, one at a time, from a 52-card pack ranking A K Q J 10 9 8 7 6 5 4 3 2. There is an auction to determine the declarers and their contract. The contract is an undertaking made by the declaring partnership to win at least a certain number of tricks using a given suit (or none) as trump. For each side, a horizontal line is drawn half way down the scoresheet. A side scores points below this line for winning the contracted number of tricks, and above it for winning any overtricks and other bonuses. (See Bridge for illustration.) A game is won by the first side to reach 10 points below the line. The rubber is won by the first side to win two games.

Starting with the dealer, each in turn may pass, bid, double the previous bid, or redouble the previous double. Passing does not prevent a player from speaking next time round. The auction ends when a bid, double, or redouble is followed by three consecutive passes.

A bid states the number of tricks above six which a player proposes his partnership to take, and the suit proposed as trump. The lowest bid is 'One club'—an undertaking to win at least seven of the thirteen tricks with clubs as trump. Each bid must be higher than the last. A bid is higher if it raises the number of tricks contracted, or if it involves the same number but in a higher trump. For this purpose clubs are lowest, followed by diamonds, hearts, spades, no trump. Thus there are thirty-five possible bids, ranging from 'one club' to 'seven no trump'.

Instead of bidding, you may 'Double' the previous bid, or 'Redouble' the previous double, if the previous announcement was made by an opponent and no other bid has intervened. A double or redouble is cancelled if followed by another bid.

Following three consecutive passes, the last bid named becomes the contract. The opening lead is made by the player to the left of that member of the contracting side who first named the trump involved. You must follow suit if you can, but may otherwise play any card. The trick is taken by the highest card of the suit led or by the highest trump if any are played, and the winner of each trick leads to the next.

If the contract makes, the contracting side scores below the line 3 points per contracted trick in a trump suit, or 4 points at no trump (or 6 or 8 if doubled, 12 or 16 if redoubled). Overtricks are scored above the line at 2 each whether trump or no-trump, or 5 if doubled or 10 if redoubled. In addition, a doubled or redoubled contract, if made, scores a further 5 or 10 points (respectively) above the line.

If not, the defenders score (above the line) 10 per trick by which the declarers fell short of the contract, or 20 if doubled, 40 if redoubled.

Winning the rubber carries a bonus of 50.

☞ *Note.* Contract Whist lends itself to natural Bridge-style bidding, but less well to conventional or artificial bids, as their significance in Bridge often only becomes clear when the dummy is exposed.

Coon Can

▸▸ **Conquiàn** (Also an obsolete double-pack Rummy known as 'Colonel' in Britain.)

Coquimbert

Or 'Qui gagne perd' (English 'Losing Loadam'), a sixteenth-century ancestor of penalty-trick games such as ▸ **Hearts** and ▸ **Reversis**.

http://www.davidparlett.co.uk/histocs/lodam

Costly Colours

An elaborate relative of ▸ **Cribbage** first described in Cotton's *Compleat Gamester* of 1674 and apparently sighted in a Lancashire pub as late as 1985, according to pub-game researcher Arthur Taylor.

http://www.davidparlett.co.uk/histocs/costly.html

Coteccio

Penalty-trick game

40

Coteccio means 'reverse' and is applied to several Italian games ancestral to ▸ **Hearts**. The most interesting is that of Trieste, described below, in that it is one of the few games extant that retain the card-point system of the ancient game of ▸ **Trappola**. It is invariably played with Italian-suited cards and from left to right.

From two to seven players pay an agreed stake to a pool and start with a notional four lives. Deal five each from a 40-card pack (ideally an Italian one) pack ranking and counting A K Q J 7 6 5 4 3 2. Each Ace, King, Queen, Jack counts respectively 6, 5, 4, and 3 points. Another 6 for winning the last trick makes 78 card-points in all. The aim is either to avoid taking the most card-points, or to win all five tricks.

Eldest leads. You must follow suit if you can, but may otherwise play any card. The trick is taken by the highest card of the suit led, and the winner of each trick leads to the next. There are no trumps. If you win the first four tricks straight off you may either annul the hand, in which case the same dealer deals again, or undertake to win the fifth trick by leading to it.

Whoever takes most card-points loses a life. If two or more tie for most, they all lose a life. If you win four and successfully go for the fifth, you gain an extra life and the opponents lose one each. If you fail, you lose a life and the actual winner of the last trick gains one.

Theoretically, players drop out upon losing their fourth life, and the winner is the last left in. However, the game can be long drawn out. By agreement, a player upon losing his last life may, provided at least two other players remain alive, 'call the doctor' by paying (say) a half stake to the pool and receiving in return as many lives as remain to the player who currently has fewest.

If all live players tie for most and so 'die' simultaneously, the whole game is annulled, and restarted with four lives each and a new pool added to the old one.

The turn to lead first always passes to the next live player to the right of the previous first leader, and the deal is always made by the next live player to the leader's left.

Couillon/Couyon ▸ *Troeven*

Crapette ▸ *Spite and Malice*

Crash ▸ *Brag*

Crazy Eights
Going-out game

Crazy Eights is a children's or students' game, or rather a family of closely related games that first appeared in the early twentieth century and became prolific from about the 1960s, giving rise to a more elaborate group of games such as ▸ **Two-Four-Jack** (or Switch).

From two to five play with a single 52-card pack, which is doubled to 104 if more take part. Deal five cards each, or seven if only two play, and stack the rest face down. Turn its top card face up and place it next to the stock to start a wastepile. If it is an Eight, bury it in the stock and turn the next instead. The aim is to be the first to play off all your cards.

The player at Dealer's left goes first. On your turn to play, you may discard one card to the wastepile provided that it matches the previous discard by either rank or suit. For example, if the previous upcard is the Jack of spades, you can play a spade or a Jack.

Eights are wild: you can play one whenever you like, and nominate a suit for the next player to follow, which need not be that of the Eight itself. If you are unable (or unwilling) to match, you must draw cards from the top of the stock and add them to your hand until you do make a discard, or the stock runs out. If you can't play when the stock has run out, you can only pass.

Play ceases as soon as someone plays their last card, or when no one can match the last card. The player who went out collects from each opponent a payment equivalent to the total face value of cards remaining in the latter's hand, counting each Eight 50, courts 10 each, others face value. If the game blocks, the player with the lowest combined face value of cards remaining in hand scores from each opponent the difference between their two hand values. In the four-hand partnership game both partners must go out to end the game.

Rockaway (Crazy Aces)

The earliest form of the above, with Aces wild instead of Eights and counting 15 each at end of play.

Mau-Mau

Deal five cards each from a 32-card pack (4 × A K Q J 10 9 8 7), turn the next as a starter, and stack the rest face down. Play as Crazy Eights, except that Jacks are wild instead of Eights. You must call 'Mau' upon playing your last card, or 'Mau mau' if it is a Jack, in which case you win double. The penalty for not doing so is to draw a card from stock and keep playing. Cards left in others' hands score against them thus: each Ace 11, Ten 10, King 4, Queen 3, Jack 2 (or 20), others 0 (or face value). End when someone reaches 100 penalties.

Neuner ('Nines')

As Mau-Mau, but with a Joker added. It and all Nines are wild.

Cribbage

Matching game

52

English national card game apparently derived from ▸ **Noddy** by the addition of the lay-away, box, or 'crib'—an invention traditionally ascribed to Sir John Suckling (1609–42). A game of court and aristocracy until the mid-eighteenth century, it became a club game in the nineteenth and is nowadays played in two main forms: five-card Cribbage in pubs as a league and tournament game for two players or four in partnerships, and six-card Cribbage as a home game for two. The latter is described first.

Six-card Crib

Two players use a 52-card pack running A 2 3 4 5 6 7 8 9 10 J Q K. The aim is to be the first to score 121 over as many deals as necessary. Scores are best recorded by moving pegs round a Cribbage board ('pegging').

The deal. The player cutting the lower card deals first (Ace lowest), after which the deal alternates. Deal six cards each in ones.

The discard. Each player discards two cards face down to form a 'crib' of four cards, which will eventually count for the dealer. In discarding, both aim to keep a hand of four cards which form scoring combinations, while the dealer will throw combinable cards and the non-dealer non-combinable cards to the crib. The crib cards are placed together face down and must not be looked at yet.

Combinations. The combinations and their scores are:

- Fifteen (2): two or more cards totalling 15 in face value, counting Ace 1, numerals as marked, courts 10 each.
- Pair (2): two cards of the same rank.
- Prial (pair royal) (6): three of the same rank.
- Double pair royal (12): four of the same rank.
- Run (1 per card): three or more cards in ranking order.
- Flush: Four cards of the same suit in one hand.

Starter. Non-dealer lifts the top half of the undealt pack, the dealer removes the top card of the bottom half and places it face up on top as the starter. If it is a Jack the dealer pegs 2 'for his heels', provided that he remembers to claim it before any card is played.

Play. Starting with non-dealer, each in turn plays a card face up to the table in front of himself and announces the total face value of all cards so far played by both.

A player making it exactly 15 pegs 1 point. Each must play if able to do so without going over 31. A player unable to do so says 'Go'. The other then adds as many more cards as possible without exceeding 31 and scores 1 for the go, or 2 for making 31 exactly. If any cards remain in hand, the cards played so far are turned face down, and the next in turn to play begins a new series. When one player runs out of cards, the other continues alone.

Points are also pegged for pairs and runs made by cards laid out successively in the play. A card matching the rank of the previous one played scores 2 for the pair; if the next played also matches, it scores 6; and the fourth, if it matches, 12.

If a card just played completes an uninterrupted run of three or more in conjunction with the cards just played, the run is scored at the rate of 1 per card.

Example. Annie plays 5, Benny 7, Annie 6 and pegs 3 for the run. If Benny then plays 4 or 8 he pegs 4. If he played 2 he would peg nothing, having broken the sequence; but Annie could then play 3 and re-form it for 6.

Flushes are not scored in the play to 31, but runs are, and they need not be played in order. For example, if the first four cards played are A-4-2-3, then whoever played last scores 4 for the run. The additional of a Five would make it a run of five, while a Four would re-create a run of three. However, a run is broken by the interruption of a paired card. For example, in the consecutive play of 6-7-7-8, the second Seven prevents the Eight from completing a run of three.

The show. Each player, starting with non-dealer, picks up his four hand cards and spreads them face up. Counting these and the starter as a five-card hand, he then scores for any and all combinations it may contain—fifteens, pairs, prials, runs, and flushes. A given card may be used in more than one combination. It may even be used more than once in the same combination, provided that at least one other associated card is different each time.

Example. ♠6 ♥7 ♣7 ♦8 ♠9 scores 2 for each distinct card combination counting 15 (♠6 ♠9, ♥7 ♦8, ♣7 ♦8), 2 for the pair of Sevens, and 4 for each run of four (♠6 ♥7 ♦8 ♠9, ♠6 ♣7 ♦8 ♠9). The score is announced thus: 'Fifteen 2, 4, 6; pair 8; fours 16'.

A flush in the hand counts 4, or 5 if its suit matches the starter's. A player holding the Jack of the same suit as the starter also pegs 1 'for his nob'. (If the starter is a Jack, neither player reckons for his nob, as it is overridden by the 2 'for his heels'.)

Counting the crib. Finally, dealer turns the crib face up and pegs for it as a five-card hand exactly as above, except that a flush only counts if all five are in suit.

Muggins. (An optional rule nowadays often ignored.) A player who notices that his opponent has failed to declare a scoring feature may point it out ('Muggins!') and peg it himself.

Score. Play ceases the moment either player 'pegs out' by reaching the target score, no matter what stage of the game has been reached. If the

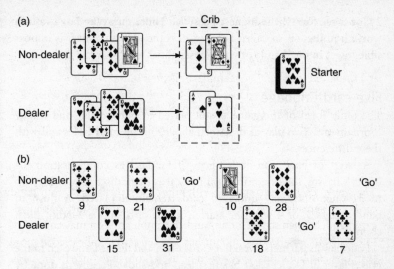

Cribbage. (a) The players each discard two to the dealer's crib and a starter is turned from the pack. (b) How the hands might be played. (c) The score. Non-dealer pegged in play 2 for the second Six and 1 for a go; in hand fifteen 2 (6 + 9), 8 9 10 J, and 1 for his nob (♥J), total 3 + 7 = 10. Dealer pegged in play fifteen 2, thirty-one 2, and 1 for the last go; in hand fifteen 2, fifteen 4 (for the Seven and each Eight), 2 for a pair (Eights), and 6 7 8 twice for 6; in the crib fifteen 2 (8 3 3 A) and a pair 2; total 5 + 12 + 4 = 21. The appropriate pegging is shown below.

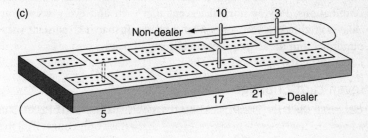

loser has less than 91 he is whitewashed (or 'lurched', or 'in the lurch'), and loses a double game or an agreed additional stake. Also by agreement, game may be set at 61 (lurch 31) or 181 (lurch 121). It is customary to play for a fixed amount per game and on-the-spot side payments for extras such as dozens and nineteen in the box. 'Dozens' means a player gets, say, a penny for scoring 12 in hand or crib, two for

24, or three for 29, the highest possible. 'Nineteen in the box'—a crib worth nothing—is so called because 19 is the lowest count it is impossible to get in one hand (other impossibilities are 25, 26, 27).

Five-card Cribbage

The older form of the game is still played in pubs, clubs, and league tournaments. Two play as described above, but up to 61 holes and with these differences.

At start of play, non-dealer pegs '3 for last' as compensation for dealer's having the first crib. Deal five cards each, discard two. Play up to 31 once only: any unplayed cards remain unplayed. A flush in hand counts 3, or 4 with the starter. In the crib, only a 5-point flush counts.

Four play as partners. Deal five cards each, and discard one each to the crib. Player at Dealer's left has first lead and show. Pegging is done by Dealer's and leader's partners. Each partnership scores the amount made by both its members.

Losing Cribbage

Two-hand six-card Cribbage in which the aim is to avoid scoring for combinations. Play as normal, except that each and every score you make is credited to your opponent, and the first to 121 wins. It may sound daft, but in fact requires equally skilful play.

Seven-card Cribbage

Deal seven each, discard two to the crib. Game is 181. Rarely played.

Auction Cribbage

Before the starter is turned, each in turn, Dealer first, states how many points he will pay (deduct from his score) in return for the privilege of the crib. The higher bidder promptly subtracts that amount, and play proceeds as in any of the above games as if he were the normal dealer. (Devised by Hubert Phillips.)

Three-hand Cribbage

1. **Cut-throat version.** Deal five cards each and one face down to the crib, to which each then discards another one, making four in all. Player at dealer's left plays and counts his hand first; dealer plays and counts his hand and crib last. Each player scores for himself.

2. **Solo version.** The dealer's two opponents play as a partnership. Deal five cards each and six to the dealer. The partners pass one card each to the dealer, who from his hand discards four to the crib. Play as above, except that each partner scores the total made by them both.

Cribbage Patience

Deal 16 cards face up to form a square of four rows and columns, placing each new card adjacent to any previous one. Turn the seventeenth up as a starter. Score for each row and column as for a five-card hand including the starter. Win if you make at least 61.

Cromwell

Patience game

A solitaire devised and named by Charles Jewell as an improved version of an old game originally called House on the Hill.

Shuffle all 104 cards together and deal them all out, face up, in twenty-six fans of four cards each.

Your aim is to get all eight Aces out, as and when they are exposed, set them up as bases, and build each up in suit and sequence until it contains thirteen cards headed by the King.

The exposed card of each fan is available either for building, or for packing on the exposed card of another fan. Packing must be done downwards and in suit. For example, you may pack ♥6 on ♥7 or ♣7 on ♣8. You may also take a packed sequence of two or more cards and shift it as a whole to the exposed end of another fan, provided that the join follows the rule. For example, if one fan consists of ♣4 ♦J ♠9, and another ends with ♠8-7-6, you may move the ♠8-7-6 to the ♠9.

Beware of emptying a fan completely, as you are not allowed to start a new one in its place.

If the game jams up completely, you are allowed one 'grace'. This consists in exchanging any two cards in the layout—whether in the same or different fans, and whether exposed or buried. Count half a win for succeeding with the aid of a grace.

Cuarenta

Fishing game

This South American member of the Cassino/Scopa family is played—with a great deal of drama and passion—in the mountainous regions of Ecuador. There is a Cuarenta web site in Spanish, which includes rules, information about the World Championship, and a downloadable software program.

Four play crosswise in partnerships, with one partner keeping score and the other storing their won cards. The cards in play are K Q J 7 6 5 4 3 2 1(= A), usually taken from a 52-card pack, of which the Eights, Nines, and Tens are used for marking scores. At start of play they are stacked face up between the two opposing scorekeepers.

Deal a single batch of five cards to each player and stack the rest face down. When five each have been played, five more are dealt.

Immediately after any deal, and before play begins, a player may declare and score for either of the following:

- **Four of a kind**: Four cards of the same rank. These are shown, and that player's side wins the game without play.
- **Ronda**: Three cards of the same rank. These are declared, but not shown or identified, and their holder's side scores 4 points.

Each in turn plays a card to the table and either captures with it or leaves it to trail. Captures are made by:

- **pairing**—that is, a Two takes a Two, a Jack a Jack, etc., or
- **summing**—that is, capturing two or more cards summing to the value of the capturing card, for which purpose each Jack counts 8, Queen 9, King 10, or
- **footing** a sequence—that is, if a table card captured by pairing is accompanied by one or more cards in ascending numerical

sequence then the whole sequence is thereby captured. For example, playing a Three captures a Three alone, or any sequence beginning Three-Four-(etc.).

Given a choice of captures, you may choose any one of them, but not more. You may also trail a card even if you could make a capture with it. A card played to an empty table, as at start of play or following a sweep, is necessarily trailed.

Caída. Capturing the card just played by the previous player by matching it is called a caída (a fall), and scores 2 points. However, it is not a caída when the first player after a new deal matches and captures the last card played at the end of the previous deal.

Limpia. Capturing all the cards on the table is a limpia ('clean-up'), and scores 2 points. Since the next player can only trail, it often happens that the player or partnership scoring for limpia also scores for caìda on their next turn, making 4 in all.

Any table cards remaining untaken at end of play do not count to either side. A player or side that took exactly 20 cards scores 6 points, but if both do, only the non-dealing side scores. For each card taken above 20, add 1 point, but round up to the nearest even number. For example, score 8 for 21 or 22 cards, 10 for 23 or 24, and so on. If both sides take fewer than 20, the side that took more cards, or the non-dealing side if equal, scores just 2 points. Game is 40 (*cuarenta*) points.

Special scoring rules. If you make a caída by capturing a card that was part of a ronda (trio), and remember this event and the rank of the ronda cards, you can score 10 points at the end of the hand for correctly announcing this fact and the rank of the ronda involved. You may not announce it before the hand ends, or after the next deal has begun.

A side standing at 30 or more cannot score for rondas, nor for capturing a card of the opponents' ronda by means of a caída. However, if the opposing team have less than 30, they may still score 10 points if they capture a card of an 'unannounced' ronda by a caída, and correctly announce it.

A side standing at 38 points cannot score for limpia. They can win only by counting cards or with a caída. Standing at 36, however, they can win the game by scoring 4 for both feats (*caída y limpia*).

Scorekeeping with eights, nines, and tens. Each of these cards represents 2 points face up or 10 points face down. Each scorekeeper takes a scorecard from the stock and places it face up before him for every 2 points scored. Upon reaching 10, four cards are returned to the stack and the fifth is turned down to represent 10 (when it becomes known as a *perro*, 'dog'.) A score of 38 is indicated by returning all one's score-cards to the stack. There are just enough cards to keep score in all situations.

Cuckoo ⇥ *Chase the Ace*

Cucumber

Penalty-trick game

52

A Baltic gambling game (Swedish *Gurka*, Polish *Ogórek*, etc.) that need not be taken too seriously, and can be scored in writing.

From three to eight players contribute equal stakes to a pot and receive six cards each dealt one at a time from a 52-card pack running 2 3 4 5 6 7 8 9 10 J Q K A. The aim is to avoid being left with the highest card at end of play.

Eldest leads any card. Each in turn must play a card equal to or higher in rank than the previous card played, regardless of suit. Anyone unable to do so must play the lowest he has. Whoever plays the highest card—or the last played of equally highest—removes the 'trick' and leads any card to the next. When five tricks have been played, everyone reveals their last card. The player with the highest card (or each of tied players) scores penalty points equal to its face value, counting Ace 14, King 13, Queen 12, Jack 11, numerals as marked.

Upon reaching −30 points you become a 'cucumber' and drop out of play. However, you may buy yourself back in for a new stake, but must restart with the same number of minus points as the player with the next highest total. No one may buy in more than once.

When only three players are left, buying-in is barred, and play continues until one of them is sliced (or cucumbered). The pot then goes to the player with the lowest total.

Curds and Whey

Patience game

This relative of ▶ **Spider**, invented by the author, introduces a rare form of packing, that of rank on rank. This leads to a good deal of breaking up and reforming of packed lines, which may put you in mind (if you go back far enough) of spooning curds and whey ('junket').

Deal thirteen cards face up in a row, then three more rows across the top of them, then spread all 52 cards downwards towards you to produce thirteen columns of four.

Your aim is to build within the layout four thirteen-card suit sequences in descending order from King to Ace.

At each turn, you may take the uncovered card of one column and place it on the uncovered card of another, provided that the card you place it on is the next higher card of the same suit ('whey') or a card of the same rank ('curd').

Similarly, you can transfer a sequence from one end of a column to another provided that the join follows the sequence rule, or a set of cards of the same rank from one column to another ending in the same rank. For example, if the end card of one column is ♥9, you can transfer to it any number of Nines from the end of another column, or the ♥8 from another column, together with any hearts in sequence to it. What you may not do, however, is to shift a number of cards consisting of both a sequence and a set. For example, you could not put ♥8 on ♥9 if ♥8 is covered by ♥7-♥6-♣6-♦6. If you empty a column, you may only restart it with a King, together with any number of cards correctly covering it. With accurate play, this game nearly always comes out.

Czech Rummy

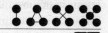

Rummy game

A relative of ▸ **Contract Rummy** with an interesting twist, in that different players may have different initial meld requirements at the same time. A knowledge of basic ▸ **Rummy** is assumed.

The aim is to make melds in order to avoid being left with counting-cards in hand, which score against. Each player drops out of the game on reaching 300 penalty points, and the winner is the last one left.

Deal 12 cards each from a 108-card pack (2 × 52 plus Jokers). Stack the rest and turn the top card face up to start a wastepile. Each draws the top card of stock or wastepile, melds or lays off subject to the rules below, and discards one to the wastepile. You may not draw and discard the upcard on the same turn.

Cards count as follows: Joker 25, King 13, Queen 12, Jack 11, numerals face value. Ace counts 1 point and is always low, forming a sequence only with 2 3 … etc.

A meld is three or more cards of the same rank or in suit and sequence. A Joker represents any desired card. The first meld you make must be worth a minimum amount. At start of play it is 15. In subsequent deals, whoever has the highest penalty score must start with a meld of at least 15, the second highest with 20, the third with 25, and so on in increments of five. If two players have the same total, their requirement is the same, but the next increment is omitted.

Example. At the end of the first deal Annie counts 0 against, Benny 28, Connie 72, Denny 28. In round two Connie may start with a sequence worth at least 15 (e.g. A-2-3-4-5, 4-5-6). But Benny and Denny must meld at least 20 and Annie at least 30 to start.

Having made an initial meld, you may on subsequent turns meld new sets or sequences of any value and lay off individual cards to any melds of your own. You may also take a Joker from any meld on the table in return for any card that leaves it legally intact.

Play ceases the moment someone plays or discards the last card from their hand. The others are then penalized by the face values of all cards left in hand, even if they form valid melds. There is no plus score for melds lying face up on the table.

If the stock runs out, leave the upcard intact but shuffle the wastepile below it and turn it face down as a new stock.

Dealer's Choice

Method of playing ▶ **Poker** whereby the version played at each deal or round of deals is chosen by the current dealer.

Delphi

Going-out game

52

A simpler development of ▶ **Eleusis** devised by Martin Kruskal of Princeton University. The aim is to play out all your cards, as at ▶ **Crazy Eights**, but without being told the rule by which each card must match the previous one.

A pool of chips is required for scoring purposes. Each player starts with one chip and a card or counter marked YES on one side and NO on the other. One player, designated the Oracle, secretly writes down a rule of card-matching and the other players seek to deduce what it is. The rule may not be related to any factors extrinsic to the cards themselves, such as the current clock time or the way in which each card is announced, but the Oracle may give a clue as to its nature before the first card is placed. A simple rule might be 'An odd card must be followed by a red card, an even card must be followed by a black'. (For numerical purposes, Jack counts 11, Queen 12, King 13.)

The pack is stacked face down and the top card is turned and placed face up beside it to start a sequence. Each subsequent card is turned face up and will eventually be placed next in the main sequence if it correctly follows the previous card in accordance with the rule. If not, it is put in a vertical line above the last card validly placed in the main sequence.

At each move the Oracle turns the top card of stock and announces its identity. Each player decides whether or not it will fit the main sequence and places their decision counter on the table with either the YES or the

NO face side up according to their decision, but as yet covered by their hand. When all are ready, their decisions are revealed simultaneously.

The Oracle then attaches the card to the main sequence if it fits, or to the vertical column if it does not, and pays one chip to each player who correctly foretold the oracular decision, and wins all the chips of those who did not.

When all the cards have been placed, each player scores (*a*) the difference between their own total of chips and the totals of all who won fewer, less (*b*) the difference between their own total of chips and the totals of all who won more. Their total for the deal may therefore be positive or negative, or zero.

The Oracle scores the sum of all the part-scores made in category (b). The scoring system ensures that the Oracle's best interests are served by formulating a rule which about half the players will correctly deduce by the end of the deal.

Ideally, a game consists of as many deals as there are players (or a multiple thereof), so that all can be the Oracle the same number of times.

Demon (Canfield)

Patience game

The American name Canfield commemorates the owner of a Saratoga gambling saloon who made a tidy profit by selling players packs of cards and paying them back according to how many cards they managed to play off in a game of Demon before getting stuck.

Deal a packet of thirteen cards face down and turn the top one face up. These form a reserve called the demon. Deal the next card face up to form the first of four base cards, then deal four more cards in a row beneath it to start the layout. As the three other cards of the same rank as the first base become available, move them up into a row next to it. Build these up in suit and sequence until each pile contains thirteen cards, turning the corner from King to Ace where necessary.

Turn cards front stock in sweeps of three at a time and play them to a single wastepile. After each sweep, see if you can play the top card of the wastepile to a building pile or to one of the four layout columns.

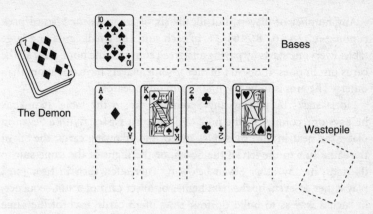

Bases

The Demon

Wastepile

Demon. A lucky start: play Ace to Two, King to Ace, Queen to King, and fill gaps from the top of the demon. Extract the other three Tens as bases when they come out, and build each one up in suit to its Nine (10 J Q K A 2 3 4 5 6 7 8 9).

In the layout, pack in descending sequence and alternating colour, turning the corner from Ace to King as necessary. You may move either one card at a time or complete sequences from column to column, provided that the join follows the rule.

Whenever you can build or pack the top card of the demon, do so, and turn the card beneath it face up.

Whenever you clear out a column of the layout, you must fill it at once with the top card of the demon—or, if none remain, with the top card of the wastepile. You may not fill it from the pack or from elsewhere in the layout.

Keep turning the wastepile and redealing until the game either blocks or comes out.

Deux Cents ▸▸ *Two Hundred*

Domino
Going-out game

52

Also called Card Dominoes, Fan Tan, Parliament, and Spoof Sevens, Domino makes a good game for children. It also forms one component of several compendium games such as ▸ **Barbu**.

Any number of players, but ideally six or seven, use a 52-card pack running A 2 3 4 5 6 7 8 9 10 J Q K in each suit. Use small cards or a large table. Everyone starts by paying an agreed sum into the pool. Deal all the cards out in ones. It doesn't matter if some players have one more than others. The aim is to be the first to run out of cards.

Eldest starts by playing any Seven face up to the table. If unable, he pays one counter to the pool and the turn passes. With a Seven in place, the next in turn must play one of the following cards: the Six of the same suit to the left of the Seven, or the Eight of the same suit to its right, or any other Seven below it. Thereafter, each in turn must play either a Seven, or the next higher or lower card of a suit-sequence, in such a way as to build up four rows of 13 cards, each of the same suit and reading from Ace at the extreme left to King at the extreme right.

If you can't make a play when it is your turn you contribute one counter to the pool. If you decline to play when able to do so, you pay three to each opponent, plus five to the holders of the Six and Eight of a suit if you hold the Seven and fail to play it. Not that you are obliged to do so: holding up Sevens is all part of the strategy.

First out sweeps the pool and gets one counter from each opponent for each card left in hand.

Variant. In Five or Nine (or Five and Nine), the first person able to play may start with a Five or a Nine. Whichever is chosen must be adhered to as the foundation rank for each row for the rest of that hand.

Don

Point-trick game

A derivative of ▸ **All Fours** (*see also* ▸ **Cinch**, ▸ **Phat**, ▸ **Pitch**) widely played on a league basis throughout England and Wales. Also called Nine-card Don, Big Don, Long Don, and (with slight variations) Welsh Don. Following are the rules of the Bolton (Lancashire) Don League.

Four players sitting crosswise in partnerships receive nine cards each dealt one at a time from a 52-card pack. The aim is to win counting cards in tricks. Game is 91 up, scores being pegged on a Cribbage board.

Cards rank A K Q J 10 9 8 7 6 5 4 3 2 in each suit. Certain cards have point-values as follows:

trump Ace	4
trump King	3
trump Queen	2
trump Jack	1
trump Nine	9
trump Five	10
each non-trump Five	5

(The non-trump Fives are called 'Dons' in South Wales.)

Eldest leads, and the suit of the led card is automatically trump. Others must follow suit if possible, otherwise may play any card. The trick is taken by the highest card of the suit led or by the highest trump if any are played. Each trick-winner leads to the next.

During play, each side pegs immediately the value of any trump counters and Fives taken in tricks. After play, the side that took a majority of card-points (by the traditional count of each Ace 4, King 3, Queen 2, Jack 1, Ten 10) pegs an additional 8, but neither does so if equal. This makes the total peggable for the whole deal 52.

☞ *Note.* Though derived from All Fours, Don has lost its traditional rules of trick play (follow suit or trump as preferred, but only discard from another suit if unable to follow). Pity.

Donkey

Collecting game

52

A children's game, ideal for five or six, Donkey is also known as Pig, or Hog, and there is a variant called Spoons.

Remove from a 52-card pack as many groups of four as there are players. For example, with five players you might use all four Aces, Fives, Tens, Queens, and Kings. Shuffle these cards together and deal them round in ones so everyone gets exactly four. The aim is to get four of a kind, or to notice when somebody else has done so.

Each one of you, all at the same time, take one card from your hand and pass it face down to your left-hand neighbour. Keep doing this till one player gets all four of a rank in his hand. He then, as slyly and quietly as possible, lays his hand of cards face down on the table and rests one finger wisely against his nose. Anyone who notices him doing so also puts his cards down and rubs his nose, even if he hasn't got four of a kind. Eventually, everybody will notice what's going on and do the same thing. The last player to do so is the donkey. (Or Pig, or Triceratops, or whatever.)

Variant 1. The donkey drops out of play, and all four cards of one rank are stripped from the pack for the next deal. Play continues until only two players remain in the game, and they are considered joint winners.

Variant 2. Use the full 52-card pack instead of reducing it to four times the number of players. Deal four each and stack the rest face down. The dealer, instead of passing a card to his left and taking one from his right-hand neighbour, passes one to the left and draws one from the top of the stock. Similarly, the dealer's right hand neighbour, before taking a card from his right-hand neighbour, starts by discarding one face down to a discard pile. As the dealer has a slight advantage, it is usually agreed that the winner of each round should deal to the next.

Spoons. This variant is played with additional equipment consisting of objects such as spoons, of which you start with one fewer than the number of players. As soon a someone collects four of a kind, they show their cards and take a spoon. Everyone else then grabs a spoon, whether they have four of a kind or not. The player who fails to get one is the loser and drops out of play, and the number of spoons is reduced by one for the next round.

Doppelkopf

Point-trick game

A popular north German alliance or 'floating partnership' game related to ▶ **Skat**. Doppelkopf (meaning 'double-head') is usually played for hard score (coins or counters) and acknowledges no authoritative code of practice, being subject to a wide range of variant bids and elaborations. It is very elaborate, and if you've never played this type of game before you might find it helpful to start with ▸ **Sueca**.

Cards. 48, a double 24-card pack with Nine low. All Queens, Jacks, and diamonds are permanent trumps, ranking and counting from high to low as follows:

♣Q	♠Q	♥Q	♦Q	♣J	♠J	♥J	♦J	♦A	♦10	♦K	♦9
3	3	3	3	2	2	2	2	11	10	4	0

Plain suits rank and count Ace 11, Ten 10, King 4, Nine 0. Note that trumps account for half the pack (twenty-four cards), and that the total value of all counters is 240.

Start. Everyone starts with the same number—at least ten—of coins or gaming chips. The turn to deal and play passes to the left. Deal 12 cards each in fours.

Aim. The holders of the two club Queens are secret partners, their partnership being discovered only from the play. Their object is to take at least 121 card-points in tricks.

If dealt both club Queens, you have various options. You may either seek someone with whom to take at least 121 card-points in partnership, or else play solo and aim to take at least 121 playing alone against the other three. Typically, you may:

1. Call for a partner by declaring a 'wedding' (*Hochzeit*). The first opponent to win a trick automatically becomes your partner. *Or*:
2. Call for a partner by naming a card you haven't got, typically a plain-suit Ace. Whoever first plays that card to a trick (there being two of them, remember) automatically becomes your partner. *Or*:
3. Say nothing, and play a secret solo. *Or*:
4. Declare a trump solo by naming as trumps a suit other than diamonds. In this case Queens and Jacks are still top trumps, followed by the eight cards of the nominated suit, but diamonds count as an ordinary plain suit.

Doubling. If a solo is announced, an opponent who thinks the contract will fail may double the amount being played for. The soloist, if confident he can win, may then redouble.

Play. Eldest leads first. You must follow suit if you can, but may otherwise play any card. The trick is taken by the highest card of the suit led or by the highest trump if any are played. Of identical cards, the first played beats the second. Each trick-winner leads to the next.

Settlement. When two play two, each member of one partnership pays one member of the other. The amount paid depends on how many card-points they took between them—the fewer they took, the more they pay.

If the Queen partners win, they get 5 if the losers took no trick, 4 if they took less than 30, 3 if less than 60, 2 if less than 90, 1 if less than 120. (The method of announcing is 'No tricks, no 30, no 60, no 90, no 120, total five'; or, if they took (say) 58, 'No 60, no 90, no 120, total 3'; etc.)

If the Queen partners lose, the other side counts in the same way but with an extra point for playing 'against the Queens'. Thus, if they took only 89, the others would count 'No 90, no 120, against the Queens, three'. (Note that 120 is a loss for the Queen-players, even though announced as 'No 120'.)

Solo games are reckoned in the same way, except that if the three partners win they do not count an extra chip for playing against the Queens. If the soloist wins, each opponent pays him the relevant amount; if not, he pays that amount to each opponent.

Notes. In the orthodox game (as distinct from the 'free' game involving variants described below) the Queen-holders will quickly seek to find each other out by leading, playing, or inviting the play of a club Queen as soon as possible. If one of them has the opening lead, a trump Ace or Ten will serve this purpose while gaining some high card-points. Once you know who your partner is, you can seek every opportunity to 'grease' (or 'fatten', or 'stuff') any trick that he or she is winning, by throwing a high-counting Ace or Ten to it.

Variants. An advanced form of the game promotes certain cards to trumps ranking above the black Queens. The top two are the diamond Nines, referred to as Jokers. (If real Jokers are used, remove both diamond Nines from the pack.) These are followed by both heart Tens, called *die Tollen*, 'the loonies'. This has the curious effect of shortening the red plain suits and increasing trumps to twenty-eight. In play, it inhibits a black-Queen partner from discovering his ally by leading an Ace, as an opponent may now win the trick with a Joker (worth 0 card-points) or a loony (worth 10).

By agreement, an additional unit may be paid as between each partner and one opponent, or the soloist and each opponent, for:

· capturing a trump Ace (a 'fox') played by an opponent;
· winning a doppelkopf—that is, a trick consisting of four 'big 'uns' (Aces and Tens);
· winning the last trick with a club Jack (Karlchen Müller, or 'Charlie Miller').

Each of these is settled independently of winning or losing the main game.

Variant solo bids include a 'Jack solo', in which only Jacks are trumps and plain suits rank A-10-K-Q-9, and a 'Queen solo', in which only Queens are trumps and plain suits rank A-10-K-J-9. In the more off-beat solo bids it may be agreed to disregard Jokers and loonies, leaving those cards in their normal positions.

Double Dummy

Plain-trick game

52

A version of ▶ **Whist** for two.

You both sit at connected sides of the table instead of opposite each other. Cut the cards to determine trumps for the deal. Deal four hands, as if for Whist or ▶ **Bridge**, one to each side of the table. Each player arranges the hand opposite him into suits and ranks like a dummy at Bridge, and takes his own cards into hand. Non-dealer leads to the first of 13 tricks. A trick consists of four cards, one from each of the four hands, with each player playing alternately from his own hand

and own dummy (or vice versa, depending on which hand wins the trick). Score 1 point for each trick taken in excess of six. Game is 5 points, or any other agreed total. Honours may be scored (as at classical Whist).

Draw Bridge ▸▸ Honeymoon Bridge

Drinking games

Simple gambling games producing not a winner but a loser, whose penalty is to buy the next round of drinks. Many children's games, such as ▸ **Cuckoo** and ▸ **Old Maid** are old drinking games from which the liquid element has been drained.

Drive Whist ▸▸ Whist (Progressive)

Dudak

Going-out game

32

A light-hearted Czech game related to the Russian ▸ **Durak** and ▸ **Svoyi Kozyri**. 'Dudak' means 'bagpipe', implying rustic simplicity.

Four players (the best number) are each dealt eight cards one at a time from a 32-card pack ranking A K Q J 10 9 8 7 in each suit. The aim is to play all your cards out. The last player left with cards in hand loses.

Eldest starts by playing any card face up to the table to start a wastepile. Each in turn thereafter may, if possible, play two cards to the wastepile. The first must be a higher card of the same suit as the top card of the pile, and the second may then be any card at all.

If you cannot or will not beat the top card you must take and add it to your hand, and keep doing this till you uncover a card that you can beat and are willing to. Having beaten it, you add any second card, and play continues as before. If, however, you thereby take the whole pile, your turn ends, and the next in turn starts a new pile with a single card.

The game gets interesting when trumps are declared. On your turn to play you may declare any suit to be your personal trump. Thereafter, the first of your two discards must be either a higher one of the same suit as the top card, or any one of your trumps. Typically, each player will choose a different suit; but it is allowed, and can be tactically interesting, for two or more players to choose the same trump.

Having declared a trump suit you must observe the following rules:

- You must keep that suit as trump for the rest of the game.
- Whenever you cannot or will not beat the top card, you may not remove cards one by one but must take the whole pile into hand. A new one is then started with a single card by the next in turn to play.

When you play your last card to the pile, you drop out of play, and the others continue from the next in turn. If you went out by playing two cards, play continues exactly as before. If, however, you had only one card at the start of your last turn, and went out by beating the top card, then the current wastepile is turned face down and put to one side. The next in turn then starts a new wastepile by playing one card only, and play continues as before.

The overall winner is the one who loses fewest of an agreed number of games. Alternatively, it is the one who has not lost a game when everyone else has lost at least one.

☛ *Comment.* Lacking rules for fewer players, I suggest three receive 10 each from a 30-card pack made by removing the black Sevens, and two 12 each from a 24-card pack with Nine low.

Dummy Whist ▶▶ *Whist for three,* or ▶ *Double Dummy for two*

Durak
Going-out game

A popular Russian game related to ▶ **Dudak** and ▶ **Svoyi Kozyri**. Other relatives are played throughout Eastern Europe and Scandinavia. The two-hand version runs as follows.

Deal six cards each, in threes, from a 36-card pack ranking A K Q J 10 9 8 7 6. Stack the rest face down, then turn the top card for trumps and slip it under the pack, face up and half exposed.

A game consists of several bouts, each followed by a draw of fresh cards if necessary. The aim is be first out of cards when the stock is exhausted. The loser is a *durak* ('fool').

In each bout, one player attacks and the other defends. Non-dealer attacks first; thereafter, the winner of each bout attacks in the next. Each bout proceeds as follows:

Attacker leads any card. Defender must respond with a higher card of the same suit, or any trump if a non-trump was led. Attacker continues with any card of the same *rank* as either of the first two, and, again, defender plays higher or trumps. This continues until all twelve cards are played, or one player can't or won't make a legal continuation.

☛ *Note*. The two players follow different requirements: the attacker's lead must always match the rank of any card so far showing, the defender's reply must always be higher in suit or a trump.

If all cards are played out, the attacker draws six cards from stock, waits for the defender to do likewise, then starts a new bout with any desired lead.

But a bout more commonly ends because one player fails to play the next card. If the attacker fails, he concedes the bout by turning the played cards face down and pushing them to one side, where they remain out of play for the rest of the game. He then becomes the defender in the next bout.

If the defender fails, he does so by gathering up all cards so far played to the bout and adding them to his hand. He will continue to defend in the next bout.

Before the next bout begins, each player (starting with the attacker) must, if necessary and if he can, restore his hand to six cards by drawing from stock. The last card drawn from stock will be the turned trump, after which play continues without further drawing until one player goes out.

Dutch Whist

Plain-trick game

52

A light-hearted ▶ **Whist** variant with a different rule of play on each deal. Both it and its three-hand equivalent Bismarck are subject to variations.

Four players, in two partnerships, receive 13 cards each from a 52-card pack ranking A K Q J 10 9 8 7 6 5 4 3 2.

First deal. The last card is turned for trump. The side taking most tricks scores 1 point per trick taken above six.

Second deal. No card is turned, and the game is played at no trump.

Third deal. No card is turned, and eldest hand announces trumps on his opening lead.

Fourth deal. Establish trumps by cutting the pack before dealing.

Bismarck

Three players each deal four times in succession, making twelve deals in all. Dealer takes the top four cards himself, then deals 16 cards to each player one at a time (including himself), then discards any four unwanted cards from his own hand.

First deal. Play at no trump. Dealer scores 8 less than the number of tricks he took, and each opponent 4 less.

Second deal. As before, but with a trump selected by cutting the pack before dealing.

Third deal. As before, but with trumps announced by the dealer before Eldest leads.

Fourth deal: *misère*. No trump; aim to lose tricks. Dealer scores 4 less, and each opponent 6 less, than the number of tricks they took.

Earl of Coventry ▸▸ *Snip-Snap-Snorem*

Ecarté

Plain-trick game

32

Fast, skilful, classic two-hander derived from fifteenth-century Triomphe or 'French Ruff'. Once popular in French casinos but nowadays played only by connoisseurs.

Deal five cards each, in batches of three and two, from a 32-card pack ranking K Q J A 10 9 8 7 (note the intermediate position of the Ace). Turn the next for trump and placed under the stock. If it is a King, you (dealer) score 1 point. The aim is to win at least three of the five tricks played, using the turned suit as trump.

You may each seek to improve your hands by drawing fresh cards, provided that both agree to do so. Elder hand, first, must either lead to the first trick or 'propose' an exchange of cards. If he proposes, Dealer either accepts the proposal, or refuses it by saying 'Play'.

If the proposal is accepted, each in turn, starting with Elder, discards at least one and up to five cards, and is dealt the same number from the stock. Elder then again either leads or proposes; and so on until either bars the exchange.

☞ *Note.* Neither of you may call for more cards than remain face down, and neither may draw the card turned for trump. When five or fewer remain, Elder may call for them all. If no cards remain to draw, whichever of you would have drawn next is obliged to play.

The holder of the King of trumps may show it and score 1 point, but must do so before playing to the first trick.

Elder hand leads first and the winner of each trick leads to the next. You must not only follow suit if you can, but also win the trick if possible. If unable to follow suit you must play a trump if you can. Only otherwise may you freely discard.

Score 1 point for taking three or four tricks, or 2 for the *vole* (all five). If no cards were exchanged, and the refuser loses, the other scores 2 invariably.

Game is five points, and is not played out if this is reached by scoring 1 for the King. By agreement, the game counts double if the loser scores less than 3, treble if he scores none.

Optional rule. Traditionally, the leader to a trick announces the suit he is leading. If the announcement does not match the suit led the other may demand that it be withdrawn and a card of the announced suit played, if possible, or else may play to the suit led exactly as if it were the suit announced.

Notes. The 'strict' rules of following to a trick are not as restrictive as they may appear, since they release valuable information as to the lie of cards, and give the leader to a trick considerable control over subsequent play.

Eight Off (Patience) ▸▸ *Freecell*

Eights ▸▸ *Crazy Eights*

Einwerfen ▸▸ *Sueca*

Eleusis
Going-out game

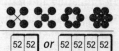

Eleusis formally resembles a game of the ▸ **Crazy Eights** type, but turns the whole idea on its head by concealing the rule of matching that determines whether a given card can legally follow the previous one. The current dealer invents the rule and the players have to deduce what it is before they can successfully play their cards off. This involves a process of inductive thinking similar to that which underlies scientific investigation into the laws of Nature: you observe what happens, hypothesize a cause, test your hypothesis by predicting the outcome of experiments, modify it until it appears to work, then accept it as a theorem so long as it continues to produce results. Eleusis was invented by American games inventor Robert Abbott in his student days and first described in Martin Gardner's Mathematical Games department of *The Scientific American* in 1959. Here is Abbott's revision of 1977.

Preliminaries. From four to eight players start by shuffling two 52-card packs together. At least one other pack should be available, but must be kept apart until needed (if ever). Cards rank A 2 3 4 5 6 7 8 9 10 J Q K. Unless otherwise stated, an Ace counts as numeral 1, Jack as 11, Queen 12, and King 13.

Deal. Nobody deals twice in the same session, but the dealership should not rotate regularly but be allocated at random to someone who has not yet dealt. The dealer receives no cards and plays a different role from the others. Deal 14 to each other player, then one card face up as a starter, and stack the rest face down.

Players' object. To be the first to get rid of all one's cards by successfully playing them to a mainline sequence extending rightwards from the starter. A card can only be played to the mainline if it matches the last card there. The rule determining whether or not a given card is playable varies from deal to deal, and is decided by the dealer. The primary object, therefore, is to discover the dealer's rule of following. This is done by formulating and testing hypotheses as to what the rule might be, on the basis of information gained by noting which cards are accepted and which rejected by the dealer.

Dealer's object. To devise a rule that is neither too easy nor too hard to deduce. A typical elementary rule is: 'If the last card is red, the next card played must be even; if it is black, the next must be odd.' The dealer writes this rule down on a piece of paper, and may refer to it at any time, but does not say what it is (though he may give clues, such as 'Colours are significant, but not individual suits'.)

Play. Each in turn tries to play a card to the mainline. If the dealer says 'Right', it stays put and the player's turn ends. If not, it is replaced below the last card played in a 'sideline' extending at right angles to the mainline. If a sideline already exists for that card, it goes at the end of the sideline.

If you think you know The Rule, you can attempt to play a 'string' of two, three, or four cards, of which you believe the first correctly follows the last mainline card and the others correctly follow that rule among themselves. Again, if the dealer says 'Right' they stay in place, but if 'Wrong' (and he won't say how many or which ones are wrong) they must be added to the latest sideline. In this case they should be overlapped, to show that they were attempted as a string and not one per turn.

When an attempt is declared wrong, and the incorrect card or cards have been added to the sideline, the dealer deals to the defaulting player twice the number of cards made in the attempt—that is, from two to eight cards as the case may be.

Can't play. If you think you know The Rule, but have no card in hand that will go, you can declare 'Can't play'. In this case you must expose your cards so everyone can see them, and the dealer will say whether your claim is right or wrong.

If you're wrong, the dealer must play to the mainline any one of your cards that will fit, then deal you five more from the stock.

What happens if you're right depends on how many cards you have left. If five or more, the dealer counts your cards, puts them at the bottom of the stock, and deals you from the top of the stock a number of cards equivalent to four less than the number you held when you made the claim. If four or fewer, they go back into the stock and the game ends.

Adding another pack. If four or fewer cards remain in stock after someone has been dealt more, shuffle them into the spare pack and set it face down as a new stock.

The prophet. If you think you know The Rule, you may, instead of simply playing all your cards out, seek to improve your eventual score by declaring yourself a prophet and taking over the functions of the dealer (who, as the Ultimate Rule-maker, is known in some circles as God). But there are four conditions:

1. There can only be one prophet at a time.
2. You cannot become a prophet more than once per deal.
3. At least two other players must still be in play (discounting yourself and the dealer).
4. You may declare yourself prophet only when you have just successfully added a card or cards to the mainline, and before the next in turn starts play.

On declaring yourself a prophet, you place a marker on the card you just added to the mainline (a coin or a chess-piece will do) and stop playing your cards (but keep them in case you get deposed and have to play again). You then proceed to act as if you were the dealer, making the appropriate announcements of 'Right' or 'Wrong' as other players attempt to play. The dealer must either confirm or negate each decision as you make it, and you remain the prophet so long as they are confirmed. As soon as you make a wrong decision, you are deposed as Prophet, must take up your hand of cards and become an ordinary player again. The dealer takes over again and immediately correctly places the attempted card or cards that you wrongly adjudicated. Furthermore, whoever played them is absolved from having to take extra cards even if their attempted play was wrong.

A trap you can fall into as prophet is to contradict a player who claims 'Can't play', and to play to the mainline a card from his hand which the dealer then declares to be wrong. (Your decision may have been right, but the actual card you played wasn't.) In this case the dealer returns the wrong card to the player's hand, plays a right one to the mainline, and deposes you as prophet. The wronged player does not have to take any extra cards.

Expulsion. There comes a point at which it is assumed that everyone has had long enough to deduce The Rule. Once that point is reached, as soon as you make a play that is rejected as illegal you are expelled from the game, and place your cards face down on the table. The expulsion point is reached when there is no prophet in operation and at least 30 cards have been played to the mainline, or, if a prophet is currently operating, at least 20 cards have been added to it since the prophet took over. To keep track, it helps to place a white piece every on every tenth card from the starter until a prophet takes over, and then a black piece on every tenth card from the prophet's marker. If a prophet is overthrown, the black pieces are removed, white pieces placed on every tenth card from the starter, and nobody can be expelled on that turn.

☛ *Note.* A round can go in and out of expulsion phases. For example, one player may be expelled when there is no prophet and more than 30 cards have been placed. But if the next player then plays correctly and becomes a prophet, and the player after that fails to place a card, the latter is not expelled, as fewer than 20 cards have been placed since the prophet took over.

Ending and scoring. Play ceases when somebody plays the last card from their hand, or when everybody except the prophet (if any) is expelled. Everybody scores 1 point for each card left in the hand of the player with the most cards, and deducts 1 point for each card left in their own hand. The player with no cards in hand (if any) adds 4 points.

A bonus also accrues to the prophet, if any. This bonus is 1 for each card on the mainline following his marker, and 2 for each card on any sideline following his marker.

The dealer, finally, gets a score equal to the highest score made by anyone else, but with one possible exception. If there is an un-deposed prophet at end of play, count the total number of cards played (to mainline and sidelines) before the prophet's marker, and double it. If this total is smaller than the highest score, the dealer scores that smaller total instead.

Game. If not enough time remains for everyone to have a turn as dealer, those players who never dealt add 10 points to their score (to compensate for the dealer's inbuilt scoring advantage which they did not enjoy).

Notes. Beginners should keep rules simple to start with. It is fatally easy to be too clever too soon. If you play regularly, it is worth keeping a notebook of rules devised and their relative success rate. The rule must be one which, on average, would give a randomly played card at least a one-in-five chance of being acceptable. For example:

- Each card must be higher than the last until a face card is reached, which must then be followed by a numeral.
- If the last card attempted by the previous player was accepted, play red; if not, play black.
- If the last two cards match colour, play a high number, otherwise a low number.
- If the last three cards form an ascending sequence, play a spade; if descending, a heart; if they go up and down, a diamond; if they contain any two of the same rank, a club. (This one is not easy!)

If a rule is not meaningful until two or more cards are down, as in examples (2) and (3), then any cards played before it takes effect must be accepted.

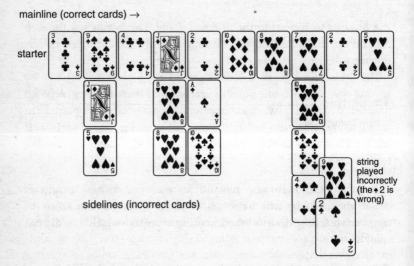

Eleusis. Sample layout (from Abbott, *The New Eleusis*). It shouldn't take more than 15 seconds to deduce the governing rule of play.

Elfern

Point-trick game

An old German card game suitable for children and beginners, especially those intending to graduate to ▶ **Bezique**. Elfern means 'making elevens'. Its alternative title, *Figurenspiel*, means 'the honours game'. *See also* ▶ **Bohemian Schneider**.

Deal six each from a 32-card pack ranking A K Q J 10 9 8 7 and turn the rest face down as a stock. The aim is to capture, in tricks, at least 11 of the 20 honours, namely, all Aces, Kings, Queens, Jacks, and Tens.

Eldest leads first. Suit need not be followed. The higher card of the suit led wins the trick. The trick-winner draws the next card from stock, waits for the other to draw, and leads to the next.

When no cards remain in stock, suit must be followed if possible in the play of the last six tricks. Count a single win for taking eleven to fourteen honours, double for fifteen to nineteen, treble for all twenty.

Variant. Before play, the top card of the stock is turned to establish a trump suit, and is slipped under the pack so as to be taken by the loser of the sixth trick. A trick can then be taken by the higher trump if any are played. In the last six tricks, a player unable to follow suit must trump if possible.

Elimination Rummy

Rummy game

A simple but exciting member of the family, also called Java Rummy, or Freeze-out.

Play as at basic ▶ **Rummy** but with these particularities. Deuces are wild, as are any Jokers that may be added. Deal seven cards each. Each in turn draws and discards without melding. This continues until one player, without drawing, goes out by melding all seven cards, or six cards provided that the seventh does not count more than five. Jokers count 25 against, Aces 15, face cards 10, others at face value. Going out by melding all seven entitles you to deduct 25 from your current penalty total. Upon reaching

100 penalties, a player drops out and pays a single stake to the pool. The pool eventually goes to the last player left in, or to the player with the lowest score if more than one reach 100 simultaneously.

Epsom

Stops game

52

A relative of ▶ **Newmarket**, as suggested by the whiff of turf in its title.

Prepare a staking layout consisting of an Ace, King, Queen, and Jack from another pack, or a piece of paper so marked. These are called 'boodle' cards.

Deal the same number of cards to each player, as many as will go round, leaving any remainder face down, out of play.

Each player, after examining his hand, stakes five counters: one for 'game', the other four distributed as he pleases amongst the boodle cards. The aim is to play the fourth Ace, King, Queen, or Jack, and to be the first out of cards.

Eldest starts by choosing any suit and playing face up to the table the lowest card he has of that suit. This starts a sequence which will be made face up and slightly spread so that all its cards are visible. Each in turn thereafter must play *either* the next higher card of the same suit *or* a card of the same rank as any card already played. A card of matching rank does not start a new sequence: it merely interrupts the main sequence.

Example. The sequence starts ♥3, ♥4, ♣3. The next required card is not ♣4 but ♥5, though any 3 or 4 may be played instead.

You may pass only if unable to play. The turn then passes to the left.

Whenever you play the fourth card of a given rank, you set them aside and start a new sequence. It may be in any suit, but you must start with the lowest you hold of it. If the fourth card is a Jack, Queen, King, or Ace, you win the counters from the corresponding boodle card.

Play ceases when one player has played his last card, thereby winning the stakes for 'game' and all remaining on the boodle cards.

Euchre

Plain-trick game

24 → 32

Of Alsatian origin, Jucker, Yuker, or Euchre became a great social card game of nineteenth-century America and Australia. It still has a wide following, chiefly in its partnership form, in North America and in the south and west of England, especially Cornwall. It is the game for which the Joker was originally invented, around 1860, to act as the top trump or 'Best Bower' (from German *Bauer*, 'farmer', denoting also the Jack at cards). Though constant in essentials, the game is played in many different formats for various numbers of players, and exhibits a bewildering range of superficial variations. The most advanced version of the game is ▸ **Five Hundred**.

Euchre basics. Unless otherwise stated, all forms of Euchre are played with a short pack of either 24 or 32 cards ranking A K Q J 10 9 (8 7) in every suit except trumps. In trumps, cards rank as follows:

1. Jack of trumps, or Right Bower,
2. The other Jack of same colour as trumps, or Left Bower,

followed by Ace, King, etc. The trump suit is therefore one card longer, and the other suit of its colour one card shorter, than the two plain suits of the opposite colour.

If you add a Joker to the pack, it is called the Best Bower and ranks as the highest trump. In England, its place is taken by the ♣2, or 'Benny'.

Players are each dealt five cards in batches of three and two, the remainder being stacked face down and not used. The aim is to win at least three of the five tricks played, with a bonus for the *march*—that is, winning all five.

Partnership Euchre (4 players)

This is now generally played with a 24-card pack plus Joker, but originally with 32 cards. A game is played up to five, seven, or ten game-points, as agreed, over as many deals as it takes.

Deal five cards each and place the remainder face down to one side, with the top one faced to show a preferred trump suit.

Auction. There is an auction to determine which side will contract to win at least three tricks in exchange for choosing trumps. A bidder who thinks he can take three or more from his own hand may offer to play 'alone'.

Each in turn, starting with Eldest, must either pass or accept the turned suit as trump. (Eldest accepts by saying 'I order it up', adding 'alone', if applicable. Second hand says 'I assist' if he intends his partner to participate, otherwise 'I play alone'. Third hand and dealer may 'order it up', adding 'alone' if applicable.) As soon as a bid is made, the auction ends.

If the turned suit is ordered up, Dealer may exercise the privilege of taking the turn-up into his hand in exchange for any face-down discard (unless, of course, his partner is playing alone).

If all pass, the turn-up is turned down and a second round of bidding follows. Each in turn may now pass, or, if the previous player passed, offer another suit as trump. (Choosing the other suit of the same colour is to 'make it next'; choosing either of the other two is to 'cross it'.) As before, a bidder may offer to play alone.

The auction ends when someone bids or all four pass. If a bid is made, the dealer may not exchange a card, as there is no turn-up. If all four pass, the cards are thrown in and a new deal made by the next in turn to deal.

Play. In a lone bid, the loner's partner lays his cards face down before the opening lead, which is made by the player at loner's immediate left. Otherwise, the opening lead is made by Eldest hand. Follow suit if possible, otherwise play any card. The trick is taken by the highest card of the suit led or by the highest trump if any are played. The winner of each trick leads to the next.

Score. If successful, the contracting side scores 1 point, or 2 for the 'march' (all five tricks), or 4 for the march if played alone. If not, they are 'euchred', and the other side scores 2.

Euchre for 2 or 3 players

As for four, but each bids individually and the player who makes trump plays alone against the other, or the other two acting in concert. If the turned suit is trump, dealer takes the turn-up in exchange for a discard.

Eldest leads to the first trick. The maker scores 1 for point, 2 for the march, or, if euchred, deducts 2 from his score. Game is 5, 7, or 10, by prior agreement.

Jackpot Euchre (4 players)

Four use 25, five 29, six 33 cards, including a Joker as Best Bower. Each plays for himself, chips one to the pool and receives five cards. Turn the top of the undealt cards for trump. The maker is not obliged to win three tricks. Instead, each player draws a chip from the pool for each trick he wins, or pays one chip if he won none. The pool is swept by the first player to win a march.

Call-Ace Euchre (4-6 players)

Four, five, or six players use 24, 28, or 32 cards respectively (Joker optional). Play as above, except that before the first trick the bidder names a suit other than trumps. The holder of the Ace of that suit thereby becomes the bidder's partner for that deal, sharing in any gain or loss he makes, but may not reveal himself except by the play. If the called Ace is in the bidder's own hand, he is in effect playing alone, but no-one else knows this. (If it is one of the undealt cards, he will not know it himself.)

Auction Euchre (best for 5 players)

Use 28 cards (omitting Sevens), deal five each, and leave a blind or widow of three face down. Alternatively, use 32 cards, make a blind of five, and leave two cards out of play. Each in turn has one opportunity to bid at least three tricks using a named trump, or to overcall a previous bid. A bid of five is overcalled by a bid of eight, which is an undertaking to play a lone hand after exchanging cards, and that by a bid of 15, which is to play alone with the hand as dealt. The maker, before play, first takes the widow and discards any three cards from his hand (unless he bid 15); then calls for an ally (unless playing alone) by naming any specific card not in his own hand. The holder of that card becomes his silent partner, revealing that fact only by his play.

Euchre for six (Cornish)

The Cornish version has two teams of three, each player flanked by an opponent. The cards are either 33 (A K Q J 10 9 8 7 + Joker) or

50 (2 × A K Q J 10 9 + 2 Jokers). In the double-pack game the second of two identical cards played to a trick beats the first, though if the Jokers are of different colours then the one matching the trump colour prevails. One member of either or both sides may play alone, in which case the other two lay their cards down. The loner may make one discard face down and ask one of his partners for a replacement, which that partner must furnish at his own discretion and without consultation.

Euchre for six (Almonte)

The Canadian six-hander uses a 31-card pack consisting of A K Q J 10 9 8 in each suit, plus three Jokers represented by low numeral spades. Trumps rank downwards ♠4 ♠3 ♠2 Right Bower, Left Bower, A-K-Q-10-9-8. Each receives five cards, leaving one turned for preference. If it is a Joker, dealer names a suit before looking at his cards. (In some circles, this obliges him to become the maker in the nominated suit should all five others pass.) The score for a march or a euchre is 3 instead of 2, or 6 if played alone. Game is 15 points.

Pepper (Hasenpfeffer) (for 4)

Hasenpfeffer ('Jugged Hare') was an early step in the direction of improving the skill factor of Euchre by reducing the number of undealt cards—in this case by dealing them all out. The modern version, currently popular in Iowa and Ohio, is now called 'Pepper'.

Preliminaries. Four players sitting crosswise in partnerships receive six cards (not five) dealt one at a time from 24-card pack (no Joker). As at Euchre, the top trumps are the Right and Left Bowers, but there is a no-trump bid where cards rank A K Q J 10 9 in every suit.

Auction. Each in turn, starting with eldest, either passes or bids a number of tricks he would commit his partnership to winning given the choice of trumps. The bids are one, two, three, four, five, Little Pepper (six), and Big Pepper, which is also six but for a doubled score. Each bid must be higher than the last. The player whose bid precedes three consecutive passes becomes the maker. The maker announces the trump suit, or declares no trump, and leads to the first trick.

Play. Players must follow suit if possible, otherwise may play any card. The trick is taken by the highest card of the suit led, or by the highest trump if any are played, and the winner of each trick leads to the next.

Score. If successful, the makers score 1 point per trick won; if not, they score −6. Big Pepper scores plus or +/−12. The other side always scores 1 point per trick won. Game is 30 points.

Double Hasenpfeffer (4 or 6 players)

Original Hasenpfeffer was often played without Bowers, cards ranking normally in all four suits. This obtains in Double Hasenpfeffer, which is for four or six players in two partnerships, and employs the 48-card Pinochle pack (A K Q J 10 9, doubled) without a Joker. Deal all the cards around. Each player has one chance to bid or overbid, the minimum being for three tricks, with no trump as yet mentioned. Dealer must bid at least three if the others pass. The high bidder may play alone, in which case he discards any two cards face down and receives from his partner any two cards the latter wishes to give him. If the making side takes at least as many as it bid it scores 1 point per trick taken; if not, it loses the amount of the bid, except that the dealer, if forced to bid, loses only half that amount. A lone player wins or loses double for his side.

Fair Lucy

Patience game

A nineteenth-century French solitaire that has attracted new fans since being made available as computer software.

Deal all the cards face up in 17 batches of three and one by itself. Each batch of three is called a fan, and is fanned out so that two cards are partly covered by one exposed card. (Traditionally, the 17 fans are arranged in rows with a smaller number in each successive row and the one odd card at the bottom, so that the whole layout has the overall appearance of a fan.)

Your aim is to release the four Aces and build each one up in suit and sequence to the King.

If any of the exposed cards is an Ace, put it out as a base, thus releasing the card beneath it. Then build on the Ace pile any exposed Two, Three, and so on.

Besides building upwards in suit on the Ace piles, you can build downwards in suit on the exposed cards. For example, you can transfer the exposed ♠8 to the exposed ♠9, and so on. But you may only transfer individual cards, not descending sequences of two or more. (You can only play ♠8 alone to ♠9, not ♠8 covered by ♠7.

The initial single card can he built up into a fan. But you may never have more than 18 fans in all, and once a fan has been emptied it may not he replaced, so the number of fans gradually decreases.

When stuck, gather up all the cards in the layout, shuffle them thoroughly, and deal them out again in as many three-card fans as possible, plus one odd fan of one or two cards if necessary. Two such redeals are allowed.

Fan Tan ▸▸ *Domino*

Farmer

Banking game

45

An old French game (*la Ferme*) reportedly played in rural America until well into the twentieth century—though not as rural as its title sounds, as 'farmer' is an old term for tax-collector.

Play with 45 cards omitting all Eights and Sixes except ♥6 (originally called *le brillant*). The aim is to get as close to 16 as possible, but not more, counting Ace 1 (only), numerals face value, courts 10. Players ante 1 unit to the farm (pool), and the farmer (or tax-gatherer, or banker) deals one card each face down. Each in turn must call for at least one card and may request more, these being dealt face down. Players may stop when they like, without stating whether or not they are bust. When all are ready, the hands are shown and anyone with a bust pays 1 unit to the farmer. Whoever has 16, or the nearest count below it, collects 1 unit from each non-bust player with a lower total. Two or more players tying for best share this equally between them. The farm and office of 'farmer' transfer to the player who gets exactly 16. In the event of a tie, priority goes to (a) the farmer, (b) the hand containing ♥6, (c) the hand with fewer cards, (d) the tied player next from farmer's left.

Faro
Banking game

52

Casanova's favourite game, and the most widespread casino game of the western world in the eighteenth and nineteenth centuries—especially and notoriously in the Wild West—Faro originated in Italy as a development of ▶ **Basset** but took its name at the court of Louis XIV from the French Pharaon, referring to the representation of one of the Kings as a Pharaoh. In the twentieth century it gave rise to simpler variants such as Stuss, but eventually gave way to ▶ **Blackjack** and ▶ **Baccara**.

To simplify a highly elaborate game requiring special equipment, there is a single layout consisting of all thirteen spades arranged in order from Ace to King. Punters place stakes on individual ranks to win or lose as the banker deals. They can bet a rank to lose by placing a special coin on chip involved ('coppering'), can arrange them in various different positions to represent combinations of two or more ranks, and can bet high or low, or odd or even—very much as at roulette.

The banker, after rejecting the top card of the pack (called *soda*), turns cards from the pack in twos. The first of each pair is the losing card, the second the winning card for that turn. If anyone has bet on either card, all bets are immediately settled, and players are free to place new ones. If both are the same rank, the banker wins all bets. If neither has been bet on there is no action and the next two cards are turned. Winning punters can let their bets ride in hopes of a third or fourth card of the same rank turning up later, earning apparently tremendous but in fact unfavourable pay-offs.

When only three cards remain a punter can either bet on any one of the cards, or 'call the turn' by betting that the three will turn up in a particular order—for example, 'Three, Queen, Four'. The 52nd card, called *hoc*, is not individually staked on.

Femkort

Plain-trick game

52

'Five-cards' is a Swedish relative of ▶ **Loo**, but has an unusual object.

From two to ten players chip an equal amount to the pot and receive five cards each (2 + 3 or 3 + 2) from a 52-card pack ranking A K Q J 10 9 8 7 6 5 4 3 2. The aim is to win the last trick.

Each in turn plays to a trick by laying his card face up in front of himself and leaving it there for the rest of the game so everyone can see who has played what. Eldest leads first. Players must follow suit and win the trick if possible, but if unable to follow may play any card. The trick is taken by the highest card of the suit led, and the winner of each trick leads to the next. There are no trumps.

The pot goes to the winner of the last trick, or to the first to win an agreed number of deals.

An optional but common rule is that anyone in course of play may call for 'better cards', i.e. for an annulment and a new deal. If anyone else refuses, play continues with the cards still held.

Fifty-One

Adding-up game

32

One of many arithmetical games popular in central European countries.

Deal five each from a 32-card pack and turn the next face up to start the count. Cards count as follows:

A	K	Q	J	10	9	8	7
1	4	3	2	−1	0	8	7

(The Tens each count *minus* 1.)

Each in turn plays a card face up to the table and announces the total value of all cards so far played, including the starter. Whoever raises the total above 50 is the loser.

Fifty-One

Rummy game

54

A Chinese game (Wushiyi-fen) looking like a cross between ▶ **Ride the Bus** and ▶ **Thirty-One**. Play rotates to the right.

From a 54-card pack including two Jokers deal five cards each in ones and stack the rest face down. The aim is to go out by collecting five cards of the same suit, preferably with a high face value. For this purpose Aces count 11, face cards 10 each, and numerals at face value. Jokers belong to any suit and count as any card of that suit not already held.

Eldest hand starts by drawing the top card of stock, adding it to his hand, and throwing out one card face up to start a discard pile.

Each in turn thereafter may either:

- draw the top card of stock and add one face up to the discard pile, which should be kept spread out so all are visible; or
- take the whole discard pile after previously discarding the same number of cards from hand to act as a replacement for it.

The pile of discards may never exceed five. When it contains exactly five, each in turn has the further option of drawing any one card from it in exchange for any replacement. As soon as one player draws from stock instead, the five discards are bunched and discarded face down from play. The discard of the player who drew from stock starts a new discard pile, and play proceeds as before.

When you have five of a suit you may, on your turn to play, either draw in the hope of increasing their total face value, or 'knock' by laying all five on the table before you. You may not draw and knock in the same turn. If the stock runs out before anyone knocks, the players reveal their cards and everyone scores for their best flush.

When someone has knocked (or the stock runs out) everyone reveals their hand. Anyone with five cards of the same suit scores their total face value, 51 being the highest possible. The knocker scores double, provided that no one else has either a higher-scoring five-flush, or one of equal face value but containing fewer Jokers. Anyone who does have such a better hand (or the best of them if more than one player has) scores the value of his own hand plus that of the knocker, who deducts the value of his own hand from his current score.

Play up to 1000, or any other agreed target.

☛ *Note.* You may prefer the following suggested modifications. (1) Jokers belong to any suit but have a face value of zero. (2) If you hold three or four cards of a suit you cannot knock but may, at a showdown, score the face value of the flush minus the face-value of any cards of a different suit. This just about makes it possible for a player who knocks with a low five-flush to be beaten, on points, by one with a shorter but higher-scoring flush.

Fildinski ▸▸ Bezique

Fishing games

A family of games of the following pattern. Four or so cards lie face upwards in a 'pool', and players try to capture one or more at a time by matching them with cards played from the hand. Cards that make no capture are simply added to the pool. There is usually a bonus for capturing all the pool cards in one sweep. Games of this type are common in China, where they are generically referred to as 'Fishing', in the Middle East, and in south-east Europe as far west as Italy. See individual entries for: Basra, Cassino, Chinese Ten, Cìcera, Cirulla, Cuarenta, Pishti, Scopa, Scopone, Tablanette, Zwicker.

Five and Nine ▸▸ Domino

Five Hundred

Plain-trick game

$32 \rightarrow 62$

Five Hundred was devised in America shortly before 1900 as a form of ▸ **Euchre** incorporating the basic principles of ▸ **Bridge**. It remains popular in America, and more so in Australia and New Zealand, of which countries it may now be described as the national card game. Australian '500' packs contain 63 cards, extended from 52 by the addition of a Joker, Elevens, and Twelves in each suit, and two Thirteens (red suits). The full pack is only required for six players, however, and is stripped of various low cards for varying numbers of participants, the basic principle being that there should be just enough for ten cards per player and three left over (or two if the Joker is omitted). Though usually played by four in partnerships, it is excellent for three or five.

Players. Three to six. Four and six play in partnerships, the latter in either two partnerships of three (sitting A B A B A B) or three of two (sitting A B C A B C).

Cards. Joker optional, plus,

- if two play, 24 cards (A K Q J 10 9);
- if three, 32 cards (A K Q J 10 9 8 7);
- if four, 42 (A K Q J 10 9 8 7 6 5 and both red Fours);
- if five, standard 52-card pack;
- if six, full 62-card pack.

The basic ranking is A K Q (J) 10 9 8 7 6 5 4, but the top three trumps are:

1. Best Bower (Joker, if used)
2. Right Bower (Jack of trumps)
3. Left Bower (other Jack of same colour),

followed downwards by Ace, King, etc.

Object. Play ceases when one player or partnership reaches either 500 or *minus* 500 points over as many deals as necessary, the winner(s) being the player or side with the highest plus score.

Deal. Deal ten cards each, in batches of 3-4-3, with a 'kitty' of three dealt face down to the table immediately before the batch of four. (If two play, the Joker is omitted and the kitty contains four cards.)

Bidding. Each in turn, starting at Dealer's left, either passes or names a contract with a higher value than the preceding one. A player may not rebid having once passed. The contract states a proposed trump and the minimum number of tricks the bidder offers to win either alone (if three play), in partnership (four or six players), or with or without the aid of a temporary partner (five players). A bid is made by suit and number (e.g. 'Six spades', the lowest possible bid) or by game value ('40', etc.), according to the following schedule:

Trump	Six	Seven	Eight	Nine	Ten
Spades	40	140	240	340	440
Clubs	60	160	260	360	460
Diamonds	80	180	280	380	480
Hearts	100	200	300	400	500
No trump	120	220	320	420	520

Misère (no trump, lose every trick): 250
Open misère (same, cards exposed): 520

Misère is overcalled by any bid of eight or more tricks; open misère overcalls everything.

The highest bidder becomes the declarer. If all pass without bidding, tricks are played at no trump and scored to the players or partnerships winning them.

The kitty. Declarer takes the kitty in hand and makes any three discards face down before play. If all passed, the kitty remains untouched.

Calling a partner. If five play, declarer either announces that he will 'go alone', or calls for a partner (except in misère) by naming any non-trump card lacking from his hand. The holder of that card immediately identifies himself.

Play. Declarer leads first, or, if everyone passed, the player at Dealer's left. (At open misère, the hand is spread face up before the opening lead.) Normal rules of trick-taking apply. The Joker is the highest card of the trump suit. At no trump, it is the only trump, and may be used to win the trick when its holder cannot follow suit to the card led. If led, its holder calls for a suit to be played to it, which may not be one in which he has already renounced.

Score. For a won contract, the bidding player or partnership (or, five-handed, each member of the temporary partnership) scores the value of the contract. There is no credit for overtricks, but winning all ten scores 250 if the contract value was less. For a lost contract, the declarer or declaring partnership deducts the contract value from their score. Whether won or lost, each opponent or opposing partnership scores 10 points per won trick. (At misère, they score 10 per trick taken by the declarer. Misères must therefore be played right through.) If no bid was made, each player or partnership scores 10 points per trick won individually. If two or more players or partnerships reach 500+ on the same deal, the declaring side wins.

Variants. Rules vary slightly from circle to circle. The Joker is often omitted in serious play, especially four-handed. In the original game, each player could make only one bid, and had therefore to bid the maximum immediately. This rule has been largely dropped from modern Australian play.

Flip-Flop

Patience game

An unusual solitaire, also known as Eight Aces.

Extract the eight Aces and set them up as a row of bases. Your aim is to build each base up into a thirteen-card sequence headed by a King, regardless of suit.

Turn cards from stock and build them if possible, otherwise discard each to any one of six possible wastepiles. The top card of each wastepile is always available for building on an Ace-pile if it fits.

Keep going till you run out of cards and cannot build another card from the top of a wastepile.

At this point you take the top card of each wastepile, turn it face down ('flip'), place it at the bottom of the pile, and start building again as far as you can from the newly exposed cards.

Keep playing and flipping in this way, so that each wastepile gradually works its way down to the face-down cards. Whenever you get to a face-down card, turn it face up ('flop') and continue play. No more flipping may be done from this point, so if the game fails to come out now there is no help for it. But it usually does.

Forty-One

Plain-trick game

52

A middle-eastern ▸ **Whist** variant popular in Syria and the Lebanon. An interesting (and ancient) feature is that partners must play in such a way as to assist each other as individuals.

Four players sitting crosswise in partnerships receive 13 cards each dealt 1-2-2-2-2-2-2 from a 52-card international pack ranking A K Q J 10 9 8 7 6 5 4 3 2. All play passes to the right.

Each partnership's object is for *one* of its members to reach 41 points over as few deals as possible, by accurately bidding how many tricks they will win, with hearts as permanent trumps.

Each in turn from the dealer's right examines his cards and states the minimum number of tricks he expects to win. If the four bids total less than 11 the cards are thrown in and the deal passes on. However, bids of seven or more count double, so any such bid automatically ensures that play will proceed.

Eldest leads first. Players must follow suit if possible, otherwise may play any card. The trick is taken by the highest card of the suit led, or by the highest heart if any are played, and the winner of each trick leads to the next.

Each player's score is recorded cumulatively. Bids of 1 to 6 score, if successful, 1 point per trick bid (even if more were made), or lose 1 per trick bid if unsuccessful. Bids of 7 or more correspondingly win or lose 2 points per trick bid.

The player who first reaches or exceeds 41 points wins for his side.

Forty-Five ➤ *Twenty-Five*

Four Jacks ➤ *Polignac*

Freecell

Patience game

Freecell has become something of a cult game since starting life as a freeware computer solitaire. It is almost identical with one called Eight Off, or Baker's Game, which dates back to the 1920s, the only difference being that packing on the layout is now done in alternating colour instead of strictly in suit, which makes it easier to get out. In fact, the amount of attention devoted to Freecell has resulted in the discovery that the chances of success are about 99 per cent in your favour, so if you want a real challenge you should play it the original way. Still, success does depend upon careful and accurate play: the slightest mistake at any point in the game can put you quickly out of business.

Deal eight cards face up in a row. Deal eight more across them, slightly overlapping so that the first cards remain identifiable. Keep dealing in rows like this till you run out of cards. There will only be four in the last row. Regard the result as eight columns, the first four containing seven and the last four six cards.

Your aim is to release the Aces as and when they become available, set them up as bases at the top of the board, and to build each one up into a thirteen-card suit-sequence headed by the King.

For this purpose the uncovered card at the nearer end of each column is available for building on an Ace-pile when it fits. Alternatively, you can pack it on the uncovered card at the end of another column in downward sequence and alternating colour—for example, a red Ten on a black Jack, a black Nine on the red Ten, and so on. You may move only one card at a time, not a packed sequence of two or more as a whole. A space made by clearing out a column may be filled with any single available card, which may then be packed on in descending sequence and alternating colour as before.

An available card may also be taken from the end of its column and set out by itself in a reserve. Up to four cards may be held in reserve at any time. Every card of the reserve is individually available for building on an Ace-pile or packing on the end of a column whenever it properly continues the sequence.

French Ruff ▸▸ *Ecarté*

French Whist ▸▸ *Scotch Whist*

Frog ▸▸ *Six-bid Solo*

Gaigel
Point-trick game

24 | 24

A multi-player extension of ▸ **Sixty-Six**, much played in Württemberg, sometimes by three but mainly by four in partnerships. Described below is the core of the German game, from which the form described in American books ultimately derives. The modern versions lack an official standard and are subject to many local variations and extras.

Use two 24-card packs shuffled together, each consisting of Ace, King, Queen, Jack, Ten, Seven. (Gaigel was originally played with 32-card packs containing Eights and Nines. When it was speeded up by the suppression of worthless ranks, Sevens were kept because they have a significant role to play. But Nines will do if it is more convenient to use a Pinochle pack.)

Four players sit crosswise in partnerships. The turn to deal and play passes always to the right. The winning side is the first to claim (correctly) that it has reached 101 points, which usually happens before all cards have been played out. Points are scored for capturing counting-cards in tricks and for declaring marriages.

Cards rank and count as follows:

A	10	K	Q	J	7 (or 9)
11	10	4	3	2	0

Deal five cards each in batches of 3+2. Turn the next face up to establish trumps, and stack the rest face down partly covering it.

Eldest leads first. So long as cards remain in stock you can play any card you like without having to follow suit. When the stock is empty, the rules change. You must now, so far as possible:

· follow suit,
· head the trick, and
· trump (and overtrump) if unable to follow suit.

A trick is taken by the highest card of the suit led, by the highest trump if any are played, or by the first played of two identical winning cards. Players must remember the cumulative value of counters their side has won in tricks, as it is not permissible to keep a written or mechanical tally.

The winner of a trick draws the top card of stock and adds it to his hand, waits for the others in turn do likewise, then leads to the next.

On playing to a trick you may declare a marriage—King and Queen of the same suit—if you have one. You do this by showing both cards and playing one of them. This adds 20 to your side's count, or 40 if in trumps. However, you can only score this if your side has already won at least one trick, or if the card you play wins the trick.

Example: The leader's side has not yet won a trick. Trump Ace is led. As this is bound to win, leader's partner may declare a marriage upon playing to it. The same principle may be extended to any other certain trick.

No single player may declare more than one marriage in the same deal. A note may be kept of declared marriages to avoid argument.

If you hold the trump Seven (*dix*) you may 'rob the pack' by exchanging it for the turn-up. You can do this at any time, provided that your side has won at least one trick, and that cards still remain in stock. Alternatively, you may place your Seven under the turn-up, thus leaving it for your partner to take in case he should have the other Seven. In this event, your partner may either take the turn-up and give you the Seven, or keep the Seven and invite you to take the turn-up. The other side may not take the turn-up, and, if anyone plays the other Seven to a trick, the player who first declared it may promptly take the turn-up to restore his hand. This must be done before the last draw of cards, and if the last draw includes a *dix* it may not be exchanged.

Play ceases when any player claims that his side has reached or exceeded 101 in counters and marriages, or that the other side has done so and failed to claim before leading to the next trick. If correct, his side wins a single game, or a double if the other has not yet won a trick. (Even if they were about to win the trick in which the winning side reached 101 by declaring a marriage.) If incorrect, the other side wins a double game, or *gaigel*. (Incorrectly claiming a win is called 'overgaigling', and incorrectly failing to do so 'undergaigling'.)

Gambling games

In card games, 'gambling', has at least three shades of meaning:

1. A game whose outcome depends wholly or almost entirely on chance and cannot therefore be significantly affected by skilful play, as is the case with most banking and casino games;

2. A game played for hard score (cash or counters), in amounts that may vary according to the outcome of previous deals, rather than for soft score (points kept in writing), in amounts that are specified by the rules of play. This category includes games of skill such as ▸ **Poker** and ▸ **Solo Whist**;

3. Any game, regardless of skill, if and when it happens to be played for money on any particular occasion.

The first two categories are gambling games intrinsically, or by definition; the third, only accidentally so. The deeper and more strategic the game, the more interest attaches to the play than to the outcome, and the less likely it is to be played for money. Therefore a game of skill with a refined scoring system, such as ▸ **Bridge** or ▸ **Skat**, is not technically a gambling game, but only accidentally so if it specifically agreed that it should be played for money.

Card games are therefore not all necessarily gambling games by defin-ition—some are by nature, some are not by nature, and some may or may not be, as agreed beforehand. It is true, however, that card games in general reflect an origin in gambling games to the extent that they tend to produce elaborate scores rather than the simple 1–0 (or ½ – ½) of abstract board games. In this connection it is interesting to note that many children's games are ancient gambling games that have lost their bite, or fallen out of fashion, and become cleaned up or watered down for family play.

Gaps

Patience game

This solitaire is also known as 'Spaces' (not surprisingly).

Shuffle the cards and deal them all out, face up and not overlapping one another, in four rows of thirteen. Remove the four Aces, thus creating four gaps or spaces.

Your aim is to convert each row into a sequence of cards running in suit from Two (left) to King (right).

At each move, fill a space with the card that is of the same suit as the one on its left and next higher in rank. For example, if there is a space with ♥J to the left of it, remove the ♥Q from wherever she is and put her to the right of the Jack. The sequence of rows is not continuous, and a space at the extreme left of a row must be filled with a Two.

When the game blocks (all spaces being to the right of Kings), gather up all cards that are not in proper sequence with their initially-placed Twos and shuffle them thoroughly. Deal them out again from left to right and top to bottom so as to bring each row up to its full complement of cards. If a row starts with a Two, leave a space to its right, or to the right of the last one of a sequence of cards starting with a Two, and deal the first new card of the row to the right of that space. If not, deal the first new card of a row immediately to the right of the first space of it. (This enables a Two to be placed in position as soon as the deal is complete.)

Play on as before. A second such redeal is allowed if the game blocks again, but not a third.

German Solo

Plain-trick game

A tidy simplification of the more elaborate classic game of ▶ **Ombre**. It bears interesting resemblances to ▶ **Solo Whist** and is a hard-score game, using coins or counters.

Deal eight cards each in batches of 3-2-3 from a 32-card pack basically ranking A K Q J 10 9 8 7. Trumps, however, when established, rank as follows, from the top down:

1. ♣Q (spadille)
2. Seven of trumps (manille)
3. ♠Q (basta)

followed by Ace, King, Queen (if a red suit is trump), Jack, Ten, Nine, Eight. Trumps therefore number nine if black, ten if red, while plain suits contain seven in black and eight in red.

There is a round of bidding to establish who will undertake to win five or more tricks, alone or with the aid of a partner, in return for naming trumps. A player dealt both black Queens is obliged to bid at least 'grand'. From lowest to highest, the bids are:

1. Call (*Frage*): The bidder will name trumps and call, as his partner, the holder of a card lacking from his own hand, usually an Ace.
2. Grand (*Grossfrage*): The bidder, holding both black Queens, calls a partner, as above, but leaves the partner to name trumps.
3. Solo: The bidder, whether or not holding black Queens, announces trumps and goes for a five-trick solo.
4. Slam declared: As solo, but the bidder undertakes to win all eight tricks.

The auction goes as follows. Eldest says 'Pass' or names a bid. If he names a bid, the next in turn may name a higher bid, which the first player must either undertake himself or else pass. This continues until one of them passes, whereupon the next in turn may name the next higher bid, and so on. If everyone passes, the holder of *spadille* is obliged to 'call'.

If the contract is a Call, the caller says, for example, 'Spades trump; call the Ace of hearts'. (He may not call a trump.) The holder of the Ace of hearts thus becomes his partner, and leads to the first trick.

In a Grand, the holder of the called card himself announces trumps and leads to the first trick.

In a solo or declared slam, the soloist announces trumps and leads first.

You must not only follow suit but also win the trick if you can. If unable to follow suit you must play a trump if you can, and only otherwise may you freely discard. The winner of each trick leads to the next.

If the soloist or contracting side wins the first five tricks straight off, they must either stop or else go for the slam. Leading to the sixth trick is automatically a slam bid, and if all eight are not then made, the whole contract is lost. (If, of course, the soloist declared a slam to start with, he may not stop at five.)

The suit of the first deal becomes the preferred trump for the rest of the session. In subsequent deals, a given bid is overcalled by the same bid 'in best', that is, in the preferred suit.

The pay-offs are: Call 2, Grand 4, Solo 4, Slam 8, Declared Slam 16. These are doubled if the preferred suit was trump (except in the first deal). The stated amount is paid by each partner of the losing side to one partner of the winning side, or as between the soloist and each opponent as the case may be.

German Tarock ▸▸ *Bavarian Tarock*

German Whist
Plain-trick game

52

▸ **Whist** for two, but no one has explained why 'German'.

Deal thirteen cards each, stack the rest face down, and turn the top card to determine trumps. Non-dealer leads first. You must follow suit if you can, but may otherwise play any card. Upon winning a trick you draw the top card of stock, wait for your opponent to draw the card beneath, then turn the new top card of stock face up before leading to the next. This does not change trumps, but it may influence strategy, in that both know what card will be drawn by the winner of a trick, but only the drawer of the card beneath can see what he has got. When the stock is exhausted, keep going till all 26 tricks have been won.

The winner is the player taking a majority of the twenty-six tricks, or, if preferred, of the last thirteen tricks only. Better still, the first thirteen tricks score one point each and the last thirteen two each. Alternatively, it is the player who *loses* the majority of the last thirteen tricks.

As it is impossible in the first half of the game to police the obligation to follow suit, the following may be preferred. After dealing, turn the top card for eventual trumps and slip it half under the stock, then turn the next card of stock as before. Play the first half at no trump, without obligation to follow suit, then play the second half with trumps and obligation to follow.

Ghent Whist

The Flemish parent of ▶ **Solo Whist**. *See also* ▶ **Belgian Whist**.

Gin

Rummy game

A development of ▶ **Conquiàn** devised early in the twentieth century but achieving maximum popularity in the 1930s and 1940s, especially in 'showbiz' generally and Hollywood in particular. There are many variations on the basic game, which is further confused by the fact that people nowadays refer to almost any form of ▶ **Rummy** as 'Gin' Rummy whether it is 100° proof Gin or not. Real Gin is only properly playable by two, usually as a gambling game, though there is a three-hand version. The classic version runs as follows.

Deal two players 10 cards each, in ones, from a 52-card pack running A 2 3 4 5 6 7 8 9 10 J Q K. Turn the next to start the wastepile, and stack the rest face down.

Object. To be the first to knock by laying out all or most of one's cards in melds.

Melds. A meld is three or four cards of the same rank, or three or more cards in suit and sequence (Ace low only). A player may only knock if the total face value of unmelded cards left in hand is 10 or less, counting Ace 1, numerals face value, courts 10 each. A 'gin' hand is one in which all ten cards are melded, and scores extra.

Play. To start, non-dealer may take the upcard or pass. A pass gives dealer the same option. If both pass, non-dealer must take the top card of stock into hand and make one discard card face up to the wastepile. Each in turn thereafter draws the top card of either the stock or the wastepile and makes one discard to the wastepile. If you take the upcard, you may not discard it in the same turn.

> ☞ *Note.* In tournament play the wastepile must be kept squared up and neither player may check through the earlier discards, but in home games this rule may be waived by agreement. However, you are always allowed to spread the stock in order to count how many are left.

Knocking. Keep playing till either player knocks, or only two cards remain in stock. In the latter case the game is a no-score draw and deal passes. You knock by making a final discard face *down* to the wastepile and spreading your other ten cards face up, separated into melds and deadwood. Your opponent then makes whatever melds he can, lays off any cards that match the knocker's melds—unless you went out 'gin', when this is not permitted—and reveals his deadwood.

The knocker normally scores the difference between the values of both players' deadwood, plus a bonus of 25 if he went gin. However, if he did not go gin, and if his deadwood equals or exceeds that of his opponent, then the latter scores the difference between the two, plus a bonus of 25 for 'undercut'.

Game. The deal alternates and scores are kept cumulatively. The winner is the first to reach or exceed a total of 100. Both players then add 25 for each hand they won, and the winner adds a further 100 for the game. The final pay-off is the difference between these end totals, and is doubled if the loser failed to win a single hand.

Variant score. Many players score 20 instead of 25 for gin, undercut, and each deal won by the overall winner.

Oklahoma Gin

As above, but the maximum deadwood permitted to the knocker is not necessarily 10 but that of the face value of the initial upcard. For instance, if the upcard is a Seven you may not knock with more than seven. Furthermore, if it is an Ace, you must go gin to knock.

Hollywood Gin

A method of playing several games simultaneously. Rule up as many double columns as there are deals to be played, and head each pair with the initials of the two players. The score for the first deal is entered only in the winner's half of the first double column. That in the second is entered at the top of the winner's half of the second and added to the same player's score in the first. Similarly, each new deal is entered at the top of the next column and accumulated to the score in any previous column that still remains open. When either player reaches a total of 100 in any column, the appropriate bonuses are added and that double column is ruled off, indicating a won game for that player.

Doubling Gin (Open Gin)

This incorporates the doubling principle of Backgammon and other games. Before drawing, a player may offer to double. If the opponent accepts, play proceeds as usual but the winner's score for that hand is doubled, or redoubled if already doubled, and so on. If the double is refused, it doesn't take effect, but the doubler must knock immediately. There are variations on this theme.

Gin for three (Jersey Gin)

Highest cut deals, next highest sits at his left. Play as at two-hand Gin, with the following differences.

1. Eldest must take the first upcard or pass; if he passes, the next in turn must take it or pass; if he also passes, dealer draws from stock and play begins.

2. At each turn you may take either of the two top cards of the discard pile, unless one of them was taken by the previous player, when you may only take the upcard.

3. The winner scores the difference between his own hand and that of each opponent.

4. There is no bonus for undercut; instead, the knocker subtracts 20 (or 25, by agreement) from his score.

5. You can only lay off cards against the knocker's original melds—not against each other's, nor against a card already laid off by the other.

6. The bonus for gin is 50.

7. If no one has melded when only three cards remain in stock, the game is a no-score draw.

8. Game is 200 up.

Gleek

A classic English gambling game of the sixteenth and seventeenth centuries. It is a sort of three-handed ▶ **Piquet**, with a round of bidding to draw fresh cards, a round of scoring for melds, and a round of trick-play.

http://www.davidparlett. co.uk/histocs/gleek.html

Go Boom

Going-out game

A simple but interesting game suitable for lighter moments, such as after a heavy meal. Related closely to ▶ **Rolling Stone** and ▶ **Sift Smoke**, perhaps more distantly to ▶ **Cucumber** and ▶ **Crazy Eights**.

Deal eight each (or seven if five play, six if six) from a 52-card pack ranking A K Q J 10 9 8 7 6 5 4 3 2, and stack the rest face down. The aim is to be the first to run out of cards by playing them to tricks, which have no value in themselves.

Eldest leads first. Everyone else must play a card of the same suit or rank as the card led. The player of the highest card, or of the first played of equally highest, turns the trick down and leads to the next.

If you can't match the led card by rank or suit you must draw cards from stock and add them to your hand till you can. If you still can't follow when no cards remain in stock, you just miss a turn.

Play ceases the moment anyone plays the last card from their hand. This player then scores, or is paid, according to the number of cards left in everyone else's.

Variants

1. You can add one or two Jokers as wild cards, or treat Deuces as wild. You can play a wild card to any suit, but it never takes the trick.

2. You may agree to score negatively for cards left over in hand, at the rate of 20 for a wild Deuce, 15 per Joker, 10 each for courts, others at face value. The winner is the player with the smallest total after an agreed number of deals, or when one player reaches an agreed 'bust'.

Go Fish

Collecting game

Even lighter than ▶ **Go Boom**, Go Fish is recorded in Italy (as *Andare à piscere*) as early as 1585.

Deal five each from a 52-card pack and stack the rest face down. The aim is to be the first to run out of cards by laying them down in sets of four of a kind (four Aces, Tens, Jacks, etc.).

Eldest starts by pointing to a player and asking for a particular card by name. It must be one of which he holds at least one other of the same rank. For example, if you ask for ♦Q, you must already hold at least one Queen already.

If the player addressed has the card required, he must surrender it in exchange for any one the questioner does not want, and the questioner gets another turn. If not, he says 'Go fish!' This forces the questioner to draw a card from stock and add it to his hand. It is then the other player's turn to ask someone for a card.

Whenever a player gets four of a kind he lays them face down on the table. Play continues until one player has run out of cards. If the stock runs out first, anyone told to 'go fish' merely ends his turn without drawing.

Going-out games

Games where the object is to play out all your cards, whether by collecting and discarding them in matched sets (early forms of ▸ **Rummy**) or by playing them to a common wastepile in such a way as to match the previous card (▸ **Crazy Eights**, etc.) or to beat it (▸ **Stops** games and others). In some, the aim is to win by being first out of cards ('First out wins'); in others, it is to avoid being the last player left with cards in hand ('Last out loses'). Those of the second type are mostly pub or drinking games, as being a way of deciding who has to buy the next round. Games described in this book as belonging to this category include Challenge, Cheat, Crazy Eights, Delphi, Domino, Dudak, Durak, Eleusis, Go Boom, Mau Mau, Muggins, Mustamaija, Old Maid, Paskahousu, Rolling Stone, S**thead, Skitgubbe, Snip Snap Snorem, Stortok, Svoyi Kozyri, Two-Four-Jack, Verish' ne Verish', War Maria.

Golf

Memory game

This bears little or no resemblance to the Patience game below, but is a relatively recent folk game, of which several differing descriptions have appeared on the Internet. The method play is that of ▸ **Rummy**—i.e. draw and discard—but the aim is different, it being to score as few points as possible over a series of nine deals or 'holes'. Here is the simplest version.

Each player is dealt four cards face down in front of them in the form of a square. You may look at the two cards that are nearest you, but must immediately lay them back face down, and may not examine the other two.

The next card is dealt face up to start the discard pile and the remainder stacked face down beside it as a stock.

This is what you do on your turn to play:

- Take either the top (face-up) card of the discard pile, or the top (face-down) card of the stock;
- Discard one of your four place-cards face up to the discard pile; and finally
- Fill the gap it leaves with the card you just drew.

If you take the top card of stock, you may examine it first, and then either place it in your layout or, if you don't want it, immediately discard it.

When you think you have the lowest score you end the round by knocking instead of drawing another card. Everybody else then has one more turn to draw and discard. When they have done so, everyone turns their place-cards face up and totals their values, counting 1 for each Ace, Two to Ten at face value, 10 for each Jack or Queen, and zero for each King.

Whoever has the lowest cumulative score over nine deals wins.

If the stock runs out before anyone knocks, the discard pile is turned to start a new one. With six or more players, it may be found more convenient to play with a doubled pack.

There is the inevitable range of ingenious scoring variations. For example, if the two cards of the same row or column are of matching rank, they count zero instead of face value. Jokers may be added, and count minus 5 each (so it is possible to end with a minus score). Some add a penalty of 10 points to a player who knocks but proves not to have the lowest score.

The point of the game, of course, is to remember what cards you have drawn, placed and discarded, and to deduce what scores other players may have by noting what they have drawn from and discarded to the discard pile.

Golf

Patience game

52

A long-popular solitaire (though it rarely comes out) and aptly named: all 52 cards are built up in a single pile representing a hole, into which the

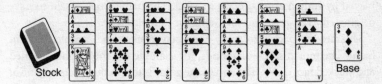

Golf. On the ♦ 3 you can build ♠2, ♥A, ♥2, ♥3.

cards of the reserve must he putted one by one. The number left unputted at the end of play is your handicap for the round.

Deal seven cards face up in a row, then another seven in a row across the tops of them, and so on, until you have dealt out 35 cards in five rows of seven. Deal the next card face up to the table, to represent the 'hole', and turn the remaining 16 cards face down as a stock. Turn the top card of the stock and deal it face up to mark the 'hole'.

Your aim is to clear all the cards off the reserve by building them into a continuous pile on the 'hole'.

At each turn, play the top card of one of the seven piles to the hole if it is one rank higher or lower than the existing hole card. For example, if the hole card is a Seven, you can play to it either a Six or an Eight, regardless of suit.

Note that Aces and Kings are not consecutive: only a Two will go on an Ace, and only a Queen on a King.

When stuck, turn the next card from the stock and play it to the main pile, regardless of whether it continues the sequence, and continue play as before.

If you run out of stock before the reserve has been emptied, you have lost. If successful, you will finish with all 52 cards in a single pile.

Gops

Card-catch game

A strange game of disputed origin. It was first described in a 1957 book on mathematics under the name Goofspiel, but games inventor Alex Randolph claims to have observed an apparently identical game (though played with numbered strips of paper rather than playing-cards) being played by Indian army officers in 1943. The name Gops is said to have originated as an acronym for Game Of Pure Strategy.

Separate the pack into suits. Each player takes one complete suit in hand. The fourth suit—diamonds, for example—is thoroughly shuffled and stacked face down. The aim of the game is to win the greatest value of diamonds, counting face value from Ace to Ten, then Jack 11, Queen 12, King 13.

A game consist of thirteen turns. At each turn the top diamond is turned face up. The players then bid for it by choosing any card from their hand and laying it face down on the table. When all are ready, these are turned face up. The player of the highest-ranking card (Ace low) wins the diamond. The bid-cards are then put aside, and the next turn played in the same way.

If both bid the same amount, the bid cards are put aside but the current diamond is held in abeyance and the next one turned as well. On the next turn, the maker of the higher bid wins both diamonds—or however many are currently in question.

The winner is the player with the higher value of diamonds. If the last card or cards are tied, they belong to neither player, unless it is agreed to credit them to the winner.

If three play, and two tie for best, the next diamond is turned, as usual, and won by whoever makes the highest bid. The previous card, however, is won by whichever of the two previously tied players bids highest, as the third player has no valid claim on it.

Hand and Foot

Rummy game

A North American extension of ▸ **Canasta** played by different circles to a variety of rules. It is usually played by four in partnerships with five packs of 54 cards (including Jokers) shuffled together. If other numbers play, the number of 54-card packs is one more than the number of players. For a good six-player equivalent, *see* ▸ **Pennies from Heaven**. Play like Canasta but with the following particularities.

Deal to each player two separate hands of 13 cards, the first designated the 'hand' and the second the 'foot'. The 'hand' is picked up and played first, while the 'foot' remains face down and unlooked at until its owner has played the last card from their hand.

At each turn you draw two cards from the stock and discard one.

There are three types of meld:

1. Natural, consisting entirely of natural cards;
2. Mixed, containing both natural and wild cards; and
3. Wild, consisting entirely of wild cards (Jokers and Deuces).

A natural meld may become 'mixed' by the addition of wild cards. When a meld contains seven cards—variously designated a 'pile' or a 'canasta'—it is squared up with a red card on top if it is natural, black if mixed, or wild if wild.

A mixed meld must always contain more natural than wild cards, and in some circles it may not contain more than two wild.

A canasta may be extended by the addition of further cards, but not in all circles.

In some circles there are four deals, for which the initial meld requirements are respectively 50, 90, 120, and 150 points, regardless of your current score.

If you play the last card from your hand to a meld, you may immediately pick up your foot and continue your turn. If, however, you empty your hand by a discard, you don't start playing with your foot until your next turn.

You go out by playing the last card from your foot, but subject to the following restrictions.

- You cannot go out by melding black Threes.
- In a partnership game, you must ask and receive your partner's permission, which will almost certainly be withheld if they have not broken into their foot (in case it contains red Threes, which are penalized if not declared).
- You (or your side) must have made at least one wild canasta.

Wild canastas score 1500 each. Other scores, bonuses, and penalties are as for Canasta. Black Threes left in hand each count 5 points against.

Some versions attach special significance to the number seven. Sevens may not be discarded. You never take the whole pack (unless it contains seven or fewer cards), but only the top seven. In order to go out, you must have made at least one natural meld of Sevens. In some circles you must also have made at least one other natural canasta, one mixed, and one wild.

Handjass ▸ *Jass*

Harjan

Point-trick game

52

A Norwegian game resembling ▸ **Sixty-Six**, but without the marriages.

Deal six cards each in threes, turn the next for trump, and half cover it with the remaining 39 cards face down. Cards basically rank A 10 K Q (J) 9 8 7 6 5 4 3 2, but the highest trump is the Jack, followed by the other Jack of the same colour. These count 12 points each, the other Jacks 2 each, and the top cards Ace 11, Ten 10, King 4, Queen 3.

Non-dealer leads first. The leader to each trick must lead three or more cards of the same suit if possible (otherwise two of one suit and an unmatched third), and the follower can only win by beating every card, either with a higher one of the same suit or a trump. Before making the next lead, draw from stock to restore each hand to six. With 10 for the last trick, the maximum possible is 150 points.

Play up to a target of 121 over as many deals as it takes. Score 1 game point for winning, or 2 if the loser fails to reach 30 (*jan*), or 3 if the loser fails to win a trick (*harjan*).

Hundreogen

('Hundred and one') is a simpler forerunner. Play as Harjan, except: deal three cards each from a 36-card pack ranking A 10 K Q J 9 8 7 6; only one card is led to a trick; and the target is 101 points. It is sometimes played with all four Jacks ranking in their normal positions and counting 2 each.

Hasenpfeffer ▸ *Euchre*

Heads and Tails

Patience game

Like many old solitaires, Heads and Tails is quite space-consuming, so you should either use proper Patience cards (two packs) for this purpose, or play on the floor.

Deal eight cards face up in a row, then eight more face up in a row beneath them, leaving enough space between the two rows for a third row to come. The upper row is designated 'heads' and the lower row 'tails'.

Deal the next eight cards face *down* in the space between the heads and the tails. Then deal eight more across them, also face down, and keep doing this until you run out of cards. This will leave eleven packets of eight cards each between the two rows, all face down.

Your aim is to extract four Aces and four Kings, one of each suit, as and when they become available, to set these out as bases, and to build the Aces up into thirteen-card suit-sequences headed by their Kings, and the Kings into thirteen-card descending suit-sequences headed by their Aces. In the interests of space it is advisable to set these out as four piles on either side of the horizontal layout.

The heads and tails are available for building on the main piles as and when they fit. They may also be packed on one another in suit and sequence, either ascending or descending ad lib, and with changes of direction allowed. (For example, part of a suit-sequence might run 6-7-8-7-6-5…etc.) So far as space allows, you may spread the cards of the heads upwards and of the tails downwards in columns so that all are identifiable.

When you make a space in the heads or tails by playing off all the cards of a column, immediately turn face up the top card of the central packet in line with it and use it to fill the vacancy. If there is no packet in line—all its cards having been played off—take instead the top card of the packet nearest to its left, or, if none, furthest from its right.

There is no redeal, but careful play should bring the game out more often than not.

Hearts

Penalty-trick game

First recorded in America in the 1880s, and ultimately derived from
▶ **Reversis**, Hearts became very popular and sprouted dozens of variations during the course of the twentieth century. It is a very good game
for three (*see also* ▶ **Black Maria**), but it is a particular four-hand
version that has become the standard and classic form, largely owing to
its popularity as a computer game shipped with Microsoft™ software.
See also ▶ **Penalty-trick games**.

   In its purest form, the aim is simply to avoid winning tricks containing
hearts. Each player counts a penalty point for each heart taken in tricks,
and the winner is the player with the lowest score after a given number of
deals, or when one player reaches a given maximum.

Hearts for four

Four players each receive 13 cards dealt one at a time from a 52-card
pack. The turn to deal and play passes to the left.

   The aim is to avoid winning tricks containing hearts or ♠Q. Alternatively, if the hand is strong enough, it is to win *all* such penalty cards—a
feat called 'hitting the moon'.

   Each player first passes three cards face down to his left-hand neighbour
and receives the same number from his right. On the second deal, three
cards are passed to the right and received from the left; on the third deal
they are passed between players sitting opposite each other; and on the
fourth there is no passing of cards. The same sequence is repeated
thereafter.

   Whoever holds ♣2 leads it to the first trick. You must follow suit if you
can, otherwise you may throw any card—except on the *first* trick, to
which, if unable to follow, you may not throw a heart or the ♠Q. The
trick is taken by the highest card of the suit led, and the winner of each
trick leads to the next.

   ☞ *Note*. You may not lead a heart to a trick until hearts have been
'broken'—that is, at least one player has already taken a heart—, or

unless your only alternative is to lead the ♠Q (though you may lead her if you wish). Some say you may lead a heart when ♠Q has been played to a trick. This point should be settled beforehand.

At end of play each player scores 1 penalty point for each heart he has taken in tricks, and 13 for ♠Q. However, a player taking all penalty cards either deducts 26 points from his current score, or adds 26 to everyone else's.

The winner is the player with fewest points when one or more players reach or exceed 100 points.

Hearts for three, five, or six

The simplest way of dealing with an odd number of cards is to deal them all out as far as they will go, then for those who have one extra card to play, two cards to the first trick. There is no preliminary exchange of cards. Three, however, may remove ♦2 from the pack, deal 17 each, pass four to the left on the first deal, four to the right on the second, and either none at all or two to each side on every third deal.

Hearts for two (Draw Hearts)

Two players receive 13 cards each and the rest are stacked face down. The winner of each trick draws from stock, and waits for his opponent to draw before leading to the next. Keep playing till none remain in stock or hand. (Most rules state that the second to a trick must follow suit if possible. As this cannot be policed, here is a suggested alternative. In the first 13 tricks the second to a trick need not follow suit, but can only lose it by playing a lower card of the suit led.)

Auction Hearts

Played with chips or counters. Players bid for the right to name the penalty suit. The highest bidder leads to the first trick. Each player pays into the pool the amount of the bid multiplied by the number of cards he has taken of the penalty suit. The pool is divided evenly among those who took no tricks, or, if everyone took tricks, among those who took none of the penalty suit.

Bleeding Hearts ▶ *Bugami*

Cancellation Hearts

Two full packs are shuffled together and dealt round evenly as far as they will go. Any extras are left face down and go to the winner of the first trick, who may look at them privately. Normal rules apply, except that each trick is taken by the highest card of the suit led only if its twin is not played to the same trick. If it is, then the trick is taken by the next best card, or the next best if that is paired, and so on. If all cards of the suit led are paired, the trick is put to one side and goes to the winner of the following trick.

Domino Hearts

Players receive six cards each and the rest are stacked face down. A player unable to follow suit must draw from stock until he can. Only when none remain in stock may he discard at will. Players drop out when they run out of cards, the turn to lead passing to the left if necessary. The last player left in adds the cards he holds to those he won in tricks. Scores are then made, or the pool divided, in the usual way.

Greek Hearts

The penalties are 50 for taking ♠Q, 15 for ♥A, 10 each per ♥K, Q, J, 1 each per lower heart.

Hearts and Flowers

All clubs count plus the same value as hearts count minus, so the overall scores in each deal cancel to zero. Game is normally 30 up.

Heartsette (Widow Hearts)

Three or so cards are dealt face down as a widow and the rest are divided evenly among the players. The widow is added to the last won trick. In some circles it goes to the winner of the first trick, who may see what it contains without showing it to anyone else.

Omnibus (or Red Jack) Hearts

The ♦J (or ♦10) reduces by 10 points the penalty score of the player who wins it in a trick. This variation is so common that its players regard it as standard Hearts and do not give it any particular title.

Pink Lady

A variety in which ♥Q, or Pink Lady, also scores minus 13 points.

Spot Hearts

The penalty score for each heart taken is the same as its face value, with Jack 11, Queen 12, King 13, Ace 14, but without a penalty for ♠Q. Penalty points total 104 in each deal.

Higgledy-Piggledy (Patience) ▸▸ *Chaos*

High Card Pool ▸▸ *Red Dog*

Hi-Lo ▸▸ *Poker*

Hoc

Ancestor of ▸ **Comet**, ▸▸ **Newmarket**, etc.

Hola

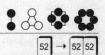

Point-trick game

Played in Poland and the Ukraine, and by Slavic communities in Canada, Hola (meaning 'nakedness') is a game of the ▸ **Sedma** type, in which you win tricks by the unusual process of matching rank.

Hola is normally played by two players, or by four in partnerships. Six can play in two partnerships of three, using a doubled pack (2×52 cards). It can also be made playable by three by removing from the 52-card pack any card other than an Ace, Ten, Seven, or Two.

Deal four cards to each player and stack the rest face down.

The aim is to win Aces and Tens in tricks. Each of these counts 10 points, while an additional 10 for winning the last trick makes 90 in all and so prevents ties.

The eldest hand leads to the first trick. You may always lead or play any card you choose: there is no need to follow suit. All Sevens and Twos are trumps. A trick is taken by the last played card of the same rank as the one led, or by the last played trump if any are played.

Examples.
1. Played: 9 J A J. The Nine wins, having been neither matched nor trumped, and the trick counts 10 for the Ace.
2. Played: 9 A A 9. The second Nine wins a trick worth 20.
3. Played: 9 7 J 10. The Seven trumps a trick worth 10.
4. Played: A 7 2 A. The Two wins a trick worth 20.
5. Played: 7 2 2 7. The last-played Seven wins a trick worth zero, unless it is the last (which counts 10).

When four cards have been played, the player who led the first card may either:

- end the trick, in which case it is won by whoever played the last matched card or the last trump, or
- fight on, by leaving the trick in place and leading to a new trick.

If he fights on, a second trick is played, following the same rules as the first, and, again, the leader may end it or fight on as before. The leader can choose to fight on up to three times, by the end of which everyone will have played out their four cards, and the leader will have no choice but to end the four-part trick.

When a trick or multi-trick ends, the player who won the last trick gathers up all the cards played and stores them face down. Each in turn, starting with the leader to the last trick, draws cards from stock until they all have four again, and the winner of the last trick leads to the next. When no cards remain in stock, play continues with those remaining in hand.

Each player or side then counts 10 for each Ace and Ten captured in tricks. Unless six play, the side winning the last trick scores an additional 10. In the rare event that one player or side took all the tricks, they score not 90 but 170 towards game. This is called a hola. If six play, the last trick does not count 10, but the total number of available points is 160, because the pack is doubled.

If the side that dealt previously scores 50 or more, the same player deals again; if not, the next deal is made by the previous dealer's left-hand opponent.

Play up to any previously agreed target, such as 200 or 300 points, or 500 if six play.

Hombre ▸▸ *Ombre*

Honeymoon Bridge

Any form of Bridge for two, such as the following.

Deal thirteen cards each and stack the rest down. Phase 1 consists of thirteen tricks, each player drawing from stock after each trick. There is no trump, and suit must be followed if possible. The aim is to finish with a thirteen-card hand suitable for Phase 2, which begins when the stock is exhausted. There is an auction to establish a contract, to which the non-declarer leads. Play and score as at Contract ▸ **Bridge**.

Hundertspiel ▸▸ *Trappola*

Hundred
Adding-up game

One of many arithmetical games popular in central European countries.
Cards count as follows:

A	K	Q	J	10	9	8	7
11	4	3	2	10	9	8	7

Divide them equally amongst the players, leaving any remainder face up on the table to start the total. Each in turn plays a card to the table, adding its value to the previous total and announcing the new one. If you make the total over 100 you lose, but for making it 100 exactly you win. You may agree to continue play with another scoring point at 200.

Hundreogen ▶▶ *Harjan*

I Doubt It ▶▶ *Cheat*

Imperial

Plain-trick game

`32`

A Provençal game related to ▶ **Piquet**, still popular in the south of France. Descriptions vary.

Two players use a 32-card pack ranking K Q J A 10 9 8 7 in every suit.

Scores can be kept in writing, but counters are better. Each starts with five reds and six whites on his left, and passes one white from left to right for each point won in play. Six points make an imperial, indicated by moving a red to the right and returning six whites to the left. Game is 36 points, being won by the first to pass all eleven counters from left to right.

Deal 12 cards each in twos, threes, or fours. Turn the twenty-fifth for trumps, and place the rest face down across it. If the turn-up is an honour (K Q J A or 7), dealer scores a white. If it is a King or an Ace, and dealer holds the Seven, he may exchange it for the turn-up.

Each in turn, starting with elder, scores for any of the following imperials he may have been dealt. All scoring combinations must be shown, any they must be declared in this order:

1. K Q J A of trumps (*impériale d'atout*)   2 reds
2. K Q J A of non-trump suit   1 red
3. All four of K Q J A or 7 (*impériale d'honneur*) 1 red
4. No face cards (*impériale blanche*)   2 reds

Next, the player with the better point scores one white. 'Point' is the total face value of all cards held in any one suit, counting Ace 11, courts 10 each, numerals as marked. If equal, Elder scores.

Elder leads to the first trick, and the winner of each trick leads to the next. 'Strict' rules apply: follow suit and win the trick if possible; if unable to follow, play a trump if possible. Score one white for leading an honour to a trick.

At end of play, you each score one white for each honour (K Q J A 7 of trumps) you have taken in tricks. Next, whoever took a majority of tricks scores one white for each trick taken above six, or two reds for *capot* if he won all twelve.

Throughout play, whenever one player scores a red—whether for an imperial or by getting his sixth white across—his opponent's odd points are promptly annulled, and he must shift all his whites back to the left. The sole exception is the *impériale blanche*, which does not annul the odd points. With this exception, however, the rule is also applied at the start of the second and subsequent deals when reds are scored for imperials in hand. Hence it is important, especially near the end of a game, that scores be made strictly in order: turned trump, imperials in hand, *impériale blanche*, the point, leading and capturing honours, number of tricks taken.

Optional extras. Some players recognize two additional imperials, each of which earns one red but does not force the opponent to cancel his whites. An *impériale de retourne* occurs when a player has all but one card of an imperial, and the card missing is the trump turn-up. This counts immediately before the score for point. An *impériale de rencontre*, or *impériale tombée*, occurs when a player wins the four top trumps in tricks without having been originally dealt all four. This counts immediately before the score for honours.

Interregnum

Patience game

A fairly challenging double-pack solitaire.

Deal two rows of eight cards each—face up, not overlapping, and with enough room between them for a third row.

The cards in the upper row are 'indicators'. Those in the lower row are the base cards of eight wastepiles.

Your aim is to build, in the space between the two initial rows, eight piles of thirteen cards each, in ascending sequence but regardless of suit. The base card of each pile is to be one rank higher than the indicator immediately above it in the top row. For example, if an indicator is a Nine, then the base card beneath it in the central row must be a Ten, on which you are to build the sequence J-Q-K-A-2-3-4-5-6-7-8. You will then complete the sequence by turning the indicator and using it to top off the finished pile.

All cards in the bottom row are immediately available for setting up as bases in the central row and building on them when possible, but do not (yet) fill the gaps they leave.

When stuck, deal eight more cards face up along the bottom row, each one either covering the previous card or filling a gap as the case may be. Having completed the deal (and not before), pause, and do any further building that may be possible. Only the top card of each position in the bottom row may be built, and its removal releases the one below it for building. You may spread the cards of the bottom row downwards towards you so that all cards remain identifiable.

Keep playing in this way until the game comes out, which it usually does.

Israeli Whist

Plain trick game

52

An elaboration of ▶ **Oh Hell**! popular in Israel, with Bridge-style bidding.

Deal thirteen cards each. There are two phases of bidding, first to determine the trump suit and then to determine the winning number of tricks.

Each in turn, starting with the dealer, either bids or passes. A bid names a number of tricks and a proposed trump. Each bid must be higher than the last. A higher number overcalls a lower, and a given number is overcalled by the same number in a higher suit. As at Bridge, the order is clubs (low), diamonds, hearts, spades, no trump. The minimum bid is 'Five clubs', the highest 'Thirteen no trumps'.

Three successive passes do not prevent the last bidder from bidding yet higher, and this phase ends only when all four pass in succession. The last bidder is the declarer.

If all four pass immediately, each player passes any three cards face down to his left-hand neighbour and then picks up the three from his right. This opens another attempt at bidding. Up to three such attempts may be made before the cards are entirely thrown in and dealt again.

If at least one player bids to become declarer, then each in turn, starting at the declarer's left but excluding the declarer himself, must announce exactly how many tricks he proposes to win, and the last bidder (at dealer's right) must avoid the number that would make exactly thirteen. If the bids total fewer than thirteen, the game is described as 'under'; if more, it is over.

The declarer leads to the first of thirteen tricks. You must follow suit if you can, but may otherwise play any card. The trick is taken by the highest card of the suit led, or by the highest trump if any are played, and the winner of each trick leads to the next.

Your score depends on whether or not you bid zero and on whether the game was 'under' or 'over'.

If you bid one or more, and succeed, you score 10 plus the square of the number you bid. For example, you score 19 for bidding and winning three tricks. For failing, you lose 10 points per over- or undertrick.

If you bid zero and succeed, you score 20 if the game was 'over' or 50 if it was 'under'. For a failed bid of zero, you score minus 50 for the first trick you won, but reduce this by 10 points for each subsequent trick won. This yields a penalty score of 40 for taking two tricks, 30 for three, and so on.

Play up to any agreed target. Scoring variations may be encountered.

Jass

Point-trick game

36

'Jass' is the name of the highest trump, the Jack, in a family of related games most widely played in Switzerland, though apparently of Dutch origin. It is also the name of the game and of the traditional 36-card Swiss-suited pack with which it is played. (Swiss suits are acorns, escutcheons, flowers, bells; its face cards are King, Over, Under; and in place of a Ten it has a banner.) By extension, it is often used of any game played in Switzerland with such cards, whether or not of the true family. The following entry gives *general* rules for all true Jass games played in Switzerland, followed by the additional *particular* rules for (*a*) Handjass, a good beginners' game for 2–4 players; (*b*) Schieber, the most popular four-hand partnership game; and (*c*) Pandur, the equivalent of Solo.

Separate entries will also be found for the related (but not specifically Swiss) games of Belote, Klaberjass, and Klaverjas.

General rules of Jass. Jass is essentially a game of points. Points are scored for three features known as *Stöck, Wys, Stich,* or 'marriages, melds, tricks'.

Marriages. A marriage is the King and Queen of trumps in one hand. Its holder claims it upon playing the second of them to a trick. Its score of 20 is recorded as if made *before* those for melds and tricks, even though it is not revealed until after melds have been declared.

Melds. A meld is a suit-sequence of three or more cards (running A K Q J 10 9 8 7 6), or a quartet of Aces, Kings, Queens, or Jacks. They score as follows:

Four Jacks	200
Five or more in sequence	100
Four A, K, or Q	100
Four in sequence	50
Three in sequence	20

A card may not be used in two melds at once (though the trump King or Queen may belong to a meld in addition to being married). For example, if you hold four Kings and a sequence of four to the Ace or King, you count only 100 for Kings, not also 50 for the sequence.

Only the holder of the best meld may score for it, but (*a*) he may also score for any other melds he holds involving entirely different cards, and (*b*) in a partnership game, his partnership also scores for those held by his partner. The holder of the best meld is found in the following way as each player contributes a card to the first trick. The leader announces the value of his best meld. The next, upon playing his card, announces a higher value if he has one, or 'Good' if he cannot equal it. If he has one of equal value, he states the number of cards it contains. A longer meld beats a shorter, so the previous player then says 'Not good' if he can beat it, 'Good' if he can't, or 'Equal'. If equal, the next states its rank if a quarter, or its top card if a sequence. A higher rank beats a lower, and the previous player again says 'Not good', 'Good', or 'Equal'. Equality must mean a sequence is in question, which the second player can then only win by (truthfully) announcing 'In trumps'. Otherwise, all else being equal, the previous player wins by prior position. The next player in turn then competes, if he can, with the winner of the first contest. As before, the pecking order is: value, length, height, trump, position.

Tricks. Won tricks are scored according to the point-value of the cards composing them. The rank and value of cards differs as between trumps and plain suits as follows:

In trumps	J	9	A	K	Q	—	10	—	8	7	6
In plain suits	—	—	A	K	Q	J	10	9	8	7	6
Card-points	20	14	11	4	3	2	10	0	0	0	0

The trump Jack, or 'Jass', counts 20 and is the highest card in the pack. The trump Nine, or 'Nell', counts 14 and is the second best. Plain-suit numerals below Ten count nothing. The total value of all counters in the pack is 152, i.e. 62 in trumps plus 30 in each plain suit. Winning the last trick scores an additional 5 points. Hence the total possible for the third scoring feature, 'tricks', is normally 157.

Play. All play, including the deal and turn to deal, passes to the *right*. Eldest leads to the first trick. Rules of play are:

- If a trump is led, you must follow suit if you can, unless your only trump is the Jass, when you may freely play it or discard.
- If a plain suit is led, you are free to follow suit or play a trump, as you prefer, but any trump played must (if possible) be higher than any other already played to the trick. Only if unable to follow suit may you discard.

The trick is taken by the highest card of the suit led, or by the highest trump if any are played, and the winner of each trick leads to the next.

Handjass

From two to four play, each for himself. Deal four hands of nine cards each in threes. If four play, the last card is turned for trump, and dealer does not take it into hand until about to play to the first trick. If two or three play, the top card of the first dead hand is turned for trump, and may be taken in exchange for the Six of trumps if anyone has it.

The aim is to score as much as possible for cards and melds. Each of you in turn must first declare whether or not you are prepared to play the hand. If not, you turn it down and sit the deal out. If all pass, there is a new deal by the same dealer. If all but one pass, he wins without playing. Otherwise, tricks are played as described above.

Two game-points are awarded at end of play, one each to the players making the highest totals. If there is a tie for second, it is broken in favour of the player cutting the higher card from the pack. If only one stayed in, he scores them both, as does the better of two players if the other failed to make 21. Any player failing to make 21 scores a negative game point (written as a zero, though actually counting minus one). As each player reaches seven game points he drops out of play, and the last left in is the loser.

Schieber

Four players; partners sit opposite each other. Precise rules vary considerably from place to place.

Deal nine cards each in threes. Eldest may nominate a trump suit or *schieben*, i.e. pass that privilege to his partner, who must then exercise it. If eldest leads without making any announcement, whatever he leads is a trump.

Follow basic Jass rules as described above. A side taking all nine tricks scores 100 extra for the 'match'. Each deal from the second onwards is made by a member of the side that won the previous deal, so that the losing side has the advantage of making trumps and leading first. Play ceases the moment one side reaches 1000 points, for which purpose it is important to remember that scores accrue in order 'marriage, melds, tricks'.

By agreement, a meld of four Nines may also be recognized. It ranks below four Jacks and counts 150.

Schieber is usually played with two additional bids, *Oben-abe*, and *Unden-ufe*, which may reasonably be translated respectively as 'tops-down' and 'bottoms-up'. Both are played at no trump, so there is no Jass or Nell, nor cards worth 20 and 14. Instead, all Eights count 8 points each when captured in tricks, thus maintaining the total of 157 for tricks, including 5 for last. In 'tops-down', cards rank from Ace high to Six low, as normal; in 'bottoms-up' their trick-taking power is reversed: Six is the highest in its suit, Seven the second highest, and so down to Ace, the lowest of all. (*Variant*: In some circles the point-value of 11 is transferred from the Ace to the Six.) Reversed ranking also applies to melds of equal length—for example, a sequence of 6 7 8 beats 7 8 9, four Kings beat four Aces, etc.; but four Jacks still count 200 and so beat all else.

When these variations are included, it is usual to double all scores made in contracts with shields or bells (spades or diamonds) as trump, treble contracts in tops-down, and quadruple those in bottoms-up. The game target may then be raised to 2500.

Pandur

Four usually play, but only three are active, as each in turn sits out the hand to which he deals. The scorekeeper deals first.

Deal eight cards each in batches of four from a 24-card pack made by stripping out all ranks below Nine.

In addition to the usual melds, you may declare a sequence of six or a quartet of Nines, each counting 150. Only the soloist may score for melds, and only if he has the best one. If any opponent has a better, it does not score itself but only prevents the soloist from scoring.

Each in turn, starting with Eldest, may bid or pass, and, having passed, may not come in again. The lowest bid is 100; higher bids must be multiples of 10. A numerical bid is the minimum amount you would undertake to make (for marriages, melds, and tricks) in return for nominating trumps and leading to the first trick.

A bid of 200 is overcalled by misère, then trump misère, then 210, etc. In misère, the soloist must lose every trick, playing at no trump. In trump misère the suit of the card he leads is automatically trump. Players are still required to trump when unable to follow suit, but are not obliged to overtrump.

A bid of 250 is overcalled by Pandur, and 300 by trump Pandur. In Pandur, the soloist must win every trick, playing at no trump. In trump Pandur, the suit of the card he leads is automatically trump.

If successful, the soloist wins a number of game-points equivalent to the bid divided by 50 (maximum 6). Misères count 4, Pandur 5, trump

Pandur 6. For a failed bid, the game value is credited to each opponent. Game is 15 points or any other agreed target. If four play, the dealer gets the value of a failed bid, but not if he stands at 13 or 14: his last point(s) must be made in active play.

Each player drops out upon reaching the target, the game being played by three, then by two. The last one left in loses.

Java Rummy ⇝ Elimination Rummy

Jeu de Vache ⇝ Aluette

Jig ⇝ Snip-Snap-Snorem

Jo-Jotte

A hybrid of ▸ **Klaberjass** and Contract ▸ **Bridge** devised in the 1930s by Ely Culbertson and named after his then wife, Josephine Dillon.

Jubilee

Adding-up game

61

A Czech member of the ▸ **Adding-up** family.

Make a 61-card pack comprising a whole suit of hearts, two whole spade suits, two each of club numerals from Ace to Nine only (no Tens or courts), and four Jokers. Aces count 15 each, courts 10, other numerals at face value, Jokers zero. Hearts count minus these amounts, black cards plus.

Deal eight each and stack the rest face down. Each in turn, starting with Eldest, plays a card face up to a common wastepile, announces the total value of all cards so far played, and draws a replacement from stock so long as any remain.

Eldest must start with a black card. No one may bring the total below zero. Anyone unable to play must show his hand and pass.

Anyone making the total an exact multiple of 25, whether by addition or subtraction, scores 10 for a 'jubilee', or 20 if it is also a multiple of 100. Anyone making the total 'jump' a jubilee, whether by addition or subtraction, instead of hitting it exactly, loses 5 points.

Keep going till the last card has been played. The final total should be 189.

Julep

Plain-trick game

40

A South American game similar to five-card ▸ **Loo**, best for five or six players. It is normally played to the right.

Deal five each from a 40-card pack lacking Eights, Nines, and Tens, and turn the next for trump. Players may pass or play. Dealer may take the turn-up in exchange for a discard, thereby undertaking to play. Those who play must win at least two tricks, but may first discard and draw any number of replacements from the undealt stock. If not enough remain, shuffle the cards of those who passed to form a new stock. If all pass but one, another can offer to 'defend the pack' by drawing six cards from stock and discarding one.

The first active player to the right of the dealer leads to the first trick. Players must follow suit and head the trick if possible; must trump and overtrump if unable to follow; and may renounce only if unable to do either.

An active player who failed to win two tricks pays an agreed stake, the *julep* (= sweet drink, or 'sweetener'), as explained below. If only one player succeeds, he wins the pot plus a julep from each active player. If two players win two each, they split the pot and the juleps. If all fail, they all pay a julep to the pot, which is then carried forwards.

If the pack was defended and lost, the lone player wins the pot but the defender does not pay a julep. If both succeed, the lone player wins half the pot, and the other half is carried forwards. If the defender wins, he gets the pot plus a julep from the lone player. If bidder is beaten, defender gets the pot, bidder pays a julep.

Jungle Bridge ⏵ *Oh Hell*!

Kaiser

Plain-trick game

A Canadian game especially popular in the Ukrainian communities of Saskatchewan and neighbouring provinces. It is a folk game, so exact details of play vary from place to place.

Four players sitting crosswise in partnerships are each dealt eight cards, in ones, from a 32-card pack basically ranking A K Q J 10 9 8 7 in each suit. However, the ♠7 is replaced by ♠3 and the ♥7 by ♥5, both remaining lowest in their respective suits.

The aim is for the side bidding highest to win at least as many points as it bid, counting 1 per trick, plus 5 for winning the ♥5 in a trick, and minus 3 for catching ♠3 in a trick (total 12 points).

Each in turn, starting with eldest, has one opportunity to speak, and may use it to pass or bid. The minimum bid is five, the maximum 12, and each must be higher than the last. No prospective trump is named when bidding, but a bidder intending to play at no trump should say so (e.g. 'Five no'). There are two exceptions to the need to bid higher. One is that a no-trump bid beats one of the same number with trump implied. The other is that the dealer can beat the previous caller by naming the same bid, not necessarily higher.

If all pass, the hands are scrapped and the deal passes round.

The highest bidder names trumps, if any, and leads to the first trick. Players must follow suit if possible, otherwise may play any card. The trick is taken by the highest card of the suit led, or by the highest trump if any are played, and the winner of each trick leads to the next.

Each side counts 1 per trick, plus 5 for ♥5 and minus 3 for ♠3. If the declarers win at least as many points as they bid, they score the number of points they actually took, doubled if played at no trump. If not, they lose the amount of their bid, also doubled at no trump.

The non-bidders score the amount they actually took, unless their cumulative score is 45 or more, in which case it remains pegged.

(But if they finish with a negative count, for example by taking only one trick containing the ♠3, then it is deducted regardless of their total.)

Game is 52 points.

Kaiserjass ▸▸ *Karnöffel*

Kalabriasz ▸▸ *Klaberjass*

Kalookie, Kaluki

Rummy game

Kalookie, under various spellings, is applied to almost any form of basic ▸ **Rummy** played with a doubled pack. A more formal and elaborate variety is currently played in Britain as follows.

Preliminaries. From two to five play, using two 52-card packs and two Jokers. The aim is to be the first to get rid of all your cards by gradually laying them out, face up, in melds (valid combinations). If you lay out all 13 at once it is a 'kalookie', which wins double if played for stakes.

Deal. Decide first dealer by any agreed means. The turn to deal and play passes to the left. Deal 13 cards each in ones. Turn the next card face up to start a discard pile and set the remainder face down beside it as a stock. The top card of the discard pile, whatever it may be at any point in the game, is called the upcard.

Melds. A meld is either:

- three or four cards of the same rank and different suits, such as ♠K-♥K-♣K (but not ♠K-♠K-♦K-♣K), or
- three or more cards in suit and sequence, such as ♥4-5-6-7. Aces are always high, so ♣A-K-Q… is valid but not ♣A-2-3….

The value of a meld is the sum of the point-values of its individual cards, as follows:

Ace	11
K, Q, J	10 each
2 to 10	face value
Joker	+(2 to 11) or −15

A Joker can stand for any desired card in a meld. In this case it assumes the point-value of the natural card that it represents, from 2 to 11 as the case may be. It counts 15 only as a penalty, when not forming part of a meld.

Play. Eldest plays first. He must take either the upcard or the top card of the stock and add it to his hand, may then lay out an initial meld if able and willing, and finally must end his turn by discarding one card face up to the discard pile.

An initial meld—that is, the first meld that each player makes—must be worth at least 40 points. For example, ♠6-7-8-9-10 is a valid initial meld, but not ♠9-10-J-Q.

Thereafter, each in turn from the first player's left plays in the same way, except that they are not allowed (unlike the first player) to take the upcard unless they have already made an initial meld, or can use the upcard to make one.

Having made an initial meld, you are thereafter (or in the same turn) free to make new melds of any value, and to extend any meld on the table by adding one or more valid cards to it. This is called building and is subject to the following rules.

- You can add an individual card to a meld of your own or to anyone else's.
- To a set of three, you can add a fourth, provided that it is of the fourth suit. For example, you can build only ♠3 to a set of ♥3-♣3-♦3. (And you cannot add a Joker to a set of four and claim that it represents an imaginary fifth suit.)
- To a sequence of three or more cards, you can add one card to either or both ends, but not more than one to either end. For example, to a run of ♣7-8-9-10 you can build ♣6 or ♣J, or both, but not ♣5-6 or ♣J-Q.

- You cannot count the value of a card you build towards the minimum of 40 needed to make an initial meld.

Jokers. A meld may contain one or more Jokers. For example, a Joker in a set of three or four cards represents the same rank and whatever suit or suits are necessary to ensure that they are all different.

If you meld both Jokers and a natural card, you must say whether they form a set or a sequence, and, if a sequence, which of the several that are possible. For example, ♥6-Jo-Jo could be three Sixes, or ♥6-7-8, or ♥5-6-7, or ♥4-5-6.

If a suit-sequence contains a Joker, whether made as part of it or built to it later, the cards of the sequence must be arranged in order and with the Joker in the position that would be occupied by the natural card it represents.

If a meld contains a Joker, and you hold the natural card it represents, you may, on your turn to play, take the Joker in exchange for your natural card. (This is why it is important to show by its position what card a Joker represents in a sequence.) However, you may only do this if (*a*) you have already made a valid initial meld, and (*b*) you can immediately use the Joker in a new meld or build it on another one. You are not allowed to take it into hand for use on a subsequent turn.

☛ *Note.* There is an oddity about taking Jokers from sets. If a set of three contains a Joker, and you hold two natural cards that would complete the set to four, you may build them both in exchange for the Joker. Similarly, if it consists of a natural card and two Jokers, you can use one of the Jokers elsewhere and replace it with any two natural cards that would turn it into a valid set of four.

General rules. Once a meld has been made, it cannot be changed or rearranged but only extended by building. If, therefore, you meld (say) ♥3-4-5 on one occasion and ♥7-8-9 on another, and then draw a ♥6, you can attach it to the appropriate end of either meld, but cannot coalesce all seven cards into a single sequence. (If you did, it would prevent anyone from building the other ♥6.) On the other hand, if you can meld a run of six or more cards at once, it is better to do so than to make two separate melds.

If a player draws the last card of the stockpile and does not call up in the same turn, he withholds his discard while the dealer shuffles the discard pile and turns it face down as a new stock, then makes his discard to start a new pile. If this happens a second time, the game is declared null and void.

If you are left with three or fewer cards in hand after ending your turn with a discard, you must announce how many cards you hold, otherwise you will not be allowed to call up on your next turn.

Ending and scoring. Play ceases the moment one player makes a final discard and is left with no cards in hand. Note that it is obligatory to make a final discard when calling up—you can't do it by melding and building all your remaining cards.

For a kalookie—melding 13 cards in one turn—you must first make a valid initial meld worth at least 40, then make any additional melds and builds you can, and finish with a final discard.

Once a player has called up, no one else may make any further melds or builds. (There is no laying off as in other Rummy games.)

Everyone else totals the value of cards left in his own hand and records these as penalty points. The game ends when all but one player have reached or exceeded a previously agreed maximum, typically 150, and the overall winner is the one player who has not done so.

Ace	11
K, Q, J	10 each
2 to 10	face value
Joker	+(2 to 11) or −15

Some players count penalty points double if the winner goes kalookie. This is appropriate when not playing for stakes, as the staking game rewards it instead by doubling the payment.

Stakes. The game is often played for fixed stakes which must be agreed in advance, specifically for the following features:

- call up—the amount received by the winner of each hand from each other player;
- kalookie—the amount received if he wins by melding all 13 cards at once;

- initial stake—the amount paid into the pool by every player at the start of the game;
- buy-in stake—the amount that a player must add to the pool in order to re-enter the game when he has reached a maximum of penalty points.

A typical schedule is 1 unit for a call-up, 2 for a kalookie, and 5 each for the initial and buy-in stakes (where 1 unit represents any agreed amount, such as 10p).

Buying in. In the staking game, a player who runs over 150 points can buy in by paying the appropriate amount into the pool. His penalty score is then reduced to equal that of the player who, having not yet reached 150, has the highest number of penalties. Nobody can buy in more than twice in the same game, nor can anyone buy in if all but one player have reached the maximum, leaving a winner.

Karma ▶ *Sh**head*

Karnöffel

(Rhyming approximately with 'kerfuffle'). The oldest identifiable European card game, first recorded in Germany in 1426, is a partnership game in which each deal is won by the first side to win three of the five tricks played. Although current before the invention of trumps (*see* ▶ **Tarot games**), Karnöffel is characterized by the assignment of special but limited quasi-trumping powers to certain individual cards. A number of European folk games have recently come to light that obviously derive from Karnöffel and continue its peculiarities. Described in this book are the relatively simple ▶ **Alkort** (Iceland), ▶ **Brus** (Gotland), ▶ **Watten** (Austria), and the more distantly related ▶ **Aluette** (France). More complicated are Kaiserjass (probably the closest surviving relative, played in Switzerland), Styrivolt (Faeroe Islands), and Voormsi or Wumps (Greenland).

http://www.pagat.com/karnoeff/

Kemps

Collecting game

52

A cross between ▸ **Commerce** and ▸ **Authors**, but with the unusual feature of being played in partnerships instead of individually. It was contributed to the Pagat website by Elena Anaya.

Any even number may play, but assume four. Before play, each pair of partners agree between themselves on a visual signal by which either can indicate to the other when he or she has collected four cards of the same rank. They can also agree on meaningless signals that merely act as camouflage. The signals may include nods, winks, grimaces, twitches, and suchlike, but may not be verbal. False signals may not be used to convey relevant information, such as having got three of a kind. The aim is to correctly call 'Kemps' when you think your partner has made four of a kind, or 'Stop Kemps' when you think an opponent has done so.

Deal four cards each and four face up to the table. Play does not take place in rotation. Anybody at any time can take from one to four cards from the table and replace them with the same number of (different) cards from their hand. If two or more players want the same card, the first one to touch it gets it.

When everyone has stopped exchanging, the dealer sweeps the spare hand away and deals four more cards from stock.

Play ceases the moment anyone calls 'Kemps' or 'Stop Kemps'. On a call of 'Kemps', the caller's partner reveals his or her hand, and, if it contains four of a kind, the opponents lose a point. If not, the caller's side loses a point. On a call of 'Stop Kemps', both members of the opposing partnership (or, if more than four play, of the partnership specifically challenged by the caller) reveal their hands. If either has four of a kind, their side loses a point; if not, the caller's side does.

The first side to get five points loses the game. The first point lost is marked as a letter K, the second as E, and so on, until a side loses by completing the name of the game. Its origin is not explained.

http:// www.pagat.com/commerce/kemps.html

King

Penalty-trick game

36

A Russian game evidently ancestral to ▸ **Barbu**. *See also* ▸ **Tyotka**.

Three players each receive twelve cards dealt one at a time from a 36-card pack ranking A K Q J 10 9 8 7 6 in each suit.

A game is twelve deals, the first six negative, the second six positive, as explained below. Eldest leads to the first trick in each deal. You must follow suit if you can, but may otherwise play any card. The trick is taken by the highest card of the suit led, and the winner of each trick leads to the next. There are no trumps.

In the first six deals you aim to avoid capturing tricks or particular penalty cards, and all scores are negative:

1. *No tricks.* Score −6 per trick.
2. *No hearts.* Score −8 per heart. You may not lead hearts unless you have no alternative.
3. *No men.* Each King and Jack taken scores −9. (*Variant*: Jacks only, −18 each.)
4. *No Queens.* Each Queen taken scores −18.
5. *No last.* The last two tricks score −36 each.
6. *No ♥King.* Score −72 for taking ♥K in a trick. In this deal you may never lead hearts unless forced, and must play ♥K as soon as you cannot follow suit or when ♥A has been played ahead of you to a heart lead.

Deals 7 to 12 follow exactly the same sequence but with plus-points instead of minus, e.g. +6 per trick won, +8 per heart won, and so on. In positive Hearts and King you may still not lead a heart unless you have no choice, but in the last deal you may play ♥K at any legal opportunity.

There are optional 7th and 14th deals called *Yeralash* (Medley). In the 7th, all penalties operate simultaneously, and in the 14th all bonuses likewise.

King and Queen (Patience) ▸▸ *Salic Law*

Kings and Queens

Rummy game

52 52

A ▶ **Rummy** game with the unusual feature of special bonus and penalty cards.

Play as ordinary Rummy with a doubled pack of 104 cards running A 2 3 4 5 6 7 8 9 10 J Q K. A meld is three or more cards in suit and sequence (Ace low) or three or more of the same rank. Deuces are wild.

The aim is to be the first to go out by melding all seven cards in one go—or six, provided that the seventh is not higher than a Seven.

When one player melds out, the others also make whatever melds they can, and whatever remains in their hands count against them. If, however, the player who went out first melded only six cards, anyone else with an unmelded card matching his seventh may lay it off, thus reducing his own penalty score and increasing that of the one who went out first.

Unmelded cards count against their holders according to their face value (Aces 1 each, courts 10). The overall winner is the last player to reach a total of 100 penalty points.

The point of the game, as indicated by its title, lies in the fact that players can reduce their penalty scores by melding Kings and Queens. Each King used in a meld reduces its holder's score by 5 points, each Queen by 3 points, and each Deuce representing a King or Queen by the appropriate amount.

☞ *Comment.* It would be sensible to (*a*) restrict the number of Deuces in a meld by insisting that every meld contain more natural cards than wild ones, and (*b*) count minus 10 for each unmelded Deuce.

Klaberjass

Point-trick game

32

A major international two-hander known in England as Clobiosh, Clobby, or Clubby, in America as Klob (notably in the writings of Damon Runyon) or Kalabriasz, and in France—with distinct differences—as ▶ **Belote**. A member of the ▶ **Jass** family, it is characterized by the promotion of the trump Jack (*Jass*) and Nine (*Menel*) to topmost position. It is a particularly Jewish game, probably of Dutch, Flemish, or Alsatian origin. Four can play Klaberjass, but its more authentic equivalent is ▶ **Klaverjas**.

Preliminaries. Whoever draws the lower card deals first, after which the deal alternates. Deal six cards each in threes and turn the next for trump. Cards rank and count thus:

In trumps	J	9	A	10	K	Q	—	—	8	7
In plain suits	—	—	A	10	K	Q	J	9	8	7
Card-points	20	14	11	10	4	3	2	0	0	0

Object. To be the first to reach 500 points by scoring for melds and winning card-points in tricks. In each deal one player becomes the 'maker' by choosing trumps and thereby contracting to score more than the other.

Bidding. There is first a round of bidding to see if either player will accept the turned suit as trump. Elder may either 'take it' or 'pass'. If he passes, Dealer may also either take it or pass.

If both pass, Elder turns the trump card down and may either pass or propose another suit as trump. If he passes, Dealer has the same options. If he also passes, the deal is annulled and Elder deals to the next hand.

Deal more. If trumps are made, dealer deals three more cards apiece, then turns the bottom card of the stock face up and places it on top. This card is for information only: it may not be taken, and plays no part in tricks or melds.

Dix. If you hold the trump Seven, and the trump suit is that of the card originally turned up, you can exchange the Seven (called *dix*, pronounced *deece*) for the trump turn-up, but must do so before you declare any melds.

Melds. A score is available for holding a sequence of three or more cards in the same suit, sequential order being A K Q J 10 9 8 7 in all four suits.

A sequence of three counts 20, of four or more 50. Only the player holding the best sequence may score, but he may then also score for any other sequences he can and will declare. A longer sequence beats a shorter. If equal, the one containing the highest cards wins. If still equal, a trump sequence beats a plain. If still equal, neither player scores. (*Variant*: If still equal, Elder scores.)

To determine which player has the better sequence, Elder announces, on leading to the first trick, 'Twenty' if he has a sequence of three cards, 'Fifty' if four or more. In responding to the first trick, Dealer announces 'Good' if he cannot match 20 or 50, or 'Not good' if he can beat it. In case of equality, he asks first 'How many cards?', then, if necessary, 'How high?', then, if still necessary, 'In trumps?' At the end of the first trick, whichever player has the best sequence (if any) must show and score for his best sequence, and may show and score for any others also held.

Tricks. Elder leads first, and the winner of each trick leads to the next. You must follow suit if you can, otherwise must trump if possible. If a trump is led, you must beat it if you can. The trick is taken by the higher card of the suit led or by the higher trump if any are played.

Bella. If you hold the K–Q of trumps, you score 20 for the marriage upon playing the second of them to a trick and announcing '*Bella*'.

Ten for last. You count 10 points extra for winning the last trick.

Score. Both players then declare their respective totals for melds and card-points. If the trump-maker made more points, both score what they make; if less (when he is said to 'go *bête*'), his opponent scores the total made by both players. If equal, the opponent scores what he took and the maker scores nothing. (*Variant*: the maker's points are held in abeyance and go to the winner of the next deal.)

The game ends at the end of the deal in which either player has reached or exceeded 500 points. (*Variant*: It ends as soon as either player correctly claims to have reached 500, the rest of that deal not being played out.) The higher total wins.

Klaverjas

Point-trick game

32

The Dutch national card game is a neat member of the ▶ **Jass** family and makes an excellent introduction to point-trick as opposed to plain-trick games. It exhibits the unusual feature of scoring for melds made 'on the table' by the cards composing the current trick, instead of for melds merely dealt to players by chance as in other varieties of Jass.

Four players sitting in crosswise partnerships receive eight dealt in batches of 3-2-3 from a 32-card pack ranking and counting as follows:

In trumps	J	9	A	10	K	Q	—	—	8	7
In plain suits	—	—	A	10	K	Q	J	9	8	7
Card-points	20	14	11	10	4	3	2	0	0	0

The trump Jack is called 'Jas', the Nine 'Nel'.

The winning side is the first to reach an agreed target, such as 1500 points, over as many deals as necessary. Points are scored (*a*) for capturing counters in tricks, according to the above schedule, (*b*) 10 for winning the last trick, and (*c*) for winning any trick containing one of the following melds:

Four of the same rank	100
Four in suit-sequence	50
Three in suit-sequence	20
Stuk (K + Q of trumps)	20

Sequence order is A K Q J 10 9 8 7 in every suit including trumps. If a sequence of three or four includes a *stuk*, both are counted. Four of a kind occurs so rarely as to be hardly worth remembering.

Each in turn, starting with Eldest, may name trumps or pass the choice to his left. If the first three pass, Dealer must name trumps. Naming trumps obligates one's partnership to take more points than the opposing side from counters and melds contained in tricks. An opponent of the trump-maker may double if he thinks the contract doubtful, and the trump-maker or his partner may then redouble. These respectively double and quadruple the eventual score made by both sides.

Eldest leads first, and the winner of each trick leads to the next. You must follow suit if you can, otherwise you must play a trump if you can. If anyone has already played a trump—whether led or played to a non-trump lead—you must, if possible, play a higher trump than the previous one. (*Variant*: You are not obliged to overtrump your partner.) The trick is taken by the highest card of the suit led, or by the highest trump if any are played.

If you win a trick containing a meld, you must claim its score before the next trick is led, otherwise it does not count.

If the trump-maker's partnership takes more points than the other, both sides score towards game the amount they have taken in tricks and melds. If not, they count nothing, and the other partnership scores 162 plus the value of melds made by both sides. Taking all 162 card-points in tricks earns a bonus of 100.

Play ceases at the end of the deal in which either side reaches or exceeds the target.

Klob ▸ *Klaberjass*

Klondike

Patience game

This game is so well known that many people just call it Patience or 'Solitaire' without realizing that it has a name of its own.

Deal seven packets of cards in a row, face down, with one card in the first, two in the second, three in the third, and so on up to seven in the last. Then turn the top card of each packet face up.

Your aim is to put out the four Aces as and when they appear, and to build each one up in suit and sequence to the King.

Turn cards from stock and play them if possible or else discard them face up to a single wastepile.

The top card of the wastepile is always available for building on an Ace-pile or packing on the end of a column, so long as it correctly continues the sequence.

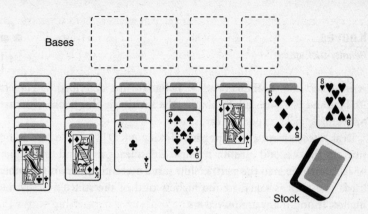

Bases

Stock

Klondike. Shift ♣A to the base line and turn up the card beneath. Then ♥8 to ♠9 leaves a space to be filled with ♦K.

Exposed cards on the packets are to be packed in descending sequence and alternating colour, with their constituent cards spread towards you in columns.

You may transfer any single exposed card, or any properly packed sequence of cards, from one column to another, provided that the join follows the descending–alternating rule.

Whenever you expose a down-card, turn it face up.

Whenever you make a space by clearing out a column, you may fill it again, but only with a King (and any other cards that may be packed upon it in proper sequence).

There is no redeal.

Note. Some players turn cards from stock in fans of three, of which only the uppermost (after turning) is available. If played, it releases the one below, and so on. If it is unplayable, all three must be discarded to the wastepile in the same order. If this method is used, the wastepile may be turned twice, giving three rounds of play in all.

Knaves

Penalty-trick game

A cross between ▶ **Hearts** and ▶ **Polignac**, first described by Hubert Phillips and B. C. Westall, combining the aim of winning tricks with that of avoiding Jacks as penalty cards.

Deal 17 each from a 52-card pack ranking A K Q J 10 9 8 7 6 5 4 3 2 and turn the fifty-second card for trumps. Eldest leads first, and the winner of each trick leads to the next. Follow suit if possible, otherwise play any card. The trick is taken by the highest card of the suit led or by the highest trump if any are played.

At end of play each player scores 1 point per trick taken, less penalty points for each Jack taken as follows: of spades 1, clubs 2, diamonds 3, hearts 4. The winner is the first to reach 20 points.

Knockout Whist

Plain-trick game

A popular British game of pub and playground, surely much older than its first printed description in 1980. No two schools play it exactly alike. The simplest rules are as follows.

Deal seven cards each and turn the next for trump. Dealer leads first, and the winner of each trick leads to the next. Follow suit if possible, otherwise play any card. The trick is taken by the highest card of the suit led or by the highest trump if any are played.

Anyone failing to take a trick is knocked out and takes no further part in the game.

Whoever took the most tricks gathers up the cards, shuffles them, deals six to each player, looks at his hand, announces trumps, and leads to the second round.

Play continues in this way, with those taking no tricks being knocked out, and the player taking most tricks dealing, choosing trumps, and leading to the next. In case of a tie for most tricks, the tied player cutting the highest card deals next.

The number of cards dealt decreases by one on each deal, so that only one is dealt on the seventh round—if it gets that far. The winner, of course, is the player left in when everyone else is out.

Of many staking methods, the simplest has each active player putting a chip in the pot at the start of each deal, and the winner taking the pot.

Labyrinth ●

Patience game 52

A solitaire with at least one unusual feature.

Take out the four Aces and lay them face up at the top of the table. Your aim is to build each Ace up into a pile of thirteen cards headed by the King, all in the same suit.

Deal the next eight cards face up in a row beneath the Aces. Do any building that can be done, using Twos, Threes, and so on, and immediately fill the space left by each built card with the next card turned from stock.

When you can go no further, deal another row of eight cards across the first eight, overlapping them slightly so all are visible, and regard the result as eight columns of two cards each. Then pause and do any more building that may be possible. From now on, you do not fill any individual spaces left by building off cards, until you can go no further and move on to the next deal. At each new deal you must deal eight cards across the columns before doing any more building.

What makes this game different from others of the same type is that you may take not only the bottom card of each column (the one not covered by another card) for building on the Ace piles, but also, if it fits, the top card of each column, which is covered by all those beneath it. The removal of a card from either end of a column naturally means that the next card that was previously covering it, or was covered by it, is now available for building on an Ace pile.

When you have made six deals in all and have run out of cards, you must hope to be able to complete the building by taking cards from the ends of the columns as before. There is no redeal.

All deals must be made in the same direction, usually from left to right. When you come to the last deal you may find that fewer than eight cards remain. Theoretically, you should deal these in the same direction as far as they will go, but, if no one is looking, you may prefer to select which columns to deal to and which to omit in order to get the game out, to compensate for the fact that there is otherwise little else to cut your mental teeth on.

Lansquenet

Banking game

52

A famous, romantic, and utterly inane gambling game once played by German mercenaries (*Landsknechte*) and at least three musketeers (according to Alexandre Dumas).

One or more players match a stake put up by the banker, who then deals the top card face up to his left and the next face up to his right. If they are of the same suit, he wins, and there is a new round with new stakes. If not, he continues dealing cards one at a time face up to the middle until one appears that matches the suit of either start-card. A left-card match wins for the banker, who may either continue banking or sell this privilege to the highest bidder. A right-card match wins for the punters, and the bank automatically passes to the next in turn.

Lanterloo ▸▸ *Loo*

Let it Ride

Banking game

52

A popular American gambling game.

You start by putting up three identical stakes and receiving from the banker three cards, which you may not show to anyone. The banker deals two face down in front of himself. Your aim—or hope—is that the three in your own hand will form a good ▸ **Poker** hand in combination with the banker's two.

Having examined your cards you may either withdraw one bet or 'let it ride'. The banker exposes one of his two cards and, again, everyone has the option of retrieving another stake or letting it ride. The banker's second card is then faced and everyone shows their hand.

If your three cards plus those of the banker make a pair of Tens or higher, you get paid on each of your remaining stakes at the following rate: Tens or better, stake 1; two pairs × 2; three of a kind × 3; straight × 5; flush × 8; full house × 11; fours × 50; straight flush × 200; royal flush × 1000.

Lift Smoke ▸▸ *Sift Smoke*

Lily Bridge

Variety of Auction ▸ **Bridge**, *c*.1910, in which spades, normally the lowest suit at 2 per trick, could be bid as 'royal spades', or 'lilies', then ranking as the highest at 10 per trick.

Linger Longer ▸▸ *Sift Smoke*

Liverpool Rummy ▸▸ *Contract Rummy*

Lodam, Loadum

Or 'Losing Lodam': an old penalty-trick game ancestral to ▸ **Hearts**.

http://www.davidparlett.co.uk/histocs/lodam

Lomber ▸▸ *Ombre*

Loo

Plain-trick game

Loo, of which many varieties are recorded, belongs to a sprawling family whose more intelligent members include ▸ **Nap**, ▸ **Euchre**, ▸ **Rams** (Rounce), and Spoil Five. It dates from the seventeenth century, was much played by the idle rich in the eighteenth, and got itself a thoroughly bad name in the nineteenth. Enthusiasts are still occasionally met with. The main forms are Three-Card Loo, Five-Card Loo, and Irish Loo, which is Five-Card Loo played with three cards. Let Five-Card be taken as typical.

Everyone contributes five chips to a pool. Deal five cards each, in batches of three then two, and turn the next for trump. Everyone's aim is to win at least one trick, under pain of increasing the pool. For this purpose cards basically rank A K Q J 10 9 8 7 6 5 4 3 2, but the ♣J or 'Pam' (short for 'Pamphilus') beats everything, including the Ace of trumps.

Before play, you each in turn announce which of these you will do:

1. Play with the hand as dealt.
2. Play after discarding any number of cards and drawing the same number from the top of the pack (which you do before the next in turn speaks).
3. Drop the hand and sit the deal out, thereby losing your stake but avoiding any further penalty. (*Variant*: In some circles, this is not permitted when clubs are trump.)

If you hold a flush, whether dealt initially or obtained by drawing fresh cards, you win the deal outright, there being no play. A flush is five cards of the same suit, or four of a suit plus Pam. If more than one has a flush, the best is a flush with Pam; failing that, a flush in trumps; failing that, the flush with the highest top card (or cards if equal). Whoever holds the winning flush wins the stakes of all other players, including those who dropped, but excluding those holding either Pam or a lower flush.

Eldest hands leads to the first trick. If he has the trump Ace (or King if the Ace is the trump turn-up), he must lead it. If not, he must lead a trump if he holds two or more, and it must be his highest trump if there is only one opponent.

Subsequent players must—so far as possible—follow suit, head the trick, and trump if unable to follow. The trick is taken by the highest card of the suit led or by the highest trump if any are played. The winner of each trick leads to the next, and must lead a trump if possible.

If the trump Ace is led, and its player says 'Pam, be civil', Pam may not be played to the same trick, unless its holder has no other trump.

Each player takes one-fifth of the pool for each trick he has won. A player who takes no trick is looed and adds five more chips to the current pool. (*Variant*: In Unlimited Loo, he doubles the pool. This is not recommended.)

Lórum

Penalty-trick game

The Hungarian ancestor of ▸ **Barbu**, dating from the early twentieth century, has some unusual and amusing features. It is normally played with German-suited cards, which I have converted thus: acorns = clubs, leaves = spades, bells = diamonds, hearts unchanged. Details vary, but all accounts contain the same core sequence of four deals.

Deal eight cards to each player from a 32-card pack ranking A K Q J 10 9 8 7 in each suit. Each player in turn deals four times in succession. Each cycle of four consists of the following part-games. The three trick games are played at no trump and eldest leads to the first trick.

1. **No hearts.** For each heart taken in tricks, pay 1 chip to the pot—or, if one or two players took no heart, pay it to each of those who took none. Hearts may not be led to the first trick.

2. **No Queens.** For taking ♣ Q pay 1 chip to the pot, for ♠ Q pay 2, for ♦ Q pay 3, and for ♥ Q pay 4, making a total of 10.

3. **No tricks.** For each trick you take, pay 1 chip to the pot—unless you win all eight, in which case each opponent pays you eight chips.

4. **Kirakó (Domino).** Eldest plays a card face up to the table as the starter of a sequence. The next higher card of the same suit will go to the right of it, the next lower one to the left of it, and so on until the eight-card sequence is complete. Each in turn must either add

the next higher or lower card to this suit sequence, or play a card of the same rank as the starter immediately above or below it. Thereafter, each player may add a card to either end of any one of the suit sequences, or start a new one with a card of the correct rank. Aces and Sevens are consecutive, so when one of them has been placed, the other can go on the vacant side of it. If you can play a card, you must. The first to run out of cards sweeps the pool and, in addition, wins from everyone else as many chips as they have cards left in hand.

Variations. One or more of the following variations may be inserted between the third deal (no tricks) and *kirakó*, which is always played last.

1. King. For taking ♥K, pay 4 chips.
2. Hairy Ape. Like King, but: Players fan their cards face down and hold them up back to front so that each can only identify those held by opponents. Each in turn plays a card at random face up to a trick. If two or more are of the same suit the highest of them takes the trick, otherwise each card 'takes' only itself. Whoever wins ♥K, the eponymous Hairy Ape, pays 10 chips to the pot (or 4, in some circles). If both King and Hairy Ape are played (rare), then ♦J is the Hairy Ape.
3. Club Jack. The player sitting opposite the one who captures ♣J pays 4 chips.
4. Seventh Trick. Whoever wins the seventh trick pays 4 chips and the eighth is not played.
5. All Bad (*Mindenrosz*). All the above applied simultaneously, except that there is no reward for taking all the tricks or all the hearts. (Compare the Russian game of ▸ **Tyotka**.)
6. Railway train (*Vonat*). An adding-up game. Each in turn plays a card to the table and announces the running total of all cards so far played, counting each Ace 11, King 4, Queen 3, Jack 2, Ten 10, others zero. The first to reach or exceed 25 adds 1 chip to the pot, likewise 2 for 50, 3 for 75, 4 for 100.
7. Quarto. A going-out game. Cards rank cyclically, Aces and Sevens being consecutive. The leader plays any card, which is to be followed by the next three consecutively higher cards of the same

suit from the player or players who hold them. The last player turns this quasi-trick face down and starts a new one with any card. Follow the same procedure, ending each trick when no more can be played to it. Whoever first runs out of cards calls 'Stop!' and receives 1 chip for each card in left in each opponent's hand.

Lowball

Any variety of ▶ **Poker** in which only the lowest hand wins the pot.

Macao

Probable ancestor of ▶ **Baccara**, but with only one card dealt.

Madrasso
Point-trick game

This most popular and widespread card game of Venice and its surrounds is a hybrid of ▶ **Tressette** and ▶ **Briscola** and is normally played with the Venetian or Trevigiane patterned 40-card Italian pack, with suits of swords, batons, cups, and coins (respectively equivalent to ♠ ♣ ♥ ♦). Anyone familiar with point-trick games will find it simple to play but strategically deep.

Four players sit crosswise in partnerships and play to the right. A game consists of at least 10 deals (*battute*) and is won by the first side to correctly claim to have reached a target score of 777 points.

The 40 cards rank and count as follows:

A	3	K	Q	J	7	6	5	4	2
11	10	4	3	2	0	0	0	0	0

Deal ten cards each in the following way: three each, two each, one (the twenty-first) face up in front of the dealer to determine trumps, then three each but only two to the dealer, and finally two each.

The dealer's faced card stays on the table until it is played to a trick. Whoever holds the trump Seven may (but need not) exchange it for the turn-up immediately before playing a card to the first trick.

Eldest leads first. You must follow suit if you can, but may otherwise play any card. The trick is taken by the highest card of the suit led, or by the highest trump if any are played, and the winner of each trick leads to the next. If a player revokes, play ceases and the opposing side scores 130 points.

At the end of a deal each side totals the value of counters they have taken in tricks, and the winners of the last trick add 10. As the two totals always make 130 it suffices for one side to write down what they have scored. Normally no running total is kept—one side simply writes their own scores for each deal in a single column.

If after 10 deals one side has scored at least 777 points, it wins. The score of the non-scorekeeping side is calculated by subtracting the scoring side's total from 1300. If neither side has that many, more deals ensue until one side reaches the target.

You can only claim to have reached 777 when you have just won a trick. This ends play and the points so far taken by the your side are counted. If the claim is upheld your side wins, otherwise you lose. If at the end of a deal both sides are found to have more than 777 and neither has declared, the side with the higher total wins.

Winning all 10 tricks in one deal (*cappotto*) wins the game outright, even if the other side has reached 777 points but failed to claim a win.

Manille ⇥ *Comet*

Manille ♠ ♦ ♣ ♦ ♣ ♣
Point-trick game

32

This classic French game derives from Spanish Malilla (Catalan Manilla), and is played mainly in the south-west of the country. Its spread to the rest of France in the early twentieth century was subsequently checked and reversed by the expansion of ▶ **Belote**. It forms a good introduction to point-trick games for players only accustomed to plain-trick games. Of many varieties for various numbers of players, the following are typical.

Manille muette (Silent Manille)

Four players; those sitting opposite each other are partners. The deal and play pass always to the right. Deal eight cards each in fours. Turn the last card (Dealer's) to establish trumps, leaving it face up until the first card has been led.

Cards rank 10 A K Q J 9 8 7 in each suit. The aim is to win a majority (35+) of the 68 points available for tricks and cards. Each won trick counts 1 point and the other 60 are scored for capturing the following cards in tricks:

Each Ten (*manille*)	5
Each Ace (*manillon*)	4
Each King	3
Each Queen	2
Each Jack	1

Eldest leads to the first trick and the winner of each trick leads to the next. You must follow suit and head the trick if you can. If unable to follow to a plain-suit lead you must play a trump if you can, and beat any previous trump if you can. However, if you can neither follow suit nor beat a trump already played you need not trump at all, but may play any card. The trick is taken by the highest-ranking card, or by the highest trump if any are played.

A common game structure is that the overall winners are the side first winning two games. Alternatively, players may agree to play up to a target score, such as 50, 100, etc., over as many deals as necessary, crediting each side with the number of points it makes at each deal, or else (if so agreed) crediting just the winning side with the number made in excess of 34.

Manille parlée (Talking Manille)

A more popular variety permitting spoken communication between partners, as the name implies; but what may be spoken is subject to stringent rules. Upon leading to a trick you may:

- give your partner a single piece of information about your hand, *or*
- request information about his, *or*
- invite your partner to do the same, *or*
- give him some instruction as to the card or suit to be led.

Such information may relate to the number of cards held of a specific suit or rank, or whether a particular card is held. Question and answer must be succinct, explicit, intelligible to the opponents, and not replaced or accompanied by any non-verbal conventions. Questions must be answered truthfully, and instructions followed if possible.

Auction Manille (1)

From three to seven may play, each for himself. Deal out all cards but two or four (depending on the number of players), which constitute a widow. Eldest has first privilege of becoming the declarer; if he declines, it passes to the right until somebody exercises it. The declarer's object is to take at least 21 points in tricks and cards, or at least 15 if more than four are playing. Before play, the declarer may keep drawing cards from the widow until he is satisfied with his hand. Each drawn card must be followed by a discard (which may be the card just drawn) before the next is taken. When satisfied, declarer announces trumps and eldest hand leads.

The amount won by the declarer from each opponent if successful, or paid to each if not, varies with the number of cards exchanged—e.g. 1-2-3-4, 1-2-4-8, 1-3-6-10, as agreed.

Auction Manille (2)

Remove as many Sevens as necessary to enable every player to receive the same number of cards. Each in turn, starting with Eldest, may pass or bid. A bid states the number of points the bidder undertakes to make in exchange for choosing trumps. Each bid must be higher than the last, and a player who has passed may not come in again. The highest bidder announces trumps (or 'No trumps'), and Eldest leads to the first trick— unless the bid was to win every trick, in which case the declarer leads. The player scores the amount of his bid if successful, or loses it if not. The winner is the player with the highest score after any agreed number of deals, each having dealt the same number of times.

Auction Manille (3)

A number of cards is dealt to each player in a particular manner, and the rest are laid some face up and some face down on the table, as follows:

Players	Deal each	Remainder
3	9 (3 3 3)	3 down, 2 up
4	7 (2 3 2)	2 down, 2 up
5	6 (2 2 2)	1 down, 1 up
6	5 (3 2)	1 down, 1 up
7	4 (2 2)	2 down, 2 up

Play as in Version 2, above, except that the highest bidder may exchange cards with the widow before naming trumps. In some circles the score is doubled if the bidder undertakes to win every trick, or plays without exchanging. (If both apply, the score is quadrupled.)

Manni

Plain-trick game

52

Manni is the Icelandic for 'chap' or 'bloke'. Following is Hornafjorður-Manni, of which its Internet contributor says 'It is one of several versions of card games called Manni …The story says that a local minister of our church is the author. This version is the most popular in Hornafjorður as in other parts of the country for the past decades.' Be this as it may, the fact that an identical game is played in Norway under the name Sprøyte, meaning 'squirt', may absolve the Icelandic minister of any such responsibility.

From a 52-card pack ranking A K Q J 10 9 8 7 6 5 4 3 2 in each suit deal a batch of four cards face down to the table to form the *manni*. Then deal batches of three cards to each hand including the *manni* until the *manni* contains sixteen and each player has twelve.

The player at dealer's right cuts the *manni*, shows the bottom card of the top half to determine what game is to be played, then places the top half face down beneath the bottom half of the *manni*. These are the possibilities:

- If the card cut is low (2 to 5), the game is *nolo*. The aim is to win as few tricks as possible. Play at no trump; Ace counts low.
- If it is intermediate (6–10), the game is *trumps*. The aim is to win tricks. The suit of the cut card is trump and Ace counts high.
- If it is high (Jack to Ace), the game is *no trump*. The aim is to win tricks. Play at no trump; Ace counts high.

Before play, eldest may exchange up to seven cards with the *manni*, second-hand can exchange up to five, and dealer up to as many as remain. (If dealer takes his full entitlement, he will get the card that decided the game.) Source does not state whether the exchange involves discarding first and then drawing replacements, or drawing the stated number and then discarding the surplus. The former seems more likely.

Eldest leads. You must follow suit if you can, but may otherwise play any card. The trick is taken by the highest card of the suit led, or by the highest trump if any are played, and the winner of each trick leads to the next.

In positive games each player scores 1 point per trick taken in excess of four, or minus 1 for each trick less than four. In nolo these scores are reversed. Game is 10 points.

Mariage, Mariáš

Mariage (French for marriage), the ancestor of trick-taking games giving a point score for holding the King and Queen of the same suit, survives in the German game now known as ▶▶ **Sixty-Six**, also in the Czech national game of Mariáš and its more elaborate Hungarian relative ▶ **Ulti**.

http://www.pagat.com.marriage/marias.html *and* .../ulti.html

Marjolet
Point-trick game

A simpler relative of ▶ **Bezique** popular in south-west France. The peculiar liaison of Jack and Queen, so characteristic of Bezique and ▶ **Pinochle**, appears here in an unusual form, perhaps suggesting an ancestral version of this feature.

Two players each receive six cards (in twos or threes) from a 32-card pack ranking A 10 K Q J 9 8 7 in each suit. The rest are stacked face down, but with the top card turned for trump and slipped face up half under the pack. If it is a Seven, dealer scores 10 for it.

Game is 500 (or 1000) points over as many deals as necessary, each dealing alternately. Scores accrue for collecting and declaring melds, as detailed below, and for winning brisques (Aces and Tens) in tricks, these counting 10 each.

Elder leads any card to the first trick. Suit need not be followed. The trick is taken by the higher card of the suit led, or by a trump to a non-trump lead. The winner of a trick draws the top card of stock, waits for his opponent to do likewise, and leads to the next. Before drawing, the trick-winner may show and score for any of the following melds:

Four Aces	100
… Tens	80
… Kings	60
… Queens	40
Trump marriage	40
Plain marriage	20

There are two sorts of marriage:

1. King and Queen of the same suit (40 trump, 20 plain).
2. The trump Jack, called 'Marjolet', and any Queen (40 trump Queen, 20 plain).

Any melds you make are left face up on the table and continue to form part of your hand for playing to tricks. So long as you keep Marjolet, you can 'marry' him at different times to different Queens; similarly, you can marry the same Queen to both Marjolet and her matching King. You can score more than one meld at a time.

If you are dealt or draw the trump Seven you may exchange it for the turn-up and score 10, but only upon winning a trick and before drawing. Whoever wins the tenth trick scores 10 for it.

The stock exhausted, players take their melds into hand for the last six tricks. You must now, so far as possible, follow suit and head the trick if possible, and trump if unable to follow. The winner of the final trick scores 10, or 50 for taking all six. You then each sort through your won cards and score 10 for each brisque you have taken.

The winner is the player with the higher score at the end of the deal in which either player reached the target.

Matching games

Games in which the aim is to match cards in some way. As the usual object is to be the first to play out all one's cards, most matching games are also ▸ **Going-out games**.

Matrimony

Gambling game

A nineteenth-century domestic gambling game.

A large sheet of paper is marked with five staking compartments labelled Matrimony, Intrigue, Confederacy, Pair, and Best. Players start with equal numbers of chips.

The dealer first distributes any number of counters in any way he likes between these five compartments, so long as each contains at least two. Each player then takes from his own store one less than the dealer's chosen quantity and distributes them with equal freedom.

The cards shuffled and cut, deal one card face down to each player, followed by a second card face up. If anyone's up-card is ♦A, he sweeps all the chips on the layout, and the cards are thrown in for the next deal by the player on the present dealer's left.

Otherwise, each in turn, starting at Dealer's left, turns up his down-card, and wins the contents of the appropriate staking compartment if his two cards form one of the stated combinations, namely:

Matrimony	Any King and Queen
Intrigue	Any Queen and Jack
Confederacy	Any King and Jack
Pair	Two cards of the same rank.

The contents of *Best* go to the player with the highest card of the diamond suit (Ace high, Two low). Any stake not claimed is carried forward to the next deal.

Mau Mau ▸▸ *Crazy Eights*

Mauscheln ▸▸ *Mousel*

Maw ▸▸ *Twenty-Five*

May I?

A form of ▸ **Contract Rummy**

Michigan

The earliest (1920s) example of a Rummy game in which players aim to score plus points for melds as well as to win by going out first. More advanced versions include ▸ **Oklahoma** and ▸ **Persian Rummy**.

Michigan
Stops game

52

A sociable and family gambling game; the American equivalent of ▸ **Newmarket**.

A staking layout is made from four 'boodle' cards from another pack: Ace, King, Queen, Jack, all of different suits. Each player starts with the same number of chips, not fewer than 20. The turns to deal and play pass always to the left. As the deal is an advantage, the game should end whenever all have dealt the same number of times.

Dealer starts by staking two of his chips against each boodle card, and everybody else stakes one. (*Variant:* Dealer's eight and others' four chips may be distributed ad lib between the boodle cards.) Deal the cards round one at a time as far as they will go, but to one more hand than there are players. The odd hand is called the widow. It doesn't matter if some players have one more card than others.

If dealer does not like his hand, he may discard it face down and take the widow instead. If he keeps it, he may sell the widow (sight unseen) to the highest bidder. Whoever takes the widow must then use it as his playing hand.

Eldest starts by playing a card face up to the table, announcing what it is. He may pick any suit, but must lead the lowest he has of it. For this purpose cards rank, from low to high, 2 3 4 5 6 7 8 9 10 J Q K A. Whoever holds the next higher card of the same suit must play it against the first, also announcing what it is; and so on. A player holding more than one card in ascending sequence may play them all.

A player who plays a card matching one of the boodle cards promptly collects all the chips staked on it in the layout.

Play continues until a stop is reached—whether because an Ace has been played, or because the next card up is in the widow, or because it has already been played. The player of a stopped card, when certain no one can follow, then starts another sequence by leading the lowest card he holds of any different suit from the one just stopped. If he can't change suit, the turn to start passes to the left until someone can play. If no one can play, the hand ends—or (*variant*): whoever played the stopped card leads the lowest card he has.

Play ends as soon as one person runs out of cards, that player collecting from everyone else one chip for each card remaining in their hand (two, in the case of unplayed boodle cards).

Michigan Rummy ▶ *Three in One*

Minnesota Whist

Plain-trick game

52

An extension of ▶ **Norwegian Whist** popular in northern Minnesota.

Four players sitting crosswise in partnerships are dealt 13 cards each, in ones, from a 52-card pack ranking A K Q J 10 9 8 7 6 5 4 3 2 in each suit. Each hand is played either high, in which case each side's aim is to win at least seven tricks, or low, in which case it is to win not more than six. In either case the play is always at no trump. Each player bids high by selecting a black bid-card from their hand, or low by selecting a red, and laying it face down on the table. When all are ready, each in turn, starting with eldest, turns up their bid-card. Since the hand is only played low if all four bid red, as soon as a black card appears the hand is fixed as high and no more cards are turned. The partnership of the player who first showed black is said to have 'granded'.

The player at declarer's right leads to the first trick. Players must follow suit if possible, otherwise may play any card. The trick is taken by the highest card of the suit led, and the winner of each trick leads to the next.

The winning side scores 1 point for each trick taken in excess of six if playing high, or short of seven if playing low. Game is 13 points.

Misère

French for 'poverty': equivalent card terms in other languages include *bettel, contrabola, devole, null, nullo, pobre.* Tricks are played, usually at no trump, and the aim is to win none at all, or as few as possible. This does not allow sufficient variety to constitute a game in its own right, but it is the basis of ▶ **Hearts** and other ▶ **Penalty-trick games**, and provides an optional contract for most games involving an auction.

Miss Milligan
Patience game

A classic Victorian solitaire. Miss Milligan was presumably some kind of recluse, as she very rarely comes out.

Deal eight cards face up in a row. If they include any Aces, take them out and set them up as bases at the top of the table. Similarly, a Two may be taken out and put on an Ace of the same suit, a Three on a Two of the same suit, and so on. Whenever you build such a card in course of dealing, deal the next card to the position that the built card would otherwise have gone to.

Your aim is to release the eight Aces as and when they appear, to set them apart as bases, and to build on each base in suit and sequence up to the Kings.

Besides building to an Ace-pile from the first row, you may also place any card in the row on top of any other that is one rank higher and opposite in colour, such as a red Eight on a black Nine, a black Nine on a red Ten, and so on.

When stuck, deal eight more cards across the ends of the columns or spaces, then pause and play further.

You may transfer cards from column to column either singly, if they are exposed, or in any length of properly packed sequence, provided always that the join follows the rule (descending sequence, alternating colour).

When all the cards have been entered into the game, play continues with building and packing in the same way, except that a space may be filled only with a King, either singly or at the base of a packed sequence.

Weaving. When no more cards remain in stock and the game gets completely blocked, you are allowed a privilege called 'weaving'. This entitles you to remove any exposed card and hold it out as a reserve while you continue building and packing front the card beneath it.

Whenever possible, you may build the reserve card on a main sequence, or replace it on an exposed card one rank higher and of opposite colour.

You may 'weave' single cards in this way as often as you like, but may not hold more than one card out at a time. If the game blocks while you have one out, you lose.

Mittlere

Point-trick game

A Swiss game of the ▸ **Jass** family with several highly unusual features. Its title takes the stress on the first syllable and can be loosely translated as 'Middleman', or possibly 'Piggy in the Middle'.

Deal 12 cards to each player, in batches of three, from a 36-card pack ranking and counting as follows:

In trumps	J	9	A	10	K	Q	—	—	8	7
In plain suits	—	—	A	10	K	Q	J	9	8	7
Card-points	20	14	11	10	4	3	2	0	0	0

The aims of the game are:

- to win at least one trick,
- to take not more than 99 of the 157 trick-points available, and
- to avoid taking the middling number of trick-points.

Note that the Jack and Nine are the highest cards of the trump suit and have special point-values that do not apply to ordinary Jacks and Nines. The total number of card-points available in the pack is 152, but another 5 attaches to winning the last trick, bringing the total to 157.

Play begins at no trump, with all Jacks and Nines ranking in their non-trump positions. As soon as one player cannot follow suit to the card led, the suit of whatever card he plays immediately and automatically becomes trump for the rest of the deal. This means that if a Jack or Nine was played earlier, and lost the trick, whoever won it will have to count it as 20 or 14 respectively instead of 2 or 0 points!

With three players there will be either one winner, who scores 2 game points to the others' minus 1 each, or one loser, who scores minus 2 to the others' plus 1 each. Specifically:

- If everyone takes at least one trick but under 100 points, the player in the middle loses.
- If you take either no tricks or 100+ points, you lose.
- If one player takes no tricks and another one takes 100+, then the third player (with the middling number) wins.
- If you take all 12 tricks, you win.

A game is 12 deals.

☞ *Note.* Sources do not state what happens if two players tie, but a logical outcome would be that the third should win if he has at least one trick and not more than 99 points, and lose otherwise.

Monte

Monte (related to *mountain*) is the Spanish for a gambler's stack of coins or gaming chips—hence 'the full monte' (or 'monty') means betting everything you have on the next turn. The name is applied to any form of three-card Poker, and also denotes a sideshow guessing game akin to Find the Lady.

Monte Bank

is a Mexican gambling game played with the 40-card Spanish pack. Two cards dealt from the bottom of the pack form the bottom layout, then two from the top form the top layout. Punters individually stake on either layout. The top card of the pack is then turned face up and placed between them. This is called the 'gate'. The dealer pays all stakes set against a layout containing a card matching the suit of the gate, and collects all stakes set against a layout not containing a card of matching suit. These five are discarded, five more are dealt, and so on until all cards have been used.

Mouche

An old French game much like Five-Card ▶ **Loo** but lacking 'Pam'.

Mousel

Plain-trick game

This popular Danish family game (also played in Germany under the name Mauscheln) is best for four. It is played for small stakes and may be regarded as a variety of ▶ **Nap**. The title means (1) to talk Yiddish, (2) to fiddle, in its non-musical sense—perhaps more like 'diddle'.

The dealer forms a kitty and deals two cards face down to each player, then one card face up to establish trumps, and finally two more each face down. Cards rank A K Q J 10 9 8 7 in each suit.

Each in turn has one opportunity to say 'I'll diddle', which is an undertaking to win at least two tricks. If no one will diddle, the cards are thrown in and the next in turn deals. Otherwise, everyone else must either 'Go along', which is an undertaking to win at least one trick, or 'Pass', in which case they take no part in the hand. If no one will go along, the diddler wins the kitty without having to play, and the cards are thrown in for the next deal.

Given two or more players, each in turn may either stand pat or discard from one to four cards face down from his hand, receiving the same number from the top of the pack. This may only be done once.

The diddler leads to the first trick. Subsequent players must, so far as possible, follow suit and head the trick, and trump if unable to follow (in which case it is not necessary to beat a previous player's trump). The trick is taken by the highest card of the suit led or by the highest trump if any are played, and the winner of each trick leads to the next.

Each trick earns its winner one quarter of the kitty. A player winning no trick, or the diddler if he wins only one, pays the amount of the kitty into the kitty for the next deal. If the diddler wins none, he is a 'diddle-twit' (*Mauschelbete*), and pays double that amount.

Optional extra. ♦ 7 ('*Belli*') may be made the second-highest trump.

Mrs Mop (Patience) ⟶ Spider

Muggins
Going-out game

52

A game played by Victorian children, including Mr Pooter (*see Diary of a Nobody*).

Deal one card face up to the table if three play, four if four, two if five, four if six, three if seven. These cards are the mugginses. Divide the rest evenly among the players. Players may not examine their cards but must stack them face down on the table in front of themselves. The aim is to be the first out of cards.

Each in turn flips the top card of his stack and places it face up on a muggins that is one rank higher or lower than the one turned—for example, a Six turned will go on a Seven or a Five. Aces and Kings may not be played on each other.

Anyone unable to place the card they turn must place it face up on the table before them to start a discard pile. Thereafter, a turned card must be played to a muggins if possible, otherwise to the next higher- or lower-ranking card on top of the faced pile of the nearest player to one's left, otherwise—if it won't legally fit anywhere—to one's own discard pile, where it need not match.

Anyone who is correctly challenged for breaking a rule—by discarding to his own pile if it will fit that of a player nearer his own left, or to a player's pile if it will fit on a muggins—is himself a Muggins. Everybody else takes the top card from their face-down pile and gives it to the offending Muggins, who must place them at the bottom of his own.

When no cards remain in your playing pile, turn your discard pile face down and continue from there. The winner is the first to have no cards remaining in either their playing or discard pile.

Mus

An unusual ▶ **Vying** game originating in the Basque country of France and Spain and now widely played throughout the Spanish-speaking world. It has the extraordinary feature of being a four-player partnership game (try introducing that into Poker!), and, as if that were not enough, partners are permitted to communicate certain card holdings to each other by means of conventional signals—a procedure that would not be countenanced in the wildest forms of Dealer's Choice. Mus is simple in structure, but complicated in detail. See:

http://www.pagat.com/vying/mus.html

Mustamaija

Going-out game

One of several Scandinavian going-out games, this one is known as Mustamaija in Finnish and Spardame ('spade Queen') in Norwegian. For a longer game, or more players, it may be played with a double pack but with one ♠Q removed. *See also* ▶ **Wan Maria** (Kitumaija).

From three to five players receive five cards each $(3 + 2$ or $2 + 3)$ from a 52-card pack ranking A K Q J 10 9 8 7 6 5 4 3 2 in every suit, except that ♠Q is not a spade but an entirely independent card. The rest are stacked face down.

The aim is play all your cards out, and especially to avoid being the last player left in and holding ♠Q, known as Mustamaija ('Black Maria').

The game is played in a series of bouts. Eldest starts the first bout by playing face up to the table from one to five cards of the same suit, which may include ♠Q if the others are spades.

Next, dealer turns the top card of the stock to establish trumps. If it is a spade, bury it and turn again until some other suit appears. Then half cover the turn-up with the remainder of the pack face down as a stock.

This is what you do on your turn to play:

1. If the previous player took cards from the table, leaving none face up, start a new bout by playing face up to the table from one to five cards of the same suit.

2. If the previous player left one or more cards on the table, you may beat as many of them as you can and will by placing upon each one either a higher card of the same suit, or, if it is a plain suit, any trump. Discard face down from the game all the cards you beat, and those you beat them with. In this connection:

   - ♠Q can neither beat nor be beaten by any other card, and must therefore always be taken up.
   - If you leave any cards unbeaten, add them to your hand.
   - If you beat them all, start a new bout (as above).

If at the end of your turn you have fewer than five cards in hand, whether you started a new bout or had to take unbeaten cards, draw from stock until you either have five again or the stock runs out.

When the stock is empty, the leader to a bout may not play out more cards than are held by the next in turn to play. Players drop out as they run out of cards. The last left in will be holding ♠Q and is designated Black Maria.

My Ship Sails
Collecting game

A children's game, possibly related to an early seventeenth-century gambling game recorded (but not described) as 'My Sow Pigg'd'. *See also* ▶ **Donkey**.

Deal seven cards each and ignore the rest. The aim is to get seven of a suit. All play simultaneously by repeatedly giving a card face down to his left-hand neighbour and receiving one from his right. The winner is the first to get seven alike, lay his hand down, and call 'My Ship Sails'.

Nain Jaune ('Yellow Nun') ▶▶ *Pope Joan*

Nap
Plain-trick game

28 → 52

Or Napoleon: a simplified relative of Euchre played widely, and with many variations, throughout Northern Europe. Despite its title and Napoleonic allusions, it is not recorded before the last third of the nineteenth century. It is best for four to five players using a stripped pack.

Deal five cards each, either in ones or as batches of 3 + 2, from a 52-card pack ranking A K Q J 10 9 8 7 6 5 4 3 2.

Eldest bids or passes first, and each in turn thereafter must bid higher or pass. A bid is an undertaking to win at least the number of tricks stated, using a trump suit of one's own choice. From low to high, the bids are: two, three, miz (lose every trick), four, Nap (five), Wellington (five, for double stakes), Blücher (five, for redoubled stakes). Wellington may only follow a bid of Nap, and Blücher a bid of Wellington.

The highest bidder leads to the first trick. The suit of the card led is automatically trump—except in a bid of miz, if players have previously agreed that miz is played at no trump. Subsequent players must follow suit if possible, but otherwise may play any card. The trick is taken by the highest card of the suit led, or by the highest trump if any are played, and the winner of each trick leads to the next.

If successful, the bidder wins from each opponent 2–4 units for bids of two to four respectively, 3 for miz, 10 for Nap, 20 for Wellington, 40 for Blücher. If not, he pays the same amount to each opponent, though it may be agreed to halve it in the case of Nap, Wellington, and Blücher.

The turn to deal passes to the left, and it is customary not to shuffle the cards until a bid of five has been won.

There are many variations on the basic theme. The skill factor may be increased by stripping the pack of lower numerals so that the number of cards in play is from six to eight times the number of players. Four would therefore use 28 or 32 cards (Eight or Seven low), five 36 or 40 cards (Six or Five low). A Joker may be added, counting as the highest trump—or, in miz, as the only trump. Many other variations may be encountered or invented.

Napoleon at St Helena

Patience game

There are several slightly differing versions of this solitaire, which is also known as Forty Thieves.

Deal 10 cards face up in a row, then 10 more face up across them, and so on until you have 10 piles of four. Spread them slightly into columns so that all are identifiable. Hold the remaining 12 face down as a stock.

Your aim is to set the Aces out, as and when they become available, and build each one up in suit and sequence to its King.

Turn cards from stock and play them if possible or else discard them face up to a single wastepile.

The top card of the stock, the top card of the wastepile, and the top card of each of the 10 layout piles are available for play. An available card may be used for starting a sequence if it is an Ace, or for continuing a sequence built on an Ace if it fits.

Alternatively, it may be placed on the top card of one of the layout piles if it is of the same suit and next lower in rank. Only one such card may he moved at a time. When a column is emptied you may fill the space it leaves with any available card—not necessarily immediately, as you may prefer to wait for a better one to become available.

There is no redeal.

Napoleon's Favourite (Patience) ▸▸ *Spider*

Neuner ▸▸ *Switch*

Newmarket
Stops game

52

A mild, sociable gambling game suitable for family play. Rules vary. Here are those of my local community centre in south London.

Each player deals in turn. Set the four Kings out in the centre as a staking layout. Deal the rest out one at a time, with the last card of each round going to an extra 'dead' hand. It doesn't matter if some players get one more card than others. Everybody stakes an agreed amount on each King and to a separate kitty.

A game is several deals and ends when all the Kings have gone.

One player may 'buy' the spare hand in exchange for the hand dealt him. Dealer has the first option, which passes to the left until someone exercises it. Whoever buys pays a fixed stake to the common kitty, except the dealer, who exchanges free.

Cards run A 2 3 4 5 6 7 8 9 10 J Q. Whoever holds the lowest diamond starts by playing it face up to the table. The holder of the next higher consecutive diamond plays it, then the next, and so on for as long as the sequence continues. Cards are played face up in front of their holders, not to a spread on the table.

Eventually the sequence will come to an end, usually because the next higher diamond is in the dead hand. In this case a new sequence is started by the player of the last card. That player must start with a suit of different colour, and with the lowest card held of it.

Example. A leads ♦ 3–4, C plays ♦ 5, B adds ♦ 6–7. No one has the Eight. B, holding ♠ 3–9–J ♥ A–2–9–Q ♣ 8–Q ♦ 2, must play either ♠ 3 or ♣ 8.

If that player has none of the required colour, the turn to start a new sequence passes to the left until someone can change colour. If no one can, the round ends and the next deal ensues.

Alternatively, the sequence ends when someone plays a Queen. That player immediately wins everything staked on the King of that suit, and starts a new sequence with the lowest card held of a different colour. The stripped King is then removed, and remains out of play till the end of the game. In subsequent deals, whoever plays the Queen of an absent King has nothing to win, and merely starts a new sequence.

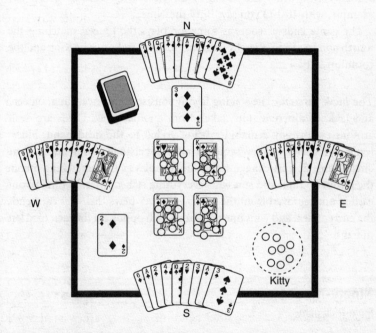

Newmarket. West dealt. No one bought the spare hand, though South should have, holding too many low cards and an imbalance of black and red suits. The lowest diamond was led by West and followed by North, who played ♠4 when the ♦4 failed to appear. The play continued ♠4–Q, ♦5–Q, ♣5, ♥A–3, ♣A–4, 'No reds', ♥9–10, ♣Q, ♥6, and East is out. It is unusual for three Kings to be dismissed in one deal.

The deal ends in either of two ways. Whoever plays the last card from their hand thereby ends the play and wins the common kitty. Alternatively, it ends when a sequence has been finished and no one can change colour to start a new one, though all have at least one card in hand. In this case the common kitty is carried forward and increased on the next deal.

When only one King remains, a new rule applies. If dealt the Queen of that King's suit you say 'Bury the Jack' (or 'Johnny'). Whoever holds the Jack, if it is not in the dead hand, must then swap their hand for the dead one, free of charge. If you hold both Queen and Jack, or any longer sequence, you order the burial of the next lower card or cards. For example, with 10-J-Q you say 'Bury the Nine'.

The game ends as soon as someone plays the Queen matching the fourth and last King, thereby winning both the stake on the King and the common kitty.

The book version. The staking layout consists of an Ace, King, Queen, and Jack, of different suits, taken from another pack. Cards are dealt around evenly, any remainder being added to the dead hand. Eldest leads. The starter of a new sequence need not change colour, but in some circles must at least change suit. Whoever plays a card matching one in the layout by rank and suit wins everything staked on it, but the layout card is not removed from the table. Whoever plays their last card ends the current deal and wins one chip from each opponent for each card left in hand.

Ninety-Nine
Plain-trick game

36 → 52

I invented Ninety-Nine as a more challenging version of three-hand ▸ **Whist**, or a three-player substitute for ▸ **Bridge**. Having found its way into many card-game books it may now be regarded as established. It is based on the historically recent idea of bidding to win an exact number of tricks rather than a minimum number. The original form is described first, followed by versions for other numbers of players.

Ninety-Nine for three

Three players use a 37-card pack ranking A K Q J 10 9 8 7 6 in each suit, plus a Joker. A game is nine deals. Deal 12 each in ones and turn the next face up to establish trumps. If it is the Joker or a Nine, play at no trump. The Joker has no permanent value of its own but adopts the identity of the card turned for trump: whoever holds it treats it exactly as if it were that card.

You each discard three cards face down and play the other nine to tricks. Your aim is to win exactly the number of tricks indicated in code by the suits of your discards. For this purpose, each discarded—

$$\spadesuit = 0 \text{ tricks}, \quad \spadesuit = 1 \text{ trick}, \quad \heartsuit = 2 \text{ tricks}, \quad \clubsuit = 3 \text{ tricks}.$$

Example: You can bid three by discarding ♠ ♠ ♠ or ♥ ♠ ♦ or ♣ ♦ ♦, nine by discarding ♣ ♣ ♣, none by ♦ ♦ ♦, and so on.

After the discard, but before the opening lead, each in turn from the dealer's left may offer to 'declare' or 'reveal', thereby increasing his potential bonus or penalty.

- To declare means to turn your bid-cards face up so that the opponents know how many tricks you are aiming for;
- To reveal means not only turning your bid-cards up but also playing with your hand of cards face up on the table.

Only one player may declare or reveal. Priority goes to the player nearest the dealer's left, but an offer to reveal takes priority over an offer to declare. Players may not change their bid-cards once anyone has stated that they will or will not declare or reveal.

Eldest leads to the first trick. You must follow suit if you can, but may otherwise play any card. The trick is taken by the highest card of the suit led, or by the highest trump if any are played, and the winner of each trick leads to the next.

If at end of play you have won exactly the number of tricks you bid you must turn your bid-cards face up to prove it. (Otherwise you are not obliged to show them.) You always score 1 point per trick taken, regardless of your bid. If you made your bid, you add a bonus of:

> 10 each if all three succeeded
> 20 if only two succeeded
> 30 if the only one to succeed

Ninety-Nine. (a)The shape of each suit shows how many tricks it stands for when bidding. (b) Five different ways of bidding the hand shown, one for each suit and one for no trumps.

There is also a bonus of 30 for declaring or 60 for revealing. This goes to the declarer if he succeeds, or to each opponent if he fails. (Thus the maximum possible score is 99, made when the only player to succeed bid and made nine, and he or another player revealed.)

A game is nine or 18 deals.

Variant. There is no Joker. The first deal is played at no trump. Thereafter, the trump suit is determined by the number of players who succeeded in their bids on the previous deal: diamonds if none, spades if one, hearts if two, clubs if three. Game is 100 points. A match is won by the first to win three game.

Ninety-Nine for four

Use 52 cards (Joker optional) and deal 13 each. A discard of three diamonds may be used to represent a bid of either zero or ten tricks: there is no need to say which was intended. There are no declarations or revelations, and if all succeed there is no bonus for doing so.

Ninety-Nine for five

This is best played with the 60-card Australian '500' pack containing Elevens and Twelves in each suit. Deal 12 each, discard three, and play nine tricks. The bonus for succeeding is 10 per player who failed.

Ninety-Nine for two

Use 24 cards (Nine low, Joker optional) and deal 12 each. There are no declarations or revelations. The first time you succeed, you get a bonus of 10. The bonus for each successive success goes up by 10—that is, 20 for the second, 30 for the third, and so on until you fail. The next time you succeed, you start at 10 again; and so on. (*Variant*: Deal 16 each from a 32-card pack, discard three, and play 13 tricks. A bid of ♦ ♦ ♦ represents 0 or 10; ♠ ♦ ♦ is 1 or 11; and so on.

Point Ninety-Nine (for two)

This is a point-trick game played with a 32-card pack ranking and counting as follows: Ace 11, Ten 10, King 4, Queen 3, Jack 2, zero each for 9-8-7. The total number of card-points is 120, there being 30 in each suit.

Deal 16 cards each, discard three bid-cards, and play 13 tricks. The suit of each bid-card represents a number of card-points as follows:

$$♦ = 0, ♠ = 10, ♥ = 20, ♣ = 30 \text{ card-points.}$$

So, for example, a discard of ♥ ♥ ♠ is a bid to capture cards totalling 50 card-points in tricks.

Non-dealer leads to the first trick. The rules of trick-taking are slightly unusual, namely: You must follow suit if you can, otherwise may play any card. There are no trumps, but each trick is taken by the higher-ranking card *regardless of suit*, or by the second played of two equally high cards. In other words, if you can't follow suit, you can 'trump' by playing an equal or higher card to the one led.

At end of play, both sets of bid-cards are revealed and each player scores 1 point for each card-point by which the other exceeded or fell short of their bid. For example, if you bid 50 and took 49 or 51 card-points, your opponent scores 1 point, and so on.

In addition, you score a bonus of 30 for taking exactly the number you bid, 20 for taking 1 more or less than your bid, or 10 for taking 2 more or less than you bid.

Game is 100 points.

☞ *Note.* Any card-points contained in the bid-cards are out of play and do not count towards either player's total. For example, if one player bids 50 with ♥K-♥9-♠J (6 card-points), and the other bids 40 with ♣A-♠9-♠8 (11 card-points), then the total number of card-points in play will be 103 (that is, 120 less 17).

Ninety-Nine

Adding-up game

Deal three cards each in ones and stack the rest face down. Play goes to the left initially (clockwise), but may change. Each in turn plays a card face up to the table, announcing the total face value of all cards so far played, and draws a replacement from stock. The total may not exceed ninety-nine. The first player unable to play without busting loses a life. The first to lose three lives is the overall loser.

Cards count as follows:

Black Ace	*Any*	Seven	7
Red Ace	1	Eight	8
Two	2	Nine	*makes* 99
Three	0	Ten	*minus* 10
Four	0	Jack	10
Five	5	Queen	10
Six	6	King	10

A black Ace brings the total to anything you like, from 0 to 99.

A Nine automatically makes the total 99, and can therefore be followed only by a Three, Four, Ten, or black Ace.

A Jack, besides counting 10, reverses the order of play—that is, the next card is played by whoever played the card preceding the Jack.

Noddy

Ancestor of ▸ **Cribbage**.

http://www.davidparlett.co.uk/histocs/noddy.html

Nomination Whist

Plain-trick game

52

A relative of ▸ **Solo Whist** reportedly popular in the Royal Navy, though the title is also used as an alternative for ▸ **Oh Hell**!

Deal thirteen each from a 52-card pack ranking A K Q J 10 9 8 7 6 5 4 3 2. Each in turn bids or passes. The lowest bid is seven, and each subsequent bid must be higher than the previous one. A bid is the number of tricks you undertake to win in exchange for naming trumps and playing either alone against the other three or with a temporary ally against the other two. The highest bidder then announces trumps and names a card, e.g. 'Hearts, Ace of spades'. The holder of the named card becomes his ally, but says nothing, revealing himself only by playing that card or obviously supporting the bidder by his play. The bidder may name a card in his own hand, in which case he is playing alone; but this fact, too, will only become known from the play.

The bidder wins from each opponent if successful, or pays to each opponent if not, one unit for each trick bid. A successful slam (13 tricks) wins or pays 26, but if the slam is made when not bid (e.g. 11 bid, 13 taken) the bidder pays 13 instead. If there was an ally, he and the bidder win from or pay to one opponent each.

Norwegian Whist

Plain-trick game

52

Trumpless trick games are typically Scandinavian. A version of this game is also played in America under the name ▸ **Minnesota Whist**.

Four players sitting crosswise in partnerships receive thirteen each from a 52-card pack ranking A K Q J 10 9 8 7 6 5 4 3 2. Each in turn, starting from the left, may pass or bid. There are only two bids, and the first to name one establishes the contract for himself and partner. If the bid is 'grand', each partnership's aim is to win most tricks (seven or more); if 'nullo', it is to win fewer tricks (not more than six). If three pass, dealer must bid.

At grand, the opening lead is made by the player at bidder's right; at nullo, at his left. Subsequent players must follow suit if possible, but otherwise may play any card. The trick is taken by the highest card of the suit led, and the winner of each trick leads to the next.

At nullo, the side taking fewer tricks scores 2 points per trick taken by the other side.

For a successful grand, the bidding side scores 4 points for each trick taken in excess of six. If unsuccessful, the other side scores 8 for each trick taken over six. (*Variant*: If the bidding side succeeds, it scores 5 for *every* trick it took; otherwise, the other side scores 6 for every trick it took.)

Game is 50 points.

Obstacle Race

Adding-up game

A German game (*Hindernislauf*), with some unusual features.

For adding-up purposes, cards count as follows:

Ace	1	Ten	10
King	4	Nine	9
Queen	3 or −3	Eight	8
Jack	2	Seven	7

☛ *Note.* Queens are the only rank able to reduce the current total.

Deal the cards out evenly. If other than four play, the two left over are laid face up on the table to start the sequence, and the dealer announces their combined point-total.

Each in turn plays a card face up to the sequence, announcing the combined total of all cards so far played. The 'obstacles' are 55, 66, 77, 88, 99, and 111. A player scores one point for bringing the total to exactly an obstacle number, but loses a point for skipping over one without making it exactly. These apply whether the obstacle is reached forwards or, by the play of a Queen, backwards.

Play continues until the total reaches or exceeds 120, then starts again at zero. The winner is the player with the highest score when all cards have been played.

Oh Hell!

Plain-trick game

Also called Blackout, Botheration, Jungle Bridge, Nomination Whist, Oh Well!, Oh Pshaw!, etc., the following party game for otherwise serious card-players first appeared in the early 1930s and is sometimes credited to Geoffrey Mott-Smith. It explores the unusual idea of bidding to take an exact number of tricks (others are listed under ▶ **Plain-trick games**) and works best for four or five players.

Use a 52-card pack ranking A K Q J 10 9 8 7 6 5 4 3 2 and appoint a scorekeeper, who should rule a sheet into as many columns as there are players and note the name or initials of one player at the head of each column. The number of deals to a game depends on the number of players.

Whoever cuts or draws the lowest card deals first. Cards are always dealt face down and one at a time. On the first deal, deal the cards round as far as they will go so that everyone receives the same number. If any remain, leave them face down to one side but turn the top card to establish trumps. If none remain, play at no trump.

Starting with Eldest, each in turn examines his hand and announces how many tricks he proposes to take, from 'none' to the maximum possible. The scorekeeper notes that number down in the appropriate column, as well as the total number of tricks to be played in that deal, and announces whether the total number of tricks bid fall short of, equals, or exceeds the number to be played. Each player's object is to take exactly the number of tricks he bid, neither more nor fewer.

Eldest leads to the first trick. Subsequent players must follow suit if possible, but otherwise may play any card. The trick is taken by the highest card of the suit led, or by the highest trump if any are played, and the winner of each trick leads to the next.

A player who took what he bid scores that number plus 10. One who failed scores nothing for that deal. The scorekeeper notes each player's total in the appropriate column, and on subsequent deals sums the score totals as he goes along.

Each subsequent deal is made after thorough shuffling by the next in turn to deal, and is played in exactly the same way as described above.

However, the number of cards dealt decreases by one at each deal, so that on the last deal (seventeenth if three play, thirteenth if four, etc.) only one card each is dealt and only one trick played.

The winner, of course, is the player with the highest score at the end of the one-card deal.

The following variations may be encountered, in various combinations:

1. One card is dealt on the first round, 2 on the second, and so on as far as possible.

2. No-trump hands may be avoided by not dealing all cards out when they could go round exactly, but, where necessary, leaving out of play as many cards as there are players.

3. The dealer, as last to bid, may be prohibited from bidding a number which would bring the total bid to the number of tricks in question, so at least one player is bound to fail.

4. Scoring: (*a*) Score 1 point per trick taken, whether bid or not. (*b*) A successful bid of zero scores 5 points, or (*c*) 5 plus the number of tricks played in that deal. (*d*) In any deal consisting of five or more tricks, there is a bonus of 50 for successfully bidding a slam (winning every trick), or 25 for a small slam (all but one).

5. Originally, the number of cards dealt was always as many as possible, and the game was played up to 100 points. Somewhere along the way Oh Hell! seems to have hybridized with Knockout Whist to produce the format described above.

Oklahoma

Rummy game

One of the few species of ▸ **Rummy** worth retaining from the Rummy explosion of the 1930s and 40s, Oklahoma (also called Arlington) has the rare merit of being good for three players.

Shuffle together two packs and (optionally) a Joker. The turn to deal and play passes regularly to the left. Deal 13 cards each one at a time, turn the next face up (the up-card) to start a wastepile, and stack the rest face down beside it to form the stock.

The aim is to make melds consisting of (*a*) three or four cards of the same rank—not more, and not necessarily of different suits; or (*b*) three or more cards in suit and sequence. For this purpose, cards run A 2 3 4 5 6 7 8 9 10 J Q K. Ace may count high or low (A-2-3 or A-K-Q), not both (K-A-2 illegal), but a sequence may be extended to fourteen cards with an Ace at each end. The Joker and all Deuces are wild, and may be used to represent any desired card in a set or sequence. Deuces, however, are 'natural' if forming part of a sequence between Ace and Three, or if melded together as a set of three or four.

Each in turn, starting at Dealer's left, has one opportunity to take the upcard, which he may do provided that he immediately incorporates it in a valid meld laid face up on the table with two or more cards from his own hand. If so, he ends his turn by replacing the upcard with a face-up discard, and play continues from his left.

If no one takes the first upcard the player at Dealer's left begins play. This is what you do on your turn to play:

- Draw the top card of stock and add it to your hand, or draw the top card of the wastepile and use it immediately in a meld. This may be a new meld, or the card may be added to a meld you have already made, either continuing the sequence, or being the fourth of a set of three. Having taken and used the upcard, you must then take the whole of the wastepile into hand.
- Start one or more new melds of three or more cards each, or lay off one or more cards to melds you have already made.
- End your turn by making one discard face up to the wastepile. You may not discard a ♠ Q unless you have no other card. The wastepile is kept squared up, not fanned out.

When using a wild card in a meld, you must state exactly what it represents, and may not later change it.

Whoever melds the Joker may later replace it with the natural card it represents, taking the Joker back into hand for future use or discard. This may only be done by the player who melded it, and Deuces may not be so replaced at all.

Play ceases the moment someone runs out of cards, whether or not they make a final discard. The player who went out scores a bonus of 100. Alternatively, it ends when someone takes the last card of the stock and reaches the end of his turn, in which case there is no bonus (unless the last player goes out).

Each player then scores plus for cards he has melded and a minus for cards left in hand, as follows:

	Plus	Minus
Joker	100	200
♠Q	50	100
Ace	20	20
Deuce (unmelded)	–	20
K Q J 10 9 8 (except ♠Q)	10	10
7 6 5 4 3 (and 2 if natural)	5	5
Deuce (as Eight or higher)	10	–
Deuce (as Seven or lower)	5	–

A player counting more against than for will get a negative score, which is deducted from his running total. The overall winner is the first to reach 1000 points over as many deals as necessary.

Old Maid

Going-out game

A popular Victorian game, often played with proprietary cards specially designed for children. Derived from an ancient gambling game in which the loser pays for the drinks, it is known in Germany as *Schwarzer Peter*, 'Black Peter', and in France as *Vieux Garçon*, 'Old Boy', the odd card being a Jack. You could add a Joker instead of removing a card, and then call it 'Old Joke'.

If more than six play, use two packs shuffled together. Remove ♠ Q from the pack and deal the rest around as far as they will go. It doesn't matter if some players have one more card than others. The aim is to get rid of all your cards, and especially to avoid being left over with an odd Queen—the 'old maid'—in your hand.

Each player starts by examining his hand and discarding, face down, any pairs of cards of the same rank he may hold (two Sevens, two Jacks, etc.). This done, Dealer starts by offering his hand of cards face down to his left-hand neighbour, who draws one and adds it to his hand. If this gives him a pair, he discards it. Whether he discarded or not, he then offers his hand face down to his left neighbour. As players empty their hands by discarding pairs, they drop out of play. Eventually there will be only one player left, holding an unpaired Queen. He is the loser, and pays a forfeit. Or (to drag it out) loses a life, a forfeit being paid by the first to lose three lives.

Ombre

English name (pronounced 'umber') for the classic Spanish game of Hombre which swept Europe in the seventeenth century and became a craze at the court of Charles II. It is still played in Spain under the name Tresillo, in South America as Rocambor, in Denmark as l'Omber, and (at time of writing) at Cambridge University under the name Tridge. It remains a brilliant game, one of the best for three players, but suffers from more needless complications than can be accommodated in these pages. For a simpler development, *see* ▶ **German Solo**.

http://www.pagat.com/lhombre/lhombre.html (*Danish game*)
http://www.pagat.com/lhombre/tresillo.html (*Spanish game*)
http://www.tridge.net (*Cambridge game*)

Pai-Gow Poker

Banking game

A banking game currently popular in American casinos, Pai-gow is not really a form of Poker, since it does not involve vying, but is based on a Chinese Domino game in which *pai-gow* denotes a seven-card hand containing no pairs. *See also* ▶ **Caribbean Stud** and ▶ **Chinese Poker** (so-called).

Each player banks in turn, unless some other method of rotating the bank is agreed.

The punters each put up a stake and are dealt seven cards apiece, face down, from a 53-card pack including a Joker. All but the dealer examine their cards and split them into two hands, one of five and one of two cards.

Your aim is to split them in such a way that *both* of them which will beat those of the banker when his turn comes to play. For this purpose your five-card hand will be rated as a ▶ **Poker** hand. The Joker, if held, is not completely wild, but may only represent an Ace, or whatever card may be necessary to complete a straight, or flush, or straight flush.

☛ *Note.* Four Aces and a Joker beats a royal flush. In some circles, A 2 3 4 5 is the second-best straight after 10 J Q K A.

In the two-card hand, a pair beats a non-pair, but no other combination counts.

The five-card hand must outrank the two-card. For example, if the two cards are a pair of Aces, the five cards must contain two pairs or better. Players may not discuss their hands at any time.

When the punters have placed their hands face down, the dealer exposes his seven cards and similarly forms them into a five-card and a two-card hand. The other players may not touch their cards once the dealer's have been shown.

As between the dealer and each punter, if both the dealer's hands beat both the punter's, the dealer wins the punter's stake; if both the punter's beat the dealer's, the dealer pays the punter the amount of his stake. If either hand is tied, the dealer's beats the punter's. If each of them wins one hand, it is a 'push' (stand-off).

Palace ⇥ *S**thead*

Pan (*Panguingue*)

A casino variety of ▶ **Rummy** much played in the American west, especially Reno and Las Vegas. It requires eight 40-card packs (A 2 3 4 5 6 7 J Q K), with ten or more spades stripped out. The most intelligible account of this elaborate game is that of Mac James, *Pan: The Gambler's Card Game* (Las Vegas 1979).

> http://www.pagat.com/rummy/panguingue.html
> http://www.bridge-information.com/panguingue.html

Pandour, Pandur ▸▸ *Jass*

Parliament ▸▸ *Domino*

Paskahousu
Going-out game

This drinking game is an elaborate and more strategic variety of ▸ **Cheat**. It comes from Finland and its name translates as 'Shitpants'. For a Russian equivalent, *see* ▸ **Verish' ne Verish'.**

Deal five cards each and stack the rest face down. The aim is to avoid being the last player with any cards left in hand.

Each in turn, starting with eldest, may either pass or start a discard pile by playing a card face down to the table and saying 'That's a Three', whether truthfully or not. If everyone passes, there is another round in which the first discard is stated to be a 'Four'; and so on until someone actually does play a first card.

After that, each in turn must play one or more cards face down to the discard pile and declare them to be any rank equal to or higher than the last rank announced (subject to restrictions below).

Whenever somebody makes such a play, and before their cards are covered by the next player, they may be challenged to prove their call by turning the card or cards in question face up. If they are what their player said they were, the challenger must add the whole discard pile to his hand, leaving an empty table. If not, the challenged player must do likewise. In either case, the turn then passes to the left of the challenged player.

Certain rules and restrictions govern particular ranks, as follows.

- You may not call a Jack, Queen, or King unless the previous call was Eight(s) or higher.
- You may not call an Ace unless the previous call was a Jack, Queen, or King, or unless the discard pile is empty.
- You may call a Two at any time, but a Two may be followed only by another Two.

- If you call a Ten or an Ace (following a Jack, Queen or King), and are not challenged, you remove the discard pile from play, face down, leaving an empty space. You then start a new pile by playing and calling any card from your hand. If the next player then calls a Ten or an Ace, the player after that must add it to their hand, leaving the next in turn to start a new pile.

Instead of playing from your hand to the table, you may draw the top card of stock, so long as any remain, and either add it to your hand, thus ending your turn, or play it face down to the table (without first looking at its face) and claim it to be any legal rank. You may even do this at the start of the game and claim it to be a Three.

The last player left with any cards in hand is designated 'Shitpants', and has to buy the next round.

Patience (Solitaire)

A card game usually (but not always) for one player, and usually (but not always) based on taking cards from one or more shuffled packs and arranging them into regular suit-sequences in accordance with rules of arrangement and rearrangement. As there are such things as competitive and interactive patiences it is more useful to apply 'patience' to any game of the arrangement type, regardless of the number of players, and solitaire to any game for one player, regardless of what type it is. Card solitaires described in this book are: Accordion, Aces Up, Bristol, Buffalo Bill, Calculation, Chaos, Clock, Cromwell, Curds and Whey, Demon, Fair Lucy, Flip Flop, Freecell, Gaps, Golf, Heads and Tails, Interregnum, Klondike, Labyrinth, Miss Milligan, Napoleon at St Helena, Penguin, Poker Patience, Pyramid, Quadrille, Salic Law, Scorpion, Spider, St Helena, Strategy. For competitive games, *see* Poker Squares, Racing Demon, Spit, and Spite and Malice.

Pelmanism

Memory game

A children's game, also called Memory.

Shuffle the cards and deal them face down at random all over the table. The aim is to collect pairs of matching ranks (two Kings, two Fives, etc). Each plays in turn. On your turn, you pick up two cards and look at them without letting the others see. If they are a two of a kind you win them; if not, you return them face down to the same positions. Winning a pair entitles you to an immediate second turn.

Penalty-trick games

Trick-taking games where the aim is to avoid winning tricks, or, more usually, to avoid winning specified penalty cards in tricks. The best-known example of its type is ▶ **Hearts**, but *see also*: Barbu, Bassadewitz, Black Maria, Bugami, Ciapanò, Coteccio, Cucumber, King, Knaves, Lórum, Polignac, Slobberhannes, Tyotka.

Penguin
Patience game

Penguin is my more challenging version of a popular old game called Eight Off. It is available as computer software, and experts have demonstrated quite convincingly that, tough as it may appear at first sight, it should with perfect play come out at least 95 per cent of the time.

Deal seven cards face up in a row from left to right (assuming you are right-handed, otherwise reverse all the following references to handedness).

The first card, at top left, is the 'beak'. As you deal, whenever you turn up a card of the same rank as the beak, put it to one side as a base.

Complete the body of the penguin by dealing seven cards face up in a row across the first row, then seven more, and so on, until you have dealt out seven rows of seven and have set aside three cards of the same rank as the beak. Spread these piles towards you so that they look like seven columns of seven, with all 49 cards identifiable.

Your aim is to build each base card up into a complete suit-sequence, turning the corner from King to Ace as necessary. For example, if the beak and the base cards are Jacks, the sequence continues Q-K-A-2-3-4-5-6-7-8-9-10. The beak itself is the fourth base card, but it cannot he put in place until you have played all the cards initially covering it.

The exposed card at the end of each column is available for building on a main sequence or for packing on another column in the layout. Pack the layout columns in suit and descending sequence, turning the corner from Ace to King where necessary.

A properly packed sequence ending in an exposed card may be shifted as a whole, provided that the join follows the rule.

A space made by clearing out a column may he filled only with a card one rank lower than the bases (a Ten, in the above example), either alone or at the bottom of a packed sequence headed by an exposed card.

During play you may move any exposed card into a reserve called the 'flipper', which at any time may contain a maximum of seven cards. Every card in the flipper is available at any time for building on a main sequence, for packing back in the layout, or for filling a space in the

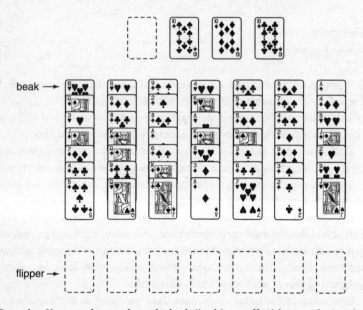

Penguin. You can always release the beak (in this case ♥10) by transferring the cards covering it to the flipper, which can hold up to seven cards at a time. But that is not necessarily the best way of starting. This particular deal came out readily enough.

layout if it is one rank lower than a base. It is therefore possible to free the beak immediately by playing the six cards that cover it into the flipper, though this usually creates more problems than it solves.

Penneech

Point-trick game

52

This nippy little game is described in detail only in *The Compleat Gamester* of 1674 and is obviously as dead as a dodo. But it contains the unique feature of changing trumps at each trick, and is too much fun to omit. Since the scoring is continuous and the target score is 61, the game is conveniently scored on a Cribbage board.

Whoever cuts the lower card deals first and the turn to deal alternates. Deal seven cards each, in ones, stack the rest face down, and turn the top card for trump. If your hand contains nothing higher than a Ten you may show it and demand a new deal.

Your aim is to win card-points in tricks, and to win the last trick.

The rank and scoring value of cards from highest to lowest is: Ace 5, King 4, Queen 3, Jack 2, followed by 10 9 8 7 6 5 4 3 2. These numeral cards have no point-value, but with this exception:

The highest card of the diamond suit is ♦ 7, called Penneech. Whenever diamonds are trump it is therefore bound to win the trick, and entitles you to peg 7 points. When diamonds are not trump it has no pegging value, but still outranks all other diamonds.

Having turned the first card for trump and pegged its value (if any), dealer leads to the first trick. When following to a trick you may either follow suit to the card led or play a trump, as you prefer, but you may not discard from any other suit unless unable to follow.

The winner of each trick pegs the scoring value of any counting-card or cards it may contain, turns down both the trick and the trump turn-up, and turns the next from stock. The suit of this card is the trump for the next trick, and if it is a counter the player who turned it pegs its value. Play continues in this way, with a new trump turned for each successive trick.

The winner of the seventh and last trick turns up the next card of stock and, if it is a counter, pegs its card-point value. If Penneech itself is turned, it pegs 14 instead of seven.

Finally, the player who won a majority of the seven tricks pegs an additional point for each card taken in excess of seven.

The game ends as soon as one player reaches 61 and pegs out.

☛ *Note.* The rules of trick play are not actually given, and it may be that you are obliged to follow suit if you can. However, the rule given here, borrowed from the contemporary game of All Fours, increases the skill factor and gives the game more bite.

Pennies from Heaven

Rummy game

| 54 | 54 | 54 | 54 |

An apparent forerunner of ▶ **Hand and Foot**, typically played in partnerships and preferably by six players, with partners sitting alternately.

Jokers (eight of them) and Deuces are wild. Deal each player 13 cards as the initial playing hand, then deal 11 cards face down in a stack. Only when you have completed a canasta do you pick these 11 up and add them to your hand. Though playing in partnership, you keep your own melds in front of you. You may lay cards off to your own or a partner's melds, but the seventh card to your qualifying canasta must come from your own hand before you can take up your 11 'pennies from heaven'.

At each turn draw two from stock and discard one. If the upcard is wild you cannot take the pack; otherwise, you can only take it by melding the upcard with two natural cards from hand. Wild-card melds are valid, and a wild canasta scores 1000 points.

Sevens are significant. No canasta may contain more than seven cards. Both partnerships must have completed at least one canasta of Sevens before any Seven can be discarded, and you cannot discard a Seven in going out. The canasta of Sevens may be natural or mixed, and in either case scores 1500 points.

Pepper ▶▶ *Euchre*

Perdivinci ▶▶ *Ciapanò*

Persian Rummy
Rummy game

56

Few Rummies are designed for partnership play. This is one of the best. It dates from the 1930s, and may be regarded as a relatively sober forerunner of the more elaborate ▸ **Canasta**.

Partners sit crosswise. A game is two deals. Use a 56-card pack, including four Jokers with backs identical to one another and the rest of the pack. Deal seven each one at a time. Turn the next face up to start the discard pile, and stack the rest face down beside it.

The aim is to collect and display melds. A meld is three or four cards of the same rank, or three or more cards in suit and sequence from 2 3 4 5 6 7 8 9 10 J Q K A. Ace counts only high. Jokers are not wild, but may only be melded together as a set of three or four. Each in turn, starting from the player left of Dealer, must draw, may meld, and must then discard.

Draw. You can always draw the top card of the stock and add it to your hand. Alternatively, you may draw the top card of the discard pile (which should be fanned slightly so that all remain visible), provided that you immediately use it either to start a new meld or to lay it off to an existing meld made by either side. In this case you must also take all the other cards of the discard pile, and may meld as many of them as you can and will. Any that you cannot meld are not added to your hand but must be left face up on the table before you. These, however, still count as part of your hand and may therefore be melded or discarded as if you were in fact holding them.

Meld. Having drawn a card, you may make as many melds and lay-offs as you can, laying all such cards face up on the table before you. A new meld must contain at least three of a kind or three in suit-sequence. If you meld four of a kind in one turn, they count double, and you indicate this fact by squaring them up instead of fanning them out. You may lay off a card that matches any meld on the table, regardless of who made it, but must place any such lay-off on the table before you as part of your own scoring cards. You must also, therefore, announce which meld it belongs to. For example, if there are melds of three Fives and of ♥6 7 8 on the table, and you lay off ♥5, you must state whether it extends the set or the sequence. If the sequence, any player may subsequently lay off ♥4 to it, otherwise not.

Discard. You end your turn by making one discard face up to the discard pile—unless you have none left to discard, in which case play ceases.

Play continues until one player goes out by melding, laying off or discarding his last card. If the stock runs out, players continue by drawing from the discard pile as long as they can and will. Play ceases when the player in turn goes out, or cannot legally draw, or will not do so.

Score. Cards count at face value from Two to Ten, courts 10 each, Aces 15, Jokers 20. Each player scores these values for all cards in his melds (remembering that immediate fours of a kind count double), and from this total subtracts the total face value of all cards left in hand, even if they could be used to start or extend melds.

A partnership's score is that of both its members added together. If one member ended the play by going out, his side counts 25 extra. At the end of the second deal (dealt by the player to the left of the first dealer), the side with the greater total scores, for settlement, 50 plus the margin of victory.

A nice feature of this game is the possibility of signals, or conventional plays. Early on, the discard of an Ace—unless immediately following a meld—asks one's partner to discard a Joker if possible; similarly, discarding a card worth 10 calls for an Ace.

Phat

Point-trick game

This variety of ▸ **Don** was first described in print in 1976 by pub-game researcher Arthur Taylor, who found it 'played on a highly organized league basis in and around Norwich'. Recent information on the Internet suggests that it is more popular in Scotland and northern England.

Four players sitting crosswise in partnerships are dealt 13 cards each, in ones, from a 52-card pack ranking A K Q J 10 9 8 7 6 5 4 3 2 in each suit.

The aim is to score points for capturing certain cards in tricks. There are two sets to be scored, known respectively as the Phat and the Muck. Points for the Phat are pegged as and when tricks are won containing the specified cards. Points for the Muck are not scored until all the tricks have been played and won. Scores are recorded by pegging on a yard-long Phat board, which resembles a Cribbage board but is half as long again, with 90 holes on each side. (They can, of course, be recorded equally well on an actual Crib board, or in writing.)

The phat		**The muck**	
trump Ace	4	each Ace	4
trump King	3	each King	3
trump Queen	2	each Queen	2
trump Jack	1	each Jack	1
trump Nine	18	each Ten	10
trump Five	10		
each other Nine	9		
each other Five	5		

(In Scotland, the trump nine is called the 'Big Don' and the trump five is the 'Wee Don'.)

The player at dealer's left is the 'pitcher' and leads to the first trick. The suit of the card pitched automatically fixes trumps for the deal. You must follow suit if you can, but may otherwise play any card. The trick is taken by the highest card of the suit led, or by the highest trump if any are played, and the winner of each trick leads to the next.

During play, a side that wins a trick containing one or more cards of the phat immediately pegs their scoring value.

After play, each side calculates the card-point value of all the cards of the muck that they have taken in tricks, as listed above, and the side counting the greater aggregate value pegs an additional eight holes. If both sides tie with 40 (there being 80 card-points in all), the eight-point bonus is carried forward to the next deal.

Game is twice round the board—that is, 181 holes. This usually takes four deals. If it runs to a fifth, one side is bound to peg out before all the tricks have been played.

Pig ▸▸ Donkey

Pink Nines
Stops game

A pub game collected by Arthur Taylor (*see also* ▸ **Phat**), this time in Bletchley. Related to ▸ **Newmarket**, it more closely resembles its seventeenth-century French ancestor ▸ **Comet**.

Everyone stakes an agreed amount to a pool. Deal thirteen cards each if two or three play, and stack the rest face down. If more play, deal four face down to one side and the rest around as far as they will go.

The aim is to run out of cards by playing them to a single sequence on the table. The running order for this purpose is A 2 3 4 5 6 7 8 9 10 J Q K A 2...etc.

Eldest leads by playing out his longest sequence of cards, regardless of suit. When unable to continue, the next in turn carries on, if he can, from the next numeral in sequence. For example, if the first played J-Q-K-A-2 and stopped, the next in turn would start with Three. If the next player cannot continue, the turn keeps passing until someone can. If no one can, the person who played last may play any card or sequence ad lib.

'Pink Nines' are ♥ 9 and ♦ 9. These are wild, and can be used to represent any desired card.

First out of cards wins the pool.

Pinochle
Point-trick game

This all-American game was originally introduced by German immigrants under its name Binokel, from French Binocle, a variety of ▸ **Bezique** still played in Württemberg and parts of Switzerland.

Two-hand Pinochle is in effect two-hand Bezique played without the Sevens and Eights. Auction Pinochle is considered the best three-handed form, if not the best version altogether. As adaptations for more than five seem somewhat artificial, the four-hand partnership game is worthiest of description here. This, too, comes in several basic forms, each with its own local variant rules.

Partnership Auction Pinochle

Four players sit crosswise in partnerships. The turn to deal and play passes always to the left. The 48-card pack is a double pack of 24, with no cards lower than Nine. The rank of the cards for trick-taking purposes, and their point-values when captured in tricks, are:

	Ace	Ten	King	Queen	Jack	Nine
Modern	10	10	5	5	0	0
Traditional	11	10	4	3	2	0

Decide first whether to follow the modern American or traditional European count. Then deal 12 cards each in batches of three.

Each side aims to score 1000 or more points over as many deals as necessary. Points are scored for cards captured in tricks, at the rates shown above, plus 10 for winning the last trick, making 250 in all. Extra points may be scored in advance of play by individual players (on their partnership's behalf) for holding any of the following card melds:

Flush (A 10 K Q J in trumps)	150
Royal marriage (K Q in trumps)	40
Plain marriage (K Q in non-trump suit)	20
Hundred Aces (four Aces, one per suit)	100
Eighty Kings (four Kings, likewise)	80
Sixty Queens (four Queens, likewise)	60
Forty Jacks (four Jacks, likewise)	40
Pinochle (♠ Q ♦ J)	40
Dix ('deece') (= trump Nine)	10

☛ *Note.* If you score for a flush, you may not additionally score for the royal marriage it automatically contains.

An auction follows the deal. A bid is the minimum point-score a player declares that his partnership will make from melds and tricks if allowed to name trumps. Eldest is obliged to make an opening bid of at least 100. (*Variant*: 200.) Each in turn may pass or name any higher bid that is a multiple of 10. A player who has once passed may not bid again. A bid followed by three passes becomes the contract, and the declarer then names trumps.

Eldest leads to the first trick. (*Variant*: Declarer leads first.) As each person plays to the first trick, he announces, shows, and scores for any melds that he may have and wish to count. Subsequent players must follow suit and head the trick if possible; if unable to follow, they must play a trump, and beat any trump already played if possible. The trick is taken by the highest card of the suit led, or by the highest trump if any are played. Of identical winning cards, the first played beats the second. The winner of each trick leads to the next.

The bidding side counts its score first. If they took at least the amount bid, they score whatever they make; if not, the amount of their bid is deducted from their score. If the bidding side thereby reaches or exceeds 1000, they win, and the opponents do not then score. Otherwise, the opponents score everything they make—unless they fail to win a single trick, in which case their melds are annulled and they score nothing.

Auction Pinochle for three

The following is typical of several similar versions.

Deal 15 cards each in threes. After the first three, lay three aside, face down, as a *widow*.

Eldest bids first. The minimum bid is 300 (variable by agreement). Each in turn must either raise by any multiple of ten or else pass, in which case they cannot bid again. The highest bidder aims to score at least as many as he bid by (*a*) scoring for melds, and then, if necessary, (*b*) completing the deficit by winning counters in tricks.

The bidder turns the widow face up and announces trumps. From the eighteen cards in his possession he shows and scores for as many as possible of the following melds listed in the table above (for Partnership Pinochle).

If the bidder has already fulfilled his bid, there is no play and he scores the value of his game (*see* below). If not, and he doubts whether he can, he may concede immediately. He then loses only his game value (*single bête*), as opposed to twice that amount for playing and failing (*double bête*).

To play, the bidder takes all 18 cards into hand and discards face down any three which have not been used in melds. Any counters among them will count in his favour at end of play. He then leads to the first trick. On a plain-suit lead, follow suit if possible, otherwise trump if possible. On a trump lead, follow suit and head the trick if possible. A trick is taken by the highest card of the suit led, the highest trump if any are played, or the first played of two identical winning cards. The side winning the last trick scores 10.

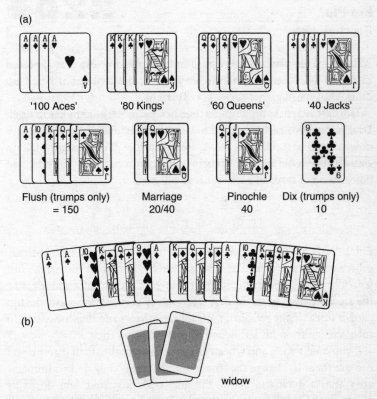

(a)

'100 Aces' '80 Kings' '60 Queens' '40 Jacks'

Flush (trumps only) = 150   Marriage 20/40   Pinochle 40   Dix (trumps only) 10

(b)

widow

Pinochle. (a) Melds and scoring features. (b) In three-hand Auction Pinochle, this hand melds 210 (80 Kings, pinochle, royal marriage, two common marriages, dix) and should certainly be bid up to 350. Any one of five cards in the widow will increase this by anything up to 150, so a bid of 400 would not be extravagant.

If successful, you score or receive from each opponent an agreed game value related to the size of the bid; if not, you lose or pay it double. A game valuation scheme might be 1 unit or game-point for a bid of 300–40, 2 for 350 +, 3 for 400 +, 5 for 450 +, 7 for 500 +, and so on.

All scores are doubled when spades are trump; many also rate hearts triple. Some award side-payments for special melds, such as 5 for a 'roundhouse' (four marriages, one per suit), flush 4, double pinochle 2, hundred Aces 2, four different Kings 1, likewise Queens or Jacks.

Pip-Pip

Point-trick game

52 | 52

A fun game for players experienced in trick-play, Pip-Pip first appeared in the 1920s. It sounds thoroughly English, but looks as if based on central European games such as ▶ **Tysiacha**.

Two 52-card packs are shuffled together. Each deal is complete in itself. Deal seven cards each, turn the next for trumps, and stack the rest face down on top of it. The aim is to score points for (*a*) changing the trump suit when possible and (*b*) capturing card-points in tricks. The rank and point-value of cards in each suit is as follows:

$$\begin{array}{ccccccc} 2 & A & K & Q & J & 10\,9\,8\,7\,6\,5\,4\,3 \\ 11 & 10 & 5 & 4 & 3 & 0 \text{ each} \end{array}$$

Eldest leads to the first trick. You must follow suit if you can, but may otherwise play any card. The trick is taken by the highest card of the suit led, or by the highest trump if any are played. Of identical winning cards, the second played beats the first. The winner of each trick draws the top card of stock (if any remain), waits for the others to do likewise—each in turn starting from his left—then leads to the next trick.

If you hold a King and Queen of the same suit other than trumps, you can use them to change the trump suit. You may only do this immediately after a draw and before the next trick is started. You do so by placing them both face up on the table before you and calling 'Pip-pip!'. This gives you an immediate score of 50 points. The two cards remain on the table but continue to belong to your hand until played to tricks. Neither of them may be used individually to 'pip' a second time, but the same suit can be 'pipped' again with the other marriage pair after the trump has been changed to a different suit. If two players pip before the same trick, both score 50, and the suit is changed to that of the second one called. If both are called simultaneously it changes to that of the elder of the players concerned (the one reached first counting round to the left of the dealer).

When the last card is drawn from stock, play continues until everyone has played out all their cards. It does not matter if some players have one fewer card than others and so cannot play to the last trick.

Everyone scores all their pips plus the total of card-points they have taken in tricks.

☞ *Comment.* You may prefer to follow this more natural scoring schedule:

A	10	K	Q	J	10 9 8 7 6 5 4 3
11	10	5	4	3	0 each

Piquet

Plain-trick game

32

Piquet (or Picket, if you prefer traditional English pronunciation and terminology), is widely regarded as one of the greatest of all two-player card games, the others being ▸ **Cribbage**, ▸ **Sixty-Six**, and possibly ▸ **Gin Rummy**. It is also considered to be of French origin and the national card game of France, though the origin is debatable and the French now prefer ▸ **Belote**. The fact that rules vary but slightly from country to country is remarkable, given the many centuries over which it has been played throughout Europe.

Rubicon Piquet

The following description is based on the English rules of 'Rubicon Piquet' as laid down by the Portland Club in 1882.

A game, or *partie*, is six deals. If the loser fails to reach 100 points by the end, he is 'rubiconed' and loses extra.

Cards rank A K Q J 10 9 8 7 in each suit. The player cutting the higher card deals first and the deal alternates. The dealer is known as Younger hand and the non-dealer as Elder.

Deal 12 each in twos or threes. (Not twos and threes mixed, and whichever you choose on the first deal you must stick to throughout the partie.) Spread the remaining eight face down between the two players. These form the 'talon'.

In each deal, players discard and draw replacements with a view to forming scoring combinations and to winning a majority of twelve tricks at no trump. Scores are carried forward in writing at the end of each deal, but as they are made little by little it is convenient to use a mechanical marker or Cribbage board.

Blank (*carte blanche*). If you are dealt nothing but numerals (no face cards), you may score 10 for a blank. You must declare it immediately, and subsequently prove it by dealing your cards rapidly, one by one, face up to the table. As Younger, however, you need not prove it until Elder has exchanged.

The exchange. Elder must discard, face down, at least one card and not more than five. He then replenishes his hand by drawing the same number from the top of the talon. If he exchanges fewer than five, he may secretly look at those he would have been entitled to take but did not. Younger may then (but need not) discard any number of cards up to as many as remain—usually three, sometimes more. If he leaves any untaken, Younger may either show them to both players or leave them unseen, but may not see them alone.

Combinations. The players now state what combinations they hold in the following order. In each class, Elder always declares first. If Younger has a higher combination of the same class, or any combination of a class in which Elder has none, he says 'Not good' and scores it himself. If he cannot match it, he says 'Good', and Elder scores. If he says 'Equal', neither scores.

1. *Point.* Whoever has the longest suit scores 1 point for each card in it. If equal, the point goes to whichever of the matched suits has the highest value, counting Ace 11, courts 10, numerals at face value. If still equal, neither scores for point.

2. *Sequences.* A sequence is three or more cards in suit and sequence. Whoever has the longest sequence scores for it and any other sequences he may declare. If both tie for longest sequence, it goes to the one with the higher-ranking cards. If both still tie, neither scores for sequences. Sequences of three and four score 3 and 4 respectively, five to eight score 15 to 18 respectively.

3. *Sets.* A set is three or four cards of the same rank but not lower than Tens. Three is a *trio* and scores 3, four a *quatorze* and scores 14. Any quatorze beats any trio, and as between equal sets a higher-ranking beats a lower. A tie is impossible.

Elder then summarises the scores he has made so far, leads a card to the first trick, and adds 1 point 'for leading'. Younger, before playing a card, then fully identifies and scores for any combinations he holds which enabled him to describe Elder's as 'Not good', and announces his total score for combinations.

Repique. If either player reaches 30 for combinations before the other has scored any, he gets a bonus of 60 for *repique*. For this purpose, points accrue strictly in order blank, point, sequence, sets.

Examples

1. Suppose Elder scores a point of 7, sequences of 15 and 4 and 3, and 3 for a trio, total 92. Normally this would give him an extra 60 for repique. However, if Younger had already called a blank, the repique would be thwarted because the blank counts first.

2. Suppose neither scores for point or sequence because Younger replied 'equal' to both. If Younger then calls two quatorzes and a trio for 31 he wins the repique. But he would not do so if Elder had scored for blank, point or sequence, which all count first.

Pique. If Younger scores nothing for combinations, and Elder reaches 30 as the result of scoring 1 point for each card he leads to a trick in unbroken succession, then Elder gains a bonus of 30 for *pique*. Younger cannot score for pique, being prevented by Elder's '1 for leading'.

Tricks. Elder leads to the first trick. Follow suit if possible, otherwise play any card. There is no trump. The trick is taken by the higher card of

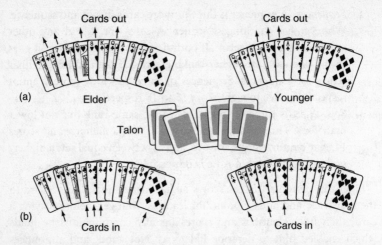

Piquet. (a) Elder keeps his diamond point and hopes for the fourth King. Younger, having to keep his King and Queen suits guarded and wishing to retain three Tens for a possible fourth, could discard three hearts, or an Eight and two Sevens. (b) After an unhappy draw, Elder calls first. E: Point of five.—Y: Worth?— E: 47.—Y: Not good.—E: Three Kings.—Y: Not good. Elder leads ♦A. Younger declares 'Point of five, *5;* (sequence of) three in spades 8; fourteen Tens 22' and follows Suit. Elder's bare ♠K causes him to lose seven tricks, leaving him a net score for the hand of 8 to Younger's 22 plus 8 for tricks and 10 for cards, total 40.

the suit led, and the winner of each trick leads to the next. In play, either player scores 1 for leading to a trick, and 1 for capturing a trick led by the opponent. The winner of the last trick scores '1 for last'.

Cards and capot. Winning seven or more tricks scores 10 'for cards'. Winning all twelve scores an additional 30 (40 in all) for *capot*.

Game. In the unlikely event of a tied score after six deals, two more deals are played. If the loser has reached the rubicon of 100, the winner's final game score is 100 plus the difference between their two scores. If not, it is 100 plus the *total* of their two scores.

Scoring variations. Some countries award 50 for *carte rouge*—a hand in which every card forms part of a scoring combination.

I have developed and recommend the following variations. First, you can seek to acquire a void suit after the exchange. A void counts as a 'point of nought' counting 50½ and scores 5 if good, and as a 'sequence of nought' ranking between an Ace-high and King-high sequence of five for a score of 15 if good. The play of tricks is considerably enlivened by awarding the bonus of 10 points not for winning a majority of tricks but for winning the last trick.

Piquet au Cent

Piquet was originally played up to 100 points over as many deals as it took, as opposed to the Rubicon game of exactly six deals—in fact, the original name of the game was Cent, or Saunt, meaning one hundred.

Pirate

Bridge variant

A variety of ▸ **Bridge** which replaces fixed with floating partnerships, so that you all play for yourselves in the long run. It was first described in 1917 by R. F. Foster, one of its principal developers. Critics say the players with the best-matched hands in each deal will always find each other and usually make their contract, but if you dislike fixed partnerships you may prefer to find this out for yourself. The following outline of basic essentials assumes a knowledge of Bridge.

Dealer bids first. If all pass, the hands are thrown in. When a bid is made, each in turn thereafter must either accept it, thereby offering himself as dummy in partnership with the bidder, or pass. If no one accepts, the bid is annulled, and the turn to bid passes to the left of the player who made it. There is no need to overcall an unaccepted bid. For example, if South opens 'two diamonds', and no one accepts, West may call anything from 'one club' upwards. If no one accepts any bid, the hands are thrown in.

Once a bid is accepted, players to the left of the accepter may bid higher, double, or pass. If all pass, the accepted bid becomes the contract. A new bid need not differ in suit from an accepted bid, and may itself be accepted by its previous bidder or accepter, thereby denying the originally proposed alliance. An accepted bidder may himself try to break an alliance by naming a new contract when his turn comes round; but that alliance stands if no higher bid is accepted.

A double reopens the bidding, giving the would-be allies a chance to bid themselves out of the alliance by naming another bid in the hope that someone will accept it. Or they can stay with the accepted bid, and redouble if confident enough to do so.

A contract established, declarer leads to the first trick, his partner lays his hand down as a dummy, and play proceeds as at Bridge. Auction or Contract scoring may be followed, the score being noted above or below the line in the column of each of the players involved.

Pishti

Fishing game

52

A Turkish member of the fishing family, also called Pashta. Four may play singly or as partners.

Deal four cards each, four face down in a pile, and turn the top card of the pile. You each in turn play a card face up to the pile, and if it matches the top card by rank (not suit), you win all the cards in the pile, leaving the next player with no option but to start a new one by playing any card. When each has played four cards, four more are dealt, and so on until all cards have been played and won. Capturing a pile consisting of a single card ('pishti') scores 10 points immediately. At end of play, you each sort through your won cards and add any of the following scores that may apply:

For taking most cards	3 (unless tied)
For the ♦ 10	3
For the ♣ 2	2
For each Ace taken	1
For each Jack taken	1

The winner is the first to reach 100.

Optional bluffing rule. When a pile contains only one card, the next to play may play a card face down and claim 'pishti'. If unchallenged, he wins it and scores 10. Otherwise, the card is revealed. If it matches, he wins both and scores 20; if not, the challenger wins them for 20.

Pitch

Point-trick game

52

An American development of ▸ **All Fours**. *See* ▸ **Cinch**.

Deal four players six cards each, in two rounds of three, from a 52-card pack ranking A K Q J 10 9 8 7 6 5 4 3 2.

The aim is to win as many as possible of the four points for High, Low, Jack, and Game.

- **High** scores to the person dealt the highest trump in play.
- **Low** scores to the player capturing the lowest trump in play.
- **Jack** scores to the player capturing the Jack of trumps (if in play).
- **Game** scores to the player taking in tricks the greater value of card-points, counting each Ace 4, King 3, Queen 2, Jack 1, and Ten 10.

Each in turn, starting with Eldest, may pass or make a higher bid than any so far made. Bids range from 1 to 4, representing the number of points for high, low, Jack, and game, which the bidder offers to win in return for choosing trumps.

The highest bidder starts play by leading to the first trick. This is called 'pitching', and the suit of the card pitched automatically becomes trump. You are free to follow suit or play a trump, as you prefer, but may only discard if unable to follow suit. The trick is taken by the highest card of the suit led, or by the highest trump if any are played, and the winner of each trick leads to the next.

The points for high, low, Jack, and game go to whoever wins them. There is no point for Jack if the trump Jack was not dealt, nor is there for game if players tie for taking the most card-points. If the pitcher fails to score as many as he bid, his bid is deducted from his score. In this case he is said to be set back, and Setback is an alternative name for the game.

Game is 7 or 11 up, as agreed. If two or more reach the target in the same deal, the pitcher wins if he is one of them; if not, the winner is the first to reach seven on the basis of counting points strictly in order (high, low, Jack, game). The winner receives 1 unit from everyone else, or 2 from whoever scored less than one.

Variations.

1. Dealer may become the pitcher by equalizing the last bid made. If all pass, however, he must bid at least one.

2. A player with a negative cumulative score may 'smudge'—i.e. bid four and, if successful, thereby win the game outright. This may not be taken over by Dealer.

3. 'Racehorse Pitch' is Auction Pitch played with a 32-card pack, Seven low.

Plain-trick games

Games in which all tricks are equal in value, so that win or loss depends solely on the number of tricks taken. The term contrasts with ▶ 'point-trick' and ▶ 'penalty-trick' (or 'trick-avoidance') games. The following are described in this book:

For two players: Bohemian Schneider, Chinese Whist, Double Dummy, Ecarté, German Whist, Honeymoon Bridge, Imperial, Piquet, Put, Truc, Watten. (Imperial and Piquet also involve melds.)

For three players: Bismarck, Booby, Chinese Whist, Five Hundred, Manni, Mousel, Ombre, Ninety-Nine, Preference, Sergeant Major, Tribello, Watten.

For four players (solo): Belgian Whist, Boston, Brandle, German Solo, Mousel, Nomination Whist, Pirate, Solo Whist.

For four players (partnership): Alkort, Aluette, Auction Forty-Fives, Bid Whist, Biritch, Bridge, Brus, Calypso, Cayenne, Chinese Whist, Contract Whist, Dutch Whist, Euchre, Five Hundred, Forty-One, Israeli Whist, Kaiser, Minnesota Whist, Norwegian Whist, Pepper, Ruff, Spades, Truc, Vint, Whist (classical).

For six players (partnership): Brus, Euchre, Five Hundred, Sizette, (solo) Sixte.

For any number of players, including five: Beast, Best Boy, Bourré, Euchre, Femkort, Five Hundred, Forty-Five, Julep, Knockout Whist, Loo, Nap, Ninety-Nine, Oh Hell!, Rams, Romanian Whist, Sift Smoke, Toepen, Twenty-Five (best for five players).

Play or Pay

Stops game

A simple relative of ▶ **Newmarket**.

Deal all the cards out as far as they will go. Eldest starts by playing any card face up to the table to start a discard pile. Each in turn thereafter must either play the next higher card of the same suit or else pay a counter to a pool. The sequence ends when it reaches an Ace, or any other card that can't be followed. Whoever played the last card of the sequence starts a new one with any card. First out of cards wins the pool, plus 1 chip for each card left in other players' hands.

Plus and Minus ▸▸ *Red and Black*

Poch

Gambling game

Poch or Pochen is a popular German gambling game, still played but now quite domesticated, of great antiquity, being first mentioned in 1441. It subsequently spread throughout Europe in several different forms, giving rise to—amongst others—the French game of Poque, from which Poker derives. (*See also* ▶ **Three in One**.) It has two striking and distinctive features. One is that it involves a circular board of traditional design containing several staking compartments, one for each winning card or combination. The other is its division into three phases of play. The first stake goes to whoever has been dealt the highest cards, or certain specified cards. The second is won by successfully vying or bragging (*pochen*) as to who holds the best combination. The third is won for either drawing to 31 or, at a later date, playing the cards to a sequence as at Newmarket. This structure underlies such other historic games as Belle, Flux, Trente-et-Un, and the original three-stake form of Brag. The second element, that of vying or bragging, has since become isolated as the sole mechanism of modern Brag and Poker, which latter derives its name from *pochen*, 'to knock', via the French game of Poque.

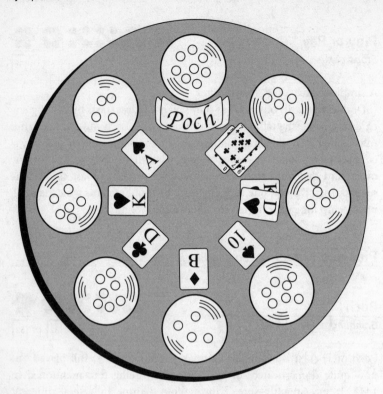

Traditional Poch board.

From two to four players use a 32-card pack (A K Q J 10 9 8 7); more than four use 52. There are three phases to the game.

1. **Betting.** Players dress the board by placing chips in the first seven of eight compartments labelled Ace, King, Queen, Jack, Ten, Marriage, Sequence, and Poch. Five cards each are dealt and the next is turned for trump. The stakes for Ace, King, Queen, Jack, and Ten go respectively to the players dealt those particular trumps. That for marriage goes to the holder of both King and Queen of trumps, in addition to the individual stakes for King and Queen. Sequence is won by anyone dealt the 7-8-9 of trumps. Unclaimed stakes are carried forward to the next deal.

2. **Vying.** Next, players vie as to who holds the best combination. A quartet beats a triplet, a triplet a pair, and a pair an unpaired hand,

with ties determined by the highest card. The first to bet places a stake in the poch compartment, saying '*Ich poche eins*' ('I bet one', or however many). Each in turn must either add the same amount or drop out of this phase of play. The opener may raise it when his turn comes round again. When he does not, there is a showdown and the best hand wins everything staked on Poch.

3. **Outplay.** Finally, the cards are played out in sequences. The winner of the previous round starts by playing the lowest card of his longest suit. The next higher card of the same suit (in order 2 3 4 5 6 7 8 9 10 J Q K A) is then played by whoever holds it, and the next, and so on, until the sequence ends either because the Ace is played or because the next card up has not been dealt. The player of the last card then begins a new sequence (and, in some circles, receives one chip from each opponent). This continues until a player wins by playing out the last card from his hand. The others pay him one chip for each card left in hand.

Point-trick games

Games in which win or loss depends on the point-value of certain cards captured in tricks, rather than on the mere number of tricks taken. An obvious schedule is the Ace 4, King 3, Queen 2, Jack 1 of All Fours (and its elaborations in such derivatives as Don and Phat); a far commoner one is the Ace 11, Ten 10, King 4, Queen 3, Jack 2 of Skat, Sixty-Six and many other games of continental Europe. The term contrasts with ▸ 'plain-trick' and ▸ 'penalty-trick' games. The following are described in this book:

For two players: All Fives, All Fours, Belote, Bezique, Binage, Bondtolva, Briscan, Briscas, Briscola, Briscolone, Bura, California Jack, Chouine, Elfern, Fildinski, French Whist, Gaigel, Handjass, Harjan, Hola, Jo-Jotte, Klaberjass, Mariage, Marjolet, Penneech, Pinochle, Pitch, Ristiklappi, Schnapsen, Scotch Whist, Sedma, Sixty-Six, Tausendeins, Trappola, Tute, Yukon.

For three players: Alcalde, Bavarian Tarock, Frog , Mariáš, Mittlere, Pandur, Reunion, Six-Bid Solo, Sjavs, Skat, Spanish Solo, Tausendeins (3p), Terziglione, Tysiacha, Zwikken.

For four players (solo): Belote, Botifarra, Briscola, Bura, French Whist, Gaigel, Handjass, Manille, Pip-Pip, Pitch, Scotch Whist, Yukon.

For four players (partnership): All Fours, Belote, Bondtolva, Briscas, Cinch, Coinche, Don, Doppelkopf, Gaigel, Hola, Klaverjas, Madrasso, Manille, Phat, Pinochle, Quinto, Ristiklappi, Roque, Schieberjass, Schnapsen, Sedma, Sixty-Six, Spády, Sueca, Tressette, Two Hundred.

For five or more players: Briscola, Bura, French Whist, Hola, Manille, Pip-Pip, Pitch, Scotch Whist, Yukon.

Poker

Vying game

52

Poker was born in or around New Orleans in the 1820s, of ancestry including Primero(*see* ▶ **Primiera**), ▶ **Brag**, ▶ **Bouillotte**, ▶ **Poch**, ▶ **Poque**, and others. The basis of modern Poker evolved by about 1870, and it has since become virtually America's national card game. Unlike most great games, especially ▶ **Bridge**, it is played in many different forms—often deliberately, at the same table and in the same session—which can disconcert the beginner. Poker is a game of skill, in that it offers the player considerable choice of play. The chance element of the deal can be negated, in the long run, by a conscious or intuitive grasp of mathematical principles, the accurate management of financial resources, and the application of practical psychology. The mark of Poker's greatness, like that of Bridge, is not that some people play it very well, but that so many play it very badly.

This entry can only cover the most basic forms of Poker: Draw, Stud, and one or two variations applicable to them all. Other possibilities are outlined, and with prior experience of the basic forms it is a simple matter to work ways of putting them into practice. It helps that Poker does not have official rules, only basic principles.

Some gambling games involve Poker hands but are not true Poker variants (though they may be introduced as variant rounds in Dealer's Choice). See separate entries for so-called ▶ **Caribbean Stud Poker**, ▶ **Chinese Poker**, ▶ **Let it Ride**, ▶ **Pai-Gow Poker**.

Basic principles

Two sets of basic principles must be understood from the outset, namely (a) the definition of Poker hands, or combinations, and (b) the mechanics of staking and betting.

Poker hands. In all forms of Poker, players bet as to which of them has the best hand. A Poker hand, by definition, is five cards. More may be dealt or held, but only five count in a showdown. These five may be totally unmatched, or may form one of the following universally recognized combinations. The value of each type of hand is indicated by the odds against receiving one when dealt five cards from a thoroughly shuffled pack. Figures above 100 are rounded to the nearest 50.

1. **High card.** No combination. Of two such hands, the one with the higher top card wins, or second higher if tied, etc. Cards rank (high–low) A K Q J 10 9 8 7 6 5 4 3 2. Odds: 1–1 (evens).

2. **One pair.** Two of the same rank, the rest unmatched. Of two such hands, the one with the higher-ranking pair wins. If equal, go by highest top card. Odds: 1½–1.

3. **Two pair(s).** Self-explanatory. Of two such hands, the one with the higher-ranking pair wins; if equal, that with the higher-ranking second pair; if still equal, go by the higher odd card. Odds: 20–1.

4. **Three of a kind (triplets, trips).** Three of the same rank, two unmatched. Of two such hands, the higher-ranking triplet wins. Odds: 46–1.

5. **Straight.** Five cards in numerical sequence, but not all in one suit. Ace counts high (A K Q J 10) or low (5 4 3 2 A). Of two straights, that with the higher-ranking cards wins. Odds: 250–1.

6. **Flush.** Five cards of the same suit, but not all in sequence. Of two flushes, that with the higher top card wins, second higher if tied, etc. Odds: 500–1.

7. **Full house.** A triplet and a pair. Of two fulls, that with the higher triplet wins. Odds: 700–1.

8. **Four of a kind (fours).** Four cards of the same rank, the fifth irrelevant. Odds: 4150–1.

9. **Straight flush.** Five cards in suit and sequence, from A 2 3 4 5 to 9 10 J Q K Odds: 65,000–1.

10. **Royal flush.** Name given to the highest possible straight flush, namely A K Q J 10 of a suit. Though unbeatable, it can in theory be be tied, as no suit is better than another.

Betting procedure. Play does not take place with cards but with money, or with chips representing money, which are bought from a 'banker' before play. Chips should be of at least three different colours. Typically, whites count as one agreed monetary unit, reds as two, blues as five. (Other possible scales begin 1, 5, 10; 1, 5, 20, etc., and additional colours may be used.) To bet, a player moves one or more of the chips from the 'stack' in front of him towards the centre of the table, where they become part of the pool or 'pot' being played for. Chips once staked cannot be retrieved, except by winning the pot. Throughout play, individual players' stakes must be kept separate from one another and not physically combined into a single pile of chips, as it is essential to know exactly how much each one has staked.

In all forms of Poker, someone makes the first or opening bet. Rules vary as to (*a*) who has the first chance to open, (*b*) what minimum combination, if any, he must hold in order to open, and (*c*) the least and greatest amount he is allowed to make as his opening bet. If no one opens the pot, the hands are thrown in and there is a new deal. Before the pot is open, each in turn may bet (thereby opening it), pass ('check'), or fold (drop out). A player who folds lays his cards face down on the table, takes no further part in the deal, and has no claim on the current pot. Once the pot is open, each in turn must either match, raise, or fold, but may not pass. To match ('stay' or 'call') is to increase his stake so that it matches that of the previous active player. To 'raise' is to match the previous stake and increase it further. This continues until either:

(*a*) The player who last raised has been called by the other players still left in the pot. All bets now being equal, the last raiser may not raise again, and the 'betting interval' is at an end. Depending on the variety of Poker in question, this is followed by the next phase of play or by a final showdown. In a showdown, those still playing reveal their hands, and the player with the best hand wins the pot. Or:

(*b*) The last raise has not been called by any of the players, all having folded. The last raiser thereby wins the pot without having to show his hand.

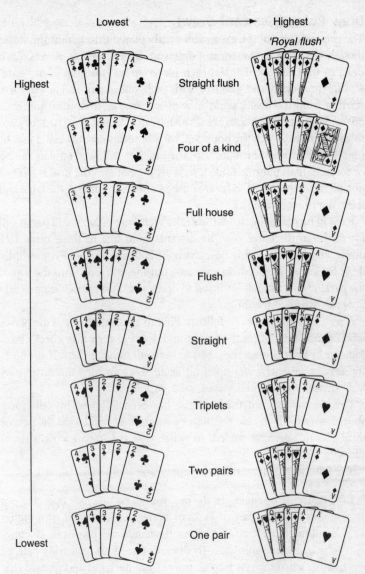

Lowest ⟶ Highest

'Royal flush'

Highest

Straight flush

Four of a kind

Full house

Flush

Straight

Triplets

Two pairs

One pair

Lowest

Poker hands.

Draw Poker (Five-card Draw)

The original form of the game, still widely played throughout the world though less so in its American homeland, is best for five players. Each deals in turn. Before the deal each player stakes one chip as an 'ante'. Shuffle thoroughly and deal five cards each, one at a time. Each in turn, starting from the dealer's left, may open, pass, or fold, until someone opens. If all pass, the hands are thrown in and the pot is carried forward to the next deal. With the pot open, each in turn may only call, raise, or fold. Play continues until the last raise has been followed only by calling or folding. If all but one folded, he wins the pot and the deal is over. If not, all the chips staked so far are pushed into the middle of the table and there is a draw, as follows.

Each in turn, starting from the dealer's left, may either stand pat or call for cards. In the latter case, he discards from one to three cards face down, announcing clearly how many he is discarding, and is promptly dealt by way of replacement the same number of cards from the top of the pack. Dealer himself is the last to draw, and must himself state clearly how many he is discarding.

A second betting interval follows. First to speak this time is the player who opened the pot on the first round. Each in turn may check (pass, indicate by knocking on the table) or bet until someone bets. If all check, the original opener must open up again. Each in turn thereafter may 'call' (match the previous stake), raise, or fold.

This continues until the last raise has been followed by calls for a showdown, in which case the player with the best hand wins the pot, or until all but one have folded, in which case the last in wins without showing his hand.

The following general rules also apply unless otherwise agreed.

1. **Qualifying openers.** In the first round, no one may open the pot unless he has a pair of Jacks or better (a higher pair or a higher combination). If no one opens, the hands are thrown in. If someone opens and subsequently discards one of his qualifying pair, he must, when the pot is won, prove from his hand and discard that he was entitled to open.
2. **Lower and upper limits** should be set on the amount of any opening bet or raise. A logical lower limit is one white. The

upper limit may be a fixed amount (e.g. five), or it may be set at the whole or half the amount currently in the pot.

3. **Ending the session.** The best way of ending the game is to agree a time limit and to finish at the end of the hand being played when that limit is reached. A player who runs out of chips must either buy more to continue, or drop out, in which case he loses all claim to the pot. (But he may be allowed to 'tap out'—i.e. pay as much as he has to the pot, any extras by other players then going to a side pot won by the second-best hand if the tapped-out player wins the main pot.)

Draw Poker variants

Hi-Lo Draw. The only draw variant much in use today. The pot is split evenly between the holders of the highest and the lowest hands. For the latter purpose, a hand lacking any combination obviously beats a pair or better. As between two low hands, decide which is the higher on a high-card basis, and the other one is automatically lower. The lowest possible hand is a Seventy-Five (7 5 4 3 2 of mixed suits), unless it is agreed to count Ace low, in which case it is a Sixty-Four (6 4 3 2 A).

Lowball. In this variety, the pot is won exclusively by the lowest hand. Straights and flushes are then ignored, so the lowest possible is 5 4 3 2 A, known as a 'wheel' or 'bicycle'.

Seven-Card Draw. Poker does not work well for fewer than four players. Two may work out their own rules for Strip Poker, and three may play Seven-Card Draw. In this case each player is dealt seven cards. In the draw, each must discard at least two, and receives as many as necessary to restore his hand to five.

Stud Poker

Stud Poker livens the game up by increasing the amount of information available and the number of players to eight. In Five-Card or 'Short' Stud, the dealer antes as many chips as there are players and deals each player one card face down (his 'hole'-card) and one face up. Everyone examines his hole-card and places it face down and half covered by his up-card. First to speak is the player showing the highest card or, if equal, the matching player nearest from the dealer's left. When bets have all been equalized, a second card is dealt face up, then a third, and finally a fourth, with a betting interval after each. At each deal the opening bet is made by the player showing the best combination (pair, three of a kind, etc.), or, if none, the highest card or cards, or, if equal, by the player nearest from the dealer's left. If all pass on the last round there is a showdown, at which everyone reveals their hole-card and the best hand wins.

Seven-card or 'Long' Stud. Deal 2 cards face down and 1 face up. After a betting interval, deal a second, a third, and a fourth face up, then a third face down, with a betting interval after each. In a showdown, each player selects the best five of his seven cards as his final hand.

English Long Stud. A hybrid of Stud and Draw. Play as above until each has been dealt 5 cards and that betting interval is closed. Each in turn may then either stand pat or make one discard in return for a replacement. The replacement is dealt face down or up depending on whether the abandoned card was down or up. A betting interval follows. Anyone who discarded on the previous round may then either stand pat or make one more discard, which again matches up or down the card it replaces. A final betting interval follows.

Variants. Any form of Stud may be played Hi-Lo or Lowball as described for Draw Poker. Also appropriate are wild-card variants, the most basic being Deuces wild.

Flop Poker

There are several varieties of Poker in which one or more cards are dealt face up to the table and counted by each player as if they were part of his own hand. These communal cards constitute the 'flop'. The classic game is:

Hold 'em (Texas Hold 'em, Hold me Darling). This has been the professionals' high-stakes game for many years now and is annually featured in major tournaments such as The World Series of Poker and the Carnivale of Poker, both at Las Vegas.

Deal two cards face down to each player, followed by a round of betting. Deal three cards face up to the centre of the table, and bet again. Then deal two more flop cards face up, one at a time, with a betting interval after each one. When all bets are equalized, the pot is won by the player who can make the best five-card hand, counting for this purpose any five out of seven—i.e. his own two and the five flop cards. The average winning hand is in the straight-to-flush region, usually a full house if the flop include a pair.

Other forms of Poker

Dealer's Choice. Each player deals in turn and each dealer chooses which form of Poker shall be played on his deal, or for a round of deals, one by each player, of which he is the first. It may be any standard Poker variant, or anything involving Poker hands (Caribbean Stud, for example), or even a variant he has made up on the spur of the moment.

Spit Poker. Any form of Poker in which one or more cards dealt face up to the table are counted by each player as if they were part of his own hand. The ancestral game, called Spit in the Ocean, is basically a form of Draw designed for up to eight players. Each receives four cards, the next is dealt face up to the table, and everyone counts this—the 'spit'—as his fifth card. For fun, the spit itself, or all four cards of the same rank, may be designated wild.

Wild-card Poker. A wild card is one which its holder may count as any natural card lacking from his hand. Any form of Poker may be played with one or more wild cards. The purpose is to increase the chances of making the higher and more interesting combinations, such as four or five of a kind and a straight flush. Which cards are made wild depends on how many are wanted: the more there are, the higher the winning hands, and the more incalculable the mathematics involved. For one wild card, add a Joker; for two, specify 'one-eyed Jacks'; for four, any given rank; for eight, any two ranks; and so on. Even wilder are variable wild cards, as exemplified by the Stud rule that any card subsequently dealt to a player that matches the rank of his hole-card is wild, but for that player only.

Although wild cards alter the mathematics, they do not normally change the relative ranking of hands. They do, however, introduce a new hand consisting of four of a kind and a wild card counting as the fifth. By agreement, 'five of a kind' either beats everything or is beaten only by a royal flush. Of tied hands, one with fewer wild cards beats one with more.

Freak hand Poker. Freak hands, nowadays not so popular, are additional combinations designed to spice up games like basic Draw in which most winning hands are low. Widely recognized in the late nineteenth century was the *blaze*—any five face cards other than four of a kind, ranking below it but above a full house. The self-explanatory four-flush, if recognized, ranks between two pair and triplets.

Short-pack Poker. Poker is often played with short packs where these are customary—32 in France, 40 in Italy, Spain, and South America, and so on. Like wild cards, short packs change the mathematics but not the relative ranking of hands.

Poker Patience

Competitive Patience

52

Poker Patience is the best known of a group of one-player games following a similar format, which can easily be extended to almost any game with distinctive scoring combinations. The competitive form (*see end of entry*) is called Poker Squares.

Turn 25 cards one by one from a shuffled pack and place each one face up on the table in such a way as gradually to build a square of five rows and columns. Cards once placed may not be moved in relation to one another. At end of play score for each row and column (ten in all) according to the Poker combination it makes, regardless of the actual order of cards within the line. There are two possible scoring schedules, of which the American (right-hand column) values hands according to their frequency in Poker while the English (left-hand column) does so on the basis of their frequency in Poker Patience, and is therefore more accurate.

One pair	1	2
Two pair	3	5
Triplet	6	10
Straight	12	15

Flush	5	20
Full house	10	25
Four of a kind	16	50
Straight flush	30	75
Royal flush	30	100

The target score is 70 by the English system or 200 by the American.

Poker Squares

Each player has a complete pack and arranges the cards in order for ease of identification. One person has a shuffled pack and plays any game of Poker Patience, calling out the name of each card as he turns it. Everyone else picks out the same card and arranges it in their own square. Whoever makes the highest-scoring square wins.

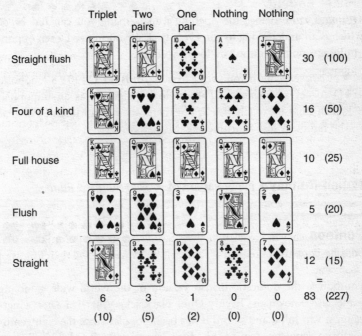

	Triplet	Two pairs	One pair	Nothing	Nothing		
Straight flush	K♠	Q♠	10♠	A♠	J♠	30	(100)
Four of a kind	K♥	5♥	5♣	5♠	5♦	16	(50)
Full house	K♣	Q♥	K♦	Q♣	Q♦	10	(25)
Flush	6♥	9♥	3♥	J♥	2♥	5	(20)
Straight	J♦	9♣	10♦	8♣	7♦	12	(15)
	6	3	1	0	0	83	(227)
	(10)	(5)	(2)	(0)	(0)		

=

Poker Square. This Poker Square contains one of each combination, scoring 83 by the English count or 227 by American.

Polignac

Penalty-trick game

32

An old but not uninteresting French forerunner of ▶ **Hearts**, best for four players.

Unless four play, remove the black Sevens. Deal all the cards around in twos and threes. The aim is to avoid capturing any Jacks in tricks, and especially ♠ J, called Polignac. Cards rank K Q J A 10 9 8 7.

Eldest leads first. You must follow suit if you can, but may otherwise play any card. The trick is taken by the highest card of the suit led, and the winner of each trick leads to the next. There are no trumps.

Lose 2 points for capturing ♠J, and 1 point for each other Jack. The first to reach an agreed total of penalties, either 10 or 20, is the loser.

Optional rule. Before the opening lead is made you can bid *capot*, which is an undertaking to win every trick. If you succeed, each opponent loses 5 points; if not, you lose 5 yourself.

☛ *Comment.* But if you prefer to rank cards A K Q J 10 9 8 7, appoint ♠Q to act as Polignac. (The original Polignac was an unpopular French minister of Charles X, but there was also a Mme de Polignac who famously lost a fortune at cards.)

Polish Rummy A minor variant of ▶ *Five Hundred Rum*

Pontoon

Banking game

52

Pontoon is the domestic British version of the world-wide gambling game also known as Twenty-One, Blackjack, Vingt-Un (*not* 'vingt-et-un'), Van John, and so on. It has been popular since the eighteenth-century Napoleon whiled his time away with it when exiled at St Helena—and goes back to the even earlier game of Thirty-One. In the twentieth century it became the most popular game of the armed forces of English-speaking nations. The home game is described first, followed by the casino game called Blackjack in Britain and Twenty-One in America.

Players. Decide who banks first by dealing cards around face up till someone gets a Jack. The bank remains with that player till someone gets a pontoon, thereby taking it over. (*Variant:* The bank passes to the left after as many deals as there are punters, or when the current banker accepts an offer to purchase it.) All staking is done with chips, counters, or any equivalent objects. Decide in advance what is the minimum and maximum initial stake.

Cards. Use a single 52-card pack. Numerals Two to Ten count at face value, face cards count 10 each, and an Ace counts either 1 or 11 as its holder prefers. Suits are irrelevant.

Object. To acquire a hand of cards totalling more than the banker's but not more than 21. A bust hand (over 21) always loses to the banker, regardless of his own total, as does any hand of equal count to the banker's.

Pontoon. A two-card hand counting 21, necessarily consisting of an Ace and a 10 or face card, is a pontoon and wins double unless tied. A banker's pontoon is therefore unbeatable.

Deal. Shuffle the cards thoroughly at start of play. Thereafter, they are not shuffled before each deal but only after one in which a player gets a pontoon. Deal one card face down to each player and to the banker (last), then a second card face up to each player but face down to the banker.

Stakes. The banker may not yet examine his cards, but everyone else examines their own and places a stake on them in accordance with the agreed minimum and maximum. If anyone has a pontoon, he turns the Ace face up and may not stake any more in that deal.

Splitting. The following option does not apply to the banker. If you have been dealt two cards of the same rank you may, if you wish, split them and play each one as a separate hand, turning them both up to show your entitlement to do so. You must stake on them separately, but not necessarily the same amount (unless otherwise agreed in advance). If either of them is paired again, you can split again and play three hands, or even (improbably) four. Some schools only allow Aces to be split, others allow you to split anything *but* Aces. If a split Ace becomes a pontoon, some schools do not pay it double or allow its holder to become the banker.

More cards. The banker then addresses himself to each player in turn and asks whether they want more cards. When he gets round to you, these are your options:

- Stick. This means you are satisfied with your hand and don't want any more cards. You must have a count of at least 16 to do this.
- Buy. In this case you increase your stake and are dealt another card face down. Your extra stake must be not less than your previous one, nor more than the total amount you have staked so far. (*Variant:* Each new buy may be for less but not more than the previous one.) If you reach a count of 11 or less on four cards you may not buy a fifth but may only twist.
- Twist. In this case you are dealt one card face up, free of charge. Having once twisted, you may twist further cards but may not subsequently buy.

You continue buying or twisting until you bust or stick, or reach a total of five cards without busting, which obliges you to stick. If you bust, you lose your total stake and return your cards to the banker, who places them at the bottom of the pack.

When playing a split hand you become two players(or more), and deal with each one separately before passing on to the next.

Showdown. When everyone has been served, the banker turns his two cards face up, and may, if he wishes, turn more cards face up until he is satisfied with his count, or busts. If he gets:

- A pontoon, he wins all the stakes.
- Twenty-one on three or more cards, he pays double to anyone with a pontoon, but wins all the others' stakes.

- Under twenty-one, he pays anyone with a higher count (double for a pontoon) but wins all the other stakes.
- A bust, he keeps the stakes of those who also bust, but pays anyone with a count of 16 to 21 (double for a pontoon).

When a punter gets a pontoon and the banker does not, the bank passes to the pontoon holder, who may play it or sell it to the highest bidder.

Optional extras. The following optional extras may be included.
Five-card trick. A five-card hand worth 21 or less beats everything except a banker's pontoon, and wins double.
Royal pontoon. A hand consisting of three Sevens beats everything except a banker's pontoon, and is paid treble.

Blackjack (the casino version of Pontoon)

In casinos the house is the bank and its croupier the permanent dealer. Casino play involves a number of 52-card packs shuffled together and dealt from a 'shoe'. An Ace initially counts 11 and only reduces to 1 if 11 would create a bust. A two-card 21 is called a natural or a blackjack.

The punters place their bets and the dealer deals two cards face up to each of them. He then deals himself either one card face down (British practice) or one face up and one face down (American).

Naturals. If you have a natural and the dealer's upcard is a numeral from 2 to 9, you are paid off at 3 to 2 and retire. If the dealer's upcard is an Ace or 10-card, nothing happens until his second card is turned. You then get 3-2 only if the dealer does not have a blackjack: if he does, it is a stand-off.

Insurance. If the dealer's upcard is an Ace, you can make a separate side bet (usually restricted to half your main stake) that he has a natural. If he has, when the time comes to show it, you win this stake double; if not, you lose it single. Insurance is usually a sucker bet, and British rules allow it only if you have a natural.

Splitting pairs. House rules vary as to which ranks you are allowed to split. British rules prohibit splitting Fours, Fives, and Tens, thereby preventing you from making a fool of yourself.

The following conditions usually apply:

1. You cannot re-split a card already split (British rules).
2. If you split Aces, you cannot draw more than one more card.
3. In a split, a two-card 21 does not count as a blackjack.

Doubling. If you have a count of 9, 10, or 11, but not a blackjack, you may double your stake (British practice. American rules may allow you to double on any first two cards.)

Drawing. If you have not got a blackjack and have neither split pairs nor doubled down, you may then call for more cards to be dealt face up, one at a time, until you either stand (stop drawing) or bust (exceed 21). If you bust, you lose your cards and your stake.

Dealer's count. If one or more players remain in play, the dealer deals himself a second card face up (or, in America, turns his hole card face up).

- If the dealer has a blackjack, he beats anyone who has not.
- If not, he must draw more cards so long as he has a count of 16 or less, and stand when he has 17 or more.
- If he busts, he pays evens to anyone who did not bust.

If not, he pays evens to anyone showing a higher count and wins the single stake of showing a lower. If equal, it is a stand-off.

Optional extras. Some house rules allow you to drop out of play after receiving your first two cards. You then get half your stake back unless the dealer has a blackjack, when you lose it all.

Some allow you to make a side bet that your first two cards will total less than 13, or more than 13. Both pay evens, but both lose if the total is exactly 13.

Pope Joan

Stops game

52

A once popular Victorian family game, since replaced by its less elaborate relative ▸ **Newmarket**.

Pope Joan traditionally involves a circular staking board with eight compartments labelled Ace, King, Queen, Jack, Game, Pope (♦9), Matrimony (K–Q of trumps), and Intrigue (Q–J of trumps). Such a board can easily be drawn on a sheet of paper. Each player is equipped with a number of chips or counters, and ♦8 is removed from the pack.

The dealer 'dresses the board' by placing a stake of six counters in the compartment labelled Pope, two each to Matrimony and Intrigue, and one to each of the others. He then deals the 51 cards round as far as they will go, but to one more hand than there are players. It doesn't matter if some have one more card than others. The last card dealt to the dead hand is turned for trumps. If it is Pope, or the Ace, King, Queen, or Jack, Dealer wins the contents of the appropriate compartment.

Play begins, the aim being to run out of cards before anyone else.

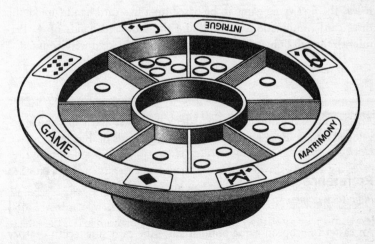

Pope Joan. An original staking board.

Eldest plays a card face up to the table. It may be of any suit, but must be the lowest he has of it. For this purpose, cards run A 2 3 4 5 6 7 8 9 10 J Q K. If he has the next higher card of the same suit, he plays this too, and so on until he can go no further. The sequence is then continued by the player who holds the next card up.

If no one can play the next card up because it is in the dead hand, or because a King has been reached, a new sequence is started by the person who played the last card (the 'stop'). As before, it may be of any suit, but must be the lowest he has of it.

The content (if any) of the Ace, King, Queen, and Jack compartments goes to the person playing the said trump card, as does that for Pope. That for Intrigue can only be won if the same person is able to play Queen and Jack, as does Matrimony for King and Queen. If any stake is not won, it is carried forward to the next deal.

The first to play out all his cards wins the stake for Game, plus one chip from each other player for each card remaining in his hand—except that anyone holding the Pope is excused payment.

Poque

Eighteenth-century French ancestor of ▶ **Poker**, derived from ▶ **Poch**. It was the first vying game to be based on a five-card hand (unlike the three-card combinations of Brag and the four-card hands of ▶ **Primiera**), though only pairs, triplets, and fours of a kind were counted.

Post

Ancient English gambling game, later called Post and Pair, which developed into ▶ **Brag** by the addition of wild cards or 'braggers'.

Preference
Plain-trick game

32

An eastern European game popular since the early nineteenth century and generally regarded as Russia's national card game. As the Russian game is too complicated and space-consuming to describe in detail, the following description is of the somewhat simpler Austrian version.

Preliminaries. Three take part in each deal, but the game is often played by four, each dealing in turn and sitting his own deal out. It may be played for a hard or soft score (cash or writing): if hard, players should agree a basic stake consisting of a multiple of ten units.

The 32 cards rank A K Q J 10 9 8 7 in each suit. If playing for hard score, the dealer places a single stake in the pot, then deals (face down) three each, two to the table, four each, and again three each, so that everyone receives 10 cards. The two odd cards constitute the talon.

Auction. An auction determines who will play alone against the other two. The soloist will name trumps, may take the talon and discard two cards, and must then win at least six tricks in play.

The basic bids are from one to four. 'One' entitles the bidder, if he becomes the soloist, to name any suit as trump. 'Two' allows him to entrump any suit other than clubs, 'three' allows him to entrump only a red suit, and 'four' allows only hearts as trump.

Each in turn, starting with Eldest, may pass or bid, and, having passed, may not come in again. The first bid is 'one'. Each thereafter must either pass or bid one higher—'jump-bidding' is not allowed. However:

1. An earlier player may 'hold' the bid of a later player. *Example*: If Annie bids 'one', Benny must pass or bid 'two'. If he bids 'two', Connie must pass or bid 'three'. Benny and Connie may not hold the previous bid, as they speak later in the auction. Annie, however, may then hold Connie's bid of three, as he is the earlier of two players willing to bid the same amount. If Annie passed, Benny would be able to hold Connie's three, and Connie would then have to bid 'four' or pass.

2. Any player in turn to bid may declare 'hand' or 'preference'. 'Hand' is an undertaking to play with the hand as dealt, without first seeking to improve it by taking the talon and making two discards. If two players are willing to bid 'hand', they name their suits, and the higher-ranking wins the bid. For this purpose, hearts beat diamonds beat spades beat clubs. 'Preference' is a bid of hearts, hand, which cannot be overcalled.

Play. Unless playing from the hand, the soloist then picks up the talon, adds it to his hand, discards any two cards face down, and announces trumps.

Before leading, he asks the player to his left, then to his right, whether they will stay in or drop out. A player who stays in must win at least two tricks, or else will be penalized. If one drops out, the other plays alone against the soloist. If both drop out, the soloist wins without playing at all.

The soloist now leads to the first trick—unless he thinks his game unwinnable, in which case he can throw it in. Subsequent players must follow suit and head the trick if possible; if unable to follow, they must play a trump, and beat any trump already played if possible. The trick is taken by the highest card of the suit led, or by the highest trump if any are played, and the winner of each trick leads to the next.

An additional rule of trick-play is important and unusual enough to require special attention. When three are active, and the soloist leads, the second must—if possible—win the trick with the *lowest* card that will do so. This is called 'indulging' (*largieren*), its purpose being to enable the partner to take his requisite two tricks. Failing to indulge when able to constitutes a revoke. (*Variant*: Some schools suspend this rule when the second partner has already taken his two tricks.)

Score. A player taking the requisite minimum of tricks—soloist six, partner two—wins one-tenth of the pot, or scores 1 point, for each trick taken. If a partner fails, he doubles the pot or loses 10 points. If the soloist fails, he triples the pot or loses 20 points. If he threw the hand in before the first trick, he pays each opponent the equivalent of three-tenths of the pot, or five-tenths if only one was active, and the pot remains unchanged.

If anyone revokes—i.e. fails to obey any of the rules of trick-taking, including 'indulging', when able to do so—play ceases and settlements are made without recourse to the pot. If the soloist revokes, he pays the others the equivalent of three-tenths of the pot, or five-tenths if only one opponent was playing. If an opponent revokes, he pays the soloist the full amount of the pot, and his partner (if active) the equivalent of four tenths.

When scoring in writing, for 'tenth' read 'point', and ignore references to the pot. (Pot scoring is, in fact, so unwieldy that complicated rules obtain to prevent anyone from winning too much after the pot has been fattened by a series of losses.)

Variants. If one partner drops and the other plays alone, the lone partner must take four tricks to avoid penalty.

If one wishes to drop, the other may invite him to stay. If, then, they fail to take four tricks between them—not necessarily two each—the one who issued the invitation will pay the dues from both.

Some schools pay the soloist a bonus, independent of the pot, for playing with, or (more rarely) without, all four Aces in hand.

Bettel is a bid to lose every trick. There is no trump, but players must still head the trick if possible. It usually outbids 'four', but its bidding position and value are variable. It may be played with exchange or from the hand, and 'open' (face up) for a higher score.

Mord, or *Durchmarsch*, is a bid to win every trick, following the same rules as Bettel.

Sans atout appears in one account (Claus D. Grupp, *Kartenspiele*, Wiesbaden, 1975) as a bid in which the soloist, playing at no trump, must win at least six tricks in succession. If they are the first six, the seventh must be won as well.

In these additional bids, some schools forbid either opponent to drop out, but allow them to double the value of the game, which the soloist may then redouble.

Another optional feature is that when a player has made an ordinary suit bid, taken the talon, and discarded, an opponent may then take over as soloist by bidding one of the higher games, taking the new talon, and discarding in its place.

☞ *Comment.* The obligation to head the trick, combined with the 'indulging' rule, has some subtle repercussions on the play. Suppose, as soloist, you lead the Queen from ♥Q-J-10-9; second hand, with ♥K-9, must play the King; third, with ♥A-7, must likewise play the Ace. The rules of following thus make your heart sequence good for three tricks once the Queen has gone. But reverse the holdings of second and third hand. Now second must play the Ace, but third can discard low, thus retaining the King and leaving your hearts good for only two tricks.

President

Climbing game

The best-known member of a group of oriental games that reached western Europe and America in the 1980s and is known by many different names, most commonly A**ehole or A**hole. The group takes its name from a Chinese game whose name translates as 'Climbing up', in the sense of social climbing. They are all characterized by the prominence they attach to the relative social status of the winners and losers, which also accounts for their common range of graphic titles. Following the pattern of some old four-hand games in which the place-holders are designated, in descending order, King, Nobleman, Poorman, Beggar, western games exhibit such characters as Boss, Foreman, Worker, Bum, or President, Vice, President, Citizen, A**hole, or, in a Hungarian six-player equivalent, King, Big Landowner, Small Landowner, Big Peasant, Small Peasant, Swamp-dweller. A peculiarly western innovation is requiring each of these characters to occupy a particular seat, ranging from a comfortable armchair to a rickety old crate, and for these to remain fixed so that players have to physically change places. In some versions they also wear different hats.

The following rules are typical rather than definitive.

From a 54-card pack including two Jokers deal all the cards round one at a time. It doesn't matter if some players have one more card than others. From highest to lowest, cards rank Jo 2 A K Q J 10 9 8 7 6 5 4 3.

Jokers not only outrank Twos (and everything else), but also, if they are distinguishable—for example, a red Joker and a black Joker—one of them outranks the other. Jokers may also be used as wild cards, but in this case are beaten by the equivalent natural combination. Thus 6 Jo Jo beats 5 5 5 but is beaten by 6 6 6.

The aim is to play all your cards out as soon as possible.

In the first deal, Eldest leads by playing face up to the table any single card, or two, three or four cards of the same rank. (*Variant*: The player holding ♣3 leads.) Each in turn thereafter may pass or play. (*Variant*: You must play if you can.) If you play, you can only do so by putting out the same number of cards as the leader, and they must all be of the same rank, which must be higher than that or those of the previous player.

(*Variant*: They may be equal in rank, but may not be lower.) If you pass, you will still be allowed to play if the turn comes round to you again. (*Variant*: No, you won't.)

The round finishes when one person plays and everyone else passes. The person who played last may not play again but must turn all the played cards face down and lead to the next round. If he has run out of cards, the lead passes round to the next player who has any left. Play ceases when all but one player have run out of cards.

The first and second to run out of cards are designated, respectively, Boss and Foreman (or President and Vice-President, whatever titles may be agreed). The last to run out of cards is the Worker (or Citizen), and the one left with cards in hand is the Bum (or A**hole). Intermediate positions may be graded accordingly.

The Boss/President scores 2 points, and in the next round occupies the most comfortable chair. The Foreman/Vice-President scores 1 point, and occupies the next best chair, which should be at the Boss's left. The others score nothing; the Bum sits at the Boss's right, and the Worker/ Citizen at the Bum's right—opposite the Boss, if four play.

Once the positions have been established, the Bum is entirely responsible for gathering cards in and shuffling and dealing, getting the others' drinks, wiping their noses, and so on.

☞ *Note*. In some circles, anyone else who so much as touches a card between deals, even accidentally, is obliged promptly to swap places with the Bum.

Dealing proceeds from the Bum's left, starting with the Boss/President. After the deal but before the play, the Bum gives the Boss the highest card in his hand, and the Boss gives the Bum any card he doesn't want. (*Or*: The Worker and Foreman exchange respectively their highest and least wanted card, the Bum and Boss their two highest and two least wanted cards.) The Boss then leads to the next round. (*Or*: The Bum leads.)

Play up to any agreed target, preferably at least 11, as the system of card exchange makes it hard for the Bum and the Boss ever to change positions in the short term. (*Variant*: Ignore point-scores and play for final position after any previously agreed number of rounds.)

Variations. A vast range of variations will be encountered. Many include rules and features borrowed from related games. The following may be worth mentioning.

Single or multiple sequences may be played. A variety called Big Two includes Poker combinations.

A given play may be followed by one containing more cards, provided that it is the same type of combination and higher in rank.

The play of a given card or combination may induce a change in the rotation of play (clockwise becomes anti-clockwise, and vice versa), or in the ranking of subsequent combinations (each new one must be lower instead of higher), or both.

Cards other than Jokers may be declared wild.

Suits may be ranked as at Bridge (♠ ♥ ♣ ♦). Consequently, ♦5 may be followed by ♥5 or ♠5, but not ♣5, and competing pairs of equal rank are won by the pair containing the spade.

Primiera (Primero)

Vying game

40

The modern Italian game of Primiera (also called Goffo, Bambara, and no doubt by other names) differs little from its sixteenth century ancestor, played under the title Primero by Henry VIII. It is a forerunner of
▶ **Poker** but based on four-card instead of five-card combinations. The eponymous *primiera*, or 'prime', consists of exactly one card in each suit—the exact opposite of a flush.

Each player stakes a previously agreed amount (the ante) and receives four cards dealt in twos from a 40-card pack lacking Eights, Nines, and Tens.

Anyone dealt a winning combination calls for an immediate showdown, and the player with the best hand wins the pot. From lowest to highest, the winning combinations are:

1. *Primiera.* One card of each suit.
2. *Fifty-five.* Seven, Six, Ace of the same suit, the fourth card any.
3. *Flush.* Four cards of the same suit.

As between equal combinations, the best is that totalling the greatest point-value, counting for this purpose

Seven	21	Four	14
Six	18	Three	13
Ace	16	Two	12
Five	15	K, Q, J	10

If still equal, the deal is annulled and the pot carried forward to the next. (*Variant*: Flushes and fifty-fives may be decided on a best-suit basis: hearts highest, then diamonds, clubs, spades.)

Example. Aldo declares a primiera: ♠K ♥Q ♣3 ♦3. Bruno counters with a fifty-five: ♠7 ♠6 ♠A ♦A. This is beaten by Carlo's flush, ♣7 ♣2 ♣Q ♣J. Dino, however, sweeps the pool with ♥6 ♥5 ♥4 ♥3, counting 60 to Carlo's 53. Four such hands are, of course, most unlikely to occur in a single, honest deal.

If no one has a winning combination, each in turn makes one or more discards and receives the same number from the top of the pack. An additional stake may be required at this point. If there is still no claim, there is a showdown, and the pot is won by the player with the best 'point', i.e. highest value of cards in one suit. (*Example*: ♥7 ♥4 ♣A ♠K, counting 35 in hearts, beats ♦K ♦Q ♦4 ♠7, counting 34 in diamonds.)

In some schools, the period between a draw and final showdown may be filled with a round of stake-raising as at Poker, or there may be further draws until a win is claimed or the pack runs out.

Note. Pairs and sequences do not count, but three or four of a kind will often win in their capacity as a prime. The sixteenth century treatise on gambling by Girolamo Cardano has four of a kind beating a flush.

Progressive Rummy

Rummy game

An early form of ▸ **Contract Rummy**. Seven deals of 10 cards each. The contract requirements may be met with sets or sequences or one of each. Meld (1) three cards, (2) four cards, (3) five cards, (4) two threes, (5)

three and four, (6) three and five, (7) two fours. Sets of three must be of three different suits; sets of four or more must include all four suits. You can only go out by discarding. Deuces 15, Aces 11, courts 10, numerals face value. Drop out when you reach 100 penalty points.

Punto Banco ▸▸ *Baccara*

Put

Plain-trick game

First recorded in the sixteenth century as a tavern game of ill repute and in the seventeenth as played only by menials, Put is still fun to play and has the merit of being very fast. Its French equivalent, ▸ **Truc**, is more elaborate and still extant.

Cards rank 3 2 A K Q J 10 9 8 7 6 5 4 (Three high, Four low). Two players put up an equal stake and the one cutting the higher Put card deals first, after which the deal alternates. Deal three cards each in ones. Non-dealer leads first. There is no rule of following: any card may be played to any trick, which is taken by the higher-ranking of the two. If both are equal, the trick is tied and discarded. The winner of each trick, or the leader of a tied trick, leads to the next. A player who wins two tricks, or one trick to two ties, scores a point. If all three are tied, or both win a trick and the third is tied (known as 'trick and tie'), neither player scores. Game is five points.

Either player, when about to play a card, may instead call 'Put'. The other may then resign, in which case the putter scores the point without further play. If the non-putter insists on playing it out, then whoever wins the point jumps to five and wins the game outright. No one scores if the point is put and the result a tie.

Pyramid

Patience game

An old but still popular solitaire.

Take out the Aces, shuffle the rest, and deal fifteen cards face up in the form of a pyramid, with one at the top, two in the next row, and so on up to five in the fifth row. Place two Aces on either side of the bottom row (for the sake of symmetry).

The aim is to build each Ace up in suit to its King.

Turn cards from stock and build them if possible or play them face up to a single wastepile if not. Whenever a card of the pyramid can be built on an Ace-pile, play it off and replace it with the top card of the stock or the wastepile.

When you run out of stock you may turn the wastepile and play through it again, but only once.

Quadrille

Patience game

●

A classic solitaire that requires only attention and patience rather than skill, but is pretty to look at.

Arrange the four Queens in a symmetrical pattern at the centre of the playing area. They are for decoration only.

Extract the Fives and Sixes of each suit and arrange them in a circle surrounding and radiating outwards from the central Queens.

Your aim is to build in suit upwards on the Sixes as far as the Jacks (6-7-8-9-10-J), and downwards on the Fives as far as the Kings (5-4-3-2-A-K).

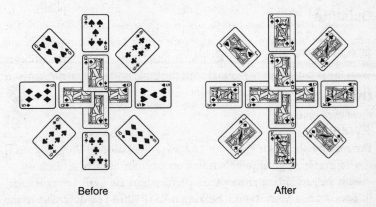

Before   After

Quadrille. (Patience).

Hold the rest of the shuffled pack face down and turn cards one by one from the top. Build each one on a Five or Six pile whenever you can, otherwise discard it face up to a single wastepile. You may always take the top card of the wastepile and add it to a building pile whenever one or more cards built from the hand enable it to continue a sequence.

When you run out of cards from stock, take the wastepile, turn it upside down, and continue play as before, using it as a new stock.

If you keep doing this long enough the game will always come out. The usual restriction is that you may not turn the wastepile more than twice, leaving you with three deals in all.

Quadrille

This classic plain-trick game, directly ancestral to ▶ **Boston** and ▶ **Solo Whist**, was devised in early eighteenth-century France as a four-handed version of l'Hombre (▶ **Tresillo**), and remained popular—especially in female society—for over a hundred years in France and England until ousted by partnership Whist. It is extremely complicated and needs to be played with a vast treasure-chest of chips and counters that few modern players are likely to have readily to hand.

http://www.davidparlett.co.uk/histocs/quadrill.html

Quintille

Five-hand adaptation of ▶ **Quadrille**.

Quinto
Point-trick game

Invented by 'Professor Hoffman' (Angelo Lewis) around 1900, Quinto is too enjoyably original to be omitted on grounds of mere artificiality.

Four players sitting crosswise in partnerships are dealt 12 cards each, in ones, from a 53-card pack ranking A K Q J 10 9 8 7 6 5 4 3 2 plus Joker. The last five are dealt face down to the table to form a *cachette*. They may not be examined until they are (eventually) credited to the winners of the last trick.

The aim of each side is to score 250 points over as many deals as necessary. Points are scored for winning tricks (5 each) and especially for any 'quints' contained in them. The best quint is the Joker, or 'Quint royal', scoring 25 points. Additional quints are the Five of each suit, and two cards of the same suit totalling five (Ace and Four, Three and Two) falling to the same trick. A quint in hearts scores 20, diamonds 15, clubs 10, spades 5.

Before play, each has one turn in which to pass, double, or redouble an opponent's double. A double increases the value of won tricks from 5 to 10 points in the current deal, a redouble further increases them to 20 each.

Eldest leads to the first trick, and the winner of each trick leads to the next. You must follow suit if you can but may otherwise play any card. There is no single trump suit. Instead, the suits rank in order from low to high: spades, clubs, diamonds, hearts. If you can't follow suit to the card led, you may either discard from a lower suit (if any) or 'trump' by playing from a higher suit (if any). The trick is therefore taken by the highest card of the highest suit played.

If you hold the Joker, you may not lead it to a trick, but you may otherwise play it at any time even if able to follow suit to the card led. It cannot win a trick.

During play, the side winning a trick containing a quint (Joker, Five, A + 4, 3 + 2) scores for it immediately according to its suit. If this brings them to the 250-point target, they win the game without any further play.

Otherwise, the side winning the last trick also wins the *cachette*, which counts as a thirteenth trick, and scores for any quint or quints it may contain.

If neither side has reached or exceeded 250, the thirteen tricks are then counted at 5 points each, or 10 if the game was doubled, or 20 if redoubled. If both sides are still under 250, or both are over but tied, there is another deal.

(Hoffman does not cover the remote possibility that the holder of the Joker may eventually be forced to lead it. As it is illegal to do so, the trick is presumably credited by default to the opposing side.)

☛ *Note*. A neat effect of doubling and redoubling is that it increases the value of tricks relative to that of quints, which are not affected by it. In an extreme case, a side winning all thirteen tricks, redoubled, would thereby score 260 points and the game.

Quinze

An old game equivalent to ▶ **Pontoon** for two players. Players match stakes and receive one card each. Cards count Ace 1, numerals face value, courts 10 each. A hand counting more than 15 is bust. Non-dealer draws further cards, one at a time, until either satisfied with his hand or bust. Dealer then does likewise. The player with the higher non-bust total wins. If one busts, the other wins. If both tie or bust, the stake is doubled and a new deal played.

Rabouge ▶▶ *Spite and Malice*

Racehorse ▶▶ *Pitch*

Racing Demon

Everybody simultaneously plays a game of ▶ **Demon** with their own pack of cards and the winner is the first to get it out, or the player who succeeds in getting most cards played off.

Rams

Plain-trick game

32

A widespread European drinking game related to ▶ **Nap** and ▶ **Loo**; also called Rounce. The basic idea is fairly constant, but scoring systems vary.

Each player starts with five, seven, or ten counters (or marks drawn on paper), and the general aim is to lose counters by winning tricks. Each player drops out as they pay their last counter, and the last left in is the overall loser. Alternatively, the first to run out of counters wins.

The 32 cards rank A K Q J 10 9 8 7 in each suit. A first dealer is selected at random. Deal five cards, in batches of three and two, to each player also face down to the table to form a spare hand or 'widow'. Turn the next card up for trumps.

Anyone who thinks he can win all five tricks immediately announces 'General Rams'. No one may then drop out, and play begins. Otherwise, each player in turn from Dealer's left announces whether he will pass, i.e. throw the hand in without penalty, or play, thereby undertaking to win at least one trick. Another option is to throw the hand in and take the widow in its place. Only the first player to bid this may do it, and he must then play.

There must be at least two active players. If all pass up to the player at Dealer's right, both he and the dealer must play. The dealer may not pass if only one previous player has undertaken to play.

Before play, dealer may take the trump turn-up and throw out any unwanted card face down. The opening lead is made by the player at dealer's left, unless anyone declared a General Rams, in which case the declarer leads. Subsequent players must follow suit and head the trick if possible; if unable to follow, they must play a trump, and beat any trump already played if possible. The trick is taken by the highest card of the suit led, or by the highest trump if any are played, and the winner of each trick leads to the next.

Each player removes a counter for each trick he wins. Anyone who played but failed to win a trick is saddled with five more. The declarer of a General Rams loses five counters if successful, and everyone else takes five more. If unsuccessful, the declarer takes five more, the others drop one counter for each trick they have won, and a player who took none is exempt from penalty.

Alternative scoring. By another method, the dealer puts five chips in the pool, and each player takes a counter for each trick won, or adds five to the pool for taking none.

Bierspiel is a variant in which ♦7 is the second best trump.
Rounce is an American variety played with 52 cards.

Ramsch

A German penalty-trick game mostly played as a round of ▸ **Skat** in the
event that everyone passes, though it is also played by itself.

Ranter-go-Round ⇥ *Chase the Ace*

Red and Black
Vying game

Red and Black, also called Plus and Minus, is played like Draw Poker but
without Poker combinations. Instead, cards count at face value from 1 to
10, with face cards 10 each. Red cards count plus, black cards minus. The
hand with the highest point total wins. Often played High-low.

Red Dog
Banking game

Its title is sometimes applied to ▸ **Yablon**, but the original Red Dog, also
known as High Card Pool, was the game those newspaper reporters were
always playing in the background of old black-and-white classics like *His
Girl Friday*.

All contribute equally to a pot, which is replenished when empty. Deal
five each, or four if nine or ten play. Each in turn, starting with eldest,
either pays a chip and throws his hand in, or bets a specific amount that
at least one of his cards will be of the same suit and higher in rank (Ace
highest) than the top card turned from the pack. If so, he wins what he
staked, otherwise he loses.

Variant 1. The actual top card is burnt (replaced at the bottom without
being shown), and the next one turned to settle the bet.

Variant 2. A punter may 'copper' his bet—that is, bet that none of his cards will win.

Reunion

Point-trick game

32

The point-trick equivalent of ▸ **Euchre**, Reunion is an old Rhenish game too interesting to omit even if no longer played. It makes a good springboard for more complex games like ▸ **Skat**.

Cards rank from high to low in the following order, and bear the stated point-values:

RB	LB	A	10	K	Q	(J)	9	8	7
12	12	11	10	4	3	2	—	—	—

RB and LB stand for Right Bower and Left Bower, which are, respectively, the Jack of trumps and the other Jack of the same colour as trumps, and are the two highest cards of the trump suit. In plain suits, Jacks rank between Nine and Queen, and count 2 each. With an additional 10 for the last trick, the total number of points in play is 150. A game is three deals, one by each player. The aim is to win a majority of card-points and especially to avoid taking fewer than 100 in all.

The player cutting the lowest card deals first, and the turn to deal and play passes to the left. Deal 10 each in batches of 3 4 3, and turn the second of the final two for trump. The dealer then makes two face-down discards, which may not include an Ace or a Bower. Any card-points they contain will count for him at end of play as if he had won them in tricks. The two undealt cards belong to him, and he may take the face-down card immediately, but must leave the turn-up in place until the second trick is over.

Eldest leads to the first trick, and the winner of each trick leads to the next. A player unable to follow suit must play a trump if possible. The trick is taken by the highest card of the suit led, or by the highest trump if any are played. If both Bowers fall to the same trick, the holder of the Left Bower immediately pays one unit to whoever played the Right.

At the end of the game, an opponent with 100–149 points pays the winner one unit. One with 150 or more pays nothing, but the other then pays double. Anyone with under 100 pays double, under 50 triple. If two tie for most, the loser pays each one accordingly.

Reversis
Penalty-trick game

The earliest known ancestor of ▶ **Hearts**, popular with the French aristocracy in the seventeenth and eighteenth centuries, and much played elsewhere, though not in Britain. Its unusual features make it interesting and exciting to play. Unfortunately, it involved vast quantities of counters and sported so complex a system of pools and side-payments as to require a disproportionate amount of space to describe.

http://www.davidparlett.co.uk/histocs/reversis.html

Ride the Bus

Gambling Game

Known as Scat in America, Ride the Bus (related to Stop the Bus—*see* Bastard ▶ **Brag**) is a cross between ▶ **Thirty-One** and ▶ **Rummy**. A more interesting equivalent is the Chinese game of ▶ **Fifty-One**.

Deal three cards each and the next one face up to start the discard pile, and stack the rest face down. Each in turn takes the top card of either the stock or the discard pile, and makes one discard.

The aim is to get cards totalling 31, or as close as possible, in a single suit. Ace counts 11, courts 10 each, numerals face value.

Examples. ♠A ♠K ♠J counts 31, ♥5 ♥3 ♥2 counts 10, ♣8 ♣9 ♦J counts 17, ♦A ♠9 ♥9 counts 11.

Play continues until either of the following happens:

- someone gets 31 exactly, in which case they call for an immediate showdown, and everyone else loses a life; or
- someone with less than 31 knocks instead of drawing a card, in which case everybody gets one more turn before the showdown, and the player with the lowest flush score loses a life.

Drop out of play when you lose your third and last life. The last player left in wins.

Lives are usually represented by pennies or chips, but (to quote from the Pagat website), 'Ride the Bus has a different way of keeping track of wins and losses. All players start out "seated" at the back of the bus. Players who lose a hand move toward the front in a sequence. The sequence is usually: first, you stand at the back of the bus, then you are in the middle of the bus, then at the front of the bus, then you are on the stairs, then you are off the bus. Players who are no longer "riding the bus" are out of play. Winning a hand simply keeps your position; you do not move back a step if you win a hand.'

Ristiklappi

Point-trick game

52

A Finnish game (it translates as 'Crossclap') with an unusual twist.

Four players sitting crosswise in partnerships are dealt five cards each in batches of three and two from a 52-card pack ranking and counting as follows:

A	10	K	Q	J	9-8-7-6-5-4-3-2
11	10	4	3	2	0 each

The rest go face down as a stock.

The total of card-points available is 120 and the aim is to be the first side to reach 121 from the capture of counting-cards over as many deals as necessary.

Eldest leads to the first trick and the winner of each trick leads to the next. You can play any card to any trick—there is no need to follow suit. The trick is taken by the last-played card of the same rank as the one led, or by the card led if nobody duplicates it.

If any cards remain in stock, each in turn, starting with the trick-winner, draws the top card of stock before playing to the next trick.

When you win a trick and draw from stock, you have the privilege of 'spicing' the trick by adding to it the card you just drew and returning to your hand the card you won the trick with. Furthermore, any player upon playing to a trick need not play from hand but may instead turn the top card of stock and play that instead. In this case the turned card must be played—it cannot be taken into hand.

Rocambor ▶ Ombre

Rockaway ▶ Crazy Eights

Rolling Stone

Going-out game

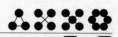

32 *or* 52

A simple but maddening game known in French as *Enflé* and in German as *Schwellen*—i.e. 'inflation', from the way one's hand tends to grow in size. More advanced relatives include ▶ **Durak**, ▶ **Stortok**, and ▶ **Svoyi Kozyri**.

Cards rank A K Q J 10 9 8 7 6 5 4 3 2. Ideally, the number of cards in use should be eight times the number of players, so strip out as many lower numerals as necessary to produce this effect. Then shuffle thoroughly and deal eight each in ones.

The aim is to be the first to run out of cards.

Eldest hand leads any card face up. Each in turn thereafter must play a card of the same suit if possible. Whoever plays the highest card wins the trick (worthless in itself) and leads to the next. A player who cannot follow suit takes all the cards so far played, adds them to his hand, and leads to the next.

Play ceases the moment somebody wins by playing the last card from their hand.

Variant. Deal 10 cards each from a full pack and stack the rest face down. If you cannot follow suit you must draw cards from stock till you can, or, when none remain in stock, must take up all the cards so far played and lead to the next trick.

Romanian Whist

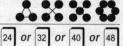

Plain-trick game

24 *or* 32 *or* 40 *or* 48

The game known as 'Whist' in Romania is actually an advanced form of ▶ **Oh Hell!**, one of the few trick games in which the aim is to win a precise number of tricks rather than a minimum number.

From three to six players use a pack stripped to eight times as many cards as players—e.g. 24 if three play (A K Q J 10 9), and so on. The first few deals consist of one card each, and there are as many of these as there are players. Thereafter, the number of cards dealt increases by one until it reaches a maximum of eight, then it decreases by one and finishes again with as many one-card deals as there are players. For example, if four play there are 21 deals: 1-1-1-1-2-3-4-5-6-7-8-7-6-5-4-3-2-1-1-1-1.

Deal the appropriate number of cards and turn the next for trump. If none remain, play at no trump. Each in turn, starting at dealer's left, announces exactly how many tricks he undertakes to win. Dealer, who bids last, may not bid a number that would enable everyone to fulfil their bid.

Eldest leads. You must follow suit if you can, but may otherwise play any card. The trick is taken by the highest card of the suit led, or by the highest trump if any are played, and the winner of each trick leads to the next.

If you win exactly the number you bid, you score that number plus 5 points. If not, you lose the number you bid plus 1 point for each overtrick, if any.

☛ *Comment.* The one-card deals are repeated in order to spread fairly the dealer's potential disadvantage of having to bid a 'wrong' number.

Rook

Game played with a proprietary pack of cards first published in the early twentieth century by Parker Brothers (now Hasbro), but, like most proprietary card games, probably derived from one originally played with standard cards, or at least with standard Chinese cards, as there are several Chinese games of its type. Rook cards consist of four suits each containing numerals 1 to 14, plus one card depicting a Rook, making 57 in all. For comparable games played with standard cards, *see* ▸ **Roque** (below) and ▸ **Two Hundred**.

Roque

Point-trick game

52

An Iranian game derived either from ▸ **Rook** or from the same source as Rook. Contributed by 'Babak' on the internet.

Four players, sitting crosswise in partnerships and playing to the right, are dealt 12 cards each, in batches of four, from a 52-card pack ranking A K Q J 10 9 8 7 6 5 4 3 2. The last four are dealt face down to the table.

The aim is for the declaring side to win at least the number of points it contracted in exchange for nominating trumps. Points are scored for winning tricks (5 each), Aces and Tens (10 each), and Fives (5 each)—a total of 165.

Each in turn, starting with eldest, bids to win a minimum number of points, which must exceed than that of any previous bid. The lowest bid is 85. No trump suit is mentioned in the auction.

Declarer takes the four table cards, discards any four face down, which will count as a won trick to the declaring side, and leads to the first trick. The suit of the card led is automatically trump. You must follow suit if you can, but may otherwise play any card. The trick is taken by the highest card of the suit led, or by the highest trump if any are played, and the winner of each trick leads to the next.

The non-declaring side always scores what it makes. So do the declarers if successful, with a special score of 250 for winning all 13 tricks. For going down, they lose the amount of their bid, doubled if they take less than their opponents. Scores are recorded as shown in the three left-hand columns below (their explanation is in parenthesis):

125 /　　 135　30　(= bid 125, made 135 to opponents' 30.)
125 /　 −125　50　(= bid 125, made only 115 to opponents' 50.)
125 /　 −250　90　(= bid 125, made only 75 to opponents' 90.)

Play up to 505 points, or any other agreed total.

Roque for three

Omit ♣2, deal 15 each and six face down to the table. The lowest bid is 95, the highest 185. As in the four-hand game the counting cards total 100, but there are 15 tricks at 5 points each, and the declarer's six discards count 10, making 185 in all. The slam score is 350. Game is 650.

Rouge et Noir (R & N) ▸ *Trente et Quarante*

Rounce ▸ *Rams*

Rovescino ▸ *Ciapanò*

Rubicon

Tag denoting any variety of game (chiefly ▸ **Bezique** and ▸ **Piquet**) in which the losing player or side is penalized more heavily for failing to 'cross the Rubicon' of a minimum point-score—similar to the 'lurch' or 'Skunk' at ▸ **Cribbage**, the 'schneider' at ▸ **Skat**, and so on.

Ruff

Sixteenth-century ancestor of ▸ **Whist**. Twelve cards each were dealt and the remaining four left face down as a stock, with its top card turned for trump. If anyone held the trump Ace they could 'ruff' by taking these four cards into hand and discarding any four in their place. Ruff became Ruff and Honours, in which the Deuces were omitted, 12 cards each were dealt, and extra payments were made for holding certain high cards or 'honours'. This became Whisk and Swabbers, in which 13 each were dealt, and the 'swabbers' (honours) were ♥A, ♣J, and the Ace and Deuce of trumps. With the loss of swabbers, Whisk became classical partnership Whist.

Rummy

Rummy game(s)

52 *or* 52 52

A large family of games in which players alternately draw and throw out cards with a view to forming their hands into matched sets of cards or 'melds'. Early forms, such as ▶ **Conquián** and ▶ **Gin**, are basically 'Going-out' games, in that you do not score for melds but merely aim to go out by playing off all your cards in melds. In later developments, leading to ▶ **Canasta**, you do score for melds, and therefore aim to keep melding as much as possible until you have a high enough score to make it worth your while to end the game by going out.

There was a vast expansion of Rummy games in the early twentieth century (partly influenced by the craze for the probably ancestral game of Mah-Jong), culminating in the highly elaborate partnership game of Canasta in the 1950s. That bubble has burst, leaving different groups of players practising a variety of informal games under an equal variety of interchangeable rules and titles. To some, all forms of Rummy are 'Gin'; to others, they are 'Kalookie'; and so on.

The most basic form of Rummy is described below. There are typical variations which players may adopt or adapt to suit their own tastes. Separate entries will be found for these more specialized members of the family: Arlington, Bolivia, Canasta, Compartment Full, Conquián, Continental Rummy, Contract Rummy, Czech Rummy, Elimination Rummy, Fifty-One Rummy, Gin, Hand and Foot, Kalookie, Kings and Queens, Oklahoma, Pennies from Heaven, Persian Rummy, Progressive Rummy, Rummy, Samba, Tonk, Vatican, Whisky Poker, Zetema.

Two to four players use one 52-card pack, five to eight use two packs shuffled together. Thorough shuffling is essential before each deal in all Rummy games. Decide first dealer by any agreed means.

Deal seven cards each in ones, turn the next face up to start the discard pile, and stack the rest face down beside it to form the stock.

The aim is to 'go out' or 'knock' by eliminating all the cards in your hand. This is done by collecting sets of matching cards and laying them face up on the table in 'melds'. A meld may be a *set* or a *sequence*.

- A set is three or more cards of the same rank (Aces, Sixes, Jacks, or whatever).
- A sequence is three or more cards of the same suit and in numerical order. For this purpose, cards run A 2 3 4 5 6 7 8 9 10 J Q K.

No card may belong to more than one meld, and once a card has been melded it may not be moved from one meld to another.

On your turn to play draw the top card of either the stock or the discard pile, add it to your hand, and throw one card face up to the discard pile. (If you drew the top discard, you may not discard it again on the same turn.)

Whenever you have a meld you may lay it face up on the table before you immediately after drawing a card and before discarding one. When you have made at least one meld, you may subsequently play off single cards from your hand by matching them to melds already made, regardless of who made them. For example, you could lay off ♥7 to a set of Sevens, or ♥Q to a set of Queens, or either of them to the sequence ♥8-9-10-J. You may make as many melds and lay-offs as you can between drawing and discarding in a single turn.

Play ceases the moment someone goes out by playing the last card from his hand, whether as part of a new meld, a lay-off, or a discard. That player wins, and scores (or is paid by the other players according to the face value of cards left unmelded in their hands. Numerals count at face value from Ace 1 to Ten 10, and face cards 10 each.

Russian Bank ⟫ *Spite and Malice*

Salic Law

Patience game

52 52

This classic double-pack solitaire takes its rather obscure theme from a medieval law of the Franks that prevented the royal succession from passing through the female line.

Flick through the pack till you find a King, and deal him face up near the top of the table and to one side, but leaving enough room for two rows to go above.

Your aim is to finish with a row of eight Queens at the very top, a row of Jacks beneath them, and a row of Kings below the Jacks. The Jacks will actually be the top cards of piles of eleven-card sequences based on Aces.

Start dealing cards face up from stock in a column upon the King, spreading the cards towards you so that all remain identifiable.

When an Ace appears, set it out above the King in a row reserved for Aces. The Aces are to be built up in sequence to the Jacks, regardless of suit. When a card appears that can be built on an Ace pile to continue the sequence, take it out and do so.

When a Queen appears, set her out above the first Ace to start the row of Queens, and complete the row with further Queens as and when they appear.

When a King appears, start a new column by setting him out next to the King at the head of the previous column.

When you run out of stock, you will have a row of Queens at the top, a row of piles under construction below, and eight King-headed columns of varying lengths below the piles.

The exposed cards at the nearer ends of the columns are now available for building on the Ace-piles. They may not be built on one another, but when a King is exposed it may be treated as a temporary space for the accommodation of any single card from the end of a column. (Or, in a variant called King and Queen, for the accommodation of up to three such cards.)

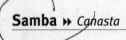

Samba ▸ *Canasta*

Sant (Saunt) ▸ *Piquet*

Scarto

Tarot game

A good introduction to ▸ **Tarot games** is afforded by the Piedmontese game of Scarto ('Discard'). It is now on the wane but has the advantage of being less complicated than most Tarot games.

Scarto is normally played with the 78-card *Tarocco Piemontese* pack, in which the Angel trump, #20, is actually the highest, beating #21. But any 78-card Italian-suited pack will do, and the 21 can then resume its normal high position. The pack consists of:

- The Fool (Matto).
- Twenty-one trumps, headed by the Angel (20), followed by 21, 19, 18, and so numerically down to No 1, called Bagatto.
- Fifty-six plain cards, fourteen in each of the four suits, swords, batons, cups, and coins. The highest cards are King (*Re*), Queen (*Dama*), Cavalier (*Cavallo*), Jack (*Fante*). These are followed by the ten numerals. In swords and batons they rank downwards from Ten high to Ace low. In cups and coins they rank in reverse order from Ace high to Ten low.

A game is three deals, each dealing in turn. Points are scored for capturing certain cards ('counters') in tricks. They are the Angel, The Bagatto, the Fool, and all sixteen courts. Each plays for himself, and whoever has the lowest cumulative score after three deals is the loser.

Deal. Choose first dealer by any agreed means. The turn to deal and play then passes to the right. Deal all the cards around in fives, Dealer himself taking the remaining three.

Discard. Dealer examines his hand and discards three cards face down which will count for him at end of play as if he had won them in tricks. He may not discard the Angel, the Fool, or any King, and may only discard The Bagatto if he holds no other trump or the Fool. Every player now has twenty-five cards.

Play. Eldest leads to the first trick. Subsequent players must follow suit if possible, otherwise trump if possible, otherwise may play any card.

Scarto is played with Italian (Piedmontese) tarocchi. Shown here are the Nine of swords and Three of trumps (The Empress).

The trick is taken by the highest card of the suit led, or by the highest trump if any are played, and the winner of each trick leads to the next. Tricks need not be kept separated: everyone just makes their own pile of the cards they win.

Playing the fool. Whoever holds the Fool may play it at any time, in contravention of any of the above rules. It cannot win the trick, but neither can it be lost. Instead, its player simply shows it as his played card, then adds it to his own pile of winnings, where it stays for the rest of the deal. It is legal, if pointless, to lead it to a trick. If you do, any card may be played second, and the third player must follow suit to that.

Score. At end of play, everyone sorts through their won cards and reckons their values in batches of three at a time. The counting cards and their values are:

The Angel (#20)	5	Kings	5 each
The Bagatto (#1)	5	Queens	4 each
The Fool	4	Cavaliers	3 each
		Jacks	2 each

A batch of three counters scores 2 less than the total value of its individual counters. Two counters and a blank score 1 less than the two counters together. One counter and two blanks score just the value of the counter, and three blanks score exactly 1 point. Whoever played the Fool counts 4 for it without including it in a batch. Whoever won the trick to which the Fool was played will have two odd cards left over. He counts these exactly as though they were three, the third being a non-counter.

No matter how the cards are batched in threes, the total of points distributed between the three players will always be 78. Since the average score is 26, each player counts towards game the difference between 26 and the points he took. Thus, if the counters divide 30, 27, 21, the respective scores are +4, +1, and −5.

The player with the lowest score after three deals pays a small stake to each of the others.

☞ *Comment.* The scoring is typical of Tarot games. There are two ways of simplifying it. One is to try to make all batches of three contain at least two blanks, as these give the simplest scores, namely, 1 point or the value of the single counter. The other is to assume a notional value of 1 point per blank, in which case any three cards count 2 less than their total face value. For example: Angel, Cavalier, Ten counts $(5 + 3 + 0) - (1) = 7$ by the first method, and $(5 + 3 + 1) - (2) = 7$ by the second.

Scat ▸▸ *Ride the Bus*

Schafkopf

The Bavarian national card game, also played to a limited extent in America under the name Sheepshead, or Shep. It was an immediate ancestor of ▸ **Skat** and subsequently gave rise to the more elaborate game of ▸ **Doppelkopf**.

http://www.pagat.com/schafk/schafkopf.html

Schieber ▸▸ *Jass*

Schmaus ▸▸ *Mousel*

Schnapsen, Schnapser ▸▸ *Sixty-Six*

Schwimmen ▸▸ *Thirty-One (2)*

Scopa, Scopone

Fishing game

Scopa and Scopone, its partnership equivalent, are two of Italy's major national card games.

Scopa

Two or three players use a 40-card pack running A 2 3 4 5 6 7 J Q K in each suit. Decide first dealer by any agreed means. The turn to deal and play passes always to the right.

Deal three cards each in ones, face down, and four face up to the table. When everyone has played their three cards, deal three more each from stock. Continue until all cards have been used and captured.

Each in turn plays a card from hand with a view to capturing one or more table cards. Table cards may be captured by *pairing* or *summing*.

1. **Pairing.** An Ace takes an Ace, a Two a Two, and so on. Only one card may be paired in one turn, and if the hand-card can capture in either way it must do so by pairing. For example, if the table cards are

and you play a Seven, you capture only the Seven, not the Three and Four.

2. **Summing.** A hand-card takes two or more table cards totalling the same as itself. For this purpose, cards count at face value from Ace 1 to Seven 7, followed by Jack 8, Queen 9, King 10. Thus a Seven will capture two or more cards totalling 7 (A + 6, 2 + 2 + 3, etc), a Jack two or more totalling 8, and so on. Only one such combination may be made at a time. For example, if the table cards are

and you play a Six, you capture either A + 5 or 2 + 4, but not both.

When you make a capture you place both the captured and the capturing cards face down in front of you and end your turn. If you capture all the cards on the table, leaving none for the next player to take, it is a *scopa* or 'sweep'. You indicate this by leaving the capturing card face up in your winnings pile, and will score 1 point for it at end of play.

If you play a card that can make a capture, the capture must be made. If not, you must 'trail' by playing any card face up to the table and leaving it there. This is inevitable after a sweep.

When no cards remain in stock, the last player to make a capture (not necessarily the last to play, since he may be forced to trail) takes all the other table cards with it. This does not count as a sweep, even if, technically, it happens to be one.

Players then sort through their won cards and score as follows:

> 1 for taking the most cards. If tied, no one scores.
> 1 for having captured ♦7, or *sette bello*.
> 1 for taking the most diamonds. If tied, no one scores.
> 1 for *primiera* (*see* below).
> 1 per *sweep*, as indicated by face-up cards.

For *primiera*, each player extracts the highest-scoring card he has in each of the four suits, and the player whose four have the highest combined value scores the point. A player who took only three suits cannot compete. For this purpose only, cards count as follows: Seven 21,

Six 18, Ace 16, Five 15, Four 14, Three 13, Two 12, face cards 10 each. (Swiss variant: King 10, Queen 9, Jack 8.)

The winner is the player with the highest score at the end of the deal in which anyone reaches 11 points.

Variants. Scopa is rich in alternative rules and optional extras.

In *Scopa d'assi*, an Ace from the hand sweeps all the cards from the table. This may or may not be permitted if the table cards include an Ace, and may or may not score as a sweep.

In *Scopa de quindici*, a card from the hand may capture one or more cards on the table which, together with the capturing card, total fifteen. For example, with A 3 7 K on the table, a Five could be played to capture the 3 + 7 (or, less profitably, the King). In some versions, point-count captures may be made only in this way, to the exclusion of other forms of addition.

Scopa de undici is the same, but with 11 as the key total.

Some start by dealing nine cards each. In this case, immediately after playing a card you draw a replacement from stock (so long as any remain) before playing again.

Points may be scored for capturing particular cards in addition to ♦7, notably ♠2; and for capturing a sequence of three cards, typically ♦A-2-3, ♠A-2-3, or ♦J-Q-K.

In some circles, points are remembered as they accrue, and the winner is the first to claim correctly that he has reached 11. A false claim loses the game.

Some use a 52-card pack, and count Jack 11, Queen 12, King 13.

Scopone

The four-hand partnership form of Scopa differs in the following respects. Players sitting opposite each other are partners. Each receives nine cards, and four are dealt face up to the table. Alternatively, each receives ten, and the first player can only trail. Both versions have staunch devotees. Beginners will probably be happier with the former.

Scorpion

Patience game

One of several solitaires invented by Albert Morehead and Geoffrey Mott-Smith, Scorpion is a version of ▶ **Spider** but with a sting in its tail. *See also* ▶ **Curds and Whey**.

Deal seven cards in a row—the first four face down, then three face up. Deal two more rows in the same way across them. Then deal four more rows of seven across them all, this time all face up.

Spread them down towards you into columns so all the faced cards are identifiable. You now have 49 cards out in seven columns of seven each, with 12 face down and the rest face up. Put the last three cards on one side, face down, as a reserve. (They are the 'sting in the tail'.)

Your aim is to build four thirteen-card suit sequences running downwards from King to Ace within the layout, and to eliminate each one as it is completed.

Within the layout, you can transfer any face-up card (except a King) to the uncovered end of a column, provided that:

- it is of the same suit and one rank lower than the card you play it to, and
- you take with it all the cards lying above it (that is, all those covering it, not the ones it covers).

Whenever this process leaves a down-card uncovered, turn it face up.

A space made by clearing out a column may be filled only by a King, together with any and all cards that may be covering it.

When stuck, deal the three reserve cards face up across the exposed ends of the first three columns and continue play. You can do this before getting stuck, if you prefer, but you must deal all three in the same turn, not one at a time on different turns.

Whenever you complete a suit-sequence of 13 cards from King to Ace, remove it from the layout and continue play.

You win if you get all four out.

Scotch Whist

Point-trick game

An old Scottish game also called Catch the Ten. Dr Johnson's Scottish biographer Boswell called it Catch-Honours.

Cards rank A K Q J 10 9 8 7 6 except in trumps. If five or seven play, omit a Six; if eight, omit all Sixes, or (better) add the Fives. Four, six, or eight may play in partnerships as arranged by agreement.

Deal all the cards out one at a time, turning the last for trumps. If two or three play, deal (respectively) three or two 6-card hands face down to each. Each hand is picked up and played separately, the others remaining face down until the previous hand has been played out.

The aim is to win tricks, especially those containing any of the top five trumps, which rank and count as follows:

Jack	11
Ace	4
King	3
Queen	2
Ten	10

(If you are used to continental games you may prefer Ace 11, King 4, Queen 3, Jack 2, Ten 10. It makes no difference to the play, and is easier to remember.)

Eldest leads to the first trick and the winner of each trick leads to the next. You must follow suit if you can, but may otherwise play any card. The trick is taken by the highest card of the suit led or by the highest trump if any are played.

Each player scores the point-value of any top trumps won in tricks, plus 1 point per card taken in excess of the number originally held. Game is 41 points. If previously agreed, play ends when anyone reaches 41 by winning a counter; otherwise, play the last hand out.

French Whist

Like Scotch Whist, but played with 52 cards. Score 10 extra for capturing ♦10, nothing for non-counting cards. Game is 40 points, the maximum available.

Sechsundsechzig ▸ *Sixty-Six*

Sedma

Point-trick game

Sedma, Czech for 'Seven', is an appropriate title for this Bohemian game with rules both simple and highly unusual. A slightly more elaborate version is its Hungarian equivalent, ▸ **Hola**. The four-hander is described first, as seeming more natural.

A game is typically twelve deals. Although each plays for himself in the long run, the players sitting opposite each other at each deal are partners. Partners are changed after every four deals, so that everyone partners everyone else an equal number of times throughout.

A 32-card pack is used, with cards ranking A 10 K Q J 9 8 7 in each suit. Deal eight cards each, one at a time. The aim is to win Aces and Tens in tricks, each counting 10 points. A further 10 for winning the last trick makes 90 in all and so prevents ties.

Eldest leads to the first trick, and the winner of each trick leads to the next. You may always lead or play any card you choose: there is no need to follow suit. All Sevens are trumps. A trick is taken by the last played card of the same rank as the one led, or by the last played trump (Seven) if any are played.

Examples

1. Played: 9 J A J. The Nine wins, having been neither matched nor trumped, and the trick counts 10 for the Ace.
2. Played: 9 A A 9. The second Nine wins a trick worth 20.
3. Played: 9 7 J 10. The Seven trumps a trick worth 10.
4. Played: A 7 7 A. The second Seven wins a trick worth 20.
5. Played: 7 7 7 7. The last-played Seven wins.

Each player scores the points made by his own partnership. These scores are carried forward, and the winner is the player with the highest total after 12 deals, or any other agreed number.

Sedma for two

Deal four cards each and stack the rest face down. Non-dealer leads first, and the winner of each trick leads to the next. A trick may contain any even number of cards, each playing alternately. The follower may play any card. If it fails to match or trump the lead, he says 'Pass', and the leader wins the trick without further play. If it does match or trump, the leader must himself then either match or trump—unlike his opponent, he may not play a losing card. If he passes, the follower wins the trick.

This continues until an even number of cards have been played, and the original leader has either won the trick or passed. The trick is taken by the last played card of the same rank as the one led, or by the last played Seven if any are played.

Each in turn, starting with the winner, then draws from stock until he has four cards again, and the previous trick winner leads to the next. The stock exhausted, continue until all cards have been played.

Sequence Rummy

A form of ▶▶ **Continental Rummy**

Sergeant Major

Plain-trick game

Also called 8-5-3 or 9-5-2, Sergeant Major is a sort of three-player ▶ **Whist** popular in the armed services, with relatives found in India and the Middle East. *See also* ▶ **Bismarck** and ▶ **Tribello**.

Cards rank A K Q J 10 9 8 7 6 5 4 3 2 in each suit. Deal 16 each in ones and four face down as a kitty. Dealer names a trump suit, discards four, and takes the kitty in their place. Eldest leads, and tricks are played as at Whist. The dealer's target is eight tricks, that of eldest five, the other's three (whence the title '8-5-3'), and each wins or loses 1 point (or stake) per trick taken above or below his quota. A player who took more than his quota is 'up', one who took less 'down'.

In subsequent deals, after the cards have been dealt but before the kitty is taken, if just one player was up in the previous deal he gives to each opponent who was down one unwanted card from his hand for each trick by which the other fell short. For each card received, the recipient must return to the donor the highest card he holds of the same suit (the same card, if he has no other). If two players were up, they each do this to the third, starting with the one who has the higher target to reach in the current deal. After any such exchanges, dealer discards four and takes the kitty, as before.

The game ends when somebody wins 12 or more tricks in one deal. Variations are inevitable. In a Canadian version, the targets are 9-5-2.

Setback ▸▸ *Pitch*

Seven and a Half

Banking game

Italian equivalent of ▸ **Pontoon** or Twenty-One played with 40 cards lacking Eights, Nines, and Tens. Numerals count face value, courts each, ♦K is wild, and the aim is to get as close as possible to 7½ without exceeding it. Each punter antes and receives a card face down. After looking at it he may either stick or call for more cards, dealt face up, until he either sticks or busts. Banker then does likewise. If he busts he pays those with less than 8 the amount of their stake, doubled to the player who has a two-card 7½ count. If not, he collects from anyone with a bust hand or a lower count than himself, and pays anyone with a better count. A tie is a stand-off. A two-card 7½ beats one with more than two and entitles its holder to replace the banker, unless the latter also has one.

Seven Up ▸▸ *Pitch*

Shanghai Rummy ▸▸ *Contract Rummy*

Shasta Sam ▸▸ *California Jack*

Shed ▸ S**thead

Sheepshead (Shep)

The American version of ▸▸ Schafkopf

S**thead

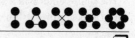

Going-out game

52

A folk-game also called Karma, Palace, Shed, etc. It resembles ▸ **Skit-gubbe** and other Scandinavian games.

Preliminaries. Two or more players use a 52-card pack ranking A K Q J 10 9 8 7 6 5 4 3 2 in each suit. Two Jokers are optional, or, if six play, essential.

Additional equipment. Brown paper bag. (Warning: do not use a plastic bag.)

Object. To avoid being left with cards in hand when everyone else has run out.

Deal. Each is dealt three cards face down in a row (down-cards), then one card face up on each of them (up-cards), and finally three cards as a playing hand (hand-cards). The rest are stacked face down. Before play, each player may exchange one or more hand-cards for a corresponding number of his own up-cards.

Play. Play takes place in two phases. Phase 1 ends when the last card is drawn from stock. In Phase 2, players continue by playing out all their hand-cards, then their three up-cards, and finally their three down-cards.

Eldest hand is the first player to have been dealt a Three as an up-card, or, if no one has, the first to have been dealt a Three as a hand-card. If no one has a Three, it is the person first dealt a Four; and so on as necessary.

Eldest starts by discarding from hand to a common wastepile any single card, or a pair or triplet of the same rank, and restoring his hand to three by drawing from stock. Each in turn thereafter must, if possible, play a singleton, or a pair, triplet or quartet of cards, equal or higher in rank than the top card of the wastepile. It is not necessary to match the *number* of cards played by the previous player, nor to play the whole of a matched set if it seems preferable to hold any back. If this reduces the hand to fewer than three cards, restore it to three by drawing from stock, thus ending the turn.

If unable or unwilling to discard, a player must take all the cards of the wastepile up into hand, leaving the next in turn to start a new series of discards.

Jokers. A Joker may be played at any time. It is not wild, but forces a switch in the rotation of play, so that the person who played the card before the Joker now has to match it or beat it himself. The new rotation continues till the next Joker appears.

Special rules. Deuces count high and low. You can therefore play one or more Deuces at any time, and the next player in turn can play any other rank.

When a Ten is played, the whole wastepile is turned down and left out of play, and the person who played it ends his turn by drawing to three cards (if necessary) and starting a new wastepile with one or more matching cards of any rank. (Some schools allow a Ten to be played after a Jack, Queen, King, or Ace.)

The same applies when a player leaves four of a kind on the top of the wastepile, whether by playing all four at once, or by duplicating the rank of the previous discard and so bringing the total to four.

Endgame. When the stock is exhausted, continue playing from hand. From now on:

A player with no card left in hand must play from his up-cards, if any remain. More than one may be played at a time if they are of the same rank. If forced to take the wastepile, however, he must revert to playing from the hand and may not play from the table until none remain in hand.

When a player has played his three up-cards, and has none left in hand, he must at each turn face one of his down-cards and play it if possible. If it will not go, he must add it and the wastepile to hand, and may not then attempt to play a down-card until no hand-cards remain.

The winner is the first to get rid of his last remaining down-card. The last to do so is a S**thead, and, to illustrate this fact, must wear a brown paper bag until somebody else takes over this role. (Plastic bags are dangerous.)

Variations. Many schools have their own special rules. For example, a Seven must be followed by one or more cards of equal or lower rank. If there are no Jokers, Eights switch the rotation, but are 'transparent'— that is, the next card or cards must beat the rank below the Eight, not necessarily the Eight itself. And so on.

Short Whist

Partnership Whist played up to five points, as opposed to the original 10 of so-called Long Whist.

Sift Smoke

Plain-trick game

52

Also called Lift Smoke (mistakenly) and Linger Longer (appropriately), this nineteenth-century game is simple, fun, and not devoid of depth. It is the reverse side of the coin, so to speak, of ▶ **Rolling Stone**.

Cards rank A K Q J 10 9 8 7 6 5 4 3 2 in each suit. Deal, in ones, 10 each if three play, 7 if four, 6 if five, or 5 if six. Turn the dealer's last card for trump, and stack the rest face down.

Eldest leads to the first trick, and the winner of each trick leads to the next. You must follow suit if you can, but may otherwise play any card. The trick is taken by the highest card of the suit led, or by the highest trump if any are played.

Tricks count for nothing as such, but the winner of each trick, and no one else, draws the top card of stock and adds it to his hand before leading to the next. As players run out of cards, they drop out of play, and the winner is the last player left with any card in hand. If all play their last card to the same trick, its winner wins the game.

If the stock runs out before anyone wins, the won tricks are gathered up, shuffled, and laid down as a new stock.

The winner scores a point for each card remaining in his hand. Credit is sometimes given for tricks won. For example, each may score 1 per trick taken, the winner's trick-score being then multiplied by the number of cards left in hand.

Six-Bid Solo

Point-trick game

36

An American invention associated particularly with Salt Lake City, and first recorded in 1924, Six-Bid ultimately derives from an old German game based on Tarock. It reached the United States under the name Frog (from German *Frage*), and underwent a variety of local modifications under such names as Solo, Slough, and Sluff.

Three players use a 36-card pack ranking A K Q J 10 9 8 7 6 in each suit. Cards captured in tricks count Ace 11, King 4, Queen 3, Jack 2, Ten 10, others zero.

Each player starts with 120 chips, or scores may be kept in writing and settled up later if desired. Choose first dealer by any agreed means. Deal 11 cards each in batches of 4-3-4, with an extra batch of three face down to the table as a blind (or skat, widow, slough, etc.). The blind remains untouched throughout play.

There is an auction to decide who will play alone against the others. Each in turn, starting with Eldest, must pass or name a higher bid than any previous one. From low to high, the six bids are:

1. *Solo.* The bidder will name a trump suit other than hearts and aim to take at least 60 card-points in tricks.
2. *Heart solo.* The same, but with hearts as trump.
3. *Misère.* Playing at no trump, the bidder aims to take no counting cards in tricks. (He may take tricks, provided they count for nothing.)

4. *Guarantee solo.* The bidder will name any suit as trumps and guarantee to take at least 80 in tricks, or 74 if hearts are trump.
5. *Spread misère.* As misère, but the bidder will lay his hand of cards face up on the table immediately before he plays to the first trick.
6. *Call solo.* The bidder will name trumps and aim to win all 120 points in tricks (not necessarily all eleven tricks). Before choosing trumps, he 'calls' any card, the holder of which must give it to him in exchange for any discard. If the called card is in the blind, there is no exchange. (*Variant*: he may call a different card.)

Eldest leads to the first trick, and the winner of each trick leads to the next. Follow suit if possible, otherwise trump if possible, otherwise play any card. The trick is taken by the highest card of the suit led, or by the highest trump if any are played.

In a positive bid, the blind is turned face up at end of play and any card-points it contains count for the soloist.

In a solo game, the soloist scores, or wins off each opponent, 2 units for each card-point he took over 60, or 3 in a heart solo. A 60–60 outcome is a tie. The other bids have fixed values: misère 30, guarantee solo 40, spread misère 60, call solo 100, call solo in hearts 150.

If the contract fails, the soloist loses, or pays each opponent, 2 or 3 units per point taken short of 60 in a solo, or the prescribed amount for any other bid.

Frog

The same, but with only three bids:

1. *Frog.* Hearts are trump; the bidder takes the blind before play and makes any three discards face down.
2. *Chico.* The bidder names any suit but hearts as trump, and plays without taking the blind.
3. *Grand.* The same, but with hearts as trump.

In each case the bidder aims to take at least 60 card-points in tricks, including any that may be contained in the blind or discard. He wins or loses the amount taken above or below 60 in frog, doubled in chico, quadrupled in grand.

Sixte

Plain-trick game

36 *or* 52

An old French game worth mentioning because it is uniquely designed for six players and very easy to learn. Sizette is the partnership version.

Sixte

Cards rank A K Q J 10 9 8 7 6 (5 4 3 2) in each suit. The turn to deal and play passes to the right. Deal six cards each in ones. If 36 cards are used, turn the dealer's last card for trump; if 52, stack the rest face down and turn the topmost card for trump.

Eldest leads to the first trick. You must follow suit if you can, but may otherwise play any card. The trick is taken by the highest card of the suit led, or by the highest trump if any are played, and the winner of each trick leads to the next.

One point is scored by the first player to win three tricks, or, if everybody wins one trick, by the winner of the first; otherwise there is no score. The overall winner is the first to reach six game points; but winning all six in one deal wins the game outright.

Sizette

There are two partnerships of three each, and each player is flanked by two opponents. Deal six each from a 36-card pack, turning the last for trump. Play as described above. The first side to win three tricks scores 1 point, or 2 if it wins all six. More interesting scoring schedules are easily devised.

Also recorded is a variant in which all the players of a side sit consecutively—i.e. A A A B B B instead of A B A B A B. You could also play a three-partnership version, with players sitting A B C A B C.

Sixty-Six (Schnapsen)

Point-trick game

24

One of the best games for two, the German *Sechsundsechzig* is almost as old as Cribbage. It was originally called *Mariage* (Marriage) and is ancestral to other marriage games such as ▶ **Bezique**, ▶ **Bondtolva**, ▶ **Gaigel**, ▶ **Tute**, etc. It is especially popular in Austria under the name Schnapsen (with slight differences: see below). Four may play Auction Sixty-Six (see later).

Cards rank and count in each suit as follows:

A	10	K	Q	J	9
11	10	4	3	2	0

The deal alternates, and the winner is the first to reach 7 game points over as many deals as it takes. Deal six each in threes; turn the next for trumps; stack the remainder face down on top of but not completely covering it.

Object. In each deal, to be the first to claim (correctly) to have reached at least 66 points for counters captured in tricks plus any marriages that may have been declared. Players must keep track of their scores mentally: it is forbidden to write them down or use a scoring device.

Tricks. Non-dealer leads to the first trick, and the winner of each trick leads to the next. Suit need not be followed. The trick is taken by the higher card of the suit led, or by the higher trump if any are played.

Trump Nine. If you are dealt the trump Nine, or draw it from stock, you may exchange it for the turn-up at any time, provided that:

- you have won at least one trick,
- at least three cards remain in stock, and
- the trump turn-up has not been turned down.

Marriages. A marriage is the King and Queen of the same suit in the same hand, counting 40 in trumps or 20 in a non-trump suit. If you are dealt one, or acquire one by drawing from stock, you may show it and claim the appropriate score, provided that:

- you have won at least one trick,
- you are about to lead to a trick,

- at least two cards remain in stock, and
- the trump turn-up has not been turned down.

Upon scoring for a marriage you lead one of the marriage cards to the trick and return the other to your hand. If you are dealt a marriage and declare it on your opening lead, but thereafter fail to win any trick, the score for your marriage is annulled.

Last six. When the last card of stock (the turn-up) has been taken, the last six tricks are played to different rules. You must now follow suit if you can and win the trick if you can, and if unable to follow suit must play a trump if you can. Marriages may no longer be declared. The winner of the twelfth and last trick scores 10.

Foreclosure (Shut-out). If, before the stock is exhausted, you think you can reach 66 with the cards remaining in hand, you may foreclose or shut the game by turning the trump turn-up face down. You may do this before or after both players have drawn. The last six tricks, or five as the case may be, are then played as above, but without the 10 for last.

Score. Play ceases when the last trick has been taken, or when either player claims to have reached 66. If both have 65, or if it is found that one player reached 66 without declaring, it is a draw, and the next deal carries an extra game point. A player correctly claiming 66 scores

1 game point, or
2 if the loser failed to reach 33, (*schneider*), or
3 if he took no trick (*schwarz*).

If one player claims 66 incorrectly, or fails to reach 66 after shutting, the other scores 2 game points, or 3 if he took no trick.

☞ *Note.* The whole point of the game lies in knowing when to foreclose. Expert players foreclose more often than not.

Schnapsen (Schnapser)

As Sixty-Six, but played with a 20-card pack lacking Nines. Deal five each (3 + 2 or 2 + 3) and play as above, except that it is the trump Jack that may be exchanged for the turn-up.

Auction Sixty-Six

(4 players, 24 cards) American partnership version. Game is 666 points over as many deals as necessary, compiled from the actual point-scores made for counting-cards, marriages, and last tricks. Deal six each, leaving no stock. Each in turns bids for the right to name trumps, but without actually naming a suit until a contract is established. The lowest bid is 60, succeeding bids are made in multiples of 6 (66, 72 etc) or 10 (70, 80), jump-bids are allowed, and the highest bid is 130. A player who passes may not bid again unless his partner did.

When three players pass in successions, the last (highest) bidder declares trumps and leads first (not necessarily a trump). Players must follow suit if possible, otherwise may play any card. The trick is taken by the highest card of the suit led, or by the highest trump if any are played, and the winner of each trick leads to the next.

If the bidding side takes at least what it bid, it scores what it makes. If not, the other side scores what it makes plus the amount of the bid. The 'grand bid' (130), won or lost, counts 260 to the scoring side.

Tausendeins

(2 players, 32 cards) This Austrian variant is played also in Switzerland under the name *Mariage*, in Denmark as *Deliriumseksogtres*, and in the Ukraine as a three-hander called ▶ **Tysiacha**. Deal six each from a 32-card pack ranking A 10 K Q J 9 8 7, and stack the rest face down. Play as at Schnapsen, but at no trump until a marriage is declared. This is done by leading a King or Queen to a trick and showing its partner. The first marriage establishes a trump suit, and each subsequent marriage changes it. The score for a marriage is 40 in diamonds, 60 in hearts, 80 in spades, 100 in clubs. Marriages may not be made in the last six tricks, and there is no score for winning the last. The winner is the first to reach 1001 over as many deals as it takes, and play ceases the moment either player claims to have done so.

Mariage

(2 players, 24 cards) As above, but deal five each from a 24-card pack. The first marriage declared scores 20, regardless of suit, the second 40, the third 60, and the fourth 80. There is a bonus of 100 for winning the

last five tricks. Actual scores are divided by ten, remainders are ignored, and the winner is the first to reach 100.

(Mariage also denotes several similar but slightly varying games. One, the ancestor of Sixty-Six is virtually identical, but is played with 32 cards, and recognizes, in addition to the marriage, a combination called *amour*. It consists of the Ace and Ten of a suit, and scores 30 points, or 60 in trumps.)

Chouine

(2 players, 32 cards) A French championship variety played especially at Lavardin, in Loir-et-Cher. Deal five each from a 32-card pack. Game is 101 points. A marriage scores 20, or 40 in trumps. A *tierce* (K-Q-J of a suit) scores 30, or 60 in trumps; a *quarteron* (A-K-Q-J) scores 40, or 80 in trumps; a *cinquante* (five 10-point cards) scores 50; and a *chouine* (A-K-Q-J-10 in any suit) wins the deal outright. A game is the best of five deals, a rubber the best of three games.

Sixty Solo ⇥ *Six-Bid Solo*

Sizette ⇥ *Sixte*

Skat
Point-trick game

Skat, one of the world's best three-handers, originated at Altenburg, near Leipzig, in the early nineteenth century, and rapidly became Germany's national card game. It is widely played, with a dozen countries affiliated to the International Skat-Players' Association and taking part in an annual world tournament. There is also a British Skat Association, founded in 2000. Other forms of the game are played in Wisconsin and Texas. The following description is of the standard German game as modified in 2002. It must be admitted that Skat not easy to learn, but it soon repays the effort. If you are not already acquainted with other games of the 'Ace 11, Ten 10' family, it might be helpful to start by playing ▸ **Sueca** or ▸ **Six-Bid Solo**.

Preliminaries. There are three active players, but usually four play together, each in turn sitting out the hand to which he deals. A 32-card French-or German-suited pack is used. A game is any number of deals exactly divisible by the number of players. Choose first dealer by any agreed means. The player at dealer's left is designated Forehand; at Forehand's left is Middlehand; and at Middlehand's left is Rearhand. If there are only three at a table, Rearhand will be the dealer. If there are four, the dealer receives no cards and plays no active part.

Deal. From a 32-card pack basically ranking A 10 K Q J 9 8 7 in each suit deal 10 cards each, starting with Forehand, in batches of 3-4-3. Between the first round of three and the round of four, deal two face down to the table to form the skat.

Cards. The rank of cards for trick-taking purposes, and their point-value when captured in tricks, is as follows:

						A	10	K	Q	9	8	7
Trumps	♣J	♠J	♥J	♦J	A	10	K	Q	9	8	7
Non-trumps	–	–	–	–	A	10	K	Q	9	8	7
Points	2	2	2	2	11	10	4	3	0	0	0

You will find it helpful to note that:

- the four Jacks normally rank as the four highest trumps and therefore belong to the trump suit, not to the individual suits marked on them;
- in suit contracts the trump suit therefore contains 11 cards as opposed to the seven of each plain suit;
- no fewer than one third of the cards in play are trumps (compared with one half in Bridge, Whist etc);
- the total number of card-points in play is 120.

Object. An auction determines who will play alone against the other two. The soloist's aim is normally to capture at least 61 card-points in tricks, but he may aim to capture at least 90, or to win all ten tricks, or to lose every trick, depending on his bid.

There are three types of game:

1. *Suit.* A suit is named as trump. The entire trump suit then contains eleven cards, headed by the four Jacks, and followed by A 10 K Q 9 8 7. The other 21 cards rank A 10 K Q 9 8 7 in each suit.
2. *Grand.* Only Jacks are trumps, forming a fifth suit of four cards, such that the lead of a Jack requires Jacks to be played if possible. The other 28 cards rank A 10 K Q 9 8 7 in each suit.
3. *Null.* This is a bid to lose every trick. There is no trump, and cards rank A K Q J 10 9 8 7 in every suit.

Any game may be undertaken in either of two ways:

1. *With the skat*: The soloist adds the skat to his hand and makes any two discards before announcing trumps, grand, or null.
2. *From the hand*: The soloist plays with the hand as dealt and announces his game immediately. He does not look at the skat until after the last trick.

Either way, any card-points contained in the skat count for the soloist at end of play, if needed.

Game values. Players bid by announcing not the *name* of the game being offered but its *value*, which is the score to be made by the bidder if he successfully undertakes the game, or lost by him if he fails. Whoever bids highest becomes the soloist. Except for nulls, which have invariable scores, games are valued as follows.

Trump games are valued by taking the *base value* of the suit selected as trump and multiplying this by a number of additional factors called *multipliers*. The base values are:

diamonds ♦ 9, hearts ♥ 10, spades ♠ 11, clubs ♣ 12, grand 24

The multipliers are:

1 per 'top' (*see* below), plus
1 for game, plus
1 for *schneider* (taking at least 90 card-points), plus
1 for *schwarz* (winning every trick), plus

1 for playing from the hand (if bid), plus
1 for *schneider* predicted (if playing from hand), plus
1 for *schwarz* predicted (if playing from hand), plus
1 for playing *ouvert* (with schwarz predicted)

'Tops' means consecutive top trumps from ♣J down. If you hold ♣J, you are playing 'with' as many tops as you hold. For example, holding ♣J but not ♠J = 'with 1'; ♣J ♠J but not ♥J = 'with 2'; and so on, to a maximum of 'with 11' in a suit game, or 'with 4' at grand.

If you do *not* hold ♣J, then you are playing 'without' (or 'against') as many tops as lie above the highest trump you do hold. For example, if your top trump is ♠J, you are without 1; if it is ♥J, you are without 2; if it is the trump Ten, you 'without 5' (since you lack four Jacks and the Ace); and so on, to a maximum of 'without 11' in suit or 'without 4' at grand.

Note that it is only the actual *number* of tops that count: whether you are 'with' or 'without' them is irrelevant.

To the number of tops you hold, add 1 multiplier for *game* if you reckon to take at least 61 card-points, or 2 for *schneider* if you think you can take 90+, or 3 for *schwarz* if you think you can win every trick.

If you intend to play from the hand instead of taking the skat and discarding before play, you further increase your game value by adding 1 for 'hand'.

If, and only if, playing 'from the hand', you may further increase your game value by announcing in advance your intention of winning *schneider* or *schwarz*, for 1 or 2 extra factors respectively—these in addition to the 1 or 2 for actually winning it.

If, and only if, playing from hand and declaring schwarz, you may add yet another multiplier for playing *ouvert*—that is, by laying your hand of cards face up on the table before the opening lead.

Given the valuations outlined above, it follows that the lowest possible game value is 18 (diamonds, with or without 1, game 2, × 9 = 18), and the highest 240 (grand ouvert with 4, game 5, hand 6, schneider 7, declared 8, schwarz 9, declared 10, ouvert 11, ×24 = 264).

Null bids. Null (misère) contracts have fixed and invariable values as follows:

Null (with skat)	23
Null hand	35
Null ouvert	46
Null ouvert, hand	59

Auction. Middlehand starts the auction by either passing or bidding against Forehand. He bids by naming successive game values from the lowest up, i.e. 18, 20, 22, 23, 24, 27, 30, 33, 35, 36, etc. (He is allowed to 'jump bid' by omitting individual values, but not to bid non-existent game values, such as 19 or 21.) To each of these, Forehand says 'Yes' if he is prepared to play a game worth at least that amount.

When one of them passes (either Middlehand because he will not make a higher bid, or Forehand because he can't accept the last bid named), Rearhand may then in like manner continue against the survivor by naming the next higher bid. When one of them passes, the survivor becomes the soloist, and must play a game at least equal in value to the last bid made.

If neither Middlehand nor Rearhand will open at 18, Forehand may play any game; but if he also passes, the deal is annulled and the next in turn to deal does so (unless it is agreed to play *Ramsch: see* below).

Game announcement. If playing with skat exchange, the soloist adds the skat to his hand, makes any two discards face down, and then announces his game, which will be either grand, a suit, null, or null ouvert. He need not announce the game he had in mind when bidding (if any), so long as what he does announce is worth at least the amount he bid.

If playing from hand, he announces his game, adding 'hand' and any other declaration that may be applicable (*schneider, schwarz, ouvert*).

If playing ouvert, he lays his hand of cards face up on the table before the opening lead.

Conceding. The soloist may concede the game at any time before he plays to the first trick. The commonest reason for conceding is when, playing with skat exchange and *without* two or more matadors, you find one or more higher matadors in the skat. For example, suppose you won the bid at 22, intending to play in hearts 'without 2, game 3, ×10, = 30'. You turn the skat and find the club (or spade) Jack. This revalues his game at 'with (or without) 1, game 2, ×10 = 20', which is lower than the 22 you bid. You now have three options:

- Announce hearts, as intended, and attempt to win *schneider* for the extra multiplier which will bring you game value to 30. There is no need to announce that you will be playing for *schneider*.
- You may attempt a different game—perhaps spades (22), null (23), clubs (24), or even grand (48).
- If none of these is playable, you will have to concede the game without play. In this case you will (of course) declare your game to be the lowest possible one consistent with your bid—in this case spades.

Play. Forehand leads to the first trick, and the winner of each trick leads to the next. You must follow suit if you can, but may otherwise play any card. The trick is taken by the highest card of the suit led, or by the highest trump if any are played.

☞ *Note.* At grand, the lead of a Jack calls for Jacks to be played, since they constitute a separate four-card trump suit. In a suit contract, the lead of any trump calls for the play of any other trump, not necessarily a Jack for a Jack.

Cards won by the partners are kept together in a single pile. All ten tricks must be played—except at null, if the soloist wins a trick—and the skat is then faced to ensure that the game is correctly valued.

Won game. The soloist wins if:
  (a) he took at least 61 card-points, or 90 if he bid *schneider*, or every trick if he bid *schwarz*, or no trick if he bid null; and
  (b) the game as revalued after play is worth at least the amount bid.
  In this event, the bidder's actual game value is added to his aggregate score.

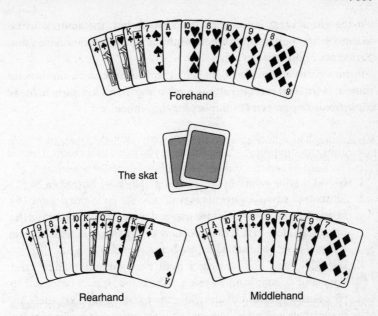

Forehand

The skat

Rearhand

Middlehand

Skat. The skat holds two Queens. Forehand can certainly think of a game in a red suit with skat exchange (worth 18 or 20), and might consider grand for 48. Middlehand bids up to 23 for a null, which Forehand accepts with grand in mind. Middlehand passes, not being prepared to play from the hand. Rearhand is willing to play in spades and bids up to 44, which Forehand accepts. He then decides to play from the hand, worth 55 (trusting that the skat will not contain a devaluing Jack). If Forehand passes at 50, it is touch and go whether Rearhand will finish with more than 59 card-points including the Queens. If he accepts Rearhand's 55 and goes for a grand hand, he should win by leading one Jack and holding the other back until he has shed his worthless cards.

- ☞ *Note.* A hand game played 'without' two or more may be reduced in value if the skat proves to contain a top trump, and may therefore be 'lost' by default.
- ☞ The skat counts as part of the hand for game valuation purposes, so it is possible to be 'with' or 'without' eleven even though only ten cards are actually held.

Lost game. If a lost game is worth at least the amount bid, its full value is first doubled and then deducted from the soloist's aggregate score.

If the game value is less than the amount bid, the amount to be doubled is the nearest appropriate multiple of the relevant base value that equals or exceeds the bid.

If the soloist is *schneidered*, by failing to take at least 31 card-points himself, there is no extra penalty—in other words, his lost game value is not increased by an extra multiplier for the schneider.

Variations. The following variations, though officially deprecated, may be encountered and preferred:

1. Grand may be valued at 20 (as it originally was) instead of 24.
2. Either of the two opponents may double the announced game (by saying *Kontra*), and the soloist may redouble (*Rekontra*), before the first trick is led. In this case the score or penalty, as detailed above, is doubled or quadrupled before being applied.
3. If Middlehand and Rearhand both pass without bidding, and Forehand doesn't want to risk a normal bid, it may be agreed to play Ramsch instead of annulling the hand. At Ramsch, there are no partners and no winner, only a loser, and cards rank and value as at grand (Jacks trump). There are several versions, the commonest being *Schieber* or Push Ramsch. Forehand takes the skat and passes two cards face down to Middlehand, who passes any two face down to Rearhand, who discards any two to the skat. (The passing of Jacks may be agreed illegal.) The winner of the last trick adds the skat to his won cards, and whoever takes the most card-points deducts from his score the number of card-points he took in tricks.

http://www.weddslist.com/skat/ (*British Skat Federation*)
http://www.pagat.com/schafk/skat.html (*Rules*)
http://www.davidparlett.co.uk/skat/ (*Background*)
http://www.skat.com (*German Skat Federation*)

American Skat

American and modern German Skat both derive from a late nineteenth-century original which offered three types of suit-game: skat exchange, tourné, and solo (hand). German Skat has retained the first and dropped the second, but American has retained the tourné and dropped the skat-exchange bid (except at grand). The hand bid, here called *solo*, remains unchanged. The games and base values of American Skat are:

Tourné. Diamonds 5, hearts 6, spades 7, clubs 8, grand 12. The soloist takes one card of the skat and may accept its suit as trump, in which case he shows it, adds the other card to his hand without showing it, and discards two to the skat. If it doesn't suit him ('Paßt mir nicht')—either because he hasn't enough of that suit, or because its value is lower than his bid—he adds it to his hand without showing it, and *must* then turn up and accept the suit of the second card as trump. In either case, if the turn-up is a Jack, he may either entrump the suit it shows, or play at grand.

Solo. Diamonds 9, hearts 10, spades 11, clubs 12, grand 20, grand ouvert 24. The soloist announces trump and plays without taking the skat first. There is no extra multiplier for this, the base values being higher instead. Extra multipliers may be added for making or declaring schneider and schwarz. Suit solos are not playable ouvert.

Guckser. The soloist may only start by taking both cards and discarding two in their place when playing grand. The bid is called *guckser* and has a base value of 16.

Null. Null may only be played solo, without skat-exchange. It counts 20, or 40 ouvert.

Ramsch. If Middlehand and Rearhand make no bid, Forehand may announce 'ramsch'. The skat is untouched, Jacks are trumps, and the player taking the fewest card-points scores 10, or 20 if he took no trick. A player careless enough to win every trick loses 30 instead of the others winning 20.

As in German Skat, game value is found by multiplying the base value by: 1 per matador, plus 1 for game (61 +), or 2 for schneider (91 +), or 3 for schwarz (win every trick), plus another 1 or 2 for schneider or schwarz predicted.

Auction, rules of play, and scoring are basically as for German Skat. But note: (*a*) the bid values begin 10 (diamonds, tourné, with or without one), 12, 14, 15, 16, 18, 20, 21, 24, 25, 28, 30 …; (*b*) to win schneider, the soloist needs at least 91 card-points, not 90 as at German Skat; and (*c*) the value of a lost guckser is doubled before being deducted, and so is that of a tourné if the soloist played *second turn*, having rejected the first suit as trump.

Skitgubbe

Going-out game

SK in Swedish is pronounced like SH in English, and the key word means 'dirty old man', in the sense of unwashed rather than obscene. It is also called Mas and Mjölnarmatte.

Deal three cards each from a 52-card pack ranking A K Q J 10 9 8 7 6 5 4 3 2, and leave the undealt cards stacked face down.

Object. In Phase 1, to win good cards for the play of Phase 2. In Phase 2, to play out all cards won in Phase 1. The last player left with cards in hand is a *skitgubbe*.

Phase 1. Tricks are played at no trump between two players at a time. Each player draws a card from stock immediately after playing one out. Eldest hand leads to the first trick against his left-hand opponent. Each may play any card regardless of suit, and the trick is taken by the higher card played. If both are equal it is a *stunsa*, or 'bounce': the same leader draws from stock and leads again, and so on until one of them manages to play higher than the other. The trick-winner takes all cards so far played, turns them face down in front of himself and leads to the next trick, to which his left-hand opponent replies. (Even if this is the same player as before.)

Either player may, instead of playing from hand, take a chance by turning the top card of stock and playing that instead. Once turned, it must be played.

When only one card remains in stock it is taken by the player in turn to draw but remains face down on the table before him. The hands are played out as far as possible, any unplayed cards remaining in hand. If the last trick ends in a 'bounce' the players retrieve the cards they played.

The last card of the stock is then turned up to establish trumps for the play of Phase 2, and added to its owner's hand.

The players pick up the cards they won in tricks and use them as their playing hands for Phase 2. They probably will not all have the same number, but that does not matter. The aim is to play out all one's cards.

Phase 2. Whoever took the last card of stock in Phase 2 leads to Phase 2, and now all three play in turn, not two at a time as before. The leader may play any single card, or a sequence of two or more cards of the same suit. For example, a Three may be led, or 3-4 of a suit, or 3-4-5, and so on. Each in turn thereafter must play a better card or suit-sequence than the previous player. 'Better' means of the same suit but higher in rank—not necessarily consecutive with the previous card—or a trump or trump-sequence to a preceding non-trump play. You may play trumps even if able to follow suit. Throughout Phase 2 it is important to keep each player's contributions separate until they are turned down.

A player who cannot or will not play better must pick up the card(s) played by the last player—which may have been himself!—and the turn passes to the left. If everyone picks up, leaving no card to beat, the next lead is made by the player to the left of the one who picked up last.

Turning tricks down. When a 'trick' contains three contributions in all—whether one each from all three, or more than one by one of them—it is turned down and ignored. Whoever played last to it leads to the next. When one player runs out of cards the others continue as before until the trick has been played to three times and turned down. Subsequent tricks require only two contributions before being turned down. When a second player plays his last card, the third player has lost, and is a *skitgubbe*.

Slapjack
Card-catch game

A children's game that tests reaction speed.

Deal all the cards round as far as they will go. Everyone keeps their cards in a neat pile face down on the table before themselves. Each in turn, as fast as possible, takes the top card of their pile and plays it face up to a pile in the middle of the table. Whenever a Jack appears, the first player to slap their hand over it wins the central pile and shuffles it in with their existing pile before playing a card out to start a new central pile.

If you slap a card that is not a Jack you must lose one of your own cards to the person who played the card you wrongly slapped. If you run out of cards you are allowed one opportunity to win a pile by correctly slapping a Jack, but if you fail to do so you are out of the game.

Play continues until only one player remains, or somebody throws a tantrum, or everyone falls asleep, whichever happens first.

Slippery Sam

Banking game

Everyone contributes equally to a pot, which is replenished when empty. Deal three cards each, which no one may yet look at, and turn the next one face up. If it is a Seven or higher (Ace high), keep turning the next until it is a Six or lower. Everyone then bets whether or not they have been dealt at least one card of the same suit as the turn-up, and higher in rank.

Slobberhannes

Penalty-trick game

The German equivalent of ▶ **Polignac** is called 'Slippery John', though the card in question is a Queen. (It was a Jack in the original game when the King was highest and the Ace ranked below the Jack. Perhaps it should be renamed Slobberhannah, or Slippery Jane.)

The 32 cards rank A K Q J 10 9 8 7 in each suit. If five or six play, remove the black Sevens. Deal all the cards out one at a time. The aim is to avoid winning the first trick, the last trick, and the trick containing ♣Q.

Eldest leads to the first trick, and the winner of each trick leads to the next. Follow suit if possible, otherwise play any card. The trick is taken by the highest card of the suit led. There are no trumps.

You lose 1 point for winning the first trick, 1 for winning the last, and 1 for winning the ♣Q in a trick. If you win all three, you lose 4 points (or, as an interesting variant, *win* 4 points). The overall winner is the player with the fewest penalty points when someone reaches a previously agreed total.

If played for hard score, everyone starts with (say) ten units, and pays the appropriate penalty into a pool immediately upon incurring it. Winners divide the pool equally when one player goes broke.

Slough, Sluff ⇥ *Six-Bid Solo*

Smoojas

Flemish forerunner of ▸ **Klaberjass**, ▸ **Clobiosh**, or ▸ **Belote**, in which two play a form of ▸ **Bezique** using the card-point system of ▸ **Jass**. The name means 'Jewish Jass'.

Snap
Card-catch game

Usually regarded as a children's game, Snap is a game of skill, though not of card sense but of reaction speed, which is nowadays more often exercised by a computer.

Deal all the cards around, face down, forming a pile in front of each player. It doesn't matter if some players have one more card than others. Each may hold his pile of cards in hand, but must keep it face down and must always play the top card. Each in turn, as fast as possible, plays the top card of his pile face up to the middle of the table. When the card played matches the rank of the previous card (Ace on Ace, Jack on Jack, etc), the first player to call 'Snap!' wins the central pile and adds it to his own pile. A player who runs out of cards drops out of play. The winner is the player who ends up with all 52 cards.

If one player snaps mistakenly, or two or more snap simultaneously, the central pile is placed to one side as a pool (or on top of an existing pool) and a new one is started. Whenever a card played to the main pile matches the top card of the pool, the pool is won by the first player to call 'Snap pool!'

Variant. There is no central pile. Instead, each plays his cards face up to a pile in front of himself on the table. Whenever a card played matches the rank of any other player's face-up pile, the first to call 'Snap!' wins his own and the other player's pile and adds them to his playing pile. Whenever a player runs out of face-down cards, he takes his face-up cards, turns them down, and continues playing from them.

Snip-Snap-Snorem

Going-out game

Snip-Snap-Snorem (or -Snorum) heads a range of children's games which certainly go back to the eighteenth century and probably derive from a more ancient and bibulous gambling game.

A pool is formed and the pack dealt round as far as it will go. The turn to play starts at dealer's left and passes to the left. The first person plays any card face up to the table. Each in turn thereafter must play a card of the same rank if possible, otherwise pass. The first to match ranks says 'Snip', the second 'Snap', and the third 'Snorem'. The third then discards the quartet face down and leads any card to the next round. Anyone unable to match pays one counter to whoever played the previous card. If two or more match consecutively, the first of them is 'snipped' and pays 1 counter to the pool if he was the leader, or 'snapped' for 2 counters if he played the second card, or 'snored' for 3 if the third. The pool goes to the first out of cards, who also receives one counter from everyone else for each card left in hand.

Earl of Coventry

The same, but played without counters for a simple win. The leader says 'There's as good as [King] can be' (or whatever rank it is); the second player 'There's a [King] as good as he'; the third 'There's the best of all the three'; the fourth 'And there's the Earl of Coventreee'.

Jig

A cross between Snip-Snap-Snorem and Stops, in that the aim of succeeding players is not to match rank but to play the next higher card of the same suit, from Ace low to King high. The leader plays any card and says 'Snip', and the next four able to continue the sequence announce respectively 'Snap', 'Snorum', 'Hi-cockalorum', 'Jig'. The last turns down the five-card sequence and starts a new one. When a sequence cannot be continued because the last card was a King or the next card has been played out, the last player says 'Jig' regardless of position, and leads to the next round. As before, the first out of cards receives 1 counter for each card left in other players' hands.

Schnipp-Schnapp-Schnurr-Burr-Basilorum

A German game almost identical with Jig, except that Kings are not stops but are followed by Ace, Two, etc.

Solitaire ▸▸ *Patience*

Solo

Solo is basically a bid or contract, common to many games, in which you undertake to play alone and with the hand as dealt, instead of calling for the aid of a temporary partner (as in Solo Whist) or of seeking to improve your hand by drawing and discarding (as in Skat). *See also* ▸ **German Solo**, ▸ **Six-Bid Solo**, ▸ **Solo Whist**, ▸ **Spanish Solo**.

Solo Whist

Plain-trick game

Solo Whist (better called English Solo) is an informal game of home and pub, usually played for small stakes. It became popular in the 1890s and remained so for much of the twentieth century, especially as a commuter game. Its subsequent decline was probably set in train by the break-up of the British railway system in the 1960s. It has much to recommend it, especially if you prefer solo games as opposed to fixed-partnership game such as Bridge. (In which case *see also* ▸ **Nomination Whist** and ▸ **Pirate**.) It originated in Belgium as an early variety of ▸ **Boston** known as *Whist de Gand* or Ghent Whist. For a more elaborate equivalent, *see* ▸ **Belgian Whist**.

Four players use 52 cards ranking A K Q J 10 9 8 7 6 5 4 3 2 in each suit. Solo is usually played for hard score, each deal being complete in itself and settled as such, rather than forming part of an overall game structure with a final settlement at the end.

Whoever cuts the lowest card deals first and the turn to deal passes to the left. Cards are shuffled before the first deal but then not again until an *abondance* has been won—instead, the tricks are gathered up in clockwise order around the table and stacked to form the next pack for dealing.

Deal 13 cards each in three batches of three and one of four cards. The dealer's last card is dealt face up and establishes a preferred suit as trump. There is an auction to determine who will be the soloist and which game will be played. The possible games are, from lowest to highest:

Proposal ('prop and cop'). A bid to win eight tricks, with the turned suit as trump, in partnership with anyone who accepts your proposal. (It presupposes that you will each win four.)

Solo. A bid to win at least five tricks, using the turned suit as trump, and playing alone against the other three.

Misère (mis). A bid to lose every trick, playing at no trump.

Abondance (a bundle, or bunny). A bid to win at least nine tricks alone, after naming as trump any suit other than the one turned. (You don't have to name the suit unless and until you become the soloist.)

Royal abondance. The same, but accepting the turned suit as trump. (You don't have to specify 'Royal' unless you are overcalling another player's bid of abondance.)

Misère ouverte (spread). As misère, but playing with his hands of cards exposed to view on the table after the first trick has been quitted.

Abondance déclaré (slam). A bid to win all thirteen tricks, playing at no trump, and leading to the first trick.

The auction proceeds as follows. Each in turn, starting with Eldest, may bid or pass, and, having passed, may not come in again. Each bid must be higher than the preceding one. If an earlier player proposes ('Prop'), a later one may accept ('Cop'), provided that no higher bid has intervened.

Eldest hand has two privileges. First, if he proposes, and no one accepts or overcalls, he may raise his bid to a solo, which may not be overcalled. Second, if he passes, and another player proposes and is not accepted or overcalled, Eldest may himself accept the proposal.

If all four pass, a 'general misère' may be played. There is no trump, and whoever wins the last trick loses. (*Variant*: Whoever takes the fewest tricks wins.) Alternatively, the cards are thrown in and the next in turn to deal does so.

Eldest leads to the first trick—except in a slam, which is led to by the soloist regardless of position—and the winner of each trick leads to the next. You must follow suit if you can, but may otherwise play any card. The trick is taken by the highest card of the suit led, or by the highest trump if any are played.

In a spread misère, the hand is not exposed until the first trick has been taken. In an abondance, many follow the practice of playing the first trick at no trump, and only then declaring which suit is trump.

Typical pay-offs are as follows.

Prop and cop pays 10 for the bid and 2 per overtrick, or a flat 20 if the partners win all thirteen. This is paid by one opponent to one partner, and by the other to the other. If the bid fails, the loss is 10 for the bid plus 2 per undertrick.

The soloist in other contracts receives the said amount from each opponent if he wins, or pays it to each opponent if he loses. Solo pays 10 for the bid, plus 2 per over or undertrick, or 20 for the slam; an abondance 30 for the bid, plus 3 per over or undertrick. The other contracts have invariable values, such as mis 20, spread 40, slam 60.

A general misère costs 10 for the last trick; or, if the aim is to take fewest tricks, the player(s) taking most tricks pays 10 to the player(s) taking fewest.

It is usual to keep a separate kitty for abondances. Everybody stakes a fixed amount to the kitty whenever it is empty, and whenever everyone passes and the hands are thrown in. When an abondance is bid, the soloist takes the kitty if he wins, otherwise increases it.

A written score may be kept as follows. At prop and cop, each partner scores 1 per trick taken between them; solo scores a basic 10, plus 1 per overtrick; abondance scores a basic 20, plus 5 per overtrick. For losing any of these games, deduct 10 per undertrick. Misère, spread, and slam win or lose respectively 20, 40, 50.

Many other variations will be (or used to be) encountered.

Auction Solo

Introduced in the 1920s under the influence of Auction ▸ **Bridge**, this form of Solo sought to expand the skill and interest by increasing the range of bids, but signally failed to displant the original game.

The bids are: five, six, seven, eight, mis, nine, ten, eleven, twelve, spread mis, no trump slam (soloist leads), trump slam (Eldest leads). Bids of five to eight are solos, and win or lose 1 unit per trick actually bid, regardless of over- or undertricks. Bids of nine to twelve are abondances, and win or lose from 15 to 18 units respectively. Mis counts 10, spread mis 20, slams 25 or 30. Any solo or abondance can be overcalled by the same number in the turned suit, but no trump suit is named before play unless necessary to distinguish a 'royal' from an ordinary trump bid.

Spaces ▸▸ *Gaps*

Spades
Plain-trick game

52

A late twentieth century game apparently originating in America, where it is the subject of numerous clubs, tournaments, and web sites. It is usually played by four in partnerships, but is easily adaptable for other numbers. As befits a genuine folk game of recent origin, it is full of variations and not subject to universally accepted official rules.

Four players sitting crosswise in partnerships are dealt 13 cards each, in ones, from a 52-card pack ranking A K Q J 10 9 8 7 6 5 4 3 2 in each suit. Spades are always trumps.

There is no competitive auction. Instead, each partnership contracts to win a certain minimum number of tricks. First, the members of the non-dealer partnership discuss how many tricks they think they can win between them. They may say how many certain, probable, or possible tricks they think they can win individually, but may not give direct information about specific suit holdings. When their contract number is agreed, it is noted down, and the dealer's side embark on the same process.

If you think you can lose every trick in your own hand alone you may declare 'Nil'. In this case your partner announces how many he proposes to win. His bid establishes your side's contract, which is lost if you personally win any trick. Only one player per side may bid nil, unless otherwise agreed in advance (*see* Variants).

'Blind nil' is a nil bid you can make *before* looking at your cards, but *only* if your side is losing by 100 or more points. In this case you pass two cards face down to your partner, who adds them to his hand and passes you two cards face down in return.

To the first trick everyone must play their lowest club. Anyone void in clubs must play any heart or diamond, but not a spade. Whoever plays the highest club wins the trick and leads to the next. Play as at Whist or Bridge, but with the restriction that trumps (spades) may not be led until the suit is broken—that is, until a player has used a spade to trump a trick when unable to follow suit. This does not, of course, apply to a player who has only spades in hand to lead.

A side that takes at least as many tricks as its bid scores 10 times its bid, plus 1 per overtrick. There is a penalty, however, for consistent under-bidding. When, over a series of deals, the overtricks of a side total 10 or more (as witnessed by the final digit of their cumulative score), their score is reduced by 100, and any overtricks above 10 carried forward to the next cycle of ten. This is called sandbagging. (*Variant*: Each overtrick counts minus 1 point and there is no sandbagging.)

Example. A side has a score of 488, and on the next deal bid five and win nine tricks. This brings them to 538 plus 4 for overtricks, making 542. For the excess of 12 overtricks they deduct 100, bringing them to 442 and leaving them with an excess of 2 towards the next cycle.

For a failed contract, a side loses 10 points per trick bid.

For a successful nil bid, the nil bidder's side scores 50 points, in addition to the score won (or lost) by his partner for tricks made. If it fails, the nil bidder's side loses 50 points, but any tricks taken by the nil bidder may be counted towards the fulfilment of his partner's contract. Blind nil scores on the same principle, but doubled to 100.

Play up to 500 points.

Solo Spades

Four can play without partnerships, each bidding individually. If you can follow suit, you must not only do so but also (if possible) beat the highest card so far played to the trick. If unable to follow suit, you must trump, and overtrump, if possible.

Spády

Point-trick game

36

The modern Czech descendant of the historically illustrious game of ▶ **Trappola**. The 36-card Trappola pack, lacking numerals from Three to Six inclusive, was a specialized version of the Italian pack featuring suits of swords, batons, cups, and coins, and face cards representing King, Cavalier, and Footsoldier. These are here translated into (respectively) spades, clubs, hearts, diamonds; King, Queen, Jack.

Four players sitting crosswise in partnerships are dealt nine cards each, in batches of three, from a 36-card pack ranking and counting as follows:

A	K	Q	J	10	9	8	7	2
6	5	4	3	0	0	0	0	0

Whoever cuts the highest card deals first, and the suit he cuts is trump for that deal. In subsequent deals, the dealer cuts a trump after shuffling but before dealing.

After the first card is led, each in turn, starting with Eldest, may claim and score for holding three or four Aces, Kings, Queens, Jacks, or Deuces, the score being 5 for a trio and 10 for a quartet. In each case the rank must be stated, but the cards claimed need not be shown; nor, if three are held, need their suits be identified. A score of 5 may also be claimed for a *blanche* (a hand containing no courts), or 10 for a *bianca* (no courts or Aces). For each 5 or 10 scored by one side for declarations, the other marks an equivalent −5 or −10, so that all scores sum to zero.

The eldest hand leads to the first trick, and may not lead trumps (unless he has no other suit). You must follow suit if possible, otherwise trump if possible; and in either case must beat the highest card so far played to the trick if possible. The trick is taken by the highest card of the suit led, or by the highest trump if any are played, and the winner of each trick leads to the next.

Points are scored by one side (and correspondingly recorded minus by the other) for each of the following feats:

Winning the first trick with the trump Deuce	20
Winning the last trick with any Deuce	10
Winning the last two tricks with Deuces	20
Winning any other trick with any Deuce	5

(Winning the last trick with a Deuce is called a Twenty-Six, and winning the first with the trump Deuce is called a Fifty-Two, reflecting a now defunct scoring tradition.)

A score for 'game' is made by whichever side takes 40 or more of the 78 card-points available for capturing counters in tricks (each Ace 6, King 5, Queen 4, Jack 3), plus 6 for winning the last trick. The 'game' score is 10, and the other side correspondingly marks −10. It is made quite independently of any score for declarations or Deuce-tricks.

If hearts are trumps, the scores for game and for tricks taken with Deuces are doubled, but not those for declarations.

If both sides take 39 of the 78 for game, settlement is made only for declarations and Deuce-tricks, but in the following deal all scores (for declarations, game, and Deuce-tricks) are doubled, or redoubled if hearts are trump.

Spanish Solo

Point-trick game

36

Spanish Solo remains more popular in South America than in its country of origin. It is a cross between ▶ **Tresillo** and **Malilla** (▶ **Manille**)

Three players use a 36-card pack, typically A K Q J 7 6 5 4 3 in each suit. Choose first dealer by any agreed means. The turn to deal and play passes to the right. It is customary to shuffle at the start of a game, but not between deals. Deal 12 cards each in fours.

The top cards in each suit rank and count as follows:

7	A	K	Q	J
5	4	3	2	1

The Seven is called *malilla* ('imp', more or less). The other numerals (6 5 4 3 2 or 9 8 6 5 4), have no point-value, but each won trick an additional counts 1 point, bringing the total available to 72.

Each in turn, starting with eldest, must pass or make a higher bid than any gone before. A player who passes adds a chip to a pool, and is then out of the auction. The bids are:

Juego (solo): To take at least 37 points in cards and tricks, or 36 if bid by Eldest. Game value 2, or 4 in diamonds.

Bola (slam): To win every trick, after first naming a wanted card and receiving it from its holder in return for any unwanted card. Value 8, or 12 in diamonds.

Bola sin pedir (no-call slam): A bid to win every trick without first calling a wanted card. Value 16, or 20 in diamonds.

The highest bidder becomes the soloist and names a trump suit. No suit is named while bidding unless the proposed trump is diamonds, as this always beats the same bid in a different suit.

If all pass, the dealer names trumps, each plays for himself, and whoever takes most points wins.

Eldest leads to the first trick, and the winner of each trick leads to the next. Follow suit if possible, otherwise play any card. The trick is taken by the highest card of the suit led, or by the highest trump if any are played.

The appropriate amount is paid by each opponent to the soloist, or by him to each opponent.

Spanish sources do not state what happens to the pool. Probably it goes to the soloist if successful, and is doubled by him if not. Nor do they state the pay-off for the case when all pass and each plays for himself. A reasonable arrangement is for whoever takes fewest points to pay 2 to whoever takes most.

Nor do the sources adequately detail two optional misère bids. In *bola pobre*, the soloist aims to lose every trick after first calling a wanted card in exchange for an unwanted one; *bola pobre sin pedir* is the same, but without calling a card. It is unstated where these fit into the bidding hierarchy, whether they are played with or without trumps, and how they are valued.

Speculation

Banking game

52

An old family gambling game played by Jane Austen and the inhabitants of *Mansfield Park*. It is fun to play and rewards competence in calculating probabilities. A banking game to the extent that the dealer has certain advantages, it plays well, and more fairly, if the winner of each hand deals to the next.

Everyone starts with the same number of chips and at the start of each deal antes one to a pot. Deal three cards face down on the table in front of each player in a stack, then turn the next card of the pack to establish a trump suit. (Not that there is any trick-play. 'Trump' here means the only suit that counts.)

The aim is to be in possession of the highest trump when all cards in play have been exposed. For this purpose cards rank from Two low to Ace high.

The trump turn-up belongs by right to the dealer, so if it is an Ace the dealer wins without further play. If it is not an Ace, but is high enough to interest anyone else, they may offer to buy it from the dealer, and the dealer may haggle about it, or auction it, or keep it, as preferred.

Each in turn, starting with the player to the dealer's left—or, if the turn-up was sold, to the purchaser's left—turns up the top card of their own stack. This continues in rotation, but omitting the player who currently possesses the highest trump. If and when a trump is turned that is higher than the one previously showing, the player who turned it may offer it for sale at any mutually agreeable price, or refuse to sell it. Either way, play continues from the left of, and subsequently omitting, the possessor of the highest trump.

Furthermore, anyone at any time may offer to buy not necessarily the best visible trump, but any face-down card or cards belonging to another player. The purchaser may not look at their faces, but must place them face down at the bottom of his or her stack and turn them up in the normal course of play. (The time to indulge in this piece of speculation is when you currently own the highest trump and want to prevent someone else from turning a higher one.)

The game ends when all cards have been revealed, or when somebody turns the Ace, and whoever has the highest trump wins the pot.

Variations.

1. Anyone turning up a Five or a Jack adds a chip to the pot.
2. A spare hand is dealt and revealed at the end of play. If it contains a higher trump than the apparent winner's, the pot remains untaken and is added to that of the next deal.

Speed ▸▸ *Spit*

Spider　　　　　　　　　　　　　　●

Patience game　　　　　　　　　　52 52

Spider is one of a family of solitaires with the unusual feature of building suit-sequences in the layout rather than on base-cards set apart from it. For single-pack relative, *see* ▸ **Curds and Whey**, and ▸ **Scorpion**.

Deal ten cards in a row, face down. Deal four more rows of ten across the tops of them, also face down, then one more card to the tops of the first four piles in the row. You will then have dealt exactly half the pack out into ten piles of cards, with six cards in each of the first four piles, and five each in the other six. Turn the ten top cards face up.

Your aim is to build eight thirteen-card suit-sequences within the layout, each headed by a King and descending to its Ace.

The exposed cards are available for packing on one another in descending sequence and regardless of suit. For example, you can play any Six from one pile to any Seven in another. You can spread the piles towards you into columns so that all faced cards are identifiable. Whenever you uncover a face-down card, turn it face up.

You may shift a packed sequence of two or more cards as a whole to another column, provided that all the cards so moved are of the same suit, though the card on which they are placed need not itself be of that suit, so long as it is (as usual) one rank higher than the top card of the sequence.

If you create a vacancy by playing off all the cards of a column, you may fill the gap with any exposed card or suit-sequence of cards.

When you can get no further, or earlier if you prefer, deal ten more cards face up in a row across the near ends of the ten columns (or four when only four remain) in the same order as the original deal, then pause and continue play.

Whenever you complete a thirteen-card suit-sequence you may remove it from the layout and put it to one side. You are not obliged to remove it as soon as it is complete, but you must eventually discard them all in order to win.

As this game is not easy to get out, count half a win for completing and discarding six sequences. (If you get seven out, you can hardly fail to finish the eighth.)

Mrs Mop

You may prefer this variation devised by Charles Jewell. Deal eight cards face up in a row, and keep dealing rows of eight across them until all 104 cards are out in thirteen columns of eight. Then follow exactly the same rules of play as described above.

Spin (Spinado)

Stops game

This simple family game lying about half-way between ▶ **Pope Joan** and ▶ **Newmarket** is marginally more subtle than it may appear.

Remove ♦ 8 and all four Deuces from the pack. Make a layout with three compartments labelled Matrimony, Intrigue, and Game. Dealer stakes twelve counters on Matrimony, six each on Intrigue and Game, other players three each in every compartment. Deal the rest round as far as they will go, with an extra, 'dead' hand left face down on the table. The running order is A 2 3 4 5 6 7 8 9 10 J Q K.

Eldest starts a sequence by playing a card face up to the table. It may be of any suit, but must be the lowest he holds of it. Whoever holds the next higher card of the same suit adds it to the first, and so on, so that a numerical sequence of cards is built up in the same suit. Eventually a card will be played which no one can follow. Aces are all stops, because the Twos are out; ♦7 is a stop because the Eight is out; Kings are all stops because there is nothing to follow them; and others may be stops because the following card lies in the dead hand. The player of a stop then starts a new sequence, again with the lowest card he holds of any suit he pleases.

Anyone who succeeds in playing a King receives immediately 1 counter from each opponent, or 2 for the ♦K.

The pool for Intrigue goes to whoever plays ♦J Q in one turn; that for Matrimony similarly goes to the player of ♦Q K, in addition to the side payment for playing ♦K. A player holding ♦J Q K can, of course, win both; but it is equally possible that no one can win either, in which case the stakes are carried forward to the next deal.

The ♦A, known as Spinado or 'Spin', has a special power. Its holder may, on playing any card in the normal course of events, play Spin at the same time, announcing (for example), 'Seven and Spin', or whatever rank it may be. Besides earning him an immediate 3 counters from each opponent, this has the effect of making the Seven (or whatever) a stop, and so entitling him to start a new sequence.

Play ceases when one player plays his last card. He thereby wins the stake for Game, and is exempt from staking in the next deal.

Spit (Speed)

Patience

A rapid-fire children's game.

Deal 26 cards to each of two players from a well-shuffled 52-card pack. From your own 26 cards each of you deals a layout consisting of five face-down piles of cards, with one card in the first, two in the second, and so on up to five in the fifth. These are the stock piles. Turn the top card of each stock pile face up. Hold your other 11 cards face down in one hand. These 11 are your 'spit' cards.

The aim is to be the first to get rid of all your cards over as many deals as necessary. You don't take turns, just play as fast as you can simultaneously.

When you are both ready, shout 'Spit!', turn the top card from your hand, and place it face up on the table between both players' stock piles. These two cards form the bases of two piles of cards called the spit piles. What you are aiming to do is get all the cards played from your stock piles to the spit piles.

At each move, you may play the top card of one of your stock piles to either of the spit piles, provided that it is one rank higher or lower than the card you play it to. On an Ace you can play either a King or a Two. Suits don't matter. Then turn the top card of the pile you played from face up. If one of your stock piles gets emptied, you can fill the space with the top card from another one (but you can never have more than five stock piles).

Sooner or later you will both get stuck. At this point you both shout 'Spit!' again and turn the next card from your hand face up on the spit pile you started before. Then play on as before.

If one player has no spit cards left when play gets stuck, the other one spits alone. They can choose either pile to spit on, but, having chosen it, must stick with it every time the same position is reached.

If neither player has any spit cards when play gets stuck, the player with fewer cards left in their stock piles spits a card from the top of a stock pile.

When one of you gets rid of all your stock-pile cards, both of you slap your hand over one of the spit piles, ideally the smaller one. Whoever gets there first takes that pile, leaving the larger one for the other player.

(If you both choose different piles, of course, there's no dispute.) Whichever of you still has stock-cards left unplayed shuffles these in with the pile you took. Both of you shuffle your cards, deal another layout as before, shout 'Spit!' when ready, and play another round.

If one of you has fewer than 15 cards, you won't be able to deal a complete set of stock piles. In this case you deal them into five piles as far as possible and turn the top card of each. In this case you won't be able to spit, so there is only one spit pile, started by the other player.

When only one spit pile remains, and one player runs out of stock cards, the other plays on until stuck, then gathers up all the cards on the table, deals a new layout, and spits again. The winner is the first player to run out of all spit and stock cards.

There are many variations on this basic theme.

Spit in the Ocean ▸ *Poker*

Spite and Malice

Patience

54 54

Spite and Malice has become the better-known title of a game previously known under a variety of names, chiefly Russian Bank, but also Crapette, Cripette, Robuse, Rabouge, and various others. This version was formalized by Easley Blackwood (originator of the Blackwood convention at Bridge) and first published in 1970. It is deeper than it looks and easier to learn than some of its predecessors, and has the sort of addictive potential which should require it to be the subject of a government health warning.

Preliminaries. Use two packs of the same size but different back colours or designs. One contains 52 cards, the other 56 by the addition of four Jokers. (But three or even two will suffice.)

Shuffle the 52-card pack very thoroughly and deal 26 each. Each player's 26 cards form his 'riddance pile' and are placed face down on the table in front of him with the top card turned face up (the 'upcard').

Shuffle the 56-card pack very thoroughly, deal five each to form a playing hand, and place the remainder face down and squared up as a common stockpile.

Cards run A 2 3 4 5 6 7 8 9 10 J Q K. The player with the higher upcard goes first. If equal, bury the upcards and turn the next ones up.

Object. The winner is the first to play out all twenty-six cards from their riddance pile. As each one is played off, the one beneath is turned face up. Riddance cards may only be played to one of eight piles which are gradually built up in the centre of the table. Each centre pile starts with an Ace, on which is built any Two, then a Three, and so on, until it contains thirteen cards headed by a King. Suit need not be followed. When a centre pile is completed, it is turned face down and put to one side.

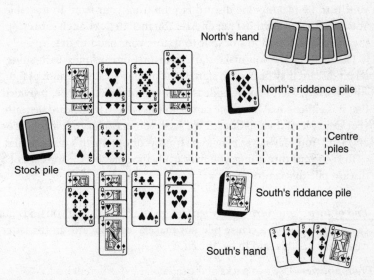

Spite and Malice. South could play ♥7 to ♠6, allowing North to play off his ♦8, and then continue the sequence to remove the ♠K from his own riddance pile. But this will be no good if North holds a Nine, as he himself could then block it by playing up to the ♦K. South will therefore play his 3–4–5 to the ♥2, discard ♠9 to ♠10, and draw four new cards, keeping the situation in tension and perhaps improving his hand.

Play. A turn consists of one or more of the following moves. On your turn to play, the following rules apply.

If your upcard is an Ace, you must play it to the centre to start a pile. If it is Two, and an Ace is already in place, you must play it to the Ace. If it is any playable card higher than a Two, you may add it to a pile headed by a card one rank lower (a Three, to a Two, a Four to a Three, etc), but are not obliged to if you can more profitably play it somewhere else.

If you hold an Ace or a card playable to a centre pile, you may play it to the centre, but are not obliged to. Playing to a centre pile entitles you to another move. If you play off all five cards to centre piles, you draw five more from the common stockpile and continue play.

Discard piles. When unable or unwilling to play to the centre, you end your turn by making one discard face up from your hand to the table. You may discard anything but an Ace. You then draw enough cards from the top of the common stockpile to restore your hand to five.

The first discard you make starts your first discard pile. Each subsequent discard may be used to start a new pile, up to a maximum of four. Alternatively, each may be added to the top of a discard pile, provided that it is either equal to or one card lower in rank than the card beneath. (For example, if the top discard is a Jack, you may play to it any Jack or any Ten.) You may never play to or from your opponent's discard piles.

To keep your turn going, you may at any time play off the top card of a discard pile to a centre pile.

End of turn. Your turn ends when you make a discard, or if you find you can neither play to a centre pile nor make a legal discard. In the latter case, your hand is said to be 'frozen'.

Frozen hands. Your hand is 'frozen' if you cannot make a legal move. In this event your opponent plays again even after making a discard, and may keep doing so until his play produces a situation in from which you can continue play.

If both players freeze, there is a redeal. All the cards in play *except the riddance piles* are gathered up, and shuffled and reshuffled very thoroughly together. Then five more each are dealt, the remainder are stacked face down, and play starts again from the beginning.

Jokers. You can play a Joker to a centre pile at any time and count it as the required card. For example, you can start a new pile by calling it an Ace, or play it as a Two to an Ace, a Three to a Two, and so on. You may not play it to a King, as this indicates a completed pile and no pile may contain more than 13 cards. A Joker once played to a centre pile cannot then be removed.

Alternatively, you may play it to a discard pile and count it as any legal card without specifying which until it is necessary to do so. (Thus, for example, if two Jokers are played to a Ten, they may be followed by a Ten, Nine, Eight, or Seven.) Although Aces themselves may not be discarded, any number of Jokers may be discarded on a Two, since they can all be counted as Twos. What a Joker stands for on top of a discard pile does not have to be kept when it is played to a centre pile: it can be played off as anything required.

Forced moves. Most moves are optional, and if both players decline to make any move from a given position then it is the same as if both hands were frozen, and a redeal is made as described above. There are, however, two exceptions:

1. If your upcard is an Ace, you must play it to the centre. If there is a bare Ace in the centre, and you have a natural Two showing as your upcard or on the top of a discard pile, then you must play it to that Ace. (But: a Joker is not so forced, even if it logically counts as a Two; and if you also hold a Two you may always play it from hand instead.)
2. If both hands are frozen, or both refuse to play, the next in turn must play an Ace or a Two from hand to the centre if he legally can, and his opponent must then do likewise.

End of stock. When the common stockpile is reduced to twelve or fewer cards, there is a pause while a new one is formed. This is done by taking all the centre piles which have been built up to the King, adding them to the existing stock, shuffling the whole lot very thoroughly, and then laying them down as a new stockpile. Incomplete centre piles are not taken for this purpose, unless *all* are incomplete, in which case *all* are taken.

End of game. The game ends as soon as one person has played off the last card from his riddance pile. The winner scores a basic 5 points, plus 1 for each card left unplayed from the loser's.

Spoof Sevens ▸▸ *Domino*

Spoons ▸▸ *Donkey*

St Helena

Patience game

One of many double-pack solitaires full of artificial Napoleonic flavour-ing. It has several names, including Napoleon's (or Washington's) Favourite, and even more variations. (One of them, though called Spider, bears no relation to the ▸ **Spider** described above.)

Put a King of each suit in a row and an Ace of each suit in a row beneath them. These are the bases. Your aim is to build the Aces up in suit to the Kings and vice versa.

Turn cards from stock and deal them in rotation as if to form a frame around the two rows, starting above the top-left King and proceeding in a clockwise direction—four above the Kings, two in a column at the right, four below the Aces, and two in a column at the left. Keep going until the stock is exhausted. But: if a turned card due to fall in the top row can be built on a King pile, take it out and build it. Similarly, a card due for the bottom row may instead be built on an Ace pile if it fits. A card due for any of the four lateral positions may be built on any suitable pile regardless of position. After building a card, fill the position it would have occupied with the next unplayable card from stock.

When the stock runs out the rules change. You can now build any uncovered card, regardless of its position. You may also pack single exposed cards on one another if they are of the same suit and consecutive in value. (Aces and Kings are not consecutive.) A vacancy may be filled with any available card.

If the game blocks, gather up the surrounding piles in reverse order of dealing, consolidate them into a new stock, turn it face down, and start playing again. The positional restrictions apply again until all have been dealt, when the rules are relaxed and packing takes place again. You are allowed two redeals, making three deals in all.

Stop the Bus ▸▸ *Brag*

Stops

A family of going-out games in which cards are played out in numerical sequence and the winner is the first player to run out of cards. A 'stop' is a card which no one can follow, whether because the sequence has reached the highest possible card (usually a King), or because the only possible cards that can legally follow the previous one have all been played out, or because some cards were not dealt to start with and are therefore unavailable for play. (The term 'stop' is commonly, but inaccurately, applied to such an undealt card rather than to the unfollowable card of a sequence.) See individual entries for: Comet, Epsom, Michigan, Newmarket, Pink Nines, Play or Pay, Pope Joan, Spin.

Stortok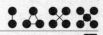

Going-out game

36

A Swedish elaboration of ▸ **Rolling Stone**.

Deal five cards each from a 36-card pack ranking A K Q J 10 9 8 7 6 in each suit and stack the rest face down. Turn the top card of stock to start the discard pile. The suit of this card is the high trump, and the other suit of the same colour automatically becomes the low trump.

Eldest starts by playing a better card than the turn-up and drawing a replacement from stock. Each in turn thereafter must similarly beat the previous card played and then draw a card from stock. A better card is a higher card of the same suit, or any trump to a non-trump, or any card of the high trump to a card of any other suit. Anyone unable or unwilling to beat the previous card must pick it up and take it into hand, but does not then draw from the stock.

If everybody plays to the trick, it is turned down and a new one started by whoever played last. If anyone picks up instead of playing, the trick is turned down and a new one started by the person to that player's left. When the stock runs out, play continues with the cards left in hand. As players run out of cards they drop out of play. The last one left with cards in hand is a *stortok*, or 'great fool'.

Strategy

Patience game
52

This solitaire by Albert Morehead and Geoffrey Mott-Smith is a more demanding version of an ancient game called Sir Tommy.

Turn cards from stock and play them one by one, face up, to any of eight wastepiles. As the table is empty to start with, the first card automatically defines the first wastepile. The next card you turn can either be placed on the first one, or used to start a second wastepile, and so on until you have a maximum of eight. Whenever you turn an Ace, do not play it to a wastepile but set it out as a base at the top of the table.

These Aces are eventually to be built up in suit and sequence to their Kings, but you may not do any building until all 48 other cards have been played face up to the wastepiles. The wastepiles should be spread towards you in columns so that their contents are identifiable.

Having dealt them all out skilfully and successfully, you now build up the four sequences on the Ace-piles by taking at each turn only the exposed card at the end of a column. If during play you have carefully considered the best column for each card, and avoided putting any card in a column already containing a card that will need to come out earlier, you should have into difficulty in getting the game out. With accurate play it should come out over 90 per cent of the time.

☛ *Note.* You needn't play the first eight cards to different wastepiles, but can delay starting a new pile for as long as you like. If successful, you can try reducing the number of piles to seven in the next game you play, or even six for more of a challenge. With a favourable distribution, Strategy has been known to come out with as few as five.

Strip Jack Naked ▸▸ *Beggar my Neighbour*

Strip Poker

A legendary but not mythical game that has yet to reach world tournament status. In the straight version, bets are made by raising the amount of promised divestiture. In Hi-Lo, the best hand specifies one such item on the part of the loser, or on the part of everyone else if all have folded. Each of these may be played by two (Honeymoon Poker) or more (Orgy Poker). The problem with the former is that it is hard to tell who has won and why; in the latter, everyone is past caring.

Stuss ▸▸ *Faro*

Sueca

Point-trick game

This Portuguese game forms an excellent introduction for beginners to point-trick games of the 'Ace 11, Ten 10' variety such as ▸ **Skat**. Although *sueca* means 'Swedish', it is virtually identical with an old German game called Einwerfen.

Four players sitting crosswise in partnerships are dealt 10 cards each, in ones, from a 40-card pack ranking and counting

A	7	K	Q	J	6 5 4 3 2
11	10	4	3	2	0 each

(The Seven, called *manilha*, may be replaced by a Ten if preferred.)

The last card is shown and its suit establishes trumps. If dealer forgets to turn it, Eldest may declare any suit trumps upon leading to the first trick. Each side's aim is to capture the greater value of counting-cards in tricks—i.e. at least 61 of the 120 available.

Eldest leads to the first trick, and the winner of each trick leads to the next. You must follow suit if you can, but may otherwise play any card. The trick is taken by the highest card of the suit led or by the highest trump if any are played.

A side scores one game point for taking 61 or more card-points, 2 for taking 90 or more, or 3 for winning every trick. A 60–60 tie doubles the value of the following game. If two successive rounds are tied, the next is quadrupled. Play up to four game points.

Einwerfen

The probable German ancestor of Sueca. The only difference is that the suit of the first deal remains 'favourite' for the rest of the game, and whenever the favourite suit is entrumped again the score for that deal is doubled.

Svoyi Kozyri

Going-out game

An exciting and easy-to-learn Russian game related to ▶ **Durak**. It is best for four and playable by three or two, but for a better two-hand equivalent *see* ▶ **Challenge** ('Besikovitch's Game'). The following description is based on that of Alexey Lobashev, an indefatigable collector of Russian folk games.

Cards. Use a 36-card pack ranking A K Q J 10 9 8 7 6 in each suit. Before play, each player announces which suit will be his personal trump for the whole game. All four must be different.

Deal. Decide first dealer by any agreed means. Thereafter, the loser of each hand deals to the next. Deal nine cards each, one at a time. (Or 12 each if three play, or 18 each if two.)

Before play, the players examine their cards to see if they have any Sixes not of their own trump suit. If so, they give them to the player or players whose trump suit they belong to. Each player will therefore start with at least one trump, and some players may have more or fewer cards than others.

Object. To play out all your cards, and especially to avoid being the only player left with cards in hand.

Play. Eldest starts by playing any card face up to the table to start a play pile. On your turn to play you have two options:

1. You may beat the top card of the play pile by playing a higher card of the same suit, or any card of your trump suit on a card of a different suit. You are allowed to trump even if you can follow suit. Having beaten it, you must then play another card on top of it. For this purpose you are free to play any card.
2. If you cannot or will not beat the top card you must instead pick up some cards from the top of the play pile and add them to your hand, thus ending your turn. How many cards you take is decided as follows:

- If the top card of the pile is not one of your trumps, you take the top three cards from the pile, or the whole pile if it contains fewer.
- If the top card of the pile is one of your trumps other than the Ace, you take the top five cards from the pile, or the whole pile if it contains fewer.
- If the top card of the pile is the ace of your trump suit, you take the whole pile.

If the previous player took the whole pile, leaving you nothing to beat, you simply play any card out to start a new pile and leave the next player to beat or take it.

The pile formed by the played cards should be stacked so that only the top card is visible. If you can beat the top card but are undecided whether to do so, you may inspect the card or cards that you would be obliged to take, and the card that would then be left on top for the next player to beat, but you may not examine any others lying below that.

If you hold an unmanageable number of cards you may spread them out face up on the table, arranged in suits, for ease of examination. This means, of course, that they must be visible to everyone else.

Endgame. When you run out of cards you drop out of play. If the player before you ran out of cards by beating the previous top card but had no free card to follow it with, you yourself may play a free card—you don't have to beat the previous beating card.

The last player left holding cards is the loser, and deals to the next hand after shuffling the cards. If, however, you are the last player and have only one card in hand, and can use it to beat the previous top card, then the game is drawn, and the next deal is made by the same dealer as before.

Variations. Details of play vary from place to place, notably as to the number of cards you must pick up when you don't beat the top card.

Swedish Rummy ▶▶ *Crazy Eights*

Switch ▶▶ *Two-Four-Jack*

Tablanette
Fishing game

52

This fishing game, popular in the Balkans, Bulgaria, and Romania, was first described by Phillips and Westall in 1939 as being of Russian origin. The name could derive from French *table nette*, 'clean table', which is how it is left when it has been swept. Four may play individually, or (better) in partnerships.

Choose first dealer by any agreed means. Thereafter, the turn to deal and play passes to the left. Deal six cards each if two play, otherwise four. Then deal four cards face up to the table, and stack the rest face down. If the table cards include a Jack, bury it in the pack and replace it with the top card of stock.

Your aim is to capture Aces, Tens, Jacks, Queens, Kings, ♣2, and ♦10. You capture table cards by matching them with cards played from your hand. You also score for making 'sweeps'. A sweep, or *tablanette*, is the capture of all the table cards in one turn.

Each in turn, starting with the eldest hand, plays a card face up to the table. The card you play can capture one or more table cards by pairing, summing, or 'jacking', in the following ways:

1. **Pairing.** An Ace captures one or more Aces, a Two one or more Twos, etc.
2. **Summing.** A played card captures two or more table cards which together total the value of the capturing card. For this purpose numerals bear their face value, Aces count 1 or 11 as preferred, Queen counts 13, and King 14.

Examples. An Eight can capture two or more cards totalling eight, such as A 7, 2 3 3, etc. A Queen can capture, for example, A 3 9 (Ace = 1) or A 2 (Ace = 11). An Ace, counting 11, can capture (say) A 4 6, with the table Ace counting one.

3. **Jacking** If you play a Jack it captures all the cards on the table in one turn, but this does not count as a sweep. Jacks have no numeral value and therefore cannot take by summing.

With one card you may make all possible captures in a single turn. For example, if the table cards are 3 5 8 10 Q, you can play a Queen to capture the Queen by pairing, and the 3 10 and 5 8 by combining, thus making a sweep. Whenever you make a sweep, you score *immediately* the total face value of all cards involved, including the capturing card.

Whenever you make a capture, you store both the card you played and the cards you captured face down on the table before you.

If you cannot or do not wish to make a capture you can 'trail' by playing any card face up to the table, where it becomes capturable on a subsequent turn. You may not, however, trail a card that is capable of capturing.

When everyone has played out their four (or six) cards, the same dealer deals each one four (or six) more from the top of the stock, but does not deal any more to the table.

The game ends when no cards remain in hand or stock. Whoever played the last card automatically wins it and all the cards left on the table, but this does not count as a sweep unless it happens to be one by definition.

Each player or partnership sorts through their won cards and scores, in addition to any sweeps they may already have made:

3 for taking the greatest number of cards (0 if tied)
1 per Ace, Ten, Jack, Queen, and King
2 for ♦ 10 instead of 1
1 for ♣ 2

Game is 251 up if played by two players or partnerships. If three or four play as individuals, a better target is 151.

Tapp ▸ *German Tarock*

Tapp Tarock

Tarot game

Once widespread in Austria, Tapp Tarock makes a good introduction to the general principles of Tarot play and serves as a springboard to more

Tarocks. Queen of diamonds.   The 12 of trumps.

advanced 54-card, French-suited games such as Point Tarock and Königsrufen.

Cards. The Austrian Tarock pack contains 22 trumps ('tarocks') and 32 plain cards, eight each in spades, hearts, clubs, and diamonds.

The highest tarock is the one bearing the figure of a Fool or Joker, known as the *Sküs* ('Excuse'). It is unnumbered.

Second highest is that numbered XXI, called *Mond* ('Moon', though from French *monde*, meaning 'world'). Others follow in descending order (XX, XIX, XVIII, etc.) to the lowest trump, I, called *Pagat*. The Sküs, Mond, and Pagat form a trio called the *trull* (from French *tous les trois*, meaning 'all three').

In plain suits, cards rank from high to low as follows:

In ♠ and ♣ King Queen Cavalier Jack 10 9 8 7
In ♥ and ♦ King Queen Cavalier Jack A 2 3 4

Deal. Whoever cuts the highest card (for which purpose any trump beats a plain suit) deals first. The deal and turn to play then pass regularly to the right.

Deal a talon of six cards face down to the table in two batches of three, the second batch lying crosswise over the first. Then 16 cards to each player in batches of eight. Anyone dealt a hand completely devoid of tarocks may demand that all hands be thrown in and a new deal made by the same dealer.

Object. There is an auction to decide who will play alone against the other two. The soloist's primary aim is to win, in tricks, cards totalling at least 36 of the 70 points available. For this purpose, cards count as follows when taken in tricks:

Sküs	5
Mond	5
Pagat	5
Each King	5
Each Queen	4
Each Cavalier	3
Each Jack	2
All others	1 each

This gives a theoretical total of 106. However, won cards are reckoned in batches of three, and each batch is actually counted as 2 less than its face value. As there are 18 batches (54/3), the final total is 70 (106–36), of which the 36-point target represents a clear majority, i.e. one more than half.

Before play, you should carefully note whether you hold two or three cards of the trull, or all four Kings. If so, you will be able to claim a score or payment for them at end of play.

Contracts. Two types of game may be bid, namely:

1. *Exchange.* In this, if you become the soloist, you will turn up the six cards of the talon, add either the top three or the bottom three to your hand, and make three discards face down in their place. These three discards will count for you at end of play as if you had won them in tricks, while the other three, which are turned face down again, will similarly count for the opponents. (Your three discards may not include a King or a card of the trull. Nor may they include any other tarocks unless you have no other choice, and in this case you must show your opponents which tarocks you have discarded.)

2. *Solo.* In a solo game, you leave the six cards of the talon unturned, and all six will count for the opponents at end of play as if they had won them in tricks.

Bidding. Although exchange and solo are the only two biddable games, the lower of them (exchange) can be bid at three different levels, namely 'threes' (*Dreier*) for a score of 3, 'lowers' (*Unterer*) for 4, and 'uppers' (*Oberer*) for 5 points. (So called because they originally referred to which of the two batches of three cards, lower or upper, the soloist was obliged to take. Nowadays he has a free choice.) These bids must be made in order. That is, 'lowers' may only be bid to overcall 'threes', and 'uppers' to overcall 'lowers'. Solo, however, may be bid at any time, and cannot be overcalled.

Each in turn, starting with eldest hand, must pass or bid. Once you have passed you may not bid again. The first bid must be either 'threes' or 'solo'. If it is 'threes', the next must be 'lowers' (or solo).

'Lowers' may be overcalled by 'solo' from either opponent, 'uppers' from the third player, or 'hold' from the first. This is because a player who comes later in the bidding order can only overcall by raising the bid, whereas one who comes earlier can overcall by agreeing to raise his previous bid to the new level, which he does by saying 'hold'. Similarly, a bid of 'lowers' is overcalled by a bid of 'solo' from either opponent, or 'uppers' from a later bidder, or 'hold' from an earlier one. 'Uppers' can only be overcalled by 'solo', or by 'hold' from an earlier bidder. Solo itself can theoretically be 'held' by an earlier player, but it is extremely unlikely that two players would both have hands strong enough to contest it.

Announcements. Unless the highest bidder is playing a solo, he next turns up the six cards of the talon, takes either the top or the bottom three, and discards as described above. Before a card is led, any of the following announcements may be made:

- The soloist may announce 'Pagat', thereby undertaking to win the last trick with the lowest trump (Roman numeral I). In this case, he is not allowed to lead or play Pagat to any earlier trick if he has any other legal choice of card, even if he might wish to do so in order to save his basic contract.
- The soloist may announce 'Valat', thereby undertaking to win every trick.
- Either opponent may announce 'double the game', 'double the Pagat', 'double the Valat' (as the case may be) if he believes the soloist will not fulfil his contract or achieve whatever feat he announced. In return, the soloist may announce 'redouble' to anything that was doubled. These announcements respectively double and quadruple whatever scoring feature is won or lost by the soloist.

Play. Eldest leads to the first trick, and the winner of each trick leads to the next. You must follow suit if you can, and if you can't you must play a tarock if you have any; only otherwise may you play any card. The trick is taken by the highest card of the suit led, or by the highest tarock if any are played. Tricks needs not be stored separately, and all cards won by the two partners are thrown face down to a single pile.

Score. Each side counts the card-points it has won as described above under 'Object'. If the soloist has reached his 36-point target he scores the appropriate game value, or is paid it by each opponent; if not, each opponent scores the appropriate game value, or receives it from the soloist. The basic game values are:

Threes	3
Lowers	4
Uppers	5
Solo	8

These amounts are doubled or quadrupled if the game was respectively doubled or redoubled.

If the soloist wins every trick, he scores the above amount four-fold, or eightfold if he previously announced 'Valat'. But if he announced Valat and failed to win every trick, he loses the above amount eightfold, regardless of how many card-points he took. This amount is doubled or quadrupled if the announcement was respectively doubled and re-doubled.

If the soloist wins the last trick with Pagat, he scores 4 points, or 8 in a solo bid. Conversely, if he plays Pagat to the last trick and loses it—or, having announced it, plays it to any earlier trick—he is deemed to have been attempting to make the bonus, and the appropriate 4 points (8 in a solo) is scored by each opponent. These amounts are doubled, won or lost, if he previously announced his intention of winning the last trick with Pagat, and further doubled or quadrupled if the announcement was respectively doubled or redoubled. Note that the score for Pagat obtains independently of the main contract: it is possible for the soloist to score for game and the partners for Pagat, or vice versa. In short, if Pagat is played to the last trick, then whoever wins it scores for it.

Finally, any player whose original hand contained one of the following features may now claim and score for it:

- for all three cards of the trull: 3 points;
- for any two cards of the trull: 1 point;
- for all four Kings: 3 points.

(In some circles, these scores are doubled in a solo game.)

Play continues for any agreed number of deals, which should be a multiple of three.

Variations. Many variations of procedure and scoring will be encountered. Some permit additional redoubles, and some credit any player with a score of (say) 2 points for capturing trump XXI with the Sküs. Of greatest interest is that whereby the holder of Pagat may bid to win the last trick with it even though he is not the soloist. In this case:

1. The soloist may double the announcement, and its maker or his partner may redouble.
2. The Pagat announcer may not lead or play it to any earlier trick than the last if he can legally avoid doing so.
3. If the Pagat holder plays it to the last trick and loses it to an opponent—or, having announced it, plays it to any earlier trick—he is deemed to have been trying to win the last trick with it, and the other side scores the appropriate bonus. (Four points, doubled in a solo, doubled if announced, and doubled or redoubled as the case may be.)

Tarot games

The pack which English-speakers call by the French name Tarot (there being no English tradition of Tarot play) is called Tarocco in Italian (plural *tarocchi*), Tarock in German, and various similar words in other languages. Contrary to popular belief, Tarot cards did not precede ordinary playing cards, and they were invented not for fortune-telling but for spicing up the play if trick-taking games by introducing the novel concept of trumps.

The Tarot was invented in Italy in about 1430–40 by adding to the existing four-suited pack a fifth suit of 21 specially illustrated cards called *trionfi*, and an extra card called the Fool. (Despite appearances, the Fool is not the origin of the modern Joker. The Joker is a glorified Jack invented in the nineteenth century for the game of ▶ **Euchre**.) From *trionfi*, or 'triumphs', comes the English word 'trumps', their original purpose being to act as cards that would beat any ordinary card played to the same trick. Only later was the word *trionfi* replaced in Italian by the inexplicable *tarocchi*, and the idea of having a special suit of trumps replaced in ordinary packs by that of turning a card and simply entrumping whatever suit it happened to be.

Tarot games subsequently spread to most parts of Europe (with the notable exception of the British Isles, the Iberian peninsula, and Greece), and still thrive in Italy, France, Austria, Hungary, Czechoslovakia, and parts of Switzerland and southern Germany. Most follow the same basic pattern, namely, that they are trick-taking games for three to five players in which win or loss is determined by the value of counting-cards captured in tricks.

As various types of Tarot playing-cards (as opposed to fortune-telling cards) are now easily obtainable from specialist games shops, this book includes three of the simpler Tarot games suitable for beginners, namely: (1) Tarot (le jeu de), the modern French game, which continues to increase in popularity; (2) Tapp Tarock, an Austrian game using the 54-card French-suited pack; and (3) Scarto, a Piedmontese game using the 78-card Italian-suited pack.

Tarot (French)

Tarot game

78

French Tarot has been gaining in popularity in France during the latter part of the twentieth century, helped largely by the fact that there is basically only one main French game, despite (or perhaps because of) the complaints of authoritarians that no official standard is universally adhered to. The following rules (for four, *see* end of entry for three) are typical rather then definitive.

Cards. Four players use a 78-card French Tarot pack, consisting of

1. the Fool, or 'Excuse';

2. 21 trumps numbered 1–21;
3. 14 cards in each of the plain suits, spades, clubs, hearts, diamonds, ranking from high to low: King (R), Queen (D), Cavalier (C), Jack (V), 10 9 8 7 6 5 4 3 2 1.

Of these, the lowest and highest trumps (1 and 21) and the Excuse have special properties and are referred to as the *bouts*.

Play centres on the winning of tricks containing counters or scoring-cards, these being the three bouts and 16 courts. All other trumps and plain cards are non-counters, or blanks. Aces, numbered '1', have no special value. The total value of all tricks and counters is 91.

Deal. The first deal is made by whoever draws the lowest card, trumps counting higher than plain suits. The turn to deal and play then passes to the right.

After cutting to the left, deal 18 cards each and 6 to the table, all face down, in the following way: 3 to the right, 3 to the player opposite, 1 to the table, 3 to the dealer; and the same again five more times. The six down-cards constitute *le chien*, 'the dog'.

If the player dealt trump 1 holds no other trump, nor the Excuse, he may annul the deal, and the next in turn to deal does so. (Other options are open to him, but the relevant rules are more complicated than the rarity of the event justifies detailing here.)

Object. There is an auction to determine who will play alone against the other three. The soloist's aim is to win a minimum number of points which varies with the number of bouts contained in his won tricks, viz.

3 bouts	36 points
2 bouts	41 points
1 bouts	51 points
0 bouts	56 points

(It will be noted that the missing value, 46, is one point more than half the total available).

Auction. Each in turn, starting with the eldest hand, must pass or name a higher bid than any gone before. A player having passed may not come in again. The bids from lowest to highest are:

1. *Petite.* To play after turning the dog cards face up, adding them to your hand, and making any six discards face down before play. These discards will count for you at end of play as if you had won them in tricks. (You may not discard a bout or a King, and may only discard trumps if you haven't enough plain cards; in this case, you must say how many you have discarded, but need not specify which.)

2. *Garde.* As above, but for a higher score.

3. *Garde sans* (Without the dog). To play without exchanging any cards or examining the dog, but with the six dog cards counting for you at end of play as if you had won them in tricks.

4. *Garde contre* (Against the dog). As above, but with the dog cards counting to the opponents as if they had won them in tricks.

Declarations. Each player, just before playing to the first trick, may make one or more of the following applicable declarations:

1. Any player holding ten or more trumps may declare a *poignée*, or bunch (literally 'fist'). The possible declarations are 'Ten', 'Thirteen', 'Fifteen', or 'Eighteen' trumps. Such a declaration must be supported by showing the stated number of trumps. The Excuse does not count as a trump unless the hand is one short of a declarable number, in which case it may be used to make it up. A player holding a bunch is not obliged to declare it; nor, if he holds cards in excess of a bunch, need he state whether or how many extra he holds; but it is not legal to declare a smaller relevant number than actually held.

(*Example*: You may declare 'Ten' if you hold ten, eleven, or twelve trumps; but if you hold thirteen, or twelve and the Excuse, you must declare, if anything, 'Thirteen'.) A bunch declared by the soloist will score for him alone if he wins, or by each opponent if he fails. One made by any partner will be credited to *each* of them if they beat the contract, or to the soloist if he wins.

2. In some circles, a partner may declare 'No trumps' if he holds neither any trump nor the Excuse; 'No courts', if he holds no court card; or 'Misère', if he has either of the above but prefers not to say which. This earns him a private and personal bonus at end of play.

3. In some circles, the soloist may declare 'slam' or 'Little slam'. A little slam is an undertaking to win at least seventeen tricks, a slam to win all eighteen.

Play. The soloist either takes the dog and discards, as detailed above under 'Auction', or moves it to his side of the table if playing 'without', or to the opposite player's side if playing 'against'.

Eldest hand leads to the first trick, and the winner of each trick leads to the next. Subsequent players must follow suit if possible, otherwise must play a trump if possible. In playing any trump—whether to a plain-suit

or a trump-suit lead—you must, if possible, play a higher trump than any so far played to the trick, even if it is already being won by a partner. The trick is taken by the highest card of the suit led, or by the highest trump if any are played. All tricks won by the partners are kept together in a single pile.

The Excuse. If you hold the Excuse you may play it at any time and in contravention of any rule stated above. If you lead it, the suit to be followed is that of the second card played. The Excuse normally loses the trick, unless you lead it to the last trick after winning all 17 previous tricks, in which case it wins.

If you are the soloist and play the Excuse, you may, when the trick has been taken, retrieve the Excuse from the won trick, and replace it with any

French tarot cards. The Knight (Cavalier) of clubs.

French tarot cards. The 20 of trumps.

card (preferably worthless) that you have won in any previous trick. If you have not yet won a trick, you lay the Excuse face up before you, and, upon winning a trick, pass one of its cards to the opposing side. In either case, the Excuse is then incorporated into one of your tricks, and cannot be played again.

If you are not the soloist and play the Excuse to a trick, and it is taken by the soloist, you have exactly the same privilege of retrieving it in exchange for a card from a trick won by your own side, and of retaining it for this purpose if your side has yet to win one.

Obviously, if the partners (or, improbably, the soloist) win not a single trick, they cannot reclaim the Excuse.

Last trick. There is a bonus for winning the last trick if it contains the lowest trump ('1', called *petit*). If the soloist plays it to the last trick, he gains the bonus from each opponent if he wins the trick, or pays it to each opponent if not. If a partner plays it to the last trick and wins, the bonus is paid by the soloist to each opponent; but if a partner loses it in the last trick, then each partner pays the soloist, even if it was a partner who captured it. (This makes it a penalty rather than a bonus.)

Score. At end of play, the opponents of the soloist count the value of all the tricks and counters they have won, including the six dog cards if the soloist played 'against'. For this purpose, cards count as follows:

Each bout	5 (trump 21, trump 1, Excuse)
Each King	5
Each Queen	4

Each Cavalier   3
Each Jack   2

Cards are counted in pairs, each pair consisting of two blanks or a blank and a counter. A pair of blanks counts 1 point; a blank and a counter take the value of the counter.

Whatever the partners count is subtracted from 91 to yield the soloist's count. As stated above, he needs 36, 41, 51, or 56 to win, depending on whether he took three, two, one, or no bouts. If he wins, he is paid the appropriate amount by each opponent; if not, he pays it to each of them. If scores are kept in writing, it is only necessary to record the amount as won or lost in the soloist's own score column, as a settlement made on the basis of the final scores will come to the same thing as if each deal had been settled in coins or counters as it occurred.

The soloist's win (or loss) is calculated as follows: (*a*) 25 points for the game, (*b*) plus the difference from the target, (*c*) plus 10 for *petit au bout* (winning the lowest trump in the last trick, if applicable), (*d*) multiply by 1, 2, 4, or 6 according to the contract. The winning side adds 20, 30, or 40 points if a 'bunch' of 10, 13, or 15 trumps was declared, plus 200 for a slam or 400 if it was announced beforehand.

French Tarot for three

The same, but with these variations. Deal 24 cards to each player in 4s, and 6 to the dog. The lowest declarable bunch is Thirteen (score 10), the highest Twenty-one (score 40). A little slam is 22 or 23 tricks. If an odd card remains after counting in pairs, ignore it.

Tausendeins (Thousand and One) ▶▶ *Sixty-Six*, ▶▶ *Tysiacha*

Terziglio ▶▶ *Tressette*

Thirty-Five

Gambling game

40 *or* 52

An American game said to be of Italian origin (*Trentacinque*), though it does not appear in any Italian book that I know of.

From two to four may use the Italian 40-card pack lacking Eights, Nines, and Tens; five need all 52. The turn to deal and play passes to the right. Players each contribute five chips, or any other agreed number, to a pool. Deal, face down and one at a time, four cards to each player and to a widow (spare hand), then five more to each player.

The aim is to get a hand containing four or more cards of the same suit totalling 35 or more points, counting courts 10 each and numerals at face value (Ace 1 only, not 11). Any player dealt such a hand may show it and claim the pool, thus ending the round. If more than one player can show 35 or more in a suit, they share the pool equally, regardless of their actual totals.

Failing that, each in turn, starting with Eldest, then bids for the right to discard four cards from his hand and replace them with the four cards of the widow, thereby aiming to acquire cards totalling 35 or more in a suit. Each bid must be higher than the last, but none may exceed the total in the pool. Bidding ends when all but one have passed, or when this limit is reached.

The highest bidder then discards four and takes the widow. If he can then show 35 or more in a suit, he wins from the pool the amount of his bid; if not, he pays that amount into the pool, which (in either case) is carried forward to the next deal. (*Variant*: If successful, the bidder wins the whole pool.)

Optional extras. A bonus of 2 chips may be claimed from each opponent by anyone showing a 'beggar' (a hand consisting entirely of numerals) or a 'royale' (K Q J of the same suit). It is said you can only claim this if you have not passed, and only after the highest bidder has been determined. But since it is only by everybody's passing that the highest bidder is determined, this proviso seems to contradict itself. Perhaps the privilege may be exercised by (*a*) those who have not passed, but have been excluded from the auction by a preceding maximum bid, or (*b*) those who made at least one bid before passing.

Thirty-One

The ancestor of Twenty-One (▸ **Pontoon**), played much like its modern descendant, but up to a target count of 31 instead of 21, and with Ace counting 1 only (not 11). It has also formed one component of several compendium games since the fifteenth century, notably Commerce, Cribbage, Trentuno, and Wit and Reason.

Thirty-One

Gambling game

This game is played in various ways under various names—*see also* ▶ **Commerce**. In its simplest form:

From a 52-card pack deal three cards each and three face up to the table as a spare hand.

The aim is to collect cards of the same suit totalling 31 or as near as possible, counting Ace 11, faces 10 each, numerals as marked. Alternatively, to get three of a kind, which counts 30½.

Each in turn draws one card from the spare and replaces it with a card from hand. As soon as anyone thinks they have the best hand they end the game by knocking. Each opponent then has one more opportunity to exchange. Cards are revealed and whoever has the highest suit-total wins the pool, unless beaten by three of a kind. Tied hands share it.

Examples ♣2 ♣3 ♣5 (counting 10) is beaten by ♥A ♣7 ♦3 (11 for the Ace), this by ♠J ♠Q ♠K (30), this by ♣9 ♦9 ♠9 (30½), and this by ♦J ♦K ♦A (31).

Versions of this game are particularly popular in Germany and adjacent parts of Austria. The following has several names, including *Schnautz*, *Knack*, and *Hosen 'runter'* ('Trousers Down'), but is best known as:

Schwimmen (Swimming). This played with 32 cards (Seven low). Everyone starts with (typically) three chips. Play as above, but three Aces counts 32 instead of 30½. Anyone dealt a 31 or 32 must show it immediately, thereby ending the play and winning. The dealer deals the spare hand face down and, if not satisfied with his own hand, may exchange it for the spare, sight unseen. Whether he does or not, the spare is then faced and eldest plays first.

Each in turn may exchange one card, or pass. If all pass, the spare hand is swept away and three more cards dealt from stock. If none remain, there is a showdown. When somebody knocks, everybody gets one more turn—though not if the knocker went down with a 31 or 32.

The worst hand loses a chip. Ties (rare) are decided in favour of the best suit, for which purpose the order is clubs (high), spades, hearts, diamonds (low). If the winner has a 32 (three Aces), everyone else loses a chip.

A player who has lost three chips is said to be 'swimming'. The swimmer may continue play, but must drop out upon losing again. (You might as well play with four chips in the first place.) The overall winner is the last player left in.

Thirty-One Rum (Scat) ▸▸ *Ride the Bus*

Three-card Monte

The American name for Find the Lady, which is not a game but a sideshow swindle.

Three in One

Modern American version of the ancient European game ▸ **Poch**, also known as Michigan Rummy, Tripoli, Calliente. A proprietary version is available under the name Tripoley®.

http://www.pagat.com/stops/3in1.html

Tieng Len

Climbing game

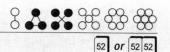

Tieng Len, meaning something like 'Speak Up', is the equivalent of ▸ **President** and may be described as Vietnam's national game. In America, to which it has not unnaturally spread, it is usually called Viet Cong, or just VC. It is playable by virtually any number, but works best for four as described here (but see after for variants).

Deal 13 cards each, in ones, from a 52-card pack ranking from high to low 2 A K Q J 10 9 8 7 6 5 4 3. The suits also rank against one another, from highest to lowest hearts, diamonds, clubs, spades. Numeral ranking takes precedence over suit ranking, so the full 52-card hierarchy runs ♥2 (highest of all) ♦2 ♣2 ♠2 ♥A … (etc.) down to … ♠4 ♥3 ♦3 ♣3 ♠3 (lowest of all).

The aim is to play out all your cards, and especially to avoid being the last player left with any cards in hand.

Decide who deals first by any agreed method. Thereafter the loser of each hand deals to the next.

In the first deal only, the player with ♠3 begins by playing it face up to the table, either as a single card or as part of a multi-card combination. In subsequent deals, the winner of the previous one plays first, and can start with any card or combination.

These are the only valid plays or combinations:

- Single card.
- Pair = two cards of the same rank, such as ♦7-♣7.
- Triple = three of the same rank.
- Four of a kind = all four of one rank.
- Sequence = three or more cards of consecutive rank, regardless of suit. Sequences cannot 'turn the corner' between Deuce and Three, a sequence may not include 3-2-A.
- Double Sequence = three or more pairs of consecutive rank, such as 3-3-4-4-5-5 or 6-6-7-7-8-8-9-9.

Each player in turn after the leader must either pass or else beat the previous play by playing exactly the same number of cards forming exactly the same type of combination, but higher in rank than that of the previous player. You cannot beat it by playing a different type of combination, or one of the same type containing a greater number of cards.

Example. The leader plays ♦3 ♠3. You must play either a higher pair (such as ♣7 ♠7), or an equal pair containing a higher suit (♥3 ♣3). If you play the pair of Sevens, the next person must play a pair higher then Sevens, or beat them with ♥7 ♣7.

If you pass (which is allowed even if you can play), you cannot subsequently play to the same round. The played card(s) are placed in a heap face up in the centre of the table. The play goes around the table as often as necessary until someone plays a card or combination that no one else beats. All the played cards are then set aside, and the person whose play was unbeaten starts again by playing any legal card or combination face up to the centre of the table.

There are four exceptions to the rule that a combination can only be beaten by a combination of the same type, and these concern only the beating of Deuces. Specifically:

1. A single Deuce is beaten by playing any four of a kind. This in turn can then be beaten by a higher four of a kind, and so on.
2. A single Deuce can alternatively be beaten by playing a sequence of three pairs, such as 7-7-8-8-9-9. This in turn can then be beaten by a higher sequence of three pairs, and so on.
3. A pair of Deuces can be beaten by a sequence of four pairs such as 5-5-6-6-7-7-8-8. This in turn can be beaten by a higher sequence of four pairs, and so on. A sequence of four pairs can then be beaten by a higher sequence of four pairs.
4. A triplet of Deuces can be beaten by a sequence of five pairs, such as 7-7-8-8-9-9-10-J-J. This in turn can be beaten by a higher sequence of five pairs, and so on.

When you run out of cards you drop out of play. If it was your turn to lead, the lead passes to the next player on your left who has not yet run out of cards. The play ends when only one player has any cards left. That player loses, and pays a previously agreed stake to each other player.

Variants for other numbers of players. If two or three play, deal 13 cards each and leave the remainder out of play. Alternatively, if three play, deal 17 each and leave one out of play (though it doesn't spoil anything if the odd card is added to the dealer's hand). If no one has the ♠3, then whoever holds the lowest card begins and must do so by leading it, either on its own as part of a combination.

With four or more players, use a doubled pack and deal either 13 each, or as many as possible so that everyone has the same number of cards, leaving the remainder of play.

Viet Cong (VC)

Play as Tieng Len but with these differences:

1. Anyone dealt four Deuces automatically wins without further play.
2. Whoever holds ♠3 always leads and must include it in his lead.
3. Deuces cannot be used in single sequences.
4. Deuces are beaten by special combinations called slams. A single Deuce is beaten by four of a kind or three consecutive pairs, a pair of Deuces by a sequence of five consecutive pairs or two consecutive fours of a kind, a triplet of Deuces by a sequence of seven consecutive pairs or three consecutive fours of a kind.

As before, a slam can be beaten by a higher slam of the same type.

Viet Cong is sometimes played with exchanging. After the deal, but before the opening lead, you can exchange one or more cards with another player for an equal number of cards, provided that they are willing to trade. In this version, four Deuces do not automatically win the game.

Toepen

Plain-trick game

A drinking, singing and whistling game popular in the Netherlands. Details vary from pub to pub, or even in the same pub as time passes.

Deal four cards each, in batches of two, from a 32-card pack ranking 10 (highest) 9 8 7 A K Q J (lowest).

In each deal the aim is to win the last trick. The overall aim is to avoid accumulating 10 penalty points, which obliges you to buy the next round of drinks.

Exchange. If you have nothing higher than an Ace, or an otherwise poor hand, you may lay it face down and draw a new one from the stock, so long at least four cards remain. (You may not exchange just one, two, or three cards.) If challenged, you turn the old hand face up. If it contains any card higher than an Ace, you incur one penalty; if not, the challenger incurs one.

Warnings. If you hold four Tens you must stand up, to warn others of this fact. With four Jacks you may stand up if you wish, to bluff them into thinking you have four Tens. Similarly, if you hold three Tens you must whistle, and if you have three Jacks you *may* whistle. If you can't whistle you may sing loudly instead. If you fail to stand up or whistle when you should, or do so when you shouldn't, you will incur one penalty when you are found out.

Play. Eldest leads. You must follow suit if you can, but may otherwise play any card. The trick is taken by the highest card of the suit led, and the winner of each trick leads to the next—or, if he then folds, the next active player to his left leads. There are no trumps. Everyone scores 1 penalty except the winner of the last trick, who becomes the next dealer.

Raising the penalty. The penalty value of each deal may be increased as follows. Any active player may, at any point in the play—in or out of turn—knock sharply on the table to notch the value up by one point. Thus the first knock increases the penalty to 2, the next to 3, and so on. When a player knocks, any still active player (other than the knocker) may immediately drop out by laying their cards face down, thereby incurring only the penalties previously obtaining. If they fail to do so before the next card is played, they must continue play at the new level. If someone knocks during the course of the last trick and you have no cards left, you can escape the new level by saying 'Fold' before the next card is played.

You may knock more than once in the same deal, but:

- not twice in succession, unless someone else has knocked in the interim, and
- not if this would raise your score above 10 should you lose. (This means that you may not knock at all when you have nine penalties.)

Pay-off. The round ends when one player reaches 10 penalties and staggers to the bar. If more than one do so, duty devolves upon the one with most penalties.

Conventions. A player who has temporarily disappeared on an errand of mercy or nature is dealt a hand *in absentia*, but is deemed to fold at the first knock. A player who is currently buying a round of drinks is exempt from all penalties while so engaged.

Tonk

Rummy game

This version of Knock Rummy has been popular in America for decades, and its terminology (words in quote-marks) is that of the black card-playing community. There are no universally agreed rules and hardly any two schools play it in exactly the same way, so the following description is typical, not definitive.

As Tonk is usually played for money, players start by agreeing a stake. Deal five cards each, in ones. Deal the next card face up to start a discard pile, and stack the rest face down.

If your cards total 49 or 50 (counting Ace 1, numerals face value, and face cards 10 each), you immediately show it and win a doubled stake from each other player. This is called 'tonking', or 'a tonk'. However, if two or more players do this, it is a tie, and neither wins. (50 does not beat 49.) In either case there is no play, and the cards are thrown in. If no one tonks the play begins. Once play has started no special advantage attaches to a hand worth 49 or 50.

The aim is either to go out by getting rid of all your cards, or to have the smallest value of card-points left in hand when someone else stops the play. You get rid of cards by forming them into 'spreads'. A spread is either three or four cards of the same rank (a book), or three or more cards in suit and sequence (a run), for which purpose the running order is A 2 3 4 5 6 7 8 9 10 J Q K. Ace is always low.

At each turn you 'pluck' (draw) the top card of either the stock or the discard pile, add it to your hand, and discard one card face up to the discard pile. Between drawing and discarding you may, if you can, 'drop' a spread by laying the appropriate cards face down on the table before you. You can also 'hit' an existing spread, whether one of your own or anyone else's, by laying off a card that extends it. For example, you could lay of ♥7 to a book of three Sevens or to a run of ♥4-5-6 or ♥8-9-10.

There are three ways of ending.

1. You automatically end the game, and win, if you get rid of the last card from your hand. If you do so by discarding it, you win a single stake from everyone else. If you do so by making or hitting a spread and having nothing left to discard, it is a 'tonk' and you win a double stake.

2. If you think the total value of the cards you hold is lower than anyone else's, you can end the game by 'dropping'—that is, by laying them all face up on the table. However, you may only do this on your own turn to play, and must do so instead of (not as well as) plucking a card. If your count is lower than anyone else's you win a single stake. If not, you must pay a double stake to everyone whose count is lower than or equal to your own. Furthermore, the player who actually does have the lowest count also receives a single stake from every other player besides yourself. If two or more tie for lowest, they are each paid by the others.

3. The game automatically ends when the stock runs out of cards and no one has dropped. In this case the player with the lowest count (or players, if tied) wins a single stake from everyone else.

http://www.pagat.com/rummy/tonk.html

Towie

An adaptation of Contract ▸ **Bridge** for three players, invented by Replogle and Fosdick in 1931. The basic idea is that four hands are dealt, six cards of the dummy are turned up, and players bid for the right to partner it. *See also* ▸ **Booby**.

Trade or Barter ▸▸ *Commerce*

Trappola
Point-trick game

This ancient Venetian game spread to other European countries and survived, under various names and in various forms, until perhaps the middle of the twentieth century. All were played with a special pack of Italian-suited cards, last reported to have been manufactured in Prague in 1944. The distinctive feature of this delightful and intelligent game, no doubt accounting for its extraordinary popularity in so many different societies, is that of leading a Deuce, the lowliest card, and winning the trick because no one can follow suit. What follows is Professor Dummett's reconstruction of two-hander outlined by the sixteenth-century scholar Girolamo Cardano. (For more than two, *see* ▶ **Spády**.)

The 36-card Trappola pack, lacking numerals from Three to Six inclusive, was a specialized version of the Italian pack featuring suits of swords, batons, cups, and coins, and face cards representing King, Cavalier, and Footsoldier. These are here translated into (respectively) spades, clubs, hearts, diamonds; King, Queen, Jack.

Cards rank and count as follows:

A	K	Q	J	10 9 8 7 2
6	5	4	3	0 each

The aim is to score points for (*a*) combinations held before play, (*b*) point-cards won in tricks, (*c*) winning the last trick, and (*d*) winning any trick with a Deuce, especially the last trick or successive tricks.

Deal nine cards each in batches of four then five, and lay the remaining 18 face down as a stock. Non-dealer, if unsatisfied with his hand, may discard it face up and take in its place the first nine cards of stock. If still unsatisfied, he may do the same again, but must then play with the last nine cards taken from stock. If he leaves any, Dealer may then exercise the same option either once or twice, depending on how many remain. Faced discards may not be taken up.

If you hold three or four Aces, Kings, Queens, Jacks, or Deuces you may declare them any time before playing one of them to a trick (provided that, having three only, you have not already captured the fourth in a trick). You need say no more than 'three' or 'four' as the case may be, unless they are Aces, when you must add 'Aces'. The appropriate scores are not made until the trick-play is over.

Non-dealer leads to the first trick, and the winner of each trick leads to the next. You must follow suit if you can, but may otherwise play any card. A trick is taken by the higher card of the suit led. There is no trump suit.

For winning a trick with a Deuce (by leading it when your opponent cannot follow suit) you score 10 points immediately. For winning the last trick you score 6, unless you win it with a Deuce. For winning the last one, two, three, or four successive tricks with Deuces you score, respectively, 26, 52, 78, and 104.

You each then add in the value of counting-cards you have taken in tricks (their total value is 72), and finally the value of any three-or four-card combination you declared at start of play. The respective scores are:

	Aces	Kings	Queens	Jacks	Deuces
Three held	12	6	6	6	10
Four held	24	12	12	12	20

The winner receives an amount proportional to the difference.

Traversone ⟩⟩ Ciapanò

Trédrille ⟩⟩ Quadrille

Treikort

Three-player version of ⟩⟩ **Alkort**

Trente et Quarante
Banking game

This traditional French casino game, also called Rouge et Noir (or R&N), is not favoured elsewhere because of its low house percentage. Essentially, the banker deals cards alternately into an upper row designated 'black' and a lower row designated 'red', stopping as soon as both have reached a count of at least 31 (and not over 40, whence the title). Punters bet, for even money, on whether the *rouge* or *noir* row will finish closer to 31, or that the first card dealt will be of the same (*couleur*) or opposite (*inverse*) colour to the winning row. A tie is a stand-off. On a 31-point tie, players may immediately forfeit half their stake or else play for 'double or quits' on the next coup.

Trentuno ▸ *Commerce*

Tresillo

The modern Spanish form of Hombre (*see* ▸ **Ombre**).

Tressette

Point-trick game

40

One of Italy's major national card games, together with ▸ **Scopone** and ▸ **Briscola**. Its title, 'three Sevens', may refer to a scoring combination no longer recognized, or to the fact that it is played up to twenty-one. Tressette is played in a full range of formats, with versions for any given number of players from two to eight, including a non-partnership version for four (Mediatore), a trick-avoidance variety (▸ **Ciapanò**), and the intriguing ▸ **Madrasso**, which is a hybrid of Tressette and Briscola unique to Venice. Described below are the standard partnership game for four and a classic three-hander popular in Lombardy under the name Terziglio, sometimes called Calabresella.

Partnership Tressette

Four players use a 40-card Italian pack (lacking Eights, Nines, or Tens) and sit crosswise in partnerships. A stake is agreed, and a first dealer chosen by any agreed means. The turn to deal and play passes to the right. Deal 10 cards each in ones (some say in fives). A player whose point-cards total less than 1 point (*see* below) may demand a fresh shuffle and deal from the same dealer.

Each side's overall aim is to reach a score of 21 over as many deals as necessary. Points are scored for winning counters in tricks, for which purpose cards rank and count as follows:

3	2	A	K	Q	J	7	6	5	4
⅓	⅓	1	⅓	⅓	⅓	0	0	0	0

In practice, complications are avoided by reckoning the ⅓-point counters at the rate of 1 point for every three taken and ignoring fractions. This gives a total of 6 for honours, which, with 1 per Ace and 1 for winning the last trick, makes 11. (Some accounts rate counters at 1 each, Aces and last trick at 3 each, making 35 in all; but as they are still counted in batches of three, and odd ones are ignored, it comes to the same thing in the end.)

Eldest hand leads to the first trick. You must follow suit if you can, but may otherwise play any card. The trick is taken by the highest card of the suit led, and the winner of each trick leads to the next. There are no trumps.

When you are leading to a trick (but not following) you may make one of the following conventional announcements or signals to your partner. False signals are illegal.

Busso (or bunch your fist on the table) = 'If possible, win the trick and return the same suit.'

Volo (or slide the card slowly onto the table) = 'This is the last or only card I have of its suit.'

Striscio (or skim the card rapidly onto the table) = 'This comes from my best suit.' (This convention is not always admitted.)

Whoever wins the last trick adds 'one for last' (*dietra*).

Normally, the game ends as soon as one side claims to have reached 21, any remaining cards being left unplayed. That side wins the fixed stake— or loses it, if the claim proves mistaken. Alternatively, any of the following special events ends the game:

1. *Cappotto*. One side wins all ten tricks in a deal. This wins a double stake.
2. *Cappottone*. A single player wins all ten tricks. This wins sixfold.
3. *Stramazzo*. One side takes all the counters, but not all the tricks. This wins treble. Its also prevents the losing side from scoring a point for winning the last trick, as also does:
4. *Strammazzone*. A single player takes all the counters, and the opposing side wins at least one trick. This wins eightfold.

Combinations (optional). It may be agreed that a player dealt a particular combination of cards may announce *buon giuoco* before the first

trick is played, then declare and score it to his partnership's credit when
that trick is over:

Four Threes, Twos, or Aces	4 points
Three Threes, Twos, or Aces	3
3 2 A of same suit (*napoletana*)	3

To score for a *napoletana* you must specify which suit it is in, and for
three of a kind which suit is missing from the trio. When honours are
included, the game is played up to a higher target, such as 31 or 51.

Some play that if you are dealt all ten of a suit (a *napoletana decima*),
your side wins the game outright. This win is called *collatondrione* and
receives a sixteenfold stake.

Terziglio (Calabresella)

Three play as above, but with these differences:

Deal 12 cards each and spread the other four face down as a
monte. The overall aim is to be the first to make a score of 21. In each
deal, one person plays against two with the aim of capturing in tricks
cards totalling at least 6 of the 11 points available for counters and the
last trick. The soloist is determined by auction. Each successive bid must
be higher than the last, and a player who has once passed may not come
in again. The bids from low to high are:

Chiamo (Call). The soloist plays after calling for a card lacking from his
hand, and receiving it from its holder in exchange for any card he does
not want—unless the called card is in the monte, in which case he does
not get a second call. Having called, he turns the monte face up for all to
see, adds it to his hand, and makes any four discards face down to restore
his hand to twelve.

Solo. The soloist does not call a card, but simply takes the monte and
discards as explained above.

Solissimo. The soloist plays without calling a card or taking the monte,
which remains face down and out of play.

Solissimo aggravato. The soloist not only plays without the monte, but
even allows the opponents to use it. If he says 'half each' (*dividete*), each

of them takes two cards without showing them, and makes any two discards face down, also without showing them. If he says 'you choose' (*scegliete*), they turn the four face up and may agree to split them 2 2, 3 1, or 4 0, in which each discards (face down) as many as he took.

Eldest hand leads to the first trick, except in a bid of *solissimo*, when players may have agreed to follow the alternative rule permitting the soloist to lead. Play as for four, except that the two partners may not communicate with one another (unless otherwise agreed).

The winner of the last trick, besides scoring one for last, also wins the *monte* as if it were an extra trick. The soloist counts the points he has won in tricks, as described above, and ignoring fractions. If he has taken at least 6 points, he scores the appropriate amount, or is paid it by *each* opponent; if not, each opponent scores the appropriate amount, or is paid it by the soloist. The appropriate amounts are: call 1, solo 2, solissimo 4, *aggravato dividete* 8, *aggravato scegliete* 16. The appropriate score is trebled for taking all 11 points but not every trick, or quadrupled for winning every trick.

Game is normally 21 points, but may be made 31 or 51 if preferred.

Optional extra. If all pass without bidding, the monte is left intact and the hands are gathered up and redealt by the same dealer without being shuffled. This time, the lowest permissible bid is solo.

Tribello

Plain-trick game

A cross between ▶ **Bismarck** and ▶ **Sergeant Major**, Tribello was contributed to the Pagat web-site by an inhabitant of Illinois, whose family (from Dekalb county) have played it since the 1930s or 40s.

Deal four hands of 13 cards, in ones. Deal first to the left, then to a spare hand called the pickup, then to the right, then to the dealer, and so on.

There are four rounds of play with three deals per round, making twelve deals in all. The turn to deal passes to the left after each hand, so that each player plays once in each of the three positions in each round. Each round of three is played in a different way as follows:

1. Before dealing, cut the cards to establish a trump suit.
2. The dealer nominates trumps after examining his hand.
3. Play at no trump.
4. Play at no trump and aim to lose tricks (nullo).

In the first three rounds the dealer has a quota of six tricks, his left-hand neighbour of four tricks, and his right-hand neighbour of three. If you take more than your quota you score 1 point per extra trick; if you take less than your quota you score minus 1 point per trick below quota.

In the fourth round (nullo), the dealer's quota is three, his left-hand neighbour's four, his right-hand neighbour's six. If you take more that your quota you score minus one point for each surplus trick; if you take less than your quota you score plus one for each trick below.

Before play, each in turn, starting with the dealer, seeks to improve his hand by discarding any number of cards up to the number remaining in the pickup and drawing the same number of replacements from the top of it. If any remain in the pickup there is another round of discarding and drawing, and so on until none remain in the pickup or nobody wishes to discard. All discards go face down in a pile and may not be examined.

Dealer leads to the first trick. You must follow suit if you can, but may otherwise play any card. The trick is taken by the highest card of the suit led, or by the highest trump if any are played, and the winner of each trick leads to the next.

The total score for each hand will equal zero, as will the total score for the twelve hands of the game. The player with most points wins.

http://www.pagat.com/whist/tribello.html

Tridge ⇥ *Ombre*

Triomphe

An old name for several related trump games, especially ▸ **Ecarté.**

Tripoli ▶ *Three in One*

Trouduc ▶ *President*

Truc

Plain-trick game

A delightful game of bluff and counterbluff that has been reasonably likened to Poker for two. With slight variations, it is played in south-western France, especially Roussillon and Pays Basque. More elaborate versions are played in Uruguay and Argentina under such names as Truco, Truque, and Truquiflor. The nearest English equivalent is ▶ **Put**.

Two players use a 32-card pack ranking 7 8 A K Q J 10 9 in each suit. A rubber is the best of three games, and a game is 12 points, which may require several deals to reach. Players deal in turn, the first being chosen by any agreed means.

Deal three cards each in ones. The aim in each deal is to win two tricks, or to win the first trick if each wins one and the third is tied.

Non-dealer may propose a redeal. If Dealer agrees, the hands are put to one side and each receives three new cards. Only one such redeal may be made, and only if both agree to it.

Non-dealer leads to the first trick, and the winner of each trick leads to the next. Any card may be played by either player. There is no trump, and the trick is taken by the higher-ranking card regardless of suit. If both play equal ranks, the trick is 'spoilt' and belongs to no one, and the same leader leads to the next. Note that Sevens are highest, then Eights, Aces, etc.

Theoretically, the winner scores one game point. Either player, however, before playing to a trick, may offer to increase the score for a win by saying 'Two more?'. The first such increase raises the value from 1 point to 2, and subsequent increases add 2 more each, raising the game value from 2 to 4, then 6, and so on. If the other says 'Yes', play continues for the increased score; if not, he throws his hand in, play ceases, and the challenger scores whatever it was worth before he offered to raise. It is possible for both to raise in the same trick—the leader before leading and, if accepted, the follower before replying. It is also legal to concede at any time, even if the other has not just offered to double.

An even more drastic raise may be made as follows. Either player, on his turn to play, may declare 'My remainder' ('*Mon reste*')—thus jump-raising the game value to whatever he needs to make 12, with a view to winning the game outright. To this, however, the opponent may either concede, in which case the increase does not take effect, or may himself announce 'My remainder', in which case whoever wins the deal wins the game.

The round finishes when one player concedes or when three tricks have been completed. Whoever took two tricks, or the first if each took one, scores the game point, or whatever value it may have been increased to. If all three tricks were spoilt, neither scores.

Variant. Sid Sackson, who was the first to describe this game in English, (*A Gamut of Games*, New York, 1969; London, 1972), proposed a variation which has since been followed by others, namely: Each increase doubles the game value (2 4 8…, not 2 4 6 8…), but neither player may double if this would give him more points than he needs for game. For example, a player with 5 may double from 1 to 2 points, or from 2 to 4, but not from 4 to 8, which would make him 13 if he won. In this case he must instead bid 'My remainder'. Conversely, a player may not bid 'My remainder' if he could instead legally double it, though this constraint does not apply to the second player if the first bids 'My remainder' legally. (This is hardly an improvement, and is cumbersome to explain.)

Partnership Truc

Four players sit crosswise in partnerships, the turn to deal and play passing to the right. Play as above, but with these differences.

The dealer acts as the governor for his partnership, and his right-hand opponent (eldest hand) for the other. Only Eldest may propose an exchange, and only Dealer may accept or refuse it. Eldest leads to the first trick, and each subsequent trick is led by the winner of the last, or by the previous leader if the trick is spoilt. Only the governor of each side may propose an increase in the game value, and then only when himself about to play to the trick. Similarly, only the governor may accept or concede when an increase is proposed.

Throughout play, the governor's partner may indicate what card or cards he holds by means of a conventional code of gestural signals, and the governor for his part may tell his partner what to play. (They may not reverse these roles.) The holding of a Seven is indicated by a grin, an Eight by a wink, an Ace by a shrug. Naturally, the signaller will attempt to signal when his governor is looking and his opponents are not. An instruction may take the form: 'Play the Seven', 'Play low', 'Leave it to me', and so on. Signals must be truthfully made, and instructions obeyed.

Sackson states that a trick is spoilt if (and, by implication, only if) the highest card played by one side is matched in rank by the highest played by the other. But neither he nor any other source comments on the case where tied winning cards are played by two partners. Presumably they win the trick, and whichever of them led to it leads to the next. But what happens if neither of them led? It would seem logical to suggest that if two partners tie for highest then the trick is spoilt, just as if one of the tied cards were played by the other side.

Trump(s)

Trump is the ancestor of ▸ **Whist**, and Trumps is ▸ **Knockout Whist**.

Trust, don't Trust ▸▸ *Verish' ne Verish'*

Tunk ▸▸ *Tonk*

Turtle ▸▸ *Golf*

Tute

Point-trick game

40

Tute (pronounce both syllables) is said to be of Italian origin and comes from *tutti*, meaning all, or everyone. It has replaced Tresillo in the card-playing affections of Spain and Latin America. It resembles ▶ **Bezique** and ▶ **Sixty-Six** and is played in many forms by two, three, or four players. What follows is the two-hander known as Tute Habañero, but no two Spanish accounts even of this specific form appear to be identical.

Two players use a 40-card Spanish pack lacking Eights, Nines, and Tens. Cards rank and count as follows:

A	3	K	Q	J	7 6 5 4 2
11	10	4	3	2	0 each

(You may prefer to replace Threes with Tens.)

Points accrue for winning counting-cards in tricks and for declaring certain combinations. These must be totalled and remembered as play proceeds, not written down. You win by being the first to announce (correctly) that you have 101 points, which may take one or two deals.

Choose first dealer by any agreed means. Deal eight cards each in ones. Turn the next for trump, and lay the rest face down as a stockpile on top of but not entirely covering the turn-up.

If the turn-up is a Jack or higher, then whoever has (or draws) the trump Seven may exchange it for the turned card, though not before winning a trick. Similarly, if it is a Seven—whether dealt or exchanged for a Jack—it may be taken in exchange for the Two. Exchanging is optional, not obligatory.

Non-dealer leads to the first trick, and the winner of each trick leads to the next. You must follow suit if a trump is led, but otherwise may play any card. If unable to follow to trumps you must lay your cards face up on the table (to prove it) and keep them there until you draw a trump, when you may take them up again. The trick is taken by the higher card of the suit led, or by the higher trump if any are played. The winner of a trick draws the top card of stock, adds it to his hand, and waits for the other to do likewise.

Before leading to a trick (but not following) you may show and score for a marriage or a *tute*. A marriage is a King and Queen of the same suit and scores 20, or 40 in trumps. A *tute* is all four Kings or all four Queens, and wins the game outright. Only one such combination can be declared per trick.

When the stock is exhausted and the turn-up taken in hand, the last eight tricks are played to different rules. Combinations may no longer be declared. You must now not only follow suit but also win the trick if you can. If unable to follow, you must play a trump if you can. Winning the last trick scores 10 extra. Before the last eight are played, either player may declare *capote*, thereby undertaking to win them all. If successful, he wins the game outright; if not, he loses.

Play ceases with a *tute* or a *capote*, or when one player claims to have reached or exceeded 101 points, or when either player is found to have reached 101 points but has failed to claim it. A correct claim of 101 wins the game, a false claim or failure to claim loses. If neither has claimed 101 by the end of play, but it transpires that both have made it, the game is won by whoever took the last trick.

If none of these applies, there is another deal, which must be made by the winner of the last trick.

Variants. Some accounts give the target score as 121. One states that the tute declaration wins outright and that capote can be won without being declared, another that capote is valid only if declared and a tute does not count at all.

Twenty-Five

Plain-trick game

52

The national card game of Ireland, and of Gaeldom in general, formerly called Spoil Five, or Five Fingers. Its sixteenth-century ancestor, Maw, was the favourite game of James VI of Scotland (I of England) and bears an obvious similarity to ▸ **Ombre**. If unacquainted with this family you may think it needlessly complicated at first sight, but for all that it is a fascinating game, which undoubtedly explains its longevity.

From two to ten can play. Four may play in two partnerships of two, and six in two partnerships of three or three of two. For non-partnership play, five is ideal. Each starts with 20 chips or counters, but scores can easily be kept in writing.

Cards. Fifty-two. There is always a trump suit, and three or four cards are always the highest trumps, namely (from the top down):

Five of trumps ('Five fingers')
Jack of trumps
Ace of hearts (♥A)
Ace of trumps (if other than hearts)

The others rank from high to low according to colour:

in ♥ and ♦ : K Q [J] 10 9 8 7 6 5 4 3 2 [A] ('high in red')
in ♠ and ♣ : K Q [J] [A] 2 3 4 5 6 7 8 9 10 ('low in black')

The bracketed cards only occupy those positions when they are not among the four top trumps.

Deal. Everyone chips one to the kitty. Deal five cards each in batches of two and three, or four and one. Stack the rest face down and turn the top card for trump.

Object. Primarily, to sweep the kitty by winning at least three tricks, and preferably all five. Failing this, to 'spoil five' by preventing anyone else from winning three, thereby increasing the size of the kitty for the next deal. If played for written scores, each trick counts 5 points and the target is *25*.

Robbing the pack. If dealt the trump Ace, you may declare that fact and then 'rob the pack' by taking the turn-up and discarding an unwanted card face down. You need not declare it if you do not intend to rob, but, if you do, you must rob before playing to the first trick. If the turn-up is an Ace, dealer may rob the pack by exchanging it for any unwanted card.

Play. The player at dealer's left leads to the first trick.

If a non-trump is led, you may follow suit or play a trump, as you prefer, but you may only play anything else if unable to follow suit.

If a trump is led, you must play a trump if possible, unless the only one you hold is one of the top three trumps (Five, Jack or ♥Ace) and is *higher* than the one led. In this case, you may 'renege' by discarding from another suit. In other words, you cannot force a player to disgorge one of the top three trumps by leading a lower trump, but only by leading a higher one of the top three, and then only if that player has no lower trump.

Example. If the trump Six is led and you hold the trump Five, trump Jack, or ♥A, but no lower trump, you needn't play it but may discard from any other suit. But you can't renege against a higher trump. For example, if the trump Jack is led, you needn't play the trump Five, but must (if you have no alternative) play ♥A, as it is lower than the Jack.

The trick is taken by the highest card of the suit led, or by the highest trump if any are played, and the winner of each trick leads to the next.

Jinking. If you win the first three tricks straight off, you sweep the kitty without further play. If instead you 'jink' by leading to the fourth trick, this counts as an undertaking to win all five, and you will lose your stake if you fail to get them all.

Score. A player who wins three or more tricks wins the kitty, and for winning all five gains an extra chip from each opponent. If nobody wins three, or a jinker fails to win five, the tricks are said to be 'spoilt'. The kitty is then carried forward to the next deal, and is increased by one chip per player.

Game. The game ends when somebody runs out of chips (hard score) or reaches 25 points (soft score).

Forty-Five

Add a Joker, which ranks between tr5 and ♥A as the third-highest trump. If, in turning the top card for trump, you turn the Joker, you take it into hand, place any unwanted card at the bottom of the pack, and turn the next instead. The aim is simply to score points, not to 'spoil five', and there is no jinking. Each won trick counts 5 points, and an additional 5 goes to the player who was dealt the best card. Normally, the best card is the highest trump, and if the tr5 appears in play its holder scores 5 immediately. If no one was dealt any trumps (rare), the best card is the highest-ranking card that actually won a trick, or the first played of cards tying for this honour. Tricks are scored as soon as taken, and the game ends as soon as one player or partnership wins by reaching the 45-point target score.

Variants. In some parts of Ireland, the best card counts 6, and the target may be set at 31 (though the game is still called Forty-Five). In Canada, a side scores 5 for winning three or four tricks, or 10 for all five. Another variant has 15 for three, 20 for four, and game for all five. The Joker, if used, ranks as the fourth highest trump, below ♥A.

Auction Forty-Fives

The auction equivalent is played in Canada and Nova Scotia, but apparently not in Ireland.

Four or six play in two partnerships, with partners sitting alternately round the table. Game is 120 points. Deal five cards each (2 + 3).

Bidding. Each in turn may bid or pass, and having passed may not come in again. Bids go from 5 to 30 in multiples of five, representing five per trick plus five for holding the highest trump in play. A side standing at 100 points to game may not bid lower than 20. The first time any given number is bid, the next in turn may 'I hold,' thereby taking over the bid at the same number. The next in turn, however, must then either raise again or pass. No suit is mentioned till all have passed after the highest bidder, who then announces trumps.

Drawing. Before play, each in turn, starting with eldest, may make any number of discards face down, receiving from dealer the same number of replacements from the rest of the pack.

Play. The ranking of cards, method of trick-play and privileges of reneging are as for Twenty-Five or Forty-Five.

Score. Count 5 per trick and 5 for whoever proves to have held the highest trump in play. The non-bidding side scores whatever it makes, or 60 if it bid and made 30. If the bidding side fulfilled its bid it scores all it made; if not, it deducts the bid from its current total. Game is 120.

Variant. In some circles the dealer, having discarded, may 'rob the pack' by examining all the undealt cards and freely selecting replacements.

Twenty-Nine

Adding-up game

Twenty-Nine, which seems to have appeared from nowhere in the mid-twentieth century, is considered a children's game, but perhaps only because its potentially interesting premise has not been adequately developed: there are so many obvious ways of improving it that they may safely be left to discover themselves. Any number may play. Four is most convenient, playing either individually or in partnerships.

From a 52-card pack, remove (unless four play) as many Tens as necessary to ensure that everyone receives the same number of cards. Deal all the cards around in ones.

Eldest plays any card face up to the table and announces its face value, for which purpose Aces and face cards count 1 each. Each in turn contributes a card to the count and announces the new total. The count may not exceed 29: if it is less, and the next in turn cannot play without going over 29, he misses a turn. Whoever makes it exactly 29 wins the cards so played and turns them face down like a won trick. The player at his left then leads to the next 'trick'.

The winner is the player (or side) who has captured most cards.

☞ *Comment.* When four play, the total pack value is 232, or 8 × 29. Eight 'tricks' will therefore be taken, each containing anything from three to a theoretical 21 cards. If other than four play, the last trick will count less than twenty-nine. The earliest source (Albert A. Ostrow, *The Complete Card-Player*, New York, 1945) states that the last trick remains untaken, though no one else seems to follow this rule.

Twenty-One ⟫ *Pontoon*

Two-Four-Jack

Going-out game

Also known as Switch, or Black Jack (as opposed to the quite different Blackjack), this elaboration of ▸ **Crazy Eights** became popular in pubs and schools during the 1970s, and spawned a proprietary version played with specially designed cards under the title Uno™. As it is essentially a folk game rather than a book game, the version described here has probably undergone many changes since.

Choose first dealer by any agreed means. Thereafter, the turn to deal passes to the left. The turn to play also starts by passing to the left, but (as described below) may be 'switched' to the right and back again as play proceeds. Deal 12 each if two or three are playing, otherwise 10. Stack the rest face down, turn the top card face up, and place it next to the stock as the start card of a sequence.

The aim is to be the first to play out all your cards.

Each in turn, starting with eldest hand, continues the sequence by playing from hand a card of the same rank or suit as the previous one, or any Ace. If you play an Ace you are entitled to specify what suit must follow it.

If you cannot make a legal play you must draw cards from the top of the stock till you can. When the stock is empty, all the cards of the sequence except the last one played are gathered up, shuffled, and laid down as a new stock next to the last card, which of course continues the sequence. The player who exhausted the stock, if still unable to play, must continue drawing until he can.

So far, the game is virtually identical with Rockaway—or (with Eights wild instead of Aces) with Crazy Eights. At this point, however, it introduces special rules relating to Twos, Fours, and Jacks.

Playing a Two forces the next in turn either to play a Two himself, or, if unable, to draw two cards from stock and miss a turn. If he draws and misses a turn, the next after him may play in the usual way; but if he does play a Two, the next after him must either do likewise or draw four cards and miss a turn. Each successive playing of a Two increases by two the number of cards that must be drawn by the next player if he cannot play a Two himself, up to a maximum of eight.

Fours have the same powers, except that the number of cards to be drawn is four, eight, twelve, or sixteen, depending on how many are played in succession.

Playing a Jack reverses ('switches') the direction of play and forces the preceding player to miss a turn, unless he, too, can play a Jack, thus turning the tables.

Twos, Fours, and Jacks operate independently of one another. You cannot escape the demands of a Two by playing a Four instead, or of a Jack by playing a Two, and so on.

The game ends when a player wins by playing his last card. A player with two cards in hand must announce 'One left' as soon as he plays one of them; otherwise, he must miss his next turn and draw one from stock instead.

The winner scores the face value of all cards left in other players' hands, with special values of 20 per Ace, 15 per Two, Four, or Jack, and 10 per King and Queen.

Play up to any agreed total, or settle each deal in coins or counters.

Two Hundred

Point-trick game

A Canadian game related to ▶ **Rook** and ▶ **Roque**.

Four players sitting crosswise in partnerships receive ten cards each, in ones, from a 40-card pack ranking A K Q J 10 9 8 7 6 5 in each suit.

The aim is for the declaring side to win at least as many as it bid of the 100 card-points available, counting 10 for each Ace and Ten, and 5 for each Five captured in tricks. The lowest bid is 50, and each subsequent bid must be a higher multiple of five. Each in turn, starting with eldest hand, either passes or makes a higher bid than any that has gone before. If you pass you cannot bid again. When three players have passed, the last bid becomes the contract and its bidder names the trump suit.

Eldest leads to the first trick. You must follow suit if you can, but may otherwise play any card. The trick is taken by the highest card of the suit led, or by the highest trump if any are played, and the winner of each trick leads to the next.

At end of play each side counts the card-points it has taken in tricks. The non-declaring side scores what it makes. The declaring side scores what it bid unless it failed to reach that total, in which case the amount of its bid is deducted from its cumulative score. (This may produce a negative number, indicated by drawing a circle round it and said to be 'in the hole'.)

Game is 200 points.

Variations. Many: three are worth mentioning.

1. Your side can only win on a bid game. That is, if you are not the declaring side but take enough card-points to bring you over 200, you do not win but keep playing till you bid and win.
2. Deal nine cards each and four face down to a kitty. The highest bidder takes the kitty and throws out four cards face down before play begins. Various rules apply to whether or not the discard may contain card-points and, if so, to which side (if either) they will be credited.
3. Add a Joker, called the Rook. In this case deal nine cards each and a kitty of five.

Tyotka

Penalty-trick game

52

Compendium games of the ▸ **Hearts** family, such as ▸ **Barbu**, often include a deal that incorporates in one go all the penalty features of the preceding deals. One of the best—and oldest—is Tyotka, which is Russian for 'Auntie', and refers to the undesired Queen.

From a 52-card pack, ranking A K Q J 10 9 8 7 6 5 4 3 2 in each suit, deal thirteen cards to each player and reveal the last card before adding it to dealer's hand. The last card is the bum card: its suit is the bum suit for that deal, and its rank is the bum rank.

The aim is to avoid incurring any of the following nine penalties:

1. Taking a Queen in a trick (1 penalty each = 4 in all).
2. An extra penalty for taking the Queen of the bum suit ('Tyotka').
3. Taking the bum card in a trick.
4. Winning the 'bumth' trick (i.e. the first if the bum card an Ace, the second if a Two, and so on).
5. Winning the last trick. (If the bum card is a King this is also the bumth trick, and so counts 2 penalties).
6. Winning the greatest number of tricks. (Or, if tied, the greatest number of cards of the bum suit, or, if still tied, the highest-ranking card of that suit.)

Eldest leads. You must follow suit if you can, but may otherwise play any card. The trick is taken by the highest card of the suit led, and the winner of each trick leads to the next. There are no trumps.

Each player scores 1 penalty point for each penalty incurred. The winner is the player with the fewest penalties when one player reaches a previously agreed target score, such as 20 or 30.

Note that several penalties may fall to the same trick. To take the most extreme and unlikely example, if a Queen is the bum card, and a player leads a Queen at trick 12, and everyone discards a Queen because unable to follow suit, the total number of penalties in that trick will be seven: 2 for Auntie, 1 for each other Queen, 1 for taking the bum card, and 1 for the bumth trick.

Tysiacha

Point-trick game

An unusual but challenging three-hander, Tysiacha is played in many eastern European countries, under a variety of different rules, and mostly under a name that means either one thousand or one thousand and one, depending on the local target score. It is ideal for anyone looking for a good three-handed equivalent of ▶ **Sixty-Six**, or for something reminiscent of ▶ **Skat** but much simpler and easier to learn. Like most three-handers of its type, it is often played by four, with each player in turn sitting out the hand to which he deals. The following version is played in Russia, Belorus, and the Ukraine.

Preliminaries. Three players use a 24-card pack ranking and counting as follows:

A	10	K	Q	J	9
11	10	4	3	2	0

Points accrue for winning counting-cards in tricks (120 in all) and for declaring marriages. A marriage is the King and Queen of the same suit and scores according to its suit as follows:

$$♠ = 40, \quad ♣ = 60, \quad ♦ = 80, \quad ♥ = 100$$

The winner is the first to reach 1000 points over several deals.

Deal. Choose first dealer by any agreed means; thereafter, the turn to deal and play passes to the left. Deal seven cards to each player, in ones, and three face down to the table to form a pick-up. (The Russian word is *prikup*, which actually means a supplementary purchase.) These three are usually dealt one at a time on the first three rounds between the second and third cards.

Auction. An auction to decide who will play alone against the other two is started by eldest hand, who *must* bid at least 100. This is an undertaking to score at least 100 points for the value of counting-cards won in tricks and for declaring marriages. Subsequent bids go up in fives and each must be higher than the last. You may not bid more than 120 unless you have at least one marriage in hand (because 120 is the most you can win in card-points). Once you have passed you cannot bid again. The survivor when two have passed becomes the soloist.

The soloist turns the three cards of the pick-up face up for all to see, adds them to his hand, and may increase the value of his bid to any higher multiple of five. He then passes one card face down to each opponent so that all have eight cards in hand.

New deal demand. If any player now holds all four Nines, he may show them and demand a new deal, which is made by the same dealer. (This makes it dangerous for the soloist to pass on a Nine, in case another player already has three.)

Play. The soloist leads to the first of eight tricks. You must follow suit if you can, but may otherwise play any card. There is no trump at first, but, as play proceeds, a trump suit may be established and changed on more than one occasion. You can only change the trump suit when you have won a trick and have a marriage in hand. You do so by showing both marriage cards, announcing their suit, and leading one of them to the next trick. This trump suit remains in force till the end of the hand unless someone else with a marriage entrumps a different suit.

☛ *Note.* You cannot declare a marriage originally held if you have already played one of its cards to a trick, even if it won the trick. It follows that the soloist cannot declare a marriage on his opening lead, since he will not yet have won a trick.

When there is a trump suit, you must trump when unable to follow suit to the card led. Only if unable to follow suit or trump may you discard from another suit. The trick is taken by the highest card of the suit led, or by the highest trump if any are played, and the winner of each trick leads to the next.

Score. At end of play each opponent scores the full value of card-points that he has taken in tricks, rounded up or down to the nearest 5, plus that of any marriages he may have declared. The soloist scores the amount of his bid if he actually fulfilled it; if not, he deducts that amount from his score.

The barrel. You cannot have a score greater than 880 but less than game (1000). If you make a score that brings you over 880 but is not enough to win, your score is raised to 880 and pegged there. You are then said to be 'on the barrel', a fact indicated by drawing a box round your score. When you are on the barrel, you cannot score more unless you bid and make at least 120, thereby winning. If you bid at least 120 and do not make it, your bid value is deducted from 880 and you are no longer on the barrel—in fact, you are said to 'fall off the barrel'.

Furthermore, as soon as you find yourself on the barrel, you are allowed just three more deals in which to bid 120 and either win or fall off. If you fail to win within three deals, and are still on the barrel at the end of that period, your score is reduced by 120 (to 760), and you are no longer on the barrel. In short, no one can win the game except by bidding and making at least 120. You can, of course, win without necessarily being on the barrel—for example, if from a score of 845 you bid and win 155.

Scoring zero. If you are not the soloist and you score zero, by winning either no tricks or just one trick consisting of three Nines, this fact is noted by drawing a line under your score. When you have accumulated three such lines, having scored nothing on three separate deals (not necessarily consecutively), your score has 120 points deducted from it. This happens on every third occasion that you score zero. But there are two circumstances in which the 120-point penalty does not apply, namely: (1) when you are on the barrel, and (2) when you take just one trick containing two Nines and a Jack. Although your score of 2 is rounded down to zero, it does not incur the penalty.

Raspisat' (redistribution of points). If you become the soloist, look at the pick-up, and decide that you cannot make your bid, you may concede without play by declaring a *raspisat'*—unless you are on the barrel, when this option is not open to you. In this event, each opponent is credited with 60 points (unless he is on the barrel) and you score nothing. This fact is recorded by writing by your score the letter P (the Russian equivalent of our R.) When you have accumulated three Ps on three separate deals (not necessarily consecutively), your score has 120 points deducted from it. This happens on every subsequent third occasion that you concede.

Tausendeins (1001)

A simpler version of Tysiacha played in Germany with a pack stripped to 20 cards by removing the Nines. Card-points are the same (Ace 11, Ten 10, etc.) but the suit hierarchy is that of Skat, namely ♦ 40, ♥ 60, ♠ 80, ♣ 100.

Deal six cards each and two to the table. The minimum bid is 40 and all bids and scores are made in multiples of 10. The highest bidder takes the pickup and discards two replacements, face down. If these contain any card-points, they will count towards his total (but if they are a marriage they do not count more than 7). Marriages are used to establish or change trumps as in Tysiacha, but you don't have to win a trick first, so the soloist can declare one upon leading to the first trick.

Scores are rounded to the nearest 10 and the winner is the first player to reach or exceed 1000.

http://www.pagat.com/marriage/1000.html

Ulti

Hungary's national card game is a complicated cross between ▶ **Mariás** (from which it derives) and ▶ **Skat**.

http://www.pagat.com/marriage/ulti.html

Up and Down the River ▶▶ *Oh Hell!*

Uruguay ▶▶ *Canasta*

Vache, jeu de ▶▶ *Aluette*

Valets, jeu des ▶▶ *Polignac*

Van John ▶▶ *Pontoon*

Vatican
Rummy game

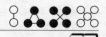

This unusual and challenging form of ▶ **Rummy** follows the modern idea of making melds common property rather than belonging to individual players. It is of eastern European origin and forms the basis of the proprietary tile game Rummikub™. Though playable by two to five, the game works best with three or four.

Shuffle together two 52-card packs and two Jokers, making 106 cards in all. Deal 13 each and stack the rest face down. There is no turn-up and no discard pile.

Your aim is to be the first to go out by playing all the cards from your hand to melds on the table.

A meld is either

- three or more cards of the same rank and all of different suits, or
- or three or more cards in suit and sequence, for which purpose the running order is A 2 3 4 5 6 7 8 9 10 J Q K A. Ace can count high and low simultaneously, so you are allowed to make a sequence that includes -K-A-2-.

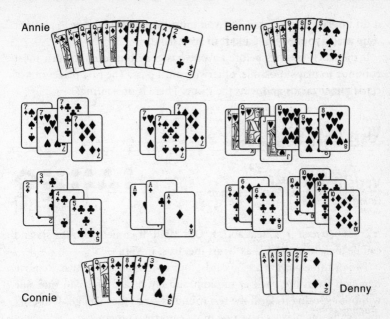

Vatican. A game in progress. Annie could lay off Kings and Queens to the King and Queen taken from the heart sequence, and ♥6 to the Sixes. Benny could make a sequence of five clubs by robbing ♣10 from the set of four.

At each turn you either draw the top card of stock and add it to your hand, or play at least one card from your hand to one or more melds on the table. If none remain in stock and you cannot play, you must pass.

The first time you play instead of drawing, you must meld a suit-sequence of at least three cards from hand. Having done so, you may, on this and any subsequent turn, add one or more cards to the table, and arrange or rearrange melds as you please. The only restriction is that, at the end of your turn, all cards on the table must remain arranged in valid melds of at least three cards.

☛ *Note.* If you find you cannot finish by leaving legal melds, you must retrieve the cards that will not fit. If none of them fit, you must take them all back and draw from stock instead (if any remain).

Jokers are wild: you can use one to represent any card you like. If you hold a card which is being represented by a Joker in a meld, you may lay it off in place of the Joker. But you must then add the Joker to another valid meld; you may not add it to your hand.

If the stock empties before anyone has gone out, each in turn must continue to play if possible, otherwise must pass. The first player out of cards thereby ends and wins the game. There is no scoring.

VC ▸▸ *Tieng Len*

Verish' ne Verish'

Going-out game

$$36 \rightarrow 52$$

A cross between ▸ **Cheat** and ▸ **Old Maid**. It comes from Russia and can be loosely translated as 'Trust me, trust me not'.

Two or three players use 36 cards, four or more use fifty-two. Remove one card from the pack at random and lay it face down to one side without exposing it. Deal the rest round as far as they will go. It doesn't matter if some players have one more card than others.

The player at the dealer's left starts by playing from one to four cards face down on the table and declaring them to be of any rank—for example 'Jacks'. Each in turn thereafter must either play one or more cards face down and declare the same rank as the previous player, or else challenge the previous player's veracity by saying '*Ne verish*' ('Don't believe you!') and turning that player's cards face up. Only the person in turn to play may challenge.

The challenger, if mistaken, or the challenged player, if caught lying, must take up all the cards so far played and add them to his hand. He may then, before play proceeds, remove any set of four cards of the same rank from his hand, reveal them to everyone, and discard them face down, thus diminishing the number of cards in play.

The next round is the started by the player to the left of the faulted player (thus the challenger himself, if correct), who may, as before, play and call any desired rank.

Eventually, all complete sets of four will be eliminated, leaving three of the initially discarded rank. Whoever is left with these in hand when everyone else has run out is the loser.

When playing instead of challenging, it is proper, but not compulsory, to say '*Verish* ('I believe you')'.

Viet Cong ▸▸ *Tieng Len*

Vinciperdi ▸▸ *Ciapanò*

Vingt-Quatre ▸▸ *Imperial*

Vingt-Un

The French equivalent of ▸ **Twenty-One** or ▸ **Pontoon**. (So called even though the French for twenty-one is normally *vingt-et-un*.)

Vint

One of several ancestors of Bridge, the Russian game of Vint is now restricted to Estonia, Finland, and Sweden, where it is also called 'Skruv'. Both names mean 'screw', from the resemblance between raising the bidding and tightening a screw.

Vira

Sweden's national card game is a dauntingly complicated three-player cross between ▸ **Hombre** and ▸ **Boston Whist**. It requires numerous counters of special sizes and shapes.

http://www.pagat.com/boston/vira.html

Vying games

Skilled gambling games in which players vie with one another as to who holds the best hand by progressively raising the stakes. The pot is won either by the player with the best hand or by the player who, by convincing others that he has the best hand ('bluffing'), forces them all to concede rather than pay for a showdown. See individual entries for: As Nas, Bouillotte, Brag, Mus, Poch, Poker, Primiera, Red and Black.

Wan Maria

Going-out game

This unusual Finnish game is actually called Kitumaija, from *kitu*, meaning to suffer pain, or pine away. So the title can be translated 'Wan Maria', as opposed to ▶ **Black Maria**.

From two to five players receive five cards each (3 + 2) from a 52-card pack, of which the next is turned to start the first spread, and the remainder are stacked face down.

The aim is to play all your cards out, and especially to avoid being the last player left in and holding ♠Q.

Cards rank A K Q J 10 9 8 7 6 5 4 3 2 in each suit, except for ♠Q, which is entirely independent. Diamonds trump spades and hearts, but not clubs, which are invulnerable.

Each in turn, starting with Eldest, plays as follows:

- If there are no cards in the spread, play any single card face up to start a new one.
- If the topmost card of the spread (the one played last) is ♠Q, take into hand the top five cards of the spread, or as many as there are if fewer than five, and end your turn.
- Otherwise, you must first play a forced card and may then play a free card. A forced card is a higher card of the same suit as the top card of the spread, or, if this is a heart or a spade, any diamond, which may be used as a trump even if the player can follow suit. A free card is any desired card. If you cannot beat the top card, you

must take the top three cards of the spread (or five if it is headed by
♠Q) and add them to your hand. The ♠Q may only be played as a
free card, not as a forced one.

- Whether or not you beat the top card, end your turn by restoring
  your hand to five cards if necessary, by drawing from the top of the
  stock, or as many as remain.

When the stock is exhausted, no 'free' cards may be played: each in
turn must either beat the top card or take the top three into hand, or the
top five if headed by ♠Q. Players drop out as they run out of cards. Last
in, holding spade Queen, is known as Wan Maria, and loses.

☞ *Comment.* As these rules stand, whoever goes into the endgame with
♠Q can never discard it, leaving the outcome a foregone conclusion. It is
quite feasible to simply ignore the change of rule and go on playing a
forced card followed by a free one. Alternatively, follow the rule but
permit ♠Q to be the only card that can be played free.

Washington's Favourite (Patience) ▸▸ *Spider*

Watten

Plain-trick game

An eccentric Bavarian gambling game belonging to an ancient family
that also includes ▸ **Karnöffel** and perhaps ▸ **Aluette**. They all have
the distinctive feature that that suit need not be followed, and that
certain individual cards act as trumps rather than there being one
whole trump suit. Despite its eccentricities, Watten is fun to play and
not too hard to learn. It is normally played with German-suited cards,
but ordinary ones will do. The four-player game is described first.

Cards and trumps. Watten is played with a 32-card pack basically
ranking A K Q J 10 9 8 7 in each suit. Before starting, it is essential to
understand the peculiar order and trick-taking value of the cards designated trumps, as follows.

Three cards are permanent top trumps. They are called *Kritischen*, which we may translate as 'matadors' (borrowing a term from comparable games). From the top down, they are:

♥K, 'Maxi'
♦7, 'Belli'
♣7, 'Spritzer'

In addition to the matadors (permanent top trumps), in each deal there are also appointed both a trump *rank* and a trump *suit*. The cards of the trump rank are called 'strikers' (*Schläger*), and the highest of these, called the Chief Striker, is the one that also belongs to the trump suit. Below it follow the other three strikers, which are all equal in rank, and below them rank the remaining cards of the trump suit in the basic order listed above, omitting any that may happen to be matadors or the Chief Striker. Here are some examples.

1. If spades are trumps and Queens are strikers, then the entire trump sequence from highest to lowest is:
   Matadors: ♥K ♦7 ♣7, *Strikers*: ♠Q (♥Q = ♣Q = ♦Q), *Suit trumps*: ♠A-K-J-10-9-8-7. (Fourteen trumps in all.)

2. If clubs are trumps and Jacks are strikers, then the entire trump sequence from highest to lowest is:
   Matadors: ♥K ♦7 ♣7, *Strikers* ♣J (♥J = ♠J = ♦J), *Suit trumps*: ♠A-K-Q-10-9-8. (Thirteen trumps in all. The ♣7 is a matador.)

3. If hearts are trumps and Sevens are strikers, then the entire trump sequence from highest to lowest is:
   Matadors: ♥K ♦7 ♣7, *Strikers*: ♥7 ♠7, *Suit trumps*: ♥A-Q-J-10-9-8. (Eleven trumps in all. The ♥K is a matador and ♥7 the Chief striker.)

If two or three strikers of equal rank fall to the same trick, the first-played ranks highest.

Object. Four players sit crosswise in partnerships, receive five cards each, and aim to score two or more game points by winning three tricks, or by bluffing the other side into conceding defeat. Game is 11 points over as many deals as necessary.

Deal. At the start of each game the dealer shuffles the cards and has them cut by his right-hand opponent. The bottom card of the top half is revealed, and if it is a matador it may be taken by the cutter as part of his hand. If the next card thereby exposed is also a matador, it goes to the dealer; and if the next is the third matador, it goes to the cutter.

The dealer then deals each player a batch of three cards (less one or two to the dealer or cutter if any matadors turned up) followed by a batch of two, so each player has five cards in all. At this point only the dealer and forehand (his left-hand opponent) may take up their cards. Those of their partners must remain face down on the table. The undealt cards go face down and remain out of play.

Announcing trumps. Forehand now examines his cards and announces which is to be the trump rank (whether A, K, Q, J, 10, 9, 8, or 7). This establishes which four cards are strikers, or three if the rank is Kings, or two if it is Sevens. Dealer then announces which is to be the trump suit. That done, their respective partners may now take up their hands and play begins.

Play. Forehand leads to the first trick and the winner of each trick leads to the next. With one exception, there is no requirement to follow suit: you can play any card you like. The exception is this. If Forehand leads the Chief Striker to the first trick (a fact to which he must draw attention by announcing 'Call for trumps'), you must play a matador or a striker or suit trump if you can. However, this obligation ceases as soon as someone beats the Chief Striker by playing a matador. If this happens, the others can revert to playing any card they like.

☛ *Note.* This rule cannot apply when there is no Chief Striker—for example, when Kings are the trump rank and hearts the trump suit.

All matadors, strikers, and suit trumps are trumps. The trick is taken by the highest card of the suit led, or by the highest trump if any are played, or by the first played of equal-ranking strikers (unless it is beaten by the Chief Striker or a matador).

Signals. Partners may signal certain card holdings to each other by means of conventional signals. For example, 'Maxi' is indicated by pursing the lips, 'Belli' by winking the right eye, 'Spritzer' by winking the left.

Raising and scoring. The side that wins three tricks gains two points, and no more tricks are played. However, any player, at any time, may raise the value of the game from 2 to 3 points by announcing 'Raise you'. At this point, play temporarily ceases, even if the trick is incomplete, while the opponents of the raiser decide which of three options to pursue, namely:

1. To concede defeat for the unraised value (2 points) by announcing 'See you'; or
2. To accept the raise and play on for the higher value (3 points) by saying 'Go on'; or
3. To re-raise the game value to 4 points by announcing 'Raise you'.

If they play on without making any announcement they are deemed to have accepted the raise.

Further raises may subsequently be made, each of them increasing the game value by 1 point if accepted, but with two constraints. First, the same side cannot raise twice in succession: each must raise in turn. Second, a side may not raise if the game value being played for is sufficient to win. For example, if your side already has 8 points, and the game value is 3, you may not raise it to 4 points. (This does not prevent you from accepting a raise to 4 from the other side.)

Watten for two
As above: Non-dealer announces the trump rank and dealer then announces the trump suit.

Watten for three
Forehand announces both the trump rank and the trump suit, and the other two play as a partnership, each of them scoring the amount scored by both of them together. The winner is the first individual to reach 11 points.

Whisk

The older name for ▸▸ **Whist**

Whisky Poker

Gambling game

52

A form of ▶ **Commerce** or **Thirty-One** but with Poker hands replacing numerical totals.

Deal five cards to each player and to a spare hand face down on the table. Everyone antes and looks at their hand. Eldest, if dissatisfied with his hand, may lay it face up on the table and take the spare in its place. If he declines, this option passes round the table till somebody exercises it or all refuse. If all refuse, the spare is turned up and play begins.

On your turn to play you may do one of the following:

· exchange one card with the spare, or
· exchange your whole hand for the spare, or
· knock.

When you knock the others have one more turn each, after which there is a showdown and the best hand wins the pot. (Or, originally, the worst hand pays for the drinks.)

Variant. You may exchange any number of cards from one to five.

Whist

Plain-trick game

52

Many games are called Whist, or have Whist in the title. They do so because they each share several (but not all) of the properties exhibited by the original and classic game of this name as described below, namely: four players, fixed partnerships, 52 cards, 13 tricks played usually with a trump suit, aim to win a majority of tricks. Separate entries will be found for the following Whist-related games, which fall into several groups:

· Partnership games with special rules: Bid Whist, Biritch, Cayenne, Contract Whist, Forty-One, Minnesota Whist, Norwegian Whist, Ruff, Russian Whist (= Biritch), Spades.

- Non-partnership games for four: Belgian Whist, Boston, Nomination Whist (but this is also another name for Oh Hell!), Solo Whist.
- Games for various numbers of players: Bismarck (3), Dummy Whist (2), French Whist = Catch the Ten (2–7), German Whist (2), Knockout Whist (2–7), Chinese Whist (2–4), Dutch Whist (3–4), Manni (3), Scotch Whist = Catch the Ten, Sergeant Major (also called 8–5–3) (3), Tribello (3)
- Bid to win a specified number of tricks: Israeli Whist, Ninety-Nine, Oh Hell!, Romanian Whist.

Though now little played, what might be called 'classical partnership Whist' was the most prestigious card game of the Western world between about 1750 and 1900, when it was relegated by Bridge. It derives from the sixteenth-century English game of Trump or Ruff, via Ruff and Honours, Whisk and Swabbers (probably a word-play on the former), Whisk, and, by about 1730, plain Whist.

Described below is the classical game of Short Whist, followed by some variants not covered in separate entries.

Short Whist

Decide partnerships, seating and first dealer by any agreed means. Four players sitting crosswise in partnerships receive 13 cards each, in ones, from a 52-card pack ranking A K Q J 10 9 8 7 6 5 4 3 2 in each suit. The last card, which belongs to the dealer, is dealt face up to establish the trump suit, and is taken into hand when the first trick is led.

The aim is to win a majority of tricks, for a score of 1 point per trick taken in excess of six. Extra points may be scored for honours (*see* below). A game is 5 points over as many deals as it takes, and a rubber is the best of three games.

The eldest hand leads to the first trick. You must follow suit if you can, but may otherwise play any card. The trick is taken by the highest card of the suit led, or by the highest trump if any are played, and the winner of each trick leads to the next.

Honours. At end of play, a side which held most of the four highest trumps (whether or not in the same hand) adds 2 points if they held three, or 4 if they held four. A side standing at 4 points to game, however, may not score for honours. Scoring for honours is traditional but may be ignored.

Variations. In Long Whist, the older game, the target score was 10 points. In American Whist it is 7 points and honours are ignored. This makes it just possible to reach game in one deal—a self-evident improvement.

Progressive Whist

The version now played in Whist drives, whereby players change tables and partners from deal to deal, ultimately producing a single overall winner. No card is turned for trump; instead, the suits rotate in order hearts, clubs, diamonds, spades. Sometimes a fifth deal played at no trump is added to the cycle.

Wumps ▸▸ *Karnöffel*

Wushiyi Fen ▸▸ *Fifty-One* (Rummy game)

Yablon

Banking game

A gambling game also known as Acey-Deucey, Between the Sheets, ▸ **Red Dog** (but see separate entry), etc. Casino play usually involves anything up to eight packs shuffled together and dealt from a shoe.

Basically, punters bet that the third card dealt from the top of the pack will be intermediate in rank between the first two. Everyone makes an initial stake and the banker deals two cards face up with enough space between them for a third. Unless the first two are of the same rank, or consecutive (running A 2 3 4 5 6 7 8 9 10 J Q K) the punters may then raise their stakes, but by not more than the original amount. A third card is then dealt between the first two. If it is intermediate, the punters win; if not, the banker wins. The odds paid to a successful punter vary with the 'spread'—that is, the number of ranks intermediate between the first two cards—as follows:

spread	odds
1	5:1
2	4:1
3	2:1
4–11	1:1

If the first two cards are consecutive, it is a tie. No one may raise, and no one wins.

If they are paired, no one may raise, but a third is turned. If matches the first two, the punters win 11:1, otherwise the bank wins.

Yellow Dwarf

The Continental forerunner of ▶ **Pope Joan** (French Nain Jaune, German Gelber Zwerg)

Yeralash

Russian forerunner of ▶ **Vint**.

Yukon
Point-trick game

52

A somewhat mysterious Canadian game, Yukon looks like a whimsical hybrid of Scotch Whist and Skat. It is not recorded in print before 1945, but card-game researcher Andrew Pennycook reports that he was brought up on it (in Canada) and that his father was playing it before the First World War. It is said (but without evidence) to have been popular in the Klondike Gold Rush of 1897.

From two to five may play, but the best format is four in partnerships. Use a 52-card pack, removing one or two Twos if three or five play. Deal five cards each and stack the rest face down.

The aim is to be the first to score 250 for card-points taken in tricks over as many deals as necessary.

The rank and value of cards is as follows, from high to low:

Jacks (Yukons)	A	K	Q	10	9 8 7 6 5 4 3 2
♠15, others 10 each	5	3	2	10	0 each

The Jacks, or Yukons, are not only highest in their suits but also act as trumps. The ♠J is known as the Grand Yukon and beats everything.

Eldest hand leads to the first trick. You must follow suit if you can, otherwise you must play a Yukon. Only if you can do neither may you discard from another suit.

The trick is taken by the Grand Yukon if it appears, or by the first played of two or more other Yukons, otherwise by the highest card of the suit led.

The winner of each trick leads to the next, after first drawing the top card of stock, adding it to his hand, and waiting for the others to do likewise. When the stock is empty, play continues until all have run out of cards.

The points taken by each player or side are not counted until the hand is played out. Play ceases when someone has reached 250 points, and the winner is the player or side that took most.

☛ *Comment.* Like any trick-and-draw game, Yukon suffers from the undetectability of a revoke (failure to follow suit or play a Yukon when able and required). If this worries you, it can be overcome by agreeing that anyone who fails to follow suit or play a Yukon should rapidly play his cards one by one face up to the table to prove his right to discard. This becomes unnecessary, of course, when no cards remain to be drawn.

Zetema
Rummy game

Zetema was marketed by J. Hunt as a proprietary game in about 1870. It was soon forgotten, but (fortunately) not before making its way into *Cassell's Book of Indoor Amusements, Card Games and Fireside Fun* (1881), from which it was rescued, revised, and promoted by Sid Sackson in *A Gamut of Games* (New York, 1969). It is in fact an excellent and unusual game, much like Rummy, but with reminiscences of Bezique and Poker, and more fun than either. The following account includes Sackson's improvements to the scoring system. It also dispenses with the word 'trick', originally used to denote a set of five discards, as it gives the impression that Zetema is a trick-play game, which it emphatically is not. I now call such sets 'zetemas' in order to make use of the otherwise redundant and apparently meaningless title.

From two to six may play. Three is ideal. Four or six play best in partnerships (six in either three of two or two of three).

The 65-card pack is made by shuffling adding in all 13 cards of one suit from a second pack, preferably of identical back design and colour. The duplicated suit—it doesn't matter which it is—is called the imperial suit.

The turn to deal and play passes to the left. Shuffle thoroughly, deal six cards each (or five if six play), and stack the rest face down.

Game is 300 points (or 200 four or more play) over as many deals as it takes. Points are scored for declaring melds in the hand and for winning zetemas. A zetema is a set of five discards of the same rank.

Each in turn, starting with eldest hand, draws a card from stock, adds it to his hand, may declare a meld if he has one, and ends (usually) by making one discard face up to the table. Discards are made in sets of the same rank. In other words, thirteen wastepiles are formed, one for each rank. Whoever adds the fifth card to a wastepile thereby completes a 'zetema' and discards it face down to a common wastepile. A zetema of Kings or Queens scores 50, Jacks 20, Aces or Fives 15, other ranks 5 each.

Upon drawing a card, you may show and score for one of the following combinations:

- Sequence (scores 20) = six cards in sequence, not all the same suit. For this purpose, cards run A 2 3 4 5 6 7 8 9 10 J Q K.
- Flush (scores 30) = six cards of the same suit, not all in sequence.
- Flush sequence (scores 50) = six cards in suit and sequence.
- Assembly = five cards of the same rank. An assembly of Kings or Queens scores 130, Jacks 120, Aces or Fives 110, other ranks 100.

Having declared one of the above, you end your turn by discarding one of the declared cards to its appropriate wastepile.

It is also possible to declare one or more marriages. A marriage is a King and Queen of the same suit. They may both come from the hand, or one of them may come from the hand and its partner be taken from the appropriate discard pile on the table. Marriages may be saved up and scored simultaneously—the more the better. One marriage scores 10, two 30, three 60, four 100, all five 150. If fewer than five are declared, each marriage in the doubled suit counts an additional ten. Having declared one or more marriages, you discard them face up to the common wastepile (they do not contribute to zetemas), and draw from stock as many cards as necessary to restore your hand to six.

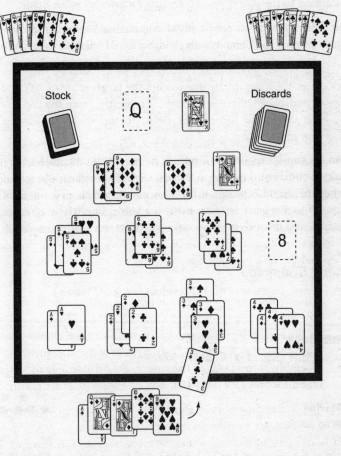

Zetema. South discards the fifth Three and scores 5 for the zetema. If he is lucky enough to draw a King, he will have a sequence to score on his next turn.

☞ *Note.* There are two ways of making a marriage: either by holding both cards in your hand, or by holding one partner and drawing the other from the appropriate wastepile. You may use either or both methods in the same turn, but may not (of course) marry two imperial Kings to one Queen or vice versa. Nor may you declare a six-card meld and marry the seventh in the same turn.

When the last card of stock has been drawn, players continue by discarding to the wastepiles and scoring for zetemas when made.

☞ *Note.* When two play, a player completing a zetema is obliged to play another card, and to keep doing so until he fails to complete one.

If some players go out before others they simply stop playing. Overall play ceases the moment anyone reaches the target score of 200 or 300, even in mid-play. Otherwise, it ends, very neatly, when the last zetema has been taken and turned face down to the wastepile, leaving an otherwise empty table.

☞ *Comment.* Assemblies originally scored 100, 90, 80, and 60; but they are so difficult to acquire that even with the revisions quoted above they are rarely worth aiming for. The exceptionally high scores for King and Queen zetemas are somewhat academic, since the declaration of any marriage prevents either wastepile from ever being completed.

Zheng Shàngyóu

The Chinese forerunner of ▸ **President** (or ▸ **A**ehole**).

Zioncheck

The original form of ▸ **Contract Rummy**.

Zwicker

Fishing game

52

A simpler version of ▸ **Cassino**, Zwicker is a popular family game of Schleswig-Holstein (Germany, bordering Denmark).

From two to four players use a 52-card pack, to which it is now usual to add six Jokers of (preferably) the same back design and colour as the main pack.

Deal four cards each face down, and four face up to the table to form a pool. Stack the rest face down.

Each in turn, starting with eldest hand, plays a card to the table, thereby capturing one or more pool cards if possible, otherwise leaving it there as part of the pool. When everyone has played four cards, four more each are dealt so long as any remain in stock, and play proceeds as before.

The aim is to capture Aces, the ♦7, ♠7, and, especially, the ♦10, and to make sweeps. A sweep is the capture, in one turn, of all the cards left in the pool.

A card played from hand to table may capture one or more pool cards by matching or summing.

Matching means an Ace captures one or more Aces, a Seven one or more Sevens, etc.

Summing means capturing two or more cards whose values sum to that of the card played from hand. For this purpose numerals Two to Ten count face value, Ace 11, Jack 12, Queen 13, King 14.

Example. The pool cards are ♠5 ♥5 ♦7 ♣J. If you play a Five you will capture both Fives. If you play a Jack, however, you will capture the Jack by matching and the Seven and one of the Fives by summing (since 7 + 5 = 12, the value of a Jack).

When you make a capture you put the capturing and captured cards together and place them face down before you like a won trick. If you capture all the cards in the pool in one turn you will score for a sweep, and must indicate this fact by leaving the capturing card face up in your pile of won cards. After a sweep, the next player has no option but to add a card to the pool.

If you can't make a capture you can only add a card to the pool. You may, however, arrange it as a separate card, or make a 'build' by placing it half over another card. In this case the build counts as if it were a single card of their combined value, and may only be captured as a whole. For example, a Five played to a Seven makes a build of 12, which can later be captured by a Jack—or, if there is also a Two on the table, by a King in conjunction with the Two, since the Two and the 12-build are equalled by the value of the King. More discards may be added to a build, so long it does not exceed 14 in total.

Jokers may be captured by matching. In addition, a Joker counts as any desired value from 2 to 14, and may be played or captured accordingly. Of course, it may only count as one value at a time: it cannot capture two different cards, or builds of different values, in the same turn.

No cards are added to the pool when extra cards are dealt. On the last deal, it does not matter that there may not be enough cards to go round. The last person to play a card from the hand also wins any cards left in the pool, but this does not count as a sweep, unless it happens to be one as defined above.

At end of play you each sort through your won cards and score for:

♦7	1 point
♠7	1
Each Ace	2
Each sweep	3
♦10	10

Play up to any agreed target.

Variants. Various restrictions may be imposed on the power of Jokers. In some circles, for instance, a Joker in the pool may not be captured at all, thus preventing any more sweeps from being made.

Zwikken

Point-trick game

An old Dutch army gambling game of ill repute but with a sufficient element of bluff to be interesting in its own right. Accounts vary; the following is typical.

Three players use a 20-card pack ranking and counting in each suit as follows: Ace 4, King 3, Queen 2, Jack 1, Ten 0. You each chip one to the pot and receive three cards dealt 1 + 2 or 2 + 1. The next card is turned for trump. If you hold the trump Ten you may eventually exchange it for the turn-up, but for now should keep quiet about it.

Each in turn has one opportunity to 'shoot' for the whole or part of the pot—typically a third or a half—or to pass. If one player shoots for less than the total in the pot, a subsequent player can take it off him by offering to shoot higher—that is, for a greater proportion of it.

The highest bidder becomes the shooter. His aim is either to have the best *zwik* (three of a kind), or to win two tricks, or one trick containing more card-points than the other two combined.

If all pass, the dealer may (but need not) require everyone to add a chip to the pool, and then turns the next card for trump. If all pass a second time, dealer has the same option. If he declines the option, or no one bids after three turns, the deal is annulled and the pool is carried forward to the next.

Otherwise, play begins as soon as someone offers to shoot. Now:

- If you hold the Ten of trump you may exchange it for the turn-up.
- If you hold a *zwik* (three cards of the same rank), you show it and win the pool. Of two *zwiks*, the higher-ranking wins.

If not, eldest hand leads to the first trick. You must follow suit if you can, otherwise must play a trump if you can. Any trump played must be higher (if possible) than any already played to the trick. The trick is taken by the highest card of the suit led, or by the highest trump if any are played, and the winner of each trick leads to the next.

The shooter wins by taking two tricks, or one trick counting more in card-points than the other two combined, equality being insufficient. If successful, he wins the amount he bid; if not, he adds it to the pot.

A wicked feature of the game is that exchanging the Ten may give a player a *zwik*.

Winning on points is virtually academic, as a single trick rarely contains enough card-points to beat the other two.

Sources vary as to how often the dealer may turn another trump and whether turning the same suit as before counts as a separate turn.

Technical terms

alliance A temporary partnership, lasting for one deal only.

ante In gambling games, an opening stake that everyone must make at the start of each deal.

auction A period of bidding to establish the conditions of the game, such as which suit shall be trump and how many tricks the bidder will undertake to win.

bid An offer to achieve a stated objective (e.g. win a given number of tricks) in exchange for choosing the conditions of play (e.g. a trump suit). If the offer is not overcalled by a higher bid, it becomes a contract.

blank In card-point games, a card worth nothing. Also = *carte blanche*.

card-points The point-scoring value of certain cards in point-trick games.

carte blanche A hand consisting only of numerals, with no face cards.

carte rouge A hand in which every card counts towards a scoring combination.

chicane A hand containing no trumps.

chip A gaming counter.

combination or **meld** A set of cards matching one another by rank or suit and recognized by the rules of the game as a scoring feature.

compendium game A game consisting of two or more different games combined.

contract *See* 'bid'.

counter (1) An object representing a score or partially won game. (2) A card with a point-value, in point-trick games such as Skat and Pinochle.

court cards (originally 'coat cards') = face cards: King, Queen, Jack, and other personages, as opposed to numerals or 'pip' cards.

cut To lift off the top portion of the pack and either (1) reveal its bottom card, so as to make a random decision such as who deals first; or (2) to replace it beneath the lower half, so as to ensure that no one knows what the bottom card is.

cut-throat All-against-all; without partnerships.

dead hand *See* 'widow'.

deadwood (Rummy) Penalty cards remaining in opponents' hands when one player has gone out.

deal (1) To distribute cards to the players at start of play. (2) The play ensuing between one deal and the next.

declare (1) To announce the contract or conditions of play (number of tricks intended, trump suit, etc.). (2) To show and score for a valid combination of cards in hand.

declarer The highest bidder, who declares and then seeks to make good the stated contract.

deuce The numeral 'Two' of any suit.

discard (1) To lay aside an unwanted card or cards from hand; (2) to play to a trick a card that is neither of the suit led nor a trump; (3) the card or cards so disposed of.

doubleton Two cards of the same suit in the same hand, no others of that suit being held.

draw To take, or be dealt, one or more cards from a stock or wastepile.

drinking game Typically, one that results in a loser rather than a winner, in order to decide who pays for the next round.

dummy A full hand of cards dealt face up to the table (or, in Bridge, dealt to one of the players, who eventually spreads them face up on the table) from which the declarer plays as well as from his or her own hand.

earlier, -est Same as elder; *see also* 'priority'.

elder, -est The player who makes the first move or bet, or who leads to the first trick, also called forehand (in games of German origin). Eldest hand is usually the player seated next to the dealer in rotation of play, and the dealer himself being 'youngest'.

exchange (1) To discard one or more cards from hand and then draw or receive the same number from stock. (2) To add a specified number of cards to hand and then discard a like number. (3) To exchange one or more cards with a neighbour, sight unseen.

flush A hand of cards all of the same suit.

follow (1) To play second, third, etc. to a trick. (2) Follow suit: To play a card of the same suit as that led.

forehand Same as 'Eldest'. (German *Vorhand*.)

frog The lowest bid in certain games of German origin. From German *Frage*, 'request'.

game (1) A series of deals or session of play. (2) The contract, or conditions of the game; e.g. 'Solo in hearts'. (3) The target score; e.g. 'Game is 100 points'.

go out To play the last card from your hand.

grand A bid equivalent to no trump in some games, a slam in others.

hand (1) The cards dealt to an individual player, which he either plays from or bets on, depending on the type of game. (2) Same as 'deal' (2).

hard score Scoring done with coins, chips or counters, as opposed to a written or 'soft' score.

head To play a higher card than any so far played to the trick, especially in games where you must do so if you can.

honours Cards attracting bonus scores or side-payments, usually to whoever holds and declares them, occasionally to whoever captures them in play.

lead To play the first card; or, the first card played.

line, above/below (Bridge) Scores made for tricks contracted and won are recorded below a line drawn half way down the sheet, and count towards winning the game; overtricks, honours, and other premiums are scored above it and mainly determine the size of the win.

marriage King and Queen of the same suit.

matadors Top trumps with special powers over ordinary trumps.

meld A combination of matching cards attracting scores or privileges, or winning the game; (2) to declare such a combination.

middlehand In three-hand games, the player of intermediate priority. (German *Mittelhand*.) *See also* 'priority'.

misère A contract or undertaking to lose every trick.

miss A dead hand, especially in Loo.

null Same as misère (German).

numerals Number cards, as opposed to face cards. Also called pip cards, spot cards, spotters, etc.

ouvert(e) A contract played with declarer's cards spread face up on the table for all to see.

overcall To bid higher than the previous bidder.

overtrick A trick taken in excess of the number contracted.

pair Two cards of the same rank.

partie A whole game, as opposed to a single deal, especially at Piquet.

partnership Two or more players whose interests are bound together as a team and who therefore play cooperatively rather than individually. A partnership may be either fixed in advance and last for the whole session, as at Whist and Bridge, or vary from deal to deal, as at Quadrille or Solo, in which case it is better referred to as an 'alliance'.

pass In trick-games, to make no further bid; in vying games, to pass the privilege of betting first but without dropping out of play.

penalty-trick games Trick-taking games where your aim is to avoid winning tricks, or at least tricks containing penalty cards (notably Hearts).

pip A suitmark printed on a card, or the number represented—e.g. the Deuce shows two pips. (Originally 'peep'.)

plain suit (side suit): A suit other than trumps.

plain-trick games Those in which importance attaches only to the number of tricks taken, regardless of the cards comprising them.

point (1) The smallest unit of value, score or reckoning. In various games distinctions may be drawn between card-points, which are notional values attached to certain cards, the object being to capture a minimum number of them; score-points, which are points credited to a player's account; and game points, which might loosely be described as 'bundles' of score-points and may be affected by other bonuses. (2) The total face value of all cards held of any one suit (Piquet).

point-trick games Those in which in which win or loss is determined not by the number of tricks taken but by the total value of counters or card-points contained in them, as opposed to plain-trick games.

pool, or pot The totality of stakes being played for in any one hand.

prial (from 'Pair-royal') A triplet; three cards of the same rank.

priority The order in which players take precedence over one another when (for example) two or more wish to make bids of equal value. Typically, an 'elder' or 'earlier' player has priority over a 'younger' or 'later'. Priority normally starts with the player sitting at the dealer's left in games played clockwise around the table, or at his right in games played counter-clockwise.

rank (1) The denomination of a card (e.g. Ace, Two, King), as opposed to its suit. (2) The relative trick-taking power of a card (e.g. 'Ace ranks above King').

rearhand The player with least priority (q.v.), usually in three-hand games. (German *Hinterhand*.)

renege To fail to follow suit to the card led, but legally so, by exercise of a privilege granted by the rules of the game (as in Twenty-Five).

renounce Strictly, to play a card of any different suit from that led—the same as 'renege' if done legally, or 'revoke' if not. Loosely, to do so only from a non-trump suit, thereby renouncing all hope of winning the trick.

revoke To fail to follow suit to the card led, though able and required to do so, thereby incurring a penalty.

riffle A method of shuffling. The pack is divided into two halves which are placed corner to corner, lifted, and allowed to fall rapidly together so that they interleave.

rotation The order in which play passes around the table, whether from right to left (clockwise) or left to right (counter-clockwise).

round (1) A period or phase of play in which all have had the same number of opportunities to deal, or bid, play to a trick, etc. (2) Round game: one playable by an indefinite number of players, typically three to seven.

rubber A series of games won by the first side to win a minimum number, such as best of three in Whist and Bridge.

ruff To play a trump to a plain-suit lead.

run (Brag, Cribbage) Same as 'sequence'.

sans prendre A bid to play with the hand as dealt, without benefit of exchanging, thereby increasing the difficulty and hence scoring value of the game. Also called 'solo'.

sequence A scoring combination consisting of three or more cards in numerical sequence or ranking order.

shoe In casino play, a box specially designed to hold several packs of cards shuffled together so that each card can be drawn without danger of exposing any other.

shuffle To randomize the order of cards in the pack. *See also* 'riffle'.

side suit (plain suit): a non-trump suit.

singleton A card which is the only one of its suit in a given hand.

skat Same as 'widow'. (German; from Italian *scarto*, 'discard').

slam The winning of every trick, or a bid to do so.

small slam As above, but every trick bar one.

soft score Score kept in writing or on a scoring device, as opposed to 'hard score' of cash or counters.

solo (Trick games). (1) Originally, to undertake a contract with the cards as dealt, rather than seeking to improve the hand by exchanging any. (2) A bid to achieve a given objective playing alone against the combined efforts of the other players.

spread Same as 'ouvert'.

squeeze In trick-taking games, a situation in which a player cannot follow suit to the card led, but either cannot play without weakening himself in another suit, or cannot tell which suit is safe to play from.

stock Cards which are not dealt initially but may be drawn from or dealt out later in the play.

stops Cards which terminate a sequence, in games of the Stops family (Newmarket, Pope Joan etc.). Sometimes applied to cards that were not dealt initially and whose absence from play prevents the completion of sequences.

straddle An obligatory stake made, before any cards are dealt, by the second player around, the first having put up an ante.

straight In Poker, a five-card sequence.

suit A series of cards distinguished by the presence of a common graphic symbol throughout; or the symbol (suitmark) itself.

talon The stock, or undealt portion of the pack.

tops Unbroken sequence of trumps from the top down.

tourné(e) A contract in which the bidder turns the top card of stock and accepts its suit as trump.

trey The numeral Three of any suit.

trick A set of cards equal to the number of players, each having contributed one in succession.

trump (1) A superior suit, any card of which will beat that of any other suit played to the trick. (2) To play such a card. (From 'triumph'.)

turn-up A card turned up at start of play to determine the trump suit.

unblock To play a high card, even if it loses, to prevent it from impeding subsequent play from one's partner's (or dummy's) long suit.

undertrick A trick less than the number required to win the deal.

upcard A card lying face up on the table, or the faced top card of the wastepile at Rummy, Patience, etc.

void Having no card of a given suit (e.g. 'void in hearts').

vole A slam; the winning of every trick played. (French, from Spanish *bola*.)

vulnerable (Bridge) Describes a side which, having won one game towards the rubber, is subject to increased scores or penalties.

wastepile A pile of discards, usually face up, as at Rummy, Patience, etc.

widow A hand of cards dealt face down to the table at start of play and not belonging to any particular player. One or more players may subsequently exchange one or more cards with it. (Also 'blind', 'miss', 'skat'.)

wild card One that may be used to represent any other card, with or without stated restrictions. Typically the Joker in Rummy games, Deuces in Poker.

Younger, -est The player last in turn to bid or play at the start of a game. See 'Eldest', 'priority'.

Oxford Paperback Reference

The Oxford Dictionary of Dance
Debra Craine and Judith Mackrell

Over 2,500 entries on everything from hip-hop to classical ballet, covering dancers, dance styles, choreographers and composers, techniques, companies, and productions.

'A must-have volume ... impressively thorough'
Margaret Reynolds, *The Times*

Who's Who in Opera
Joyce Bourne

Covering operas, operettas, roles, perfomances, and well-known personalities.

'a generally scrupulous and scholarly book'
Opera

The Concise Oxford Dictionary of Music
Michael Kennedy

The most comprehensive, authoritative, and up-to-date dictionary of music available in paperback.

'clearly the best around ... the dictionary that everyone should have'
Literary Review